RICHARD AND JOAN BRACE

ORDEAL
in ALGERIA

D. VAN NOSTRAND COMPANY, INC.

Princeton, New Jersey

Toronto   London

New York

D. VAN NOSTRAND COMPANY, INC.
120 Alexander St., Princeton, New Jersey (*Principal office*)
24 West 40 Street, New York 18, New York

D. VAN NOSTRAND COMPANY, LTD.
358, Kensington High Street, London, W. 14, England

D. VAN NOSTRAND COMPANY (Canada), LTD.
25 Hollinger Road, Toronto 16, Canada

Published simultaneously in Canada by
D. VAN NOSTRAND COMPANY (Canada), LTD.

Library of Congress Catalogue Card No. 60-53318

The authors wish to thank the publishers for permission to quote from the
following books: *Algeria in Turmoil* by Michael Clark, Frederick A. Praeger,
Inc., 1959; *On War* by Raymond Aron, Martin, Secker and Warburg, Ltd.,
1958 (Permission received from American publishers, Doubleday and
Company, Inc.); *The Question* by Henri Alleg, George Braziller, Inc., 1958,
and John Calder, Ltd.; *Economic Theory of Underdeveloped Regions* by
Gunnar Myrdal, Duckworth, 1957 (Permission received from American
publishers, Harper and Brothers who published the book under the title
Rich Lands and Poor.); *France, Troubled Ally* by Edgar S. Furniss, Jr.,
Harper and Brothers for the Council on Foreign Relations, 1960; "Monsieur
Flandin's Domaine" by A. J. Liebling in *The New Yorker*, September 13,
1958; *Les 13 complots du 13 Mai* by Merry and Serge Bromberger, Librairie
Arthème Fayard, 1959; *L'Algérie du 13 Mai* by Paul Gerin, Librairie Galli-
mard, 1958; *Secrets d'Etat* by J. R. Tournoux, Librairie Plon, 1960.

PRINTED IN THE UNITED STATES OF AMERICA

To the French and Algerian Nations,
may they reconcile their differences
and follow the path of freedom

Because of the very nature of the current French-Algerian revolution, its controversial and even prejudicial aspects, the incompleteness of evidence for both houses, and the lack of a long perspective, a historian and even his wife, should eschew it like the plague and continue to work on some safer, deader, long-gone revolution. But these characteristics which make it a difficult subject also make it passionately interesting, and they do not alter the fact of its major importance in the world of today.

Until the Gaullist coup d'état of 1958 the Western world, outside of the main participants, knew very little about the Algerian question. Partly this was a conspiracy of silence, a playing down by France of the "pacification" in Algeria, and partly it was because the western world had so many seemingly more important places on its mind. Americans particularly were unaware of the problems of the Maghrib. Recently excellent news coverage by fine reporters such as Thomas Brady, Robert Doty, and Paul Ghali has headlined the Algerian news for days at a time. Then the United Nations debates of the last few years have brought the problem out into the open. At last Americans have begun to lose their exotic notions of life in the Casbah and are viewing with increasing excitement the struggle of a Muslim nation, for many years dominated by a handful of Europeans, for its right to self-determination.

In France a spate of books have recently been published which deal with one part or another of the Algerian problem, or with

v

De Gaulle and the new Fifth Republic. But the authors do not know of any other work in France or America which has attempted objectively to present the affair from both sides. Michael Clark's book, *Algeria in Turmoil,* presents admirably the *colon* viewpoint and seems to chide France for being too lenient and indecisive rather than too late in her solutions. Charles-Henri Favrod has written what is perhaps the most sympathetic account of the battle of the Algerian rebels, *La révolution Algérienne,* and Serge Bromberger has also written an interesting study, *Les rebelles Algériens. Le Monde* and *L'Express,* when they are not censored, often carry honest Algerian news, and in America *The New York Times* reports with admirable equity. *El Moujahid,* the news organ of the Algerian "Freedom Fighters," and the publications of the Algerian office in New York are, as is to be expected, pro-Algerian sources. But almost everything else that is published has been weighted in favor of the official French position. Most important, of course, is the documentation which springs from the press and information service of the French Embassy. Copious coverage of the doctrines, legislation, and accomplishments of the Fourth and Fifth Republics and of France in the new Community stream from this source. All of it bears the official French watermark. Frenchmen such as Jacques Soustelle have written the case for the integrationists, as have colonials such as Alain de Sérigny. The Algerian press, since the suppression of *Alger Républicain,* has maintained the line of French Algeria. It is apparent, therefore, that source material is difficult to evaluate. So it is with all humility and with knowledge of the many errors which we are bound to make that we offer this work at a moment when the whole Algerian question is at rip-tide.

And then again we are *not* so humble. We have known France intimately for more than twenty years, lived with her people even during World War II, worked in the history of her earlier revolutions, studied her general thought, her politics, her art, her literature. Does it sound too simple to say that we have had a continuing love affair with France for all these years, an affair in which we were often obliged to love her more for her faults than for her excellence? When, in 1958 we again paid her a visit after a three year absence, we were instantly aware, with a sure knowledge, that this new French revolution, that of the Algerian people, was marking France as profoundly as had World War II. Soon all plans to finish a leisurely essay appraising the Girondins, "cloud compellers" of an earlier revolution, were buried beneath a passionate interest in this modern rebellion which embodied so many of the important currents of our time. We abandoned Paris for Algiers both literally and figuratively.

Not only does this question involve the internal policies of France and, of course, Algeria, but it is also a case study in the rise of non-European nationalism, one of the most striking aspects of the twentieth century. It also describes the effort of a great colonial power to meet the challenge of this surging nationalism, to channel it and construct a new framework for it. From a sociological point of view there is involved the fascinating panorama of one more underdeveloped country being pulled by a so-called civilized country, and attempting its own leap, from the primitive into the modern technical world. It is a part of the struggle between the Free World and the Iron Curtain countries. If Algeria wins her freedom can she evolve democratically or will economics force her into a totalitarian pattern? There are already rumblings of decisions to come in the heart of the Provisional Government of the Algerian Republic, and since the breakdown of the July, 1960 pourparlers with France the Algerians have announced that they will have a permanent delegation headed by Moustapha Ferrouki in China, which country has offered material aid. Certainly as long as France and the West remain impotent to solve the Algerian question, the chance of Algeria slipping from the western-oriented Maghrib, away from the benevolent influence of Morocco and Tunisia toward the East, becomes ever greater.

Moreover, the Algerian problem has complicated France's relations with the NATO powers. Almost all of France's available military forces are engaged in the fight with the rebels, and France continues to use her need for help in Algeria as a bargaining point for her agreement to NATO's program. The discovery of the great oil and natural gas treasures in the Sahara at a moment when Nasser had nationalized the Suez and bottlenecked the Near Eastern oil deliveries has involved all the great oil interests of the Western world in France's ultimate solution to the war and complicated the prospects of an equitable peace.

One of the most controversial aspects of the French Algerian question concerns the degree and nature of Pan-Arab Nasserism, and just plain Communist influence in the councils of the Provisional Algerian Government. On this, the answers come either white or black. The truth is somewhere in between, of course, and varies as the Provisional Government is repelled or pulled closer to the neighboring Maghrib states, and sometimes as those states are in a pro or anti-French state of mind. To read the greater part of the French press, even some of de Gaulle's speeches of 1958 and 1959, one might gain the idea that the whole Algerian war is a machination of the Communist Party, and that France alone is the bulwark against Communist infiltration of the North African countries, that there is, in fact, no real Algerian nationalism. To speak to Abdel Kader Chanderli, chief of the Algerian Office in New York is to hear that the Algerian National Liberation Front, the predecessor and creator of the Provisional Government, has been merciless toward those Communist rebels in its midst who put party dicta before Algerian independence. It is equally hard to know how important are the factional struggles between the Provisional Algerian Government's exterior and interior cohorts. Historians, working far away from the powder burns, at some time in the future possibly can give us the answers to these questions. At present we cannot be inside the councils of the Provisional Government any more than we can eavesdrop upon the deliberations of Premier Michel Debre's government which often seems to transform in action the speech and intent of its President into unrecognizable double-talk.

Now, at this moment, we cannot know these things. But now, more than there will be ever after, it is more important to piece together the available knowledge, read between the lines, and take some "learned guesses" about the outcome. There is satisfaction to take a stand, to throw oneself and one's evidence in the balance *now*. For it is only in so doing that the authors can become engaged in the adventure of their times, help influence

viii

direct solutions that deeply affect the world they live in. This book represents our action on the French Algerian Question of our time, our commitment not so much in the light of history's verdict, but in the light of available knowledge and a consuming interest in a just peace and the principles of national self-determination.

Summer, 1960   R. AND J. B.

ACKNOWLEDGMENT

Northwestern University and the American Council of Learned Societies supported and encouraged this project and to both the authors make grateful acknowledgment.

CONTENTS

CONTENTS

LAND, PEOPLE, AND A LITTLE HISTORY

The older handbooks tell us that Algeria is a country of North Africa, bounded on the north by the Mediterranean, on the south by the Sahara, on the east by Tunisia, and by Morocco on the west. Accounts written after 1830 claim that Algeria belongs to France by right of conquest. They tell us, too, that the boundaries are in part undetermined. The name Algeria (*Algérie*) was used in 1839 for the first time in an official French document.

Arab geographers and historians made good sense when they referred to the Maghrib, or Moghrib, meaning "the West"—the area between Bougie and Biskra westward to the Atlantic. These writers recognized the essential cultural, geographical, and economic unities of this junction of the Mediterranean with northwestern Africa. Sometimes they included the area of Tripoli eastward and, occasionally, Spain after the conquest. This older name was evidence that no natural geographic or cultural frontiers separated the modern areas of Tunisia and Morocco from Algeria. In this particular long view of history "Algeria is the Maghrib," not France. The medieval Arab writers were also aware that the Maghrib, or Africa Minor as it was sometimes called, attached itself much more intimately to the Mediterranean than to the African continent.

The recorded story of conquest and settlement has supported this view. Phoenicians, Romans, Vandals, Byzantines, Arabs, Ottoman Turks, and the French approached from the east or north. Never, in the written historic record did invasion or important migration come from the African south. The successful operation "Torch," undertaken by Anglo-American forces in 1942, originated in the west and northwest, but that was not a conquest, and, in large part it also used the Mediterranean approach.

Today's division of the Maghrib into Tunisia, Algeria, and Morocco bears the imprint of the Turkish dominion. France, too, saw the interdependence of the three states and, having "secured" Algeria, pushed as quickly as opportunity allowed into Tunisia (1881) and Morocco (1905-1912). The present ruler, Mohammed V of Morocco, agrees with this viewpoint, and in 1956 made it an argument in favor of Algerian independence. "Morocco and Tunisia are the wings of the Maghrib. . . . When the wings are free, the body frees itself."

The Algeria which France took to itself in the nineteenth century included a Mediterranean coastline of approximately 650 miles and an area four times the size of the mother country. In large part the coastline was inhospitable, particularly in the western half where the hilly rampart is rather continuous, broken infrequently with bays and valleys. East of Philippeville the mountains recede from the coast. Harbors are relatively few but those of Oran, Algiers, Bougie, and Bône are excellent and beautiful. The Bay of Algiers with its breakwaters and the White City ashore is spectacular whether viewed from seaside or from the land, and an economic godsend to Algeria. Traditionally mariners have considered this African coast to be treacherous due to the fast running easterly currents, winter gales from the north which blow straight into the harbors, and the fog-bearing summer easterlies.

Flying southward (inland) from the coast, where climate is typically Mediterranean, one sees three clearly delineated physical divisions. These are basic to all analyses of economic productivity and the reader will encounter them again in later pages. There is first a fertile, healthy area varying in depth from fifty to a hundred miles all along the Maghrib. It is rocky, mountainous, indented with rich valleys reminiscent of those of California. This

2

is the Tell, meaning "hill" in Arabic. Beyond the Tell lies the plateau or table-land zone, where elevations average 3000 feet. It is mostly arid with some grass for pasturage but lacking in good streams. In the lower Maghrib the Great Atlas Mountains rise to separate the plateau from the approaches of the Sahara. On the peaks snow can be seen any month in the year, while to the south the Sahara, literally "emptiness" or "nothing" in Arabic, takes fanatical hold.

In the lesser mountain systems (the Little Atlas) and the plateau between the coast and the Great Atlas, the guerrilla warfare which characterizes the Algerian nationalist resistance found a favorable terrain. Traversing east to west the Aurès Mountains in the Constantine, the Kabylia Mountains lying a few miles inland between Algiers and Bougie, and the Little Atlas in the Tlemçen area in the west furnish natural protection to the Algerian Freedom Fighters.

French soldiers and pioneers in Algeria in the 1830's were astonished to find many Muslims who spoke no Arabic. Anthropologists came to the rescue with the explanation that the indigenous population was almost entirely Berber. The great mystery of the origin of these people need not concern us, but there is evidence to support the conjecture that they were relatives of the Egyptians almost two thousand years before Christ, some twenty-six centuries before the first Arabic conquest. What is vitally important to anyone interested in Algeria is that throughout the centuries of invasion and conquest the Berbers held fast to their customs and even their spoken languages. As late as 1950 it is estimated that one-third of the Algerian Muslims spoke Berber languages, and many were, of course, bilingual, speaking Arabic as the second language, or even trilingual, adding French. They did accept Islam beginning in the seventh century, but they were not as devout or fanatical as the Arabs. Berbers of the Tell, particularly the Kabyles, jealously preserved their traditional political and social institutions. The Chaouia, Berber tribes in the Aurès who were not as numerous as the Kabyles, were equally independent. In the south, in the Saharan Atlas and beyond, Mzabities (or Beni-Mzab), identified by their multicolored coats and the Tua-

3

reg, both Berber peoples, lived in isolation. Tuareg society was matriarchal which possibly explains why it was monogamous and surely explains the high status of women. Their men wear veils, dyed with indigo which rubs off on their faces and they ring their eyes with blue paint, giving the appearance of blue skinned men. In contrast to most Berber groups, the Tuareg have a written language.

Older generalizations note that Berbers are blue-eyed blondes. Contemporary Berbers are fairer than Arabs, but the majority have dark hair and brown or hazel eyes. Dressed in European clothes, they would be hard to distinguish from what popularly passes for the French or Italian type. Apart from their acceptance of Islam and, in some cases, vulgarized Arabic, it would be a gross exaggeration to say they have been assimilated by the Arabs. The contrary is more likely the case, because the Berbers were (and are) essentially farmers and town dwellers rather than herdsmen-nomads as were the Arabs. Koranic theocracy never impressed them and they clung to primitive democratic ways with their *Jemaa* or tribal council of all males, reminiscent of the witenage-mot in early western Europe. Too, the unwritten Berber code, the *Kanum* protected individual liberties against community interests.

It would be equally wrong to equate the independent Berber spirit with opposition to the Algerian nationalist movement and the rebellion, as certain French writers have attempted to do, nor can Berbers be said to support France's dominion. From the Kabylia came some of the rebellion's finest military leaders and there and in the Aurès the inhabitants, alleged "Berber anarchists," clearly favored the nationalist cause.

In thinking over the history of Algeria before the French conquest, which began in 1830, several generalizations rise to the surface. The Berber people adopted what ideas they wanted from the invaders and yet held stubbornly to their indigenous culture. Islam and the Arabic language are certainly residual cultural mainstays. The Romans came, conquered, left some monuments, and departed. Ottoman Turks successfully disputed control with the Spanish in the sixteenth century and remained, in diluted strength and mastery almost until the arrival of the French. The

Holy Roman Emperor Charles V, also King of Spain, in 1541 attacked Algiers, but the great storm of October 26 destroyed his fleet, forcing him to withdraw. Spanish garrisons managed to hold Oran and Mers-el-Kebir until the Turks finally displaced them in the eighteenth century.

The chief Turkish official, the beylerbey, held forth at Algiers, and he governed the outlying domain through three beys, one in Constantine, another in Titeri in the south, and the third in Mascara and, later, Oran. In the late sixteenth century Ottoman Sultans began sending pashas for three year periods to do the work of the beylerbey. Administrative headaches were severe and life, even for the pashas and beylerbeys, was hectic and uncertain. They fought among themselves, with the indigenous population, and they contended with corsairs and the janissaries, soldiers recruited originally from slaves—the name derives from the Turkish word "yenicheri," meaning "new force." The janissaries tended to become a law unto themselves.

By the seventh decade in the seventeenth century the corsairs seized power from the pasha and installed their own dey. Thereafter direct Turkish power waned and the deys themselves fell under the control of the janissaries. This situation bothered the European powers. Corsair operations in the Mediterranean were both disagreeable and costly to the crowned heads and their commercially active subjects. Then, too, the crusading spirit was not quite dead and the crescent outranked the cross in the Maghrib. So, from Spain and France, with aid often rendered by other Christian powers and the Pope, naval expeditions set out to free the Mediterranean of piracy. Often they failed completely; at best they won temporary satisfaction. Barbary piracy was on the agenda at the Congress of Vienna (1815) and three years later at Aix-la-Chapelle.

What quickened French interest in Algeria was not an act of piracy but rather what French leaders claimed to be a diplomatic affront, incurred during negotiations over money. This was followed by reprisals by the French and retaliation from the Dey of Algiers.

5

Tension which dated back to 1797 came about this way under the Directory in France. Two Jewish merchants, Bakri and Busnach, supplied North African wheat to French armies at high prices and under conditions of delayed payments which afforded high interest rates. Bakri stationed himself in Marseilles and Busnach operated in Algiers. They also supplied the British in Gibraltar, a condition which perhaps encouraged Charles Delacroix, French foreign minister in 1797, to delay payments beyond the agreed upon limit. The Dey of Algiers became involved when Bakri and Busnach claimed they could not pay him their obligations unless they collected from France. This case dragged on until 1819 when the French government settled claims amounting to 24,000,000 francs for 7,000,000. The Restoration government of France paid 4,500,000 francs and deposited the balance of 2,500,000 francs against the outcome of hopelessly tangled litigation and claims.

Dey Husseïn had waited a long time for his money. To Pierre Deval, the French Consul in Algiers, he stated flatly, "Am I responsible for obligations contracted by two Jewish business houses. If the debt were due the King of France from one of my subjects, justice would require him to pay within twenty-four hours." A French public act intending to recognize the Dey's claim seemed in application to legalize his loss. The French and the Dey had been duped by Jacob Bakri. Husseïn wrote directly to the French king, demanding that Bakri be sent to Algiers. On April 30, 1827, Husseïn summoned Consul Deval.

"Why has not your minister written me directly, am I a peasant clod, a barefoot boy with muddy feet? You are responsible for this . . . you wicked one, you infidel, you idolater."

"My government will not write to you. It is useless."

This response infuriated Husseïn who ordered Deval to withdraw. Either the consul sat tight and tried to remonstrate or he moved too slowly. In any case Husseïn helped him on his way with three quick strokes of his flyswatter. That evening Deval wrote Paris that he had been swatted without provocation and recommended severe measures with all the éclat the incident deserved. This was the diplomatic excuse for war.

France judged three swats to be worth a blockade of the port of Algiers. The ministry in France was divided. The war minister, Clermont-Tonnere wanted war; the chief of the ministry, the comte de Villèle opposed an expedition; later, a foreign minister desired further negotiations. The blockade lasted three years and incidents multiplied. Two French ships went aground and the Kabyles killed eighty-six of the crew members. It is said they received 500 francs per man and the heads were sent to Algiers in sacks. Other French sailors were held in prison. Finally an Algiers shore battery fired eighty salvos at the French ship "La Provence" flying a flag of truce. These provocations plus blockade costs amounting to 7,000,000 francs each year forced a change in French policy.

An expedition, it was hoped, would put an end to the question. Prince Polignac wrote that Charles X took charge of the plans for it and that he served as no more than a secretary. As the new intention became generally known, Britain's interest quickened. British consuls had previously encouraged Hussein to resist French pressure. A last minute French effort to combine with Mehemet Ali, pasha of Egypt, in a joint naval expedition died in birth when it appeared to link the Near Eastern Question with the case of Algeria. Metternich knowingly observed, "It is not for a blow from a fly-swatter that one spends 100,000,000 francs and risks 40,000 men."

The decision to launch an expedition was taken in January, 1830, and on June 14 French forces landed near Sidi-Ferruch, twenty-five kilometers from Algiers. That city fell on July 5. This success did not prevent the downfall of Charles X, whose domestic policies offended the vast majority of the French nation, in the last days of July, 1830.

Meanwhile on July 10 Hussein was shipped to Naples on the frigate "Jeanne d'Arc" with his family, his harem, in all 110 persons, half of whom were women, and "considerable baggage." The dethroned Charles X left Cherbourg for England on August 16.

Many reflective French citizens and political leaders in 1830 viewed the occupation of Algiers as temporary. Thoughts of further conquest and ultimate colonization were far from their minds since not many Frenchmen wanted to exchange life in France for an adventure in North Africa. So, a temporary policy of restricted occupation of the three seaports, Algiers, Bône, and Oran satisfied most people. But continued Muslim resistance forced French commanders to enlarge the beachheads or face ultimate defeat. French troops stayed on and a few colonists arrived.

Life was hard and peace rare. For fifteen years, until 1847, Abd-el-Kader proved to be an exceedingly intelligent and fearless antagonist. Much later, beginning in 1864 in the southern Oran province, a seven year revolt plagued the military and the colonists. In 1871 a particularly bitter insurrection broke out in the Kabylia at a time when France was preoccupied with the immediate consequences of the disastrous war with Prussia and undergoing the labor pains of the Third Republic. A close view of Algeria in almost any year after 1830 reveals evidence of Muslim unrest.

A glance at French efforts to formulate policy and to administer Algeria, whose boundaries except in the south had been rounded off by 1860, reveals difficult problems and no single satisfactory solution. Almost every conceivable kind of colonial administration fell under experiment, and a great variety of encouragements were offered to permanent European settlers.

In the early years military occupation and administration were combined and the governor general, whose office was created in 1834, executed the orders of the minister of war. Some civil administrators helped the military. When France set aside the Orléanist monarchy in favor of the Second Republic in 1848, military rule in Algeria gave way to a system where public services in the colony fell under the control of the equivalent ministries in Paris. Departments and communes took shape in Algeria modeled after those in the Metropole. At the outset of the Second Empire a minister of Algeria replaced the governor general, prefects in Algeria were given enlarged responsibilities, and general councils of Europeans functioned in the departments. But in 1860 Napoleon III reestablished the office of governor general and increased the powers of the military.

The Third Republic could not decide on the amount of author-

8

ity to delegate the governor general. Sometimes the minister of interior in Paris held the reins; at other periods authority was divided among all the ministers. Between 1881 and 1896 the *rattachement* experiment, begun in 1848, governed Algeria through the equivalent ministries in Paris, reducing the governor general to a figurehead. By the twentieth century that post again resembled a proconsulship responsible to the French legislature. The Third Republic considered all Muslims in Algeria to be French "subjects." Those who accepted French civil status and abandoned Koranic law received a "citizenship" which did not include the same rights as French citizens had. Few Muslims were tempted to make the transfer.

By 1919, the point at which the more detailed narrative and analysis of this book begins, the machine of government in Algeria looked like this:

Frenchmen had begun to consider Algeria as a part of France; it was organized into similar departments. Its governor general represented the Third Republic in Algiers and had authority in most areas. He was aided by an advisory council of important European residents. Another council, composed of elected and nominated members including some Muslims, deliberated administrative questions. The Financial Delegations, created in 1898, oversaw taxes and voted the budget. This body, which is discussed later in a more specific frame of reference, brought together representatives from the rural and urban communities and included Muslim members who were always a minority.

Local government varied, being divided in the first instance between civil and military territories. The latter were usually isolated and sparsely inhabited by Europeans. Communes, the smallest units of government, were of three kinds: (1) full power communes were replicas of those in France and were European controlled; (2) mixed communes were administered by men nominated by the governor general; in these a council of Europeans and Muslims helped make decisions; often mixed communes included several villages and, where they coincided with military territories, army officers were in charge; (3) "native" communes were organized like mixed communes, but a Muslim leader (a *caïd*) ruled with the aid of a council of Muslim notables (*djemaa*) over the *douar,* or tribal division.

This brief survey of French rule does not begin to tell the whole story. It passes over the reactions of the unheard Muslim population during the first century of occupation. Nor does it discuss the vital question of land ownership, the installation of European settlers—made up of European farmers and business-men, political refugees from France, people from Alsace-Lorraine who started new lives when the tricolor was hauled down in their homeland in 1871, and the other Europeans (some retired soldiers) who for one reason or another lived in Algeria. It omits, too, most of the tensions between European and Muslim, the struggle of men against men, and the heroic stories of early settlers who lived in danger of their lives, constantly struggling against pestilence and nature's hostility. Many devoted Muslims and Europeans had built the Algeria which Clemenceau knew in 1919. Schools, public works, vineyards (in response to the ravages of phyloxera in France and the almost perfect conditions for the vine in Algeria), roads, cities, railroads, enterprises of all sort took form.

And yet deep in the soil lay the conflict, at times dormant, but always sprouting anew, which had been seeded, almost by hazard, in 1830. It is the more recent chapters in this conflict, this ordeal of the French and Algerian people fighting desperately for a solution to the Algerian question and for a renewed future in a changed world, which is our concern.

CHAPTER ONE

ALGERIA BETWEEN TWO WORLD WARS

FACTS AND FIGURES IN OUR TIME

The determined march of colonial peoples toward independence is one of the most striking and influential characteristics of world history since 1919. The mandate system which emerged from World War I took some notice of these hopes, but though it gave more than lip service to the responsibilities of trusteeship, in the eyes of the peoples of Africa, the Near East, and Asia it stood merely as an early benevolent step on freedom's road. Between the two World Wars the nationalist hopes of non-European peoples received very little encouragement. Yet they grew stronger with each passing decade.

Then came the Second War, fought on three continents and on all the oceans. The war itself brought new relationships between colonies and mother countries. At its end, nationalist movements took on greater vitality, were better led, and more insistent. And the changed international relationships, which saw the United States and the Soviet Union emerge as super powers, provided a more favorable soil for these seeds of independence. One did not have to be wise to understand the importance of the non-European world to the super power as it took stock of its resources and went about the task of increasing its world influence. The non-European world would soon hold the balance of future world power. Meanwhile, the older European imperial states, weakened by war and impoverished at home and abroad, round it increasingly difficult to contain these nationalist pressures.

In the armistice period following World War I independence movements within colonial areas were largely abstractions and without driving force. After 1945 they became hard, influential, and dynamic facts. Large areas, formerly within European empires, cut themselves free; their peoples found political independence with its attendant blessings and curses. India, Pakistan, Indonesia, former French Indo-China north of the seventeenth parallel (Vietnam), Iraq, Syria, Lebanon, Israel, Egypt, Tunisia, Morocco, Ghana, and Guinea come to mind quickly as new independent states. Independence filled the air of Africa—Nigeria, the Cameroons, Togo, and Somalia would achieve it in 1960.[1] Timetables for independence, formerly conservative in their estimates, had to be rapidly readjusted toward the present.

Nationalist pressure for political independence became desperately impelling, usually overcoming all resistance. Whether this evolution will lead toward a more peaceful world and whether the necessary increase in living standards and human welfare will in the long run accompany this evolution are questions which challenge all of our present wisdom. In one sense these are secondary, or future questions. Peoples today seek the right to make their own decisions, and to determine their own futures which will inevitably be combinations of mistakes and successes. They demand, above all, personal status combined with national existence in the form of sovereign states.

The aspirations of the people of Algeria follow this general pattern. There are, however, particular conditions and circumstances which make her case different, even from her neighbors in the Maghrib, Morocco and Tunisia, since 1956 independent of France. Algeria's association with France dating from 1830, the beginning of the conquest, is a hundred and thirty year history of coexistence interspersed with uprisings. Algeria was a colony not a protectorate, and to some persons it was (and is) considered part of France. By 1954 an important minority, roughly 10 per cent of its inhabitants, were Europeans of French citizenship. This made a tremendous difference as events unfolded and men groped for solutions.

12

This Algerian population divides itself on a religious base into Muslim and Christian. French sources tell us that approximately 9,000,000 Muslims, most of whom are of Berber origin with the remainder largely Arabic, cohabit Algeria with 1,200,000 Christian Europeans and a relatively small number of Jews. Exceptional cases of Berber-Arab Christians exist and there are some Europeans who have embraced Islam, but these cases are relatively few. Algerian nationalist spokesmen place the Muslim population at 10,000,000 and reduce Europeans, usually by not counting French armed forces, to 850,000 persons. These same spokesmen of the National Liberation Front (*Front de Libération Nationale*), F.L.N., in arguing against the "Algeria is France" view of French integrationists, point out that no more than 22 per cent of the Europeans in Algeria are of French origin. Most Europeans, they correctly note, are of Spanish descent, itself heavily Moorish in content, and there are important numbers of Maltese, Italians, and people from other Mediterranean islands including Corsica. If there are, by this count, only some 200,000 Europeans of French origin, it is well to remember that almost all the Europeans have considered themselves Frenchmen by virtue of their citizenship. This is true, too, of 140,000 Jews, given citizenship by the Crémieux Law of October 24, 1870. Though this status was denied the Jews under the Vichy Regime, beginning in 1942, it was once again guaranteed by Charles de Gaulle's French Committee of National Liberation in 1944 and subsequently by the Fourth Republic.[2]

Today's statistics are really of no more than secondary importance in the serious study of the demography of Algeria. The capital issue, which imposes itself upon any future solution of the problem, has to do with population growth. At present Algeria has a galloping population whose acceleration is one of the most rapid in the world. In 1830, when French conquest began, and a Marseilles businessman sold seats and full pension on a pleasure boat for fifteen francs a day to those sportive enough to witness the bombardment of Algiers "and the landing of our troops,"[3] there were 2,000,000 inhabitants, almost all Muslims. By 1901 the descendants of those who witnessed this nineteenth-

13

century equivalent of a "turkey-shoot" might have been surprised to learn that the Muslim population had doubled to 4,000,000. Thirty years later it had more than doubled again. Present careful projections place the Algerian population of 1980 at 20,000,000, and, if conditions remain the same, it should double once again by the year 2000. It is scarcely necessary to explain that this projected growth is confined exclusively to the Muslims. The European population remains relatively static. As early as 1891 some 501,000 Europeans lived in Algeria, thus in more than half a century the European population has scarcely doubled. What increase there is, is due to immigration, not birth rate. In the five-year period 1921-1925 the European population grew less than one-tenth of one per cent. It is interesting to note, too, that in 1891, before the "automatic naturalization law" of June 26, 1889 could be influential, 233,000 Europeans living in Algeria were not French nationals. This situation altered quickly in the direction of a solid French national European community under the impact of that law.[4]

Algerian nationalists, looking forward to the twenty-first century, when the Muslim population of their land might reach 40,000,000 thus engulfing the European minority which will remain comparatively static, feel that time is on their side. With Morocco independent on the west and Tunisia in a similar situation on the east, with the sirocco from the Sahara and "Black" Africa bearing the pollen of independence reinforced by the wind from the east bearing the same dust, the F.L.N. and its freedom fighters add present friends to their future numbers.

If the galloping population augurs a future independent Algeria, it is equally a testimonial to French public health programs on the south shore of the Mediterranean. The reduction of epidemics and the installation of preventive medicine go far to explain the increase in birthrate and greater longevity. These developments, taken in the context of a Muslim society, in which polygamy has always been accepted and where it is relatively easy for a man to dissolve a marital union, help to explain the present demographic situation. The plague is gone and penicillin, "the drug that brings children," has come. Unfortunately, food supply has not increased in the same ratio as humanity. This has led to what Germaine Tillion calls "progressive pauperization."

Diseases like malaria and typhoid, disappearing fast, have been replaced by a new one, mass starvation. It is today estimated that two-thirds of the Muslim population, some 6,000,000 or 7,000,000 persons, are paupers often forced to eat their seed crops instead of planting them, suffering constant hunger, and cut off from the archaic tribal civilization which until some twenty years ago maintained some semblance of a balance between population and food.

Today Algeria is a cultural no man's land, existing somewhere between western civilization and the primitive North African society. Modern nations produce more goods and food and raise relatively fewer children per calory of food and yard of cloth; the Algerian society of today, competing with modern techniques and at the same time clinging to ways current before the Industrial Revolution, is caught in a vacuum of change. Its living standard has therefore declined while that in most Western countries has increased.

These problems are confirmed by ethnological studies of certain areas which report serious deterioration in the villages since 1940. The French government again adds to our knowledge through its economic surveys of relationships between France and Algeria. Without the Maspétiol and Delavignette Reports of 1955, our information concerning Algerian incomes and social conditions would be exceedingly fragmentary. With these basic documents, it is possible clearly to envisage the economic problem.[5]

They tell us, for example, that 65 per cent of the total Muslim population, or 73 per cent of Muslims living off the land as rural inhabitants, were, in 1953, the year before the rebellion began, in the lowest income class where per capita income was $55 per year. Since retail prices approximated those of the United States, it is apparent that real income stood at a shockingly low point. Some 78 per cent of income in this group went for food. Above this "bottom group," where six out of ten Muslims groveled for survival, stood an urban Muslim group whose per capita annual income was $164, more than half of which was spent for food. Together these two income groups encompass 93 per cent of the Muslim population. Combining these two groups statistically and allowing for six persons per family, Professor Melvin Knight finds that such a family would have an annual income of $471 and would buy at market prices similar to those prevailing in the United States.

Above these two lowest Muslim income groups, the Maspétiol Report discusses three additional categories. Moving upward to the third level, the annual per capita income of the wage-earner, shopkeeper, and artisan, attains $372. In this mixed group more than half (53.6 per cent) are Muslim, but this same group represents no more than 6.4 per cent of the total Muslim population. In the "next to the top" class, where per capita annual income is $673, Muslims are rare, 8.6 per cent, making up less than one percent of the total Muslim population. Finally, in the "top bracket" where annual per capita incomes range as high as $4657 there are no Muslims.[6] By lumping all these figures together and making the false assumption—but the only one possible since the data does not allow a correction—that Muslim and European incomes are equal in the two mixed groups, Professor Knight places the per capita income of all Muslims at $98 per year and that of non-Muslims at $587. Since the assumption probably favors the Muslims who occupy the lower spots in the mixed income groups, it is reasonable to assume that the per capita Muslim income to the European is, at best, roughly 1:6.

The "progressive pauperization" of the Arab-Berber population which has characterized the twentieth century and which seems to be rooted in the widening gap between population growth and reduced per capita production and maldistribution may be partly understood by a careful glance at the agricultural sector of the economy. Figures argue that the annual per capita consumption of wheat for the Algerian, as distinguished from the European inhabitant in Algeria, dropped from approximately four quintals in 1900 to two and one-half in 1940, to two in 1950.[7] The situation is related directly to the question of land ownership, methods of exploitation of the land, and the choice of products grown. It is, of course, also related less directly to other aspects of the economy. If, for example, large credits from industry could be used to purchase food abroad or be reinvested in land reclamation, then the pressure upon agriculture would be reduced.

Before examining land ownership, a glance at the entire surface area of Algeria helps us to orient ourselves and to see the land problem more clearly. The boundaries of Algeria, which are vague in the south and southwest, enclose an area of approximately 850,000 square miles, a land mass more than three times the size of Texas. The Atlas Mountains divide this large territory into three longitudinal zones: the Mediterranean, the steppes or High Plateau zone, and the Sahara. Seven-eighths of the total area belong to the Sahara; the remaining one-eighth is shared between mountain and coastal land, not quite evenly, since the High Plateau zone is larger than the Mediterranean. Ever since pre-Roman times, the pleasant Mediterranean zone has attracted more inhabitants than either the High Plateaus or the Sahara. By 1957 more than 80 per cent of Algeria's 10,000,000 persons lived in the coastal zone. Although land was plentiful, good land was scarce and hard for Muslims to come by. The French conquest of 1830-1847 started the new cycle by dispossessing the Muslims and installing Europeans in the favored areas.

In 1841 General Thomas-Robert Bugeaud defined French colonization methods. "Wherever the water supply is good and the land fertile, there we must place colonists without worrying about previous owners. We must distribute the lands in full title to the colonists." [8] Early French colonial authorities, convinced of the virtues of Bugeaud's thinking, by a law of November 1, 1844 incorporated as French public domain all lands on which there were no buildings (unimproved land) when Muslim proprietors could not justify holding title before the conquest. The next year, the ordinance of July 31, 1845 allowed French military authorities the possibility of sequestering the holdings of Muslims

17

guilty of hostile acts. This imposition of European rules upon an Islamic area, enforced by conquest, deprived Muslims of good land and built a French public domain which was used to attract European settlers. The bait held out to colonists was free land or land at a ridiculously low price, including the livestock, any buildings and movable property.[9]

By the time of the revolution in late 1954, and long before, Europeans owned approximately one-third of the cultivable land. Official statistics make no distinction between fertile lands and the extensive bush and dry pasture areas. One government document, dated 1956, placed European ownership at roughly 20 per cent of the entire surface lands.[10] The Delavignette Report concluded that European holdings amounted to 32 per cent of the cultivable, as distinct from total surface, land. Raymond Aron found this situation:

LAND OWNERSHIP IN ALGERIA 1950-1951 [11]

	Europeans	Muslims
Holdings of less than 10 hectares	7,432	438,483
Holdings of more than 10 hectares	14,605	192,249
Total number of holders	22,037	630,732
Total area of holdings (hectares)	2,726,666	7,349,166

one hectare = 2.47 acres

A simple division of these last two figures places the Europeans in possession of 37 per cent of the land. According to these same estimates, the average European holding was 124 hectares against the average Muslim holding of 11 hectares, a ratio of 11 to 1 in favor of the European. Whether one accepts these statistics or those of Knight based upon interpretation of the Delavignette Report, where the ratio favors the Europeans 17 to 1, it is clear that the Muslim population is engaged almost entirely in subsistence farming while the average European agriculturist devotes himself to commercial farming.

The term "average European farmer" can be misleading be-

18

cause some 7,432 European settlers possess less than 10 hectares and are therefore also subsistence farmers. The average becomes something of a distortion because of the existence of some 300 *gros colons,* rich settlers, some dozen of whom own exceedingly large estates.

In general, the Europeans own the best land, and they exploit it by modern methods. As we have said, when they occupied the moist coastal areas, they obtained the land under exceedingly favorable terms from a government bent upon furnishing colonists with incentives, and they profited from government support for improvements, credit, and protection. While the European settlers pushed the Muslim population to less productive land and applied modern techniques, the Muslims continued to farm with primitive methods under a patriarchal system. It is scarcely surprising, then, that one-half the value of agricultural output found itself in the pockets of a European population which makes up no more than 3 per cent of the total rural population. The Muslim farmers were forced to take up agricultural work where they could find it, generally working for Europeans or deserting the land for labor in Metropolitan France. The alternatives were starvation and rebellion, and since November, 1954, the reaction of many Muslims both in Algeria and France has taken the form of revolutionary violence.[12]

It would be unjust to attribute the pauperization of the Muslims entirely to French indifference to the needs of the indigenous people of Algeria. Food production has been increased rather remarkably since 1830 when no more than 1,400,000 acres were planted in grain. By 1954, according to official French sources, 7,000,000 acres yielded various types of grains. Unproductive areas, such as the Mitidja plain near Algiers had been reclaimed. In sum, 6,000,000 acres were transformed from brush, swamp, and wasteland to productive soil.[13]

The issue is not that the French have failed in their efforts at development. But certainly they have failed to keep food production and distribution in a favorable ratio with population increase. The Algerian who gets less grain than his father and

19

grandfather cannot be satisfied with his lot, and he associates his plight with the French presence. Whether an independent Algerian state could have done better since 1830 is hard to say. Probably it would not have been able to modernize agriculture as rapidly, but on the other hand, it may have preserved the tribal economy, and it certainly would have used the land for different products. Without the marvel of penicillin, disease and death would have kept the population in check.

The growth of the wine industry in Algeria points up French insensitivity to the problem of agricultural productivity and the distribution of food. In 1953 approximately 475,000,000 gallons of wine came from almost one million acres of European-owned land. About 6 per cent of this product was consumed in Algeria, presumably by the European population, since most Muslims are alcoholic abstainers in accordance with Islamic law and practice. The great bulk of this crop went to France, where the French Institute of Demographic Studies placed the average consumption of alcohol among adults at 28 litres per head per year, a figure twice that of Italy and three times that of the United Kingdom. More important, the land devoted to vineyards in Algeria is fertile, and it is frequently held in large sections. Half of it can be considered the best land in Algeria. "There are 3 vineyards of more than 2500 acres, 20 of more than 1250 acres, 380 exceeding 250 acres." [14]

What does all this mean? On the French side it represents an occupation, an income for the *colons*, an export for Algeria. This is an asset, a source of income which can be used, at least theoretically, to develop Algeria. To the Algerian Muslim it seems a waste of fertile soil on a product which the native population cannot consume. Likewise it is doubtful that the income produced from the wine is reinvested in Algeria except in the French standard of living. It does, of course, offer employment opportunities for Algerians, both directly upon the vineyards and indirectly in enterprise which might result from wine profits. But these same opportunities would exist were this land planted in wheat, a product which the Algerians desperately need. To convert the

20

use of this land or to appropriate it for the Muslims would involve a change in human nature, at the least a change of heart and faith on the part of wealthy and powerful members of the European community in Algeria and also in France. Yet one French soldier, called from his home in Burgundy to the task of "pacification" in Algeria in 1956, raised this interesting question. "Why should we be over here fighting to defend these vintners who make such bad wine?"

Between 1830, when French armed forces entered Algiers, and November, 1954, the beginning of the current unfinished Algerian rebellion, the French have been aware of industrial possibilities in the colony. To read the official accounts of achievement in this sector of the economy by 1954 is to understand why Frenchmen are proud of the record. Algerian mines have yielded iron, phosphates, lead, zinc, antimony, copper, and other basic industrial raw materials. These products can now be transported on 50,000 miles of roads or almost 19,000 miles of highway, or the 3,000 miles of railroad track to modern ports whose ships visit the world's harbors. Airports dot the landscape, and five broadcasting stations have served about 300,000 radio sets since 1954. Coal from the Kenadsa fields in the South Oran region supplied 20 per cent of Algeria's needs, and, before the recent discoveries and exploitations in the Sahara, about 100,000 tons of oil from Aumale contributed precious energy. Thirty-five power stations generated some 800,000,000 kilowatt hours of electricity to help power some 600 industrial plants which employed more than 50 workers each. Metallurgical, electrical, and machine tool operations as well as a chemical and textile industry operated to produce goods for the local and Metropolitan market. Compared with the agricultural and pastural economy prevailing in 1830 these accomplishments can not be ignored. By 1954 Algeria's trade volume reached $1,023,000,000, with imports amounting to $623,000,000 and exports to $400,000,000. The Customs Union between Algeria and Metropolitan France accounted for 79 per cent of Algerian imports and 73 per cent of exports. Algeria's trade deficit of $223,000,000 resulted, in the French view, from determined efforts to modernize and to raise living standards.[15]

There is no doubt about it, the Algeria of 1954 bore, in several important aspects, a modern French imprint. We have no reliable statistics on industrial conditions in 1830, but it is a free assumption that, apart from such handicraft interests as rugs, embroidery, brass, and leather work, the area was undeveloped. Of course, too, the France of 1830 presented a marked contrast with that of the mid-twentieth century. Certainly the mother country developed itself more purposefully than it did the colony. This was common colonial practice throughout the nineteenth-century world, a fact of life. What interests Algerian nationalist leaders in our time is not these straw men but rather the fact that the fruits of production fell into European hands in large proportion. After 130 years of French occupation, nationalists desire, above all, status, responsibility, and opportunities to develop themselves. They think in political terms and have confidence that, in the long run, independence will lead to greater productivity and physical well being. An independent national state followed by development toward a modern economy and social order—this is the nationalist dream.

By 1954, agricultural production occupied 72 per cent of the labor force and yielded no more than 32 per cent of total output. Hand labor remained exceedingly important; unemployment and underemployment stood dangerously high. In face of a galloping Algerian population and the heavy pressure upon the French economy imposed by war and German occupation, which retarded capital investment, raising standards for Muslims was an uphill task. The problem becomes particularly acute and sensitive when one recognizes that European control of industrial and commercial enterprise was far more predominant than in agriculture where it owned the best land but not the most. Approximately 90 per cent of industry and commerce was held by Europeans who collected 92 per cent of the industrial and commercial profits (*chiffres d'affaires*) earned. This income was in direct proportion to European investment.[16]

The French are proud of their efforts to educate the Muslim

22

population. Before 1939 only very few Muslim parents agreed to send their children to the French schools. Official reports of 1954 place 17 per cent of the ordinary budget of Algeria under educational development. By this date some 500,000 children attended schools at primary, secondary, and vocational institutions. The University of Algiers ranked third in the French Union. It maintained a faculty of nearly one hundred professors and a student population of 5,000. In 1957 another official report noted "Muslim enrollment in the public schools tripled between 1945 and 1955. Total enrollment in Algeria is now 666,000 (including private schools)." [17] Accepting these statements as truth, it is also a fact that in 1954, 94 per cent of the male Muslims and 98 per cent of the females were illiterate in French. Further, in breaking down the school age population in 1954 against the numbers attending schools, no more than 1 Muslim boy in 5, and 1 Muslim girl in 16 attended school. Four-fifths of the students at the University of Algiers were Europeans. Though the regular Algerian budget spent 723 francs per inhabitant on education (against Egypt's 268) there was still a great distance to be traveled before the Muslim in Algeria had educational facilities to help him surmount the high barrier of the French language, which, as long as the French rule Algeria, will be a necessary step toward joining the modern industrialized world.

This discussion omits any consideration of instruction in Arabic, the first language of the Muslim population. The French statement of 1957 simply notes that the teaching of Arabic is being extended to Europeans and Arabs in public schools, and cites the Advanced Islamic Institute opened in 1946. By 1954 it is estimated that 150,000 Muslims attended the traditional *écoles coraniques,* which reflected the learning of Arabic civilization rather than French. Here the Muslim children did not have to recite a history lesson about their ancestors, the Gauls.

A comparison of the numbers of Muslims and Europeans in gainful employment substantiates the view that the latter dominate the most sought after and rewarding work. Unemployment is the only category where Muslims hold a great lead.

EUROPEAN-MUSLIM PERCENTAGES IN VARIOUS NONAGRICULTURAL
EMPLOYMENT CATEGORIES 1954 [18]

Socio-Professional Categories	Non-Muslims	Muslims
heads of companies or businesses	36.2	63.8
civil servants and intellectuals	92.7	7.3
lower level intellectuals and technicians	82.4	17.6
office workers and commercial workers	78.7	21.3
workers in professions	50.9	49.1
specialized workers	32.1	67.9
day laborers	4.8	95.2
apprentices	54.1	45.9
domestics	41.6	58.4
unemployed	9.6	90.4

Wherever one examines the institutions of Algeria, whether it
be in the economic zone, the social, or cultural, two interpretations
can be made. The French proudly look at their work on the
land and the cities, point to the statistics, and ask the rhetorical
question, "What would Algeria be without us?" These are the
same people whose spokesmen and literary craftsmen often find
the United States and Americans too materialistic. The other
view comes, of course, from the Algerian nationalist who asks,
"Who owns the best land, who controls industry, who spends
all the money, and who gets the education?" It points to the
misery in the "*douars*," the "villages without schools." In short, the
increasing pauperization of the Muslim population and its lack
of civil liberty blocks out the French idyllic vista.

Many myths color the picture which the casual observer of the
Algerian question carries in his mind. The European population
is not made up of a million exploiters of the Muslim. Nor are all
the Muslims anxious to cut the throats of the "exploiters."
Actually the vast majority of the European residents are not
wealthy land owners or wine merchants. Most of them are
ordinary souls who drive taxis, work as carpenters, electricians,
plumbers, small shopkeepers. Many European engineers and

24

professional people have deep love for and faith in Algeria, which has been for so many years their home and their country—a place they have built to remain in. These ordinary people have the same attitudes as the British North American of 1763. The "transplanted Englishman," while a product of Anglo-Saxon culture and tradition, by that time had undergone a mutation from exposure to a different environment. He was an American before he was an Englishman, with loyalties to the soil he had cleared or the business he had built. He had problems with the Indian natives. In Algeria these ordinary "Europeans" are really Algerians. By 1954 they occupied a position between the bitter-end *gros colon* and the Algerian nationalist. The large plantation owners, the very wealthy, number perhaps no more than one hundred families while the settler group as a whole reaches a total of 45,000 persons. Since November, 1954, the custom has been to speak in the pejorative. Thus settlers, or *colons*, or Europeans, are exploiters who deprive the Muslims of the necessities of life, and the "natives" are rebels, criminals, or traitors led by a group of fanatical nationalists.

The post-1945 period, with its difficult reconstruction in Metropolitan France, and the unfortunate and complicated demographic, economic, and social situation in Algeria, witnessed a mass emigration of Algerian workers to France. In both World Wars and in Indo-China after 1946 Algerians fought behind the tricolor. These older patriots in some cases still remain in Algeria but their numbers are few compared to the 400,000 or 500,000 young Algerians who deserted their impoverished villages and farms and sought employment in France. Coming often without money or job prospects, without even a slight understanding of basic French, these workers tried to eke out a living for themselves in the Metropole and to save a part of their wage to send home to their families. How many Algerians have come to France since 1945? This is a difficult question since a great deal of rotation takes place. Some came, stayed for a time, and returned home. Others remained. Of the adult male population perhaps two million know the other side of the Mediterranean. The striking point, and one much more important than numbers, is that the areas in Algeria where Muslims with European experience were in the majority, tended to become the centers of insurrection.[19]

In France the Algerian worker faced a host of insurmountable problems. Unskilled, without money, uneducated in the language or the ways of the labor market, he found himself performing the heaviest work, at the lowest wage scale, and without equality in matters of family allocations or social security. Housing for a Muslim was difficult because there was, and is, a housing shortage all over France since the German occupation, and there was discrimination on the part of certain landlords who did not want the *bicot* in their lodgings. That illness befell many—they often arrived suffering from paludism, trachoma, and benign syphilis— is not startling to visitors who have seen the Algerian worker asleep in the dead of winter wrapped in a blanket and lying over the Métro vents from which foul but warm air emerges.

From this experience the native Algerians had varied reactions. Some returned home with the spirit of independence burning deep. Others stayed on in the Metropole, working for one or another of the Algerian parties. Some joined the French Communist Party where they occasionally spearheaded the shock troops in demonstrations. But many, though members of the party, placed Algerian nationalism above the interests of the Communist leaders. One thing is certain, large numbers of Algerians saw in France an entirely new world in which they were determined to find a role, not a very large or remunerative role, but a modern one. They met their fate head on and saw it to be that of a people forced into the French market place because of deteriorating conditions on the land at home. Many workers hoped to return to help their native land increase opportunities for their own people. For an important section of these men who were workers or students in France the solution seemed to be independence, the practice of Liberty, Equality, and Fraternity in Algeria. They learned their lesson in French history very well. The next step would be to practice what they believed.[20]

GENESIS OF ALGERIAN NATIONALISM

Algerian political awakening evolved from various sources and pressures in the twentieth century. Two world wars speeded this process by bringing Algerian soldiers into European trenches, armored divisions, and factories. During the second war Algerians of all classes saw large numbers of Anglo-American soldiers and articulate Muslims read with keen interest the war aims of the Allies, as expressed in such statements as the Atlantic Charter. The collapse of France in 1940 pushed Algerians toward independence of action at the same time that it bound them tightly to France's future. Particularly was the precedent of the first war important to the thoughtful Muslim.

Algerian nationalist leaders knew that at the outset of war in 1914 the influential *colons* were closed-minded against any liberal alterations in the French system. They opposed conscription of the Algerians into the French army out of fear of an insurrection, and because such action would increase the wages of the workers. They also understood that patriotic support of France by her Algerian wards would open the way to civil rights, something the *colons* could not square with their continued dominance. Two years earlier, on May 18, 1912, a newspaper published in Djidjelli, *Rachidi,* carried a story in which young Algerians made the point. "We are glad to submit to the blood tax, but in compensation we demand solely the rights of French citizenship." [21] The *colons* fought the suggestion of unifying the tax system which at this time taxed Muslim differently than European. For them it was foolish and impossible to conceive of an educated Algerian population. Nor could they agree to the view that Muslims should have a hand in electing the mayors.

By the reform law of February 4, 1919, Clemenceau, in gratitude for Algerian loyalty during the war, made French citizenship more accessible and allowed those Muslims, classed as French subjects, not citizens, because they retained their personal status as Muslims, greater participation in local government.

27

Muslim municipal counsellors obtained the right to participate in the elections of mayors. Although they were far from achieving political equality or parity in the various assemblies with Europeans, the indigenous inhabitants advanced in that direction. Earlier, in November, 1918, tax equality between European and Muslim became law in Algeria but not in the Sahara. Europeans in Algeria took a jaundiced view of this program, predicting such dire future results as insurrection and the loss of French sovereignty. The opposition failed to budge the "Tiger," who, having stood firm against the German army, brooked no interference from the Algerian planters. Premiers after 1955 lacked this strength.[22]

Between the two world wars national consciousness increased noticeably among the Algerians. While an exact explanation of this defies the student of social phenomena, he can see a convergence of forces, facts, and ideas which help to explain this important change. Quite some time before World War II accelerated this reaction, such elements as a revival of Islamic religion and culture combined with increased political consciousness (itself a result of visits and work periods in France), higher education, activities in political, revolutionary, and labor movements, were producing a demand for change. This desire, conflicting with a foolishly unyielding colonial policy, culminated finally in a rebellion which began in 1954 and is not resolved six years later.

Early in the century Algeria was, of all the Islamic area, most closed to new ideas. Among the peasantry half-educated holy men (marabouts) and religious imposters preached a debased interpretation of Islam. The influence of this doctrine was social rather than religious, and it made no effort to unite its followers. The local holy men exercised power over the poor *fellahs* while the more sophisticated marabouts served the landed aristocracy whose aim was to hold the agricultural worker in check. These holy men tended to become tools of French colonial policy, "yes men," *beni-oui-oui's*. After 1930 maraboutism receded before the challenge of the Ulema (literally "learned men") who fused religious puritanism and national consciousness. The Association of Algerian Ulema, founded May 5, 1935 under the leadership of

28

Abd-al-Hamid Ben Badis, combined puritanism (Arabian Wahab-ism) and nationalist zeal.[23]

Ben Badis, descended from an old and renowned Berber family, reached, in powerful fashion, both men of letters and the masses. The ringing declaration "Islam is our religion, Algeria our country, Arabic our language," accurately expressed the Ulema objectives. Two publications, the monthly *Ech Chiheb* (*The Meteor*), and the weekly *El-Bassair* (*Future Visions*), instructed their readers in the ways of modern Islam and admonished them to discard the outmoded marabout doctrines. The Ulema viewed as apostasy the acquisition of non-Muslim (French) citizenship, and frowned upon intermarriage with Europeans. The correct direction for the Algerian Muslim was along the path of Arabic culture which now rejected the old "superstitions and fetishisms," strove for unity of purpose between Arab and Berber, and the advancement of Muslim culture. This could be accomplished through the application of traditional and modern science. The pestle and the mortar of the movement became the Arabic language. In Arabic, then, from Constantine Ben Badis expounded these ideas which so bluntly opposed the long-standing French doctrine of assimilation, and soon these views were translated into political action. It was not surprising that when World War II broke out Ben Badis refused to accept the idea that Algeria's future was necessarily linked to a French victory.

Ulema influence spread to the major cities of Algeria and reached into the rural Muslim communes (*douars*). In the department of Algiers Ben Badis' equivalent, El-Okbi, who had spent twenty-five years in Hedjaz absorbing Wahabite doctrines, provided vigorous leadership and influential oratory. Brahimi Si el-Bachir (alias Taleb el-Bachir), born in the Constantine region of a *fellah* (peasant) family, dominated the movement in the Oran area. He, too, studied Islamic theology in the east, having visited Egypt and Syria. It was he who took over the spiritual leadership of the movement from Ben Badis in May, 1940, when the latter died. The Ulema preached unity among the Muslims, and their platforms were the mosques and the Koranic schools where they instructed both children and adults. Religious instruction and canon law were taught in Arabic. In larger centers, such as the school in Constantine organized by Ben Badis, some three hundred children attended, and from there missionaries carried the program into the countryside. Teachers studied theology, philosophy, law, literature, and history. Algerian children read prepared history manuals, reminiscent of those used in the *écoles communales* of France, with the difference, of course, that the Algerian children might read about Abd-el-Kader's insurgence against the French while the French children are told about Vercingetorix's gallant fight against Caesar.

Repressive measures taken by the colonial administrators demonstrated more accurately than official statements the effectiveness of the Ulema program. French supervision of religious questions functioned largely through the bureau of *Affaires indigènes* which worked with the marabouts and *comités consultatifs de culte* in each department to keep the Muslim population docile. On February 16, 1933, an order known as the *"circulaire Michel,"* drafted by Michel, the Secretary General of the Prefecture of Algiers, asked local authorities "to watch closely communist agents and Ulema who were suspected 'of seeking to weaken the French cause.'" [24] Three decrees sought to reduce the influence of the Ulema. One deprived them of the use of the state mosques in the department of Algiers, reserving them for the *imams* and *muphtis*. Another confided the presidency of the consultative council to Michel which amounted to granting him control of Muslim religious life. These measures violated the Islamic custom of allowing any educated Muslim to comment upon the Koran. Empowering a Christian bureaucrat to oversee Muslim religious and educational activities shocked liberal Frenchmen who had fought through the separation of church and state at home and who understood the inherent danger of injecting themselves into Muslim religions questions. A future French minister of interior rightly considered this policy "a supreme blunder . . . , a lack of tact . . . , a moral error and a grave mistake." [25] The wisdom of this statement and the complete difference in attitude between Frenchmen and Muslims on

Church and State questions was reaffirmed in 1956 by Jean Brune in his argument against departmentalizing Algeria. "If France promulgates the separation of Church and State, it will inevitably lose Algeria." [26]

These stern measures hardened the Ulema and increased their nationalist fervor. Their hand could be seen in the list of grievances prepared by the Algerian Muslim Congress in June, 1936. And El-Okbi, the Ulema leader in Algiers, although his reputation did not suffer from a trumped-up charge which momentarily placed him in prison, under constant surveillance of the police became sufficiently cautious to lose his stature in the eyes of Muslim nationalists. He refused to follow the lead of Ben Badis, who, during the Munich crisis, carefully refrained from making any declaration in support of France. When war came in 1939, El-Okbi adopted a posture of loyalty to France and thus split himself from Ben Badis and El-Bachir who seized upon the war as an opportunity to oppose assimilation.

Ulema activities buoyed Islamic Arabic institutions against French efforts to drown them in less controversial doctrines. Beyond that, the Ulema stood as resistance centers against which French colonial policy and administration tried itself in a series of repressions and blunders. Finally these centers reached the general Muslim population and succeeded in depriving the French of much needed support. Here, then, stood a force unifying scholarly Islamic theologians with the proletariat of the cities, and the peasant of the *douars*. It made no distinction between Arab and Berber under the banner of Islamic purity, Algeria, and the Arabic tongue.

Another important element of Algerian national consciousness and an unmistakable sign of political maturation to be read by anyone examining the armistice period between the two world wars, was the birth of political parties. Evidence of this showed first, not in Algeria, but in the industrial outskirts of Paris where in March, 1924, Algerian workers fell under the influence of Hadj Abdelkader, a member of the French Communist Party's committee "for the defense of material, moral, and social interests of North African Muslims." Known as *L'Etoile nord-africaine*

31

(The North African Star), in 1927 the party accepted the leadership of Hadj Ben Ahmed Messali known popularly as Messali Hadj of Tlemçen, a resolute war veteran, aged twenty-nine, who had attended courses at the Sorbonne and Collège de France and possessed a simple and direct eloquence in French and Arabic. By 1929, when the French government dissolved the party for advocating a rebellion for North African independence, it claimed a membership of four thousand.

During the decade preceding the outbreak of war in 1939, Messali Hadj spent several terms in prison and his political following operated, sometimes underground, under various names. After Messali preached the independence of North Africa to ten thousand spectators gathered in the municipal stadium of Algiers on August 2, 1936, he ran against the opposition of Muslim moderates like Dr. Mohammed Salah Bendjelloul, who believed in a French Algeria. More significant, the first Popular Front Government of Léon Blum, seconded by the French Communist Party, in January, 1937, dissolved *L'Étoile nord-africaine* which had been revived in 1933. The *Etoile's* trinity of Islam, nationalism, and social reform soured even the most leftist French government of the 1930's. The Blum-Violette proposal, which foundered in 1937 upon the opposition of the *colons* in Algeria and their allies on the benches of the right in the Chamber of Deputies, pleased the *Etoile* no better. It violated Algerian nationalist dogma by projecting the gradual extension of suffrage to a small number of Muslims (21,000 initially). Assimilation and nationalism mixed badly.

Messali circumvented the Popular Front's opposition by transforming, in March, 1937, *L'Etoile nord-africaine* into a legal political party, the Algerian Peoples' Party (*Parti du peuple algérien*), the P.P.A. It scored some success in the municipal elections of 1937 in Algeria, and its members demonstrated effectively enough on Bastille Day to bring down a sentence of two years in prison upon the head of Messali Hadj for "encouraging disorderly action against the sovereignty of the state." When war came in 1939, the P.P.A. was dissolved, its leaders imprisoned or interned. Momentarily Messali Hadj tried to work out a political compromise with Vichy's rulers, but this ended in March, 1941 when he received a sentence of sixteen years of forced labor.

While the Ulema and Messali's *Etoile* and P.P.A. worked for independence, a group of French educated Algerian intellectuals, led by Dr. Bendjelloul and the very handsome pharmacist from Sétif in the Kabylia, Ferhat Abbas, sought a different goal. In the 1930's, through the *Fédération des Elus Musulmans d'Algérie,* these moderates worked, not for independence, but for fusion of the Arab-Berber population with French society. Termed variously, assimilation, integration, or progressive integration, this program called for constructive criticism of the colonial regime plus a deep-rooted faith in Muslim civilization. The answer, as Abbas saw it, involved the replacement of the old colonial order by a reform policy which recognized Algeria's evolution from a colony to a province where Muslims, while retaining their own personal status, could enjoy full French citizenship. In this program Algerian nationalism did not exist. As early as 1931 in his *De la colonie vers la province, Le Jeune Algérien,* the Sétif pharmacist wrote "Our generation owes so little to Arab literature; it is French thought upon which are based the principles of our life." [27] Five years later Abbas stated his position more eloquently and in greater depth.

> We, political friends of Dr. Bendjelloul, are [called] nationalists. The charge is not new. I have discussed this question with various people. My opinion is known: nationalism is the feeling which impels a people to live within its territorial confines, the feeling which created a network of nations. If I had discovered the *Algerian nation,* I would be a nationalist and I would not blush for my crime. Men who die for the patriotic ideal are daily honored and respected. My life is not worth any more than theirs. However, I will not die for the *Algerian fatherland* because this *fatherland* does not exist. I have not found it. I questioned history, I questioned the living and the dead; I visited the cemeteries: no one spoke to me of it. . . . One cannot build on the wind.

33

We have discarded once and for all the nonsense and chimeras to align our future definitely with that of the French work in the country. . . . No outsider believes seriously in our nationalism. What we really seek behind this word is our economic and political emancipation. Without the emancipation of the indigenous inhabitants there can be no lasting French Algeria.[28]

This antinationalist statement did not go unchallenged. Two months later Ben Badis, speaking for the Association of Algerian Ulema, came to a different conclusion.

We have searched in history and in the present and we have undeniably established that the Algerian Muslim nation is formed and exists, as all the other nations of the world. This nation has its history demonstrated by facts; it has religious and linguistic unity; it has its culture, traditions, and characteristics, good or bad, as is the case for any nation on earth. Further, we say that this Algerian nation is not France, cannot be France, and does not wish to be France. It is impossible that it be France, even if it wished assimilation. It has its fixed territory which is Algeria with its present boundaries.[29]

PARTIES AND POLITICS ON THE EVE OF WORLD WAR II

A world lay between these two Algerian statements, but within two decades that great distance was spanned. By 1956 Ferhat Abbas discarded his moderate doctrine to join the F.L.N., and two years later in the fourth year of the Algerian rebellion, he became prime minister of the Provisional Government of the Algerian Republic (G.P.R.A.). The explanation of this evolution lies in a series of "missed opportunities" on the part of French colonial policy, which, when added to the nationalist forces unleashed by World War II, resulted in a full scale independence movement.

Before France went to war in 1939, the most promising effort to conciliate men like Dr. Bendjelloul and Abbas originated in the Popular Front government of Léon Blum. Upon the advice of Maurice Violette, who served as governor general in Algeria (1925-1927), Blum accepted the principle of extending political rights of indigenous Algerians without asking them to renounce their Muslim status and the jurisdiction of Koranic law. The modest Blum-Violette proposal, which reached the floor of the Chamber of Deputies in 1937, sought in the first year of its application to admit 21,000 Muslims to full French citizenship. This élite would be chosen from among soldiers with distinguished service in the First War, teachers, officials, holders of certificates and degrees from French schools, in short from Algerians who supported France and who had an interest in holding the land for France against Algerian nationalism. They would not be required to choose between their Muslim and French civil status. In future years the offers of citizenship were to be increased.

This proposal failed because it was solidly opposed by influential *colons* who viewed this "surge through the floodgates" as the beginning of a process which would drown the Europeans in a Muslim sea. "Since 1919 we have extended maximum concessions. We should not be asked to go further because it is impossible." [30] Three hundred mayors in Algeria added their weight through a resolution passed at a meeting in Algiers (January 14, 1937). Abbé Lambert, mayor of Oran, wrote that "all the anti-French are for the Violette plan." [31] European Algeria thus vetoed a Paris proposal put forth in good faith to create a *modus operandi* in Algeria. Here a proposal which at least moved in the direction of wisdom was defeated largely through colonial influence on the Chamber of Deputies.

Rather serious consequences resulted. Relationships between Europeans and Muslims in Algeria remained frozen as of 1919, and by 1944, when General de Gaulle broke the thaw, good will between the two had markedly diminished. The failure of this early effort to insert a French-oriented screen between Algerian nationalism and the wave of Pan-Arabism across North Africa split the *Fédération des Elus Musulmans,* the one group whose interests closely coincided with those of France.

This organization had worked exceedingly hard in France and

Algeria for passage of the Blum-Violette proposal. When it failed, Bendjelloul first declared a boycott against Muslim participation in local elections and the holding of office. Later (1938), he organized the *Rassemblement franco-musulman algérien* (R.F.M.A.), momentarily bringing together such diverse groups as the Ulema under Ben Badis, the trade unions, war veterans, a part of the P.P.A., plus European trade union representatives, liberals, members of the Socialist and Communist parties. The R.F.M.A. endorsed the reform program of the All-Muslim Congress held earlier (June, 1936) in Algiers. This called for the suppression of French laws (*lois d'exception*) which applied different standards to Muslims than Europeans, attachment of Algeria to France, continuation of the Muslim personal statute, separation of church and state, amalgamation of school facilities for Europeans and Muslims, freedom to teach in Arabic and freedom for the Arabic press, equal wages for equal work performed by Europeans and Muslims, aid to the Muslim peasantry, a single electoral college (*collège électoral unique*), and universal manhood suffrage.[32]

Ferhat Abbas refused to follow Bendjelloul's R.F.M.A., organizing instead his wing of the *Fédération des Elus Musulmans* and his various other supporters into the *Union populaire Algérienne* (U.P.A.). He sought to achieve in practice what the textbooks in the French schools taught, "the conquest of the rights of man and citizen." This was to be fulfilled in the French framework by the free evolution of Muslims within Muslim traditions. "Attachment to France was not assimilation." The U.P.A., therefore, still stood apart from the nationalist-independence program of the P.P.A. and the Ulema.

Communist forces in Paris and Algeria supported the Blum-Violette project, true to the general Moscow directive to combat fascism by cooperation with republican-socialist groups. By 1936 both the Algerian Communist Party and the French Communist Party could agree upon a "free Algeria united with the French people" or a "community of interests."

Nearly fifteen years earlier, Algerian Communists, whose leaders were Europeans, had considered the Comintern's appeal for the liberation of Algeria "a dangerous folly." Moscow's influence, until 1935, was greater in the Paris party than in the Algerian. As a result, in 1934 the Moscow-Paris Communist axis cooperated with Messali Hadj's *Etoile nord-africaine* to advocate a soviet order for workers and peasants, expropriation of *colon* holdings in favor of agrarian workers. The Comintern began to heal the breach between Algerian Communists and their Paris brothers in 1935 when Jean Chaintron undertook a reorganization which placed Muslims (Ouzegane Amar, Ben Ali Boukhort) in important positions. Quickly Muslim membership quadrupled. At the same time Communist strength in the trade unions increased, and relationships with the Ulema improved.

Support of the Popular Front by French and Algerian Communist Parties implied retreating in the struggle against imperialism for the greater purpose of resisting fascism. Too, this meant breaking the alliance with Messali Hadj's P.P.A. and courting the Muslim moderates, Bendjelloul and Ferhat Abbas.[33]

On the extreme and militant right stood the *Parti Populaire Française* (P.P.F.) and the *Parti Social Française* (P.S.F.), political parties whose purpose was to vitiate the Popular Front laws disbanding fascist organizations. Of the two in Algeria, the P.P.F., which centered in Oran upon a hoped-for working agreement between the indigenous masses and other French patrons, seemed the strongest in the late 1930's. Under the leadership of the renegade communist, Jacques Doriot, it tried to make political hay of Muslim poverty. Against the Blum-Violette program it advocated collaboration with Muslims who were promised equal representation in a double electoral college without surrendering their Muslim status. Though this movement made headway at the expense of the P.S.F., its following and influence among the politically conscious Muslims who generally favored the Blum-Violette solution was minimal. Some of its *colons* had the additional disappointment of seeing their dream of forming a Muslim commando force which would take over France from Algeria, as Franco had taken Spain from his base in Morocco, come to nothing. This dream was revived in 1958 by certain colonels of the French Army in Algeria and their *colon* supporters.

37

Colonel de la Rocque presided over the congress of the P.S.F. held in Constantine in 1938. This rightist group added few members to its original following of the *Croix du Feu* in Algeria, largely because its program, while recognizing the alternate necessity of recruiting indigenous support, stood unwilling to grant "advanced" Muslims equality unless they agreed to abandon their right under the Muslim statute. Then, too, the gallant colonel seemingly did not possess the rabble-rousing qualities of Doriot whose party pulled away P.S.F. support, often upon no more original an unfulfilled promise than "bread for those who had none." [34]

By the time war broke out in Europe in September, 1939, there were two major political philosophies stemming from the Muslim population in Algeria. Messali Hadj's P.P.A. and the Ulema preached independence while the moderate groups, Bendjelloul's R.F.M.A. and Ferhat Abbas' U.P.A., still favored reform within a French order. Since the *colons* and the French right succeeded in scuttling the Blum-Violette plan for gradual assimilation and reform, the door had been abruptly closed in the faces of the Muslim moderates who hoped that Algeria's future would be linked to France's. How could these moderates cooperate with a French policy drawn by *colons* who considered the concessions of 1919 an absolute maximum? In the light of this situation the advocates of independence had a consistent position and the only dynamic program. This thought was voiced by Professor Charles André Julien, the distinguished French student of the Maghrib. He said: "The *colons* barred the road toward gradual integration of the indigenous population with the larger community of French citizenship. They thereby cultivated the seed of nationalism which grew with renewed vigor." [35]

CHAPTER TWO

THE IMPACT OF WORLD WAR II UPON ALGERIA

FROM VICHY TO "TORCH"

World War II accelerated Algerian nationalism, at the same time it rubbed French sensibilities raw. France collapsed under the German juggernaut before Algeria's contribution to the war effort could be used as a bargaining point for extended reform. The situation attending the close of the First War was not to be repeated. Instead of a Clemenceau, grateful and strong, ignoring *colon* influence to extend citizenship to loyal Algerians, there was the Vichy regime, accepted by the nation in utter desperation, and oriented, not toward France or its colonial peoples, but to Germany. While Axis radio programs drove the theme of corrupt Republican France into the attentive ears of the Muslims, Vichy promulgated anti-semitic laws and repressed Algerian political life by placing Muslim party leaders and many of their followers in concentration camps.

Vichy's ordinances against the Jews, while a marvelously convenient way of demonstrating the seriousness of the French puppets to the German overlords, found a more receptive audience among the *colons* than the citizenry of metropolitan France. These laws repudiated the Jew, Léon Blum, whose Blum-Violette plan still aroused violent antipathy among the *colons*. As a result of the suspension of the Crémieux law of 1870 and the so-called Peyrouton law, named after Marshal Pétain's minister of the interior, the Algerian Jews found themselves in a legal position

39

inferior to that of the illiterate Muslim majority which could not qualify for full French citizenship. After these decrees, Jews could not qualify for citizenship by fulfilling the conditions set forth in the law of February 4, 1919, which had admitted certain élite *indigènes* to full citizenship. Before Vichy the Algerian Jews had been among the few *indigènes* who could meet these exacting requirements. By the Peyrouton decree Algerian Jews also received a niggardly quota for admission in higher educational institutions—three per cent although they represented 14 per cent of the population at large. In the lower branches of education Jewish families were instructed to withdraw their children "so they would not feel strange among non-Jewish children." Thereafter, these families either organized their own schools privately or their children had no schooling.

The first step in dismantling these laws came on October 20, 1943, when the French Committee of National Liberation abolished Vichy's racist decrees. Not until almost a year later was the Crémieux law restored.[1]

Neither the men of Vichy; their governor general in Algeria, Yves Châtel, nor even the pleased *colons* had anticipated the major result of this extension of anti-semitic policy to Algeria. In 1943 Lieutenant-General Eisenhower quickly judged Châtel's influence to be harmful. "Nevertheless we early told Darlan he had to get rid of Châtel, governor of Algeria, and Noguès, minister to the Sultan of Morocco." [2] Muslim leaders, such as El-Okbi, did not cheer a program which withdrew citizenship guarantees of seventy years duration, practiced racial discrimination, and they drew closer to the Jewish population which in turn furnished Algerian nationalist forces with leaders and support. "Between November, 1942, and January, 1946, 'not a single anti-semitic reference could be found in the Arabic press' " of Algeria.[3]

Outwardly, Muslim political activity came to a standstill during the twenty-nine months separating the capitulation of France and the Anglo-American landings in North Africa beginning November 8, 1942. Not until the early months of 1943, after American and British journalists protested camps harboring large numbers of political prisoners, and letters from soldiers reached

40

their families, did the outside world possess even a slender idea
of political issues between European and Muslim in Algeria. The
Vichy regime, through the forceful administration of Governor
General Châtel and General Weygand, simply eliminated surface
politics by jailing contrary-minded Muslims or Europeans. Half—
and after the North American landings—all of France might be
occupied by the *Wehrmacht,* yet Algeria remained more than
ever occupied by the remnants of French military and bureau-
cratic power, frozen in colonial status. With most Muslim leaders
frightened into silence or rotting in camps, Vichy surrounded
itself with marabouts and various "notables," the precursors of
the *beni-oui-oui* (Muslim yes men) of the next decade.

Writing from notes taken in Algiers in February, 1943, A. J.
Liebling painted, as only he could, this picture:

> There were also, of course, Moslems—commonly re-
> ferred to as 'Ay-rabs'—in town, most of them working at
> the humblest jobs, but I cannot remember that they ever
> had much to say. They affected the general character of
> the place as little as the Puerto Ricans affect Rockefeller
> Center. Also, in chic bars—the Hotel Oasis was their
> favorite—there were great two-hundred-pound-and-up-
> ward dignitaries in wraparound headdresses with side
> drapes, white burnouses, which resembled shower cur-
> tains; purple silk gandurahs, which are blouses; and
> baggy white duck séroual, which are trousers, with shiny
> European shoes showing underneath like the cloven
> hoof. They smoked cigars that must have cost black-
> market fortunes, and knocked back a comfortable quan-
> tity of champagne, and all of them looked like the char-
> acter called the Sheik in the old comic strip 'Barney
> Google.' When Americans remarked, as every American
> was sure to, that they had thought Moslems didn't drink
> in public, a Frenchman who 'knew the country' was sure
> to explain that the big fellows were *chorfa*—members
> of the *cherifian,* or saintly, families, descended from par-
> ticularly venerable relatives of the Prophet. 'They do as

they please on earth; they will be judged in Heaven,'
the expert always expounded. 'It is not for mere man to
judge a hereditary saint.' He would add, 'They have
great power over political opinion. They are venerated.
They hold the people in the hollow of their hand.' (In
Paris last year [1957], though, I got a different report on
these fellows. I asked an old Algérois acquaintance, a
police inspector, why the saints with cigars didn't stop
the insurrection. 'Oh, them,' he said laughingly. 'We call
them the *Beni-Oui-Oui*—the Tribe of Yes-Men. They're
the ones we have to protect from the others.') ⁴

Ferhat Abbas survived the Vichy episode better than Messali
Hadj who, as we earlier noted, on March 17, 1941, fell under
penalty of sixteen years' imprisonment and twenty years' banishment for an "offense against the security of the state." Though
the severity of this sentence was soon moderated, first by house
arrest in the village of Reibell, some two hundred miles south of
Algiers, from which he was transferred to Brazzaville on April 30,
1945, after local disturbances, and finally by his release in June,
1946, his party, the P.P.A., was driven underground and weakened. Abbas enjoyed greater immunity until 1945 when he, too,
was arrested. For some time his record of loyalty to France had
protected him. He had served two years in World War I, reaching the grade of sergeant, was later elected to the Legion of
Honor, and again enlisted in the French army in 1939.

After the French military collapse of June, 1940, he tried unsuccessfully to induce the Vichy government to inaugurate a
reform program. In an almost obsequious letter to Marshal Pétain
(April 10, 1941) he wrote of the need to instill a feeling of "to-
getherness" between Muslim and European. As Abbas analyzed
the problem, the condition of six million Muslim farmers required immediate amelioration. They needed education in modern techniques, protection against the predatory "landed
feudality," and equality before the law. This Algerian spokesman,
a fair product of the French schools, seemed to be asking for a
true assimilation which meant equality of opportunity, educa-

tional facilities, and responsibilities in local government. He believed French occupation should be more than a military occupation; he therefore asked for the abolition of military control in the south—the area where oil has since been discovered in quantity. This suggestion came from the mind and heart of a man who, though educated by the French and tied tightly to that culture, yet understood Muslim hopes, and, above all, saw the need for modernization.

That Vichy turned a deaf ear to Ferhat Abbas should surprise no one. His program found no support among the *colons,* at whose immediate expense, they reasoned, agricultural reform must come. Further, the interests of these *colons* and the Vichy regime coincided at such points as a common belief in racist legislation, mutual dependence upon the French army, and a united front vis-à-vis the Muslim community.

All these policies underwent an important change beginning in November, 1942, when Anglo-American forces landed in North Africa. Although this military operation was aimed exclusively at defeating the Axis, the very presence of hundreds of thousands of American fighting men with their admirable equipment and seemingly endless supplies profoundly affected the Muslim and European inhabitants. The earlier Murphy-Weygand accord (February 26, 1941), which sought to buttress colonial resistance against possible Axis occupation by furnishing essential supplies to North Africa from the United States, no doubt achieved its purpose in large part.[5] Even so, its influence was small by contrast to "Operation Torch," which in the long run instilled the Muslim population with new hopes and finally reduced Vichy's influence to nil.

To the stiff-necked Vichy generals and bureaucrats in Algeria "Torch" soon became a mixed blessing. To de Gaulle and his Free French, ironically enough, it was an affront because they were neither consulted nor included in the operation. Yet, as events progressed—the "Darlan Interlude," the incapacity of General Henri Giraud, the crystallization of metropolitan resistance behind the Free French, and particularly the Anglo-American military success—there came about the creation of the French Committee of National Liberation (June 3, 1943) in Algiers and

43

finally de Gaulle's assumption of French leadership. Among Algerian independence groups, such as the P.P.A. and the moderates, too, such as Ferhat Abbas, the coming of the war to Algeria surely raised hopes.

Yet, to satisfy the French that their empire stood in no jeopardy under Anglo-American occupation and at the same time to convey to the Muslim leaders that their aspirations for a new order struck a note of sympathy in the breast of a nation which endorsed the Atlantic Charter, required a light touch. Robert Murphy in a letter to General Giraud (November 2, 1942) reassured, "It is well understood that French sovereignty should be re-established as soon as possible over all territories, Metropolitan as well as colonial, over which the French flag waved in 1939." [6] Lieutenant-General Dwight Eisenhower aimed at a broader target in an appeal to the population of North Africa at the moment of the first landings. "We come among you to save you from conquerors who would remove forever your rights of self-government, your rights to religious freedom, and your rights to live your own lives in peace." [7] Aimed to win the cooperation of both French residents and Muslim inhabitants so that military operations could move forward, this statement, with its emphasis upon rights, freedom, and peace, struck a very favorable note among Muslim leaders. General Eisenhower, however, associated the Axis with "conqueror," while to Muslim leaders in Algeria where no Axis armies had operated, the conquest dated from the 1830-1847 period and was French!

There was evidence, too, from the American summit that the problem of all the people of North Africa would obtain a future hearing. President Roosevelt's meeting in Morocco with Mohammed ben Youssef in January, 1943, to which French Governor General Auguste Noguès was not invited, surely encouraged Muslim hopes for a new order. "Father [FDR], balancing his fork, remarked cheerfully enough [to the Sultan] that the postwar scene and the prewar scene would, of course, differ sharply, especially as they related to the colonial question." [8] In the American president's world of the future, France would regain her colonies as a trustee, bearing the responsibility of reporting

44

on progress each year. He envisaged a long Allied occupation in North Africa and the drafting of new rules before the French returned to power. "I'm by no means sure in my own mind that we'd be right to return to France her colonies *at all, ever,* without first obtaining in the case of each individual colony some sort of pledge. . . . Anything must be better, than to live under French colonial rule!" [9]

These personal views of President Roosevelt, expressed to his son Elliott, could scarcely be known to the Muslim masses, but that the welfare of peoples living under colonial status concerned the United States surely filtered through to Muslim leaders in Algeria. It is, of course, exceedingly difficult to gauge accurately the effects of the Anglo-American invasion upon the politically articulate mature Muslim. Kenneth Pendar, who watched these events unfold, thinking largely about Morocco, considered the Atlantic Charter exceedingly influential. "The Atlantic Charter struck this same chord of idealism in the Arab mind. It made a truly profound impression on them, and for months they hardly talked of anything else." [10] Julien, the careful and authoritative French scholar of Socialist bent, notes, that Robert Murphy, President Roosevelt's personal representative in Algeria, exercised a "decisive influence," meeting several times with Fehrat Abbas to explore the possibilities of implementing the Atlantic Charter in Algeria. Whatever Robert Murphy's influence was at this time, Ferhat Abbas foresook the principle of assimilation in favor of a federal solution which would grant autonomy to Algeria within a French framework, a position he staunchly defended in 1946 in the Second Constituent Assembly.

AN ALGERIAN MANIFESTO AND A FRENCH ORDINANCE

But this Algerian spokesman took quick advantage of the opening presented by Admiral Darlan and the Anglo-American military leadership which immediately after the North African landings sought the cooperation of the people of Algeria in the war against the Axis. First on December 20, 1942, "A message of Muslim Representatives" addressed to "the responsible authorities," drove French officials into a fury. In its failure to address itself to the French authorities it recognized the American presence in Algeria and the inadmissible fact that continued French control existed only by grace of American moderation and concern with the war itself. It stated an awareness that the French alone could not liberate France. Finally, it made a conference of all Muslim organizations the condition for Muslim support of the war effort. The French refused to receive this communication and two days later in "A Message to the French Authorities" Ferhat Abbas assured the governor general that the Muslims of Algeria associated themselves in a peoples' war of liberation. But the message warned:

> This is not a war of liberation of all peoples without distinction of race or religion. Despite the promises which have been made to them, and the sacrifices which they have undergone, the native populations of Algeria are still deprived of the liberties and rights which others enjoy. Muslims want to be associated in the common lot otherwise than just by new sacrifices. You must show us, by tangible and immediate action, the willingness of France to institute reforms. For this, a conference must be called, . . . including representatives of all Muslim organizations, to write a new law which will give the masses a consciousness of their rights and an understanding of their duty to participate in the war effort.[11]

The unimaginative General Giraud reacted to this petition with the outworn observation that he waged war not politics, that he wanted soldiers rather than reforms. While Giraud and Marcel Peyrouton, who replaced Châtel (on January 17, 1943), as the new governor general of Algeria, and who earlier served Vichy as Minister of Interior and helped erect the anti-semitic edifice, busied themselves readying French troops to take the field against the Axis in North Africa, Ferhat Abbas, aided by some two dozen Muslim leaders, prepared the "Manifesto of the Algerian People" (February 12, 1943).

At once a sharp criticism of French colonial policy and a posi-

46

tive reform program, this statement soon became the rallying point of Algerian aspirations. Its framers respected French cultural and spiritual values; therefore they felt that Frenchmen would sympathetically receive their demands. Glancing backward to the past, the Manifesto considered the policy of assimilation a dismal failure. How could it succeed when it distinguished between the minority of citizens of France and the totally unprivileged masses? Under that policy Muslim society found itself reduced to complete servitude. True, an Algerian élite of artisans, students, peasant farmers had evolved but its numbers belied true assimilation. Further, reform efforts, such as the Blum-Violette proposal, always ran dead against the unyielding stone wall opposition of the *colons*. Assimilation, then, as it had been practiced appeared to be no more than a smoke screen for French domination and exploitation.

On the positive side, the Manifesto suggested reforms which would equalize the Arab-Berber population's rights, privileges, and duties with those of the Europeans. A new governing statute which guaranteed absolute liberty and equality without distinction as to race or religion stood as the foundation stone of the petition. From this base a broad agrarian reform to re-establish Muslims on the land, recognition of Arabic along with French as an official language, liberty of press and of association, free obligatory instruction for all children, and freedom of religion under the principle of separation of church and state took shape. Assimilation, the exhausted slogan of the last half-century, gave way to a demand for a kind of federal autonomy within the French reference frame. Independence and pan-Arabic ideas found no place in this program. In the later words of Ferhat Abbas the Manifesto makers hoped to construct "an Algerian state where Frenchman and Muslim would have the rights of citizenship without diminution of the recognition of France," "sans que le droit de regard de la France fût diminué." [12]

On March 31, 1943, Governor General Peyrouton accepted the Manifesto and agreed to study it "as a basis for future reforms." A few days later he appointed a committee to examine the economic and social condition of the Muslim population. He promised that this committee's recommendations would be included in a reform program to be launched during the war. This committee met twice (April 14 and June 23), but before it reached any conclusions on which action could be based there were two new developments.

First, a delegation representing Arabs and Kabyles drafted (May 26) a Supplement (*Additif*) to the Manifesto which increased Muslim demands. Second, General de Gaulle landed at Boufarik near Algiers on May 30. Four days later on June 3, 1943, he and General Giraud became co-chairmen of the French Committee of National Liberation. These events raised hard questions on both sides of the table. What did the Muslim population really seek? Was it autonomy within a French federalist system or was it independence? And who, if any man or any party, actually represented the Muslim population? On the French side equally embarrassing questions arose. Who spoke for the Frenchmen living in Occupied France? Did Pétain, Giraud, or de Gaulle?

No purpose can be served by probing the tortuous political situation faced by the United States and Great Britain in their relationships with the French during the year following the North African landings. Suffice it to note that military expediency often dictated decisions, and viewed from the narrow "V" for victory, this was essential. Without victory, there was no future, no liberated France, and very slender hope for any Franco-Muslim conversations or agreement in Algeria. Whether long range military expediency was actually served by the "Darlan Deal," the "Shotgun Marriage" of de Gaulle and Giraud arranged by Prime Minister Churchill and President Roosevelt can best be answered later by the military historian who can view the entire course of the war in the West, not simply the North African campaign. One conclusion seems clear and simple. Within a relatively short time de Gaulle completely outdistanced Giraud as a political force both in Algeria and France. By the time of the Normandy invasion (June 6, 1944) de Gaulle was also the more important military asset.[13]

The Supplement to the Manifesto envisaged that the "solution of the emancipation of Algeria" would come in the form of an "autonomous constitution." At the war's end there should be an Algerian state endowed with its own constitution drafted by an Algerian Constituent Assembly elected by universal suffrage. Meanwhile, the government should be transformed so that half the ministers were Muslims. The governor general, under the title "Ambassador, High Commissioner of France in Algeria," would continue to discharge the executive duties. Parity between Muslims and Europeans should be the principle in all assemblies. In the *douars,* the Muslim units of local government, autonomy was the key phrase. All public offices were hereafter to be open to Muslims and discriminatory laws abolished. The same principle applied to the army where recruitment would be identical for Muslim and European. A free press in both languages, a special office to study peasant problems, a ministry of labor, equal educational facilities, and unrestricted instruction of Arabic, rounded out the program.[14]

Both the Manifesto and the Supplement ultimately came to rest on the desk of General Georges Catroux who became Governor General of Algeria (June 3, 1943) after the resignation of Peyrouton. This officer, who had served in North Africa and the Near East, understood, without agreeing, that the French of Algeria loved Vichy because that regime stood for the most complete submission of the indigenous inhabitants to European authority and thereby safeguarded the property and special privilege of the European minority.[15] He believed, too, that acceptance of the Manifesto and the Supplement would lead to the independence of Algeria and the absorption of the European inhabitants by the Muslims. Furthermore, he feared that the preconditions stated in the Supplement would compromise the war effort. Neither Catroux nor the French Committee of National Liberation could countenance a step toward independence of Algeria. When Muslims in the *Délégations financières,* the longstanding advisory body on the budget, protested Catroux's decision to reject the Manifesto and Supplement by refusing to sit (September 22, 1943), he dissolved the Muslim section and placed its president, Saydah Abdelkader, and Ferhat Abbas under forced residence. This contretemps ended when a Muslim

49

delegation "deplored the incident" and affirmed its belief in re-forms "within legal forms, within the French community, and conforming to the democratic French ideal." [16]

Having spanked the recalcitrant child and received its profession of future good will, General de Gaulle in the name of the French Committee of National Liberation moved to conciliate the Muslims. On December 12, 1943, at Constantine in the Place de la Brèche he announced the admission "of several tens of thousands" of Muslims to full citizenship without renunciation of their special Koranic rights. He further promised them greater representation in local assemblies and increased accessibility to administrative positions.

An ordinance dated March 7, 1944, translated the Constantine promise into law. Sixteen categories of Muslims obtained full French citizenship at the same time retaining their personal status. Muslim high school and college graduates, former army officers, decorated war veterans, administrators, members of economic commissions, in all some 60,000 now joined the first electoral college, previously exclusively reserved to Frenchmen by origin or naturalization. Muslim males over the age of twenty-one not included in the first college, some 1,500,000 persons, received the right to vote within the second college. "Lastly, the proportion of those elected by the second college in the assemblies, including the French Parliament, would be increased to parity." [17] Members of the second college could aspire some day to enter the first college. Meanwhile they could elect 40 per cent of the members of the city and regional councils and the Financial Delegations.

Through this legislation de Gaulle disassociated himself completely from the Vichy administration in Algeria which had promised very little beyond domination of the Europeans, anti-semitism, and prison for Algerian political leaders. He returned to the policy of progressive assimilation—to the suggestions of Blum-Violette, rejected in 1937. The large question was, would a 1937 answer be successful to a 1944 question? De Gaulle was optimistic. Aware of the aspirations of the peoples of Asia and Africa, he seized the initiative. [18] "Of course this reform raised muffled protests, as much among the *colons* as among certain Moslem clans. But many Arabs and Kabyles felt a spur of hope and gratitude toward France. . . . I saw Dr. Bendjelloul [on the platform in Constantine December 12, 1943] and many Moslems weeping with emotion." [19]

Yet de Gaulle's hope that the most constructive piece of legislation for Algeria since 1919 would begin a new era of good will was doomed. The Ordinance of March 7, 1944, failed to satisfy all but the most Francophile of the Muslim political leaders. Too, it displeased the *colons* who, once de Gaulle left Algiers for London on June 3, 1944 to take part in the Battle of France, were free to emasculate the spirit and letter of this legislation. Finally, it seems apparent that this reform, even if applied in good faith on both sides of the Mediterranean, as well as inside and outside the casbahs could not be the final answer in Algeria. It failed to provide a common electoral roll for European and Muslim, the only political instrument for bringing the two communities to share the common rights and duties guaranteed to French Muslims and non-Muslims by the first article in the Ordinance. Admirably enough, it applied the law indiscriminately, abolishing the older policy of separating Muslims out. It did, however, provide Muslims a choice—religious or civil personal status—which Frenchmen could not enjoy. The committee of sixteen (six Frenchmen, six Muslims, and four government officials) who drafted the Ordinance, in their haste, did not foresee that in 1957 a few Muslim magistrates, living under Koranic status, might be administering French law.[20] Even if the justice of these few men might be irreproachable, the effect of this situation upon at least some persons in the European community was bound to be explosive.

The Ordinance was, however, surely a beginning, a step toward an answer, at the very least a *beau geste*, more than simply a "pitch" to recruit Muslims to de Gaulle's banner as distinct from Giraud's. The unadorned truth was that the war pushed beyond Algeria to the Continent and that de Gaulle became preoccupied with more pressing problems. Thus, after a hopeful beginning an interregnum set in.

Algeria, however, was not forgotten by the Europeans and Muslims who lived there. A new Muslim coalition opposed the Ordinance of March 7, 1944, because it did not treat all Algerians equally, and worse, insisted upon drawing Algeria tightly to France instead of preparing for independence. Both Ferhat Abbas, now free of house arrest, and Messali Hadj in his forced residence at Reibell, could agree to work against this Ordinance, and the Ulema also supported these two leaders. On March 14, 1944, at Sétif *Les Amis du Manifeste et de la Liberté* (The Friends of the Manifesto and Liberty, A.M.L.) took form as a party opposed to colonialism. Its immediate stated objective was "to make familiar the idea of an Algerian nation, to support an autonomous federal republic in Algeria federated to a revived, anti-colonial, anti-imperialist French Republic."[21] The A.M.L. brought together the Muslim urban bourgeoisie and the working class followers of Messali Hadj's P.P.A. For the first time the political evolution of Algeria was linked directly to war against the "feudatories" of European and Muslim origin.

VIOLENCE AND A DEBATE

That the Friends of the Manifesto and Liberty became exceedingly popular is proved by the more than half-million membership applications which poured into central headquarters in Algiers, stimulated by the articles in its weekly organ *Egalité*. By March, 1945, at the party congress the majority fell under the control of Messali Hadj's P.P.A. delegates who rejected federalism under France and plumbed for an Algerian Parliament and an Algerian government. The same resolution reserved the right of a future Algerian state to join any system it preferred. If this was not a declaration of independence, it was the next thing to it. This boldness on the part of the proletarian followers of Messali Hadj was doubtless related to the Congress at Heliopolis, the Egyptian university city, which coincided with the A.M.L. meeting in Algiers and declared the time to be ripe for a Pan-Arabic liberation movement. The Heliopolis meeting not only gave birth to the Arab League of thirty-six million Arab-speaking people in

Egypt, Syria, Lebanon, Iraq, Transjordan, Saudi Arabia, and Yemen, but it also prepared the fight against foreign domination and encouraged future federation of the Arab peoples. Henceforth, Algerian nationalists looked eastward for support and haven.

Against this extremist tide, Ferhat Abbas, Kessous, the editor of *Egalité,* and other moderates like Boumendjel appealed, rather effectively, for patience.[22] This ringing summons from the east with its simple, yet understandable, message reached the uneducated masses of Algeria more effectively than the more complicated and sophisticated formula of federalism. These same masses equated autonomy with independence and the departure of the French.[23]

Thus, one year after de Gaulle offered a program based upon progressive or evolutionary assimilation, the majority of the A.M.L. congress demanded an Algerian government with the authority to decide its future status. Such a formula surely led far beyond the federalist principle, to the very brink of independence. The gap between the thinking of Frenchmen like de Gaulle and an Algerian moderate like Ferhat Abbas was already considerable. Between extremists on both sides, that is, between the *gros colons* and the supporters of Messali Hadj, there stood a world.

Tension between the extremes mounted daily in the spring of 1945, the last spring of World War II. The *colons* who fought so doggedly against the Blum-Violette proposal, who loved the Vichy regime in Algeria, and detested de Gaulle's Ordinance of March 7, 1944, took their spleen out on his new governor general, Yves Chataigneau, who relieved General Catroux on September 9, 1944. They thought the new governor general had too much sympathy with Islamic culture, treated the Muslims with respect, and in return, and most unforgivably, was popular with them. Not given to intellectual solutions the *colons* labeled him "Chataigneau ben Mohammed" and awaited a suitable occasion to remove him from office. On their side, too, Muslim extremists were restless, sensing the war's end, and influenced by dreams of a resurrected Arab state. Chataigneau recognized the symptoms and warned the prefects against impending violence. In the villages, life went on at a more miserable level than before the war. In some areas such as Kabylie des Babors in the difficult terrain between Sétif and the Mediterranean this misery combined with a Berber insurrectionary tradition dating from Roman times. In Algiers and Oran the police exchanged shots on May Day, 1945, with demonstrators who demanded the release of Messali Hadj.

The spark which ignited violence struck Sétif on May 8, the day following the German surrender at General Eisenhower's headquarters in Reims. A victory parade of Muslims, authorized by the under prefect, carried the red, white, and green flag on which a crescent was inscribed—the Algerian tricolor—across which such inscriptions as "Long Live Independent Algeria," "Down with Colonialism," "Free Messali Hadj" were displayed. Some carried "Down with the Communist Party" as a slogan. The police tried to grab the nationalist banners and someone—most likely the police—began firing small arms. Most of the crowd broke up, but a street battle continued between the police and the Muslims. Some thirty people lost their lives and more were wounded. During the night, killing, pillage, and burning took place in the countryside. The insurgents directed their attacks against public buildings and officials rather than against food depots. In all, perhaps one hundred Europeans were killed. No more than 5 per cent of the Muslims in the department of Constantine took part.

Yet rumors of dire consequences, a kind of "great fear," filled the country. An Arab government was said to be installed in Algiers, and the A.M.L. was given the responsibility for this terrible uprising. Arrested Muslims later testified they were told to exterminate the French in pursuit of the objectives of the Holy War.

French military and police power moved rapidly to put down the uprising. In Sétif, placed under martial law, any Muslim found not wearing an identifying arm band exposed himself to death. The cruiser "Duguay-Trouin" needlessly bombarded the outskirts of Kerrata. The French airforce, flying American-built medium and light bombers, wiped out crowded Arab housing areas. The

American army newspaper *Stars and Stripes* reported that the French air force was sometimes flying three hundred sorties a day, and had killed or wounded more than 10,000 Muslims in nine days.[24] "During the campaign the Senegalese and Foreign Legion troops pillaged, burned, violated, and killed in complete liberty." [25] The French government officially claimed 1500 Muslims had been killed in the repression. Julien, basing his estimate upon private information from French officers, believed the Muslim dead to be between 6,000 and 8,000 persons.[26] Manfred Halpern estimated the toll at between 17,000 and 40,000.[27] After the violence, some 4,500 arrests were made, 99 persons condemned to death, and 64 given life imprisonment. "Most of the arrests were made without proof. Members of the P.P.A., A.M.L., militant trade unionists, and villagers who took no part were picked up by the authorities." [28] Ferhat Abbas and Doctor Saadane were arrested and the Association of the Friends of the Manifesto and Liberty (A.M.L.) dissolved.

Mystery and enigma surround the May uprising. Lacking any clear, probable, and simple explanation, we need no clairvoyant powers to understand the folly of tearing banners away from supercharged and authorized demonstrators. One American reporter says the authorization was given with the "express understanding that it (the parade) would be strictly non-political and that no banners would be carried." [29] Whatever the previous agreement involved, the seizure of the banners turned a parade into a bloody encounter for which the Muslim participants seemed prepared with weapons. Violence spread and repression did the rest. Yet this early police activity was scarcely more than a catalyst in an inevitable reaction.

Below the surface, lying deep in the Muslim mind, lurked fear of famine, political anxiety, and a series of hopes focused upon the war's end. Desperately hungry villagers and urban dwellers had lost hope in a French future. Messali Hadj's followers demanded his release; throughout the Muslim world there was a feeling that the era of liberation was at hand. Now, if ever, was the time to fight for it. Students of this question suggest, too, that some Muslims understood the Atlantic Charter to mean freedom after the war. The United States, they expected, would oppose continuation of colonial regimes. As if to confirm this view, did not the San Francisco Conference, held a few weeks later, claim "respect for the principle of equal rights and self-determination of peoples?" Taken together, these elements help to explain the violence. One fact is clear, old moderates turned into federalists or autonomists, like Ferhat Abbas, had no direct hand in the trouble.[30]

No mystery veils the repression. It was pitiless, possibly because a general insurrection was feared by the military and civil authorities. The uprising, which the Francophile Dr. Bendjelloul, speaking two months later in the Provisional Consultative Assembly in Paris, claimed to be the work of Vichy-fascist-*colon* reactionaries, served as an excuse for a powerful reaction against change.[31] A shrill *colon* cry of warning inveighed against reform and proposed a committee to defend French sovereignty. Governor General Chataigneau battled for his reform program against heavy local resistance from those who proclaimed "For North Africa, it is the hour of police activity," (c'est l'heure du gendarme).[32] Supported by Adrien Tixier, de Gaulle's Provisional Government's minister of interior, whose on-the-spot investigation concluded that reform must come rapidly, Chataigneau wrestled with the famine in all its variety.

Today Algerian nationalist leaders consider the events of May, 1945, of capital importance. "The revolution of 1954 was decided at the time of the events of 1945. All the nationalist leaders I met at Cairo, Tunis, Bonn, Rome, and Geneva pointed to the delusion of the days and nights of May." [33]

For nearly three years after the uprising of 1945 this energetic governor general drove forward his rural amelioration plans. Through *sociétés indigènes de prévoyance* (S.I.P.), native planning centers took form in which the *fellahs* (peasants) and their families received agricultural education. Within two years eighty-five modern sectors on which cereals and fruit were cultivated, using modern methods, were in operation. Soil reclamation and irrigation projects received equal attention; in education a three year goal of 1750 new classes sought to develop human resources.

Parallel to these economic and social reforms, ran the policy of increasing the responsibility of the *djemaa,* the Assembly of Muslim Notables, which began to discharge local powers, equivalent to the municipal councils in French villages, in the *douars,* Muslim units of government.[34] Another aspect of this reconstruction involved the strengthening of Algerian rural industry through training of the artisan class. This program included apprenticeship centers, re-location of young workers, procurement of raw materials and markets aimed to strengthen the economy, and reduce political tension. While it is true that aims were not always reached on schedule, it is nevertheless a fact that continuous reconstruction efforts characterized French policy between 1945 and the outbreak of the Algerian rebellion in November, 1954.

No miraculous results came from these programs largely because population growth swallowed up increased productivity and clamored for more. Metropolitan France, after a four-year occupation period and doomed to an eight-year adventure in Indo-China (1946-1954) found itself overextended. Political rapport between Algeria and France in the postwar decade became exceedingly strained as French and Muslim spokesmen groped for a viable solution.

ALGERIA IN TWO CONSTITUENT ASSEMBLIES

One of the reasons for the ineffectiveness of the debate on Algeria beginning on July 10, 1945, in the French Provisional Consultative Assembly meeting in Paris was the continued imprisonment of both Ferhat Abbas and Messali Hadj. Without the popular exponent of federalism and the die-hard advocate of independence the debate was so narrow as to be meaningless. Various *colons* (Paul Cuttoli, former mayor of Philippeville, and Paul Muselli) used it as a platform to criticize de Gaulle's Ordinance of March 7, 1944, while they preached suppression of the local assemblies in Algeria. Dr. Bendjelloul, president of the *Fédération des Elus Musulmans,* believed that assimilation served as a convenient façade for French dominance. If the French really meant to assimilate, if Algeria really was France, then why a governor-general, why limited citizenship for most Muslims, why special regimes in southern Algeria?[35]

In his comments, Adrien Tixier, the Provisional Government's spokesman, asked for mild political reform and emphasized economic issues. His suggestion that some of the large estates be expropriated and turned into experimental farms fell upon deaf ears. No one represented the *fellahs* in this debate.[36] A few innocuous observations on administrative reorganization, equal representation of the Muslim second college in future assemblies, and a profession of faith in the Ordinance of March 7, 1944, ended the discussion.

In July, 1945, Algerian issues were not uppermost in French minds. A new day had dawned in France itself, a new republic had to be made or the Third overhauled. The Communist party program for Algeria amounted to no more than a watered-down version of the Algerian Manifesto, a blast at the hundred great landlords "responsible" for the Constantine massacre, and a pious declaration that the people of North Africa shared common interests with France.[37]

Three months later (October 21, 1945) general elections for the First Constituent Assembly were held in France and Algeria. To many Muslims this fulfilled the promise of de Gaulle's Ordinance of March 7, 1944, since, for the first time, Muslim representatives of Algeria's second college went to Paris to be heard in the debates. An enabling act of August 17, 1945, fixed the number of representatives for each college at thirteen, and despite the boycott of the election by Messali Hadj's Algerian People's Party (P.P.A.) and The Friends of the Manifesto and Liberty (A.M.L.) of Ferhat Abbas, more than 50 per cent of the Muslim voters turned out. The results were neither spectacular nor surprising. Bendjelloul's *Fédération des Elus Musulmans* received seven seats against four for the Muslim Socialist groups and two for the Communists under Amar Ouzegane.[38]

A few Muslim delegates to the First Constituent added color along with the red fez of Amar Ouzegane and the beard and burnoose of Hachemi Benchennouf, but they could scarcely hope to exert any major influence. Still they helped the passage of the general amnesty law of March, 1946, which freed political prisoners in Algeria who had not committed violence in the May uprising of 1945. The most prominent beneficiary was Ferhat Abbas who soon drew his followers into the *Union Démocratique du Manifeste Algérien* (U.D.M.A.) under a program which posited "a new Algeria, freely federated with a new France," and renounced "assimilation, new masters, or separatism." [39]

In debating a new electoral law some of the Muslim representatives, seconded by the French Socialist party, advocated a single college (*collège unique*) for Algeria. Maurice Violette, whose earlier experience as governor general and whose position as father of the first program for gradual assimilation gave weight to his views, advocated a single college which would send thirty-five representatives to Paris. His immediate purpose was to assimilate, to reduce differences between Muslim and European.[40] The ultimate effect of it would be, of course, a Muslim-controlled assembly in Algiers. To avoid this, to allow each group to maintain its identity, became the purpose of the supporters of the two college system. They also hoped to insure French control by representing the great Muslim population at far below parity. This view captured the majority composed of the M.R.P. (*Mouvement républicain populaire*), the small parties of the right, and the Communists. Amar Ouzegane argued that a single college would offend the *colons* and thus prejudice the future. The double college stood, but the second college, the entirely Muslim college, obtained twenty-one seats in Paris against fourteen for the first college in which sat the Europeans and Muslim elite.

Bendjelloul's group of "tame" Muslims performed unspectacularly in the First Constituent. Upon one occasion, however, their spokesmen gave the assimilationists some anxious thoughts. Assimilation, or integration implied ultimately bringing Muslims into the wonderland of French citizenship on an equal political footing. Bendjelloul found it perfectly consistent therefore to ask that Algeria be given 120 deputies in Paris delegated from a single college in Algiers. Armchair assimilationists rocked out upon the floor, a position shared by the integrationists of 1958, when Raymond Aron confronted them with the same logic of equality.[41]

The rejection of the first constitutional draft in the May 5, 1946 referendum deprived the second college of its seven extra seats and automatically transferred the discussion of Algeria's future to the Second Constituent Assembly. In the June elections in Algeria a quiet revolution placed Ferhat Abbas's U.D.M.A. in control of eleven of the thirteen seats representing the second college in the Second Constituent. How had the pharmacist of Sétif obtained 71 per cent of the votes? On the positive side, his program of an autonomous Algeria associated or federated with France appealed to Algerian voters. They easily recognized that assimilation, as demanded in the First Constituent Assembly by Bendjelloul, would never succeed because Metropolitan Frenchmen could not bring themselves to face equality between Muslim and European. They knew, too, that such a formula, if fairly applied, meant the end of European dominance in Algeria itself, a condition the *colons* could not accept. Bendjelloul had tested the formula; it failed. The U.D.M.A.'s approach offered new hope, and it contained the advantage of being in tune with Algerian nationalist aspirations.

Abbas also won by default. Bendjelloul, smarting from his defeat in Paris, withdrew his party from the election. Messali Hadj was still under banishment and his P.P.A. outlawed. This left, as the sole opposition to Abbas, the Algerian Communist and Socialist parties who labored under the failures of tripartism in the First Constituent, who lacked a clear-cut program, and whose ties with the Algerian voters lacked intimacy. The U.D.M.A. therefore won eleven seats and the Socialists two.[42]

Abbas, the converted prophet of assimilation, went to Paris as the advocate of autonomy. In a real sense, too, he stood as the spokesman for independence since the P.P.A. and the Ulema had no representation. The political climate in the capital favored the Algerian delegation's influence. The second election strengthened the M.R.P. at the expense of the Socialists and Communists. So, if the Algerian delegation threw its weight behind the left, it could counterweight the M.R.P.'s electoral gain and at the very least deadlock the Assembly. Abbas decided to do this. He obtained a seat on the Constitution Committee and the support, he hoped, of the Communist and Socialist parties for an autonomous Algeria within a French Union.[43]

On paper it looked as though Ferhat Abbas and his U.D.M.A. followers might achieve their program in the Second Constituent. This illusion was dispelled soon after August 22, 1946, the day the debate on Algeria began. Out of that debate came a "buck-passing" resolution instructing the government to draft a new statute for Algeria. To this, almost everyone, including the eleven members of the U.D.M.A., could reluctantly agree. Before this postponement was reached, the debates indicated a tremendous gap in thought between right and left. The former, whose spokesmen, men like François Quilici, the *colon* representing Algeria's first college, and René Mayer, the Radical-Socialist leader who later in February, 1955, administered the coup-de-grace to his own party man, Mendès-France, saw the future of Algeria as no more than a French economic problem. "It must never be said that this provisional government and temporary assembly were the liquidators of French Algeria." [44]

The left, whose support Ferhat Abbas courted, sought first a change in political institutions. Economic and social reform could come later. Communists, acting upon the realization that they had lost precious Algerian votes supporting assimilation, and some Socialists, now recognized an Algerian nation. They demanded an Algerian Assembly elected by universal manhood suffrage, suppression of direct French administration, and its replacement by a commissioner who would coordinate foreign and military affairs between Paris and Algiers.[45] Ferhat Abbas followed with a profession of loyalty to France, a loyalty he believed secure if an autonomous Algeria freely tied to France could be created.[46] The resolution to postpone action on the status of Algeria satisfied neither right nor left. It simply recognized that the constitutional draft took precedence. Algeria would have to wait.

In debating Article 23 of the electoral law the U.D.M.A. delegation tried unsuccessfully in October, 1946 to increase the number of deputies from Algeria's second college to the future National Assembly. The U.D.M.A. amendment failed when its

Communist and colonial delegate supporters mustered no more than 158 votes against 382. The Socialist allies, divided between assimilation and autonomous federalism, voted against the amendment. Ferhat Abbas's program of autonomy proved no more successful in increasing Algeria's representation in Paris than Bendjelloul's assimilationist argument. Thirty representatives, half from each college, would sit in the National Assembly.

The game of politics in Paris went badly for the U.D.M.A. delegation. Still there remained one final inning to be played, and if it could be won, something more than face could be saved. The exact definition of the French Union remained to be formulated. The M.R.P. adopted the futuristic slogan of "progressive federalism" which proved to be scarcely more than a restatement of General de Gaulle's thoughts on the French Empire. To the M.R.P., progressive federalism began "from the top" in Paris with an Assembly of Frenchmen protecting the European colonial minority against native inundation. Such an Assembly, separate from the bicameral French parliament, would discuss rather than decide policy though in time its authority would grow. Questions of governmental structure in the colonies, the M.R.P. insisted, must be determined in Paris, and in all colonial assemblies the European minority must be guaranteed some seats. To this program the small parties of the center and right gladly adhered though some thought it too advanced.

In essence the blueprint of the left, supported by the Socialists, Communists, and Ferhat Abbas who spoke for almost all the colonial delegates, planned federalism from below—from the colonies themselves. This view started with colonial assemblies empowered to draft laws for the given colony in cooperation with Paris; then experienced delegates from these assemblies would be brought into a meaningful Union. The Constitutional Committee, on which Ferhat Abbas served and, on this issue, was particularly influential, agreed (July 31, 1946) upon a proposal passed by a twenty-one to twenty vote in committee. It outlined a "bottom to top" evolution in which after some years overseas territories would choose their relationship with the French Union from three alternatives: (1) free states associated with France by treaty, (2) autonomous units, or (3) integral departments of France. There was a fourth choice. Any territory was free to stay outside the French Union—to secede. Under this plan all residents obtained complete French citizenship and all inequalities between European minorities and native residents disappeared.

The earth-shaking victory for the colonial delegates soon foundered upon President Georges Bidault's personal intervention before the Constitutional Committee and his threat to resign. This early cabinet crisis was not the last precipitated by a colonial issue. The M.R.P.'s substitute draft fell like a subpoena upon the Constitutional Committee in September. It vitiated all possibility of secession, provided the non-Europeans with citizenship in the French Union, not French citizenship, vested all future decision of colonial status in the French parliament, and guaranteed special representation to the European minority. A crisis was at hand when Ferhat Abbas and other deputies walked out of the committee, and on the afternoon of September 20 all the native deputies left the Assembly. Under Vincent Auriol, the Socialist leader, there next ensued some very French patching up (*on va s'arranger*) of differences between Bidault and the colonial deputies who actually came off with not much more than French citizenship. Bidault and the M.R.P. restored "Papa's Algeria."

Deep resentment poisoned the U.D.M.A. for the remainder of the Second Constituent's life. They had failed as had Bendjelloul before them. This ill-will came to the surface when Ferhat Abbas spoke in the Assembly for the last time on September 28. Infuriated by a shout from the right, "What's that *salaud* doing here anyhow," and by constant interruption, the French-trained Algerian pharmacist who loved France started mildly enough but quickly gathered momentum.[47]

> We wanted France to become, not only for its own colonies, but for the colonies of the entire world, an example and a great hope. . . .
> It would be enough to renounce an impossible assimilation . . . It would be enough to renounce a direct administration which prevents the colonial peoples from

63

forming their own institutions . . . Finally, it would be enough to abandon this policy of centralization which paralyzes the initiative of the overseas territories.

The Government's text . . . has codified a neo-colonialism which is as fatal and dangerous as its predecessor, the colonial regime of yesterday.[48]

A few moments later the Algerian cast aside all inhibition to note that France lacked the strength to defend its empire in 1940. The "colonial policy of the Third Republic had been one of the worst blots on the record of the pre-war regime." [49] This offended the already wounded pride of the representatives of recently liberated France. Some walked out; others headed by Maurice Schuman, the M.R.P. leader, rushed the speaker who was stoutly defended by a cordon of Communist deputies.

No serious casualties were reported from this incident which took place during the last hours of the debate on the constitution. If one believed in prophetic symbols, one might have glimpsed a disintegrating Fourth Republic nearly twelve years later in May, 1958. One might have understood that the future of the Fourth would be plagued with colonial issues: Indo-China, Morocco, Tunisia, and finally Algeria. The sensitive person might have envisaged the "Tale of Two Cities" told twelve years after in Paris and Algiers in the month of May. Its details of plotting colonels, ex-Vichyite *colons,* young activists reminiscent of the *jeunesse dorée* of the Thermidorian Reaction, of the *Ecole Jeanne d'Arc* where army officers in Algeria studied revolutionary tactics, of busy little men in black double-breasted coats and homburgs running back and forth between the National Assembly and the Elysée, of tough paratroopers, and, alas, of torture chambers and revolutionary terrorism. And in the distance the presence could be felt of a not quite mute sphinx uttering a few grand phrases whose meaning was vague and archaic. This vision—or was it a nightmare—proved that the Second Constituent touched upon a crucial question when it debated colonial questions. Its answers, however, seemed to be those of the last century, and a little time proved them to be inadequate.

The Impact of World War II upon Algeria

THE ALGERIAN STATUTE OF 1947

Difficult problems test man's ingenuity, creativity, and generosity. The Second Constituent's failure to reach a working agreement with the U.D.M.A. meant that Muslims of moderate persuasion lost heart. They were replaced in future assemblies by men who insisted militantly upon independence or by French puppets (*beni-oui-ouis*) who really represented no one.

This situation was reflected in the elections of the National Assembly in Algeria where Messali Hadj had recently returned to active political life after seven years of prison and banishment. Still not free to enter the large cities, he established headquarters for his newly-organized *Mouvement pour le Triomphe des Libertés Démocratiques* (M.T.L.D.) at Bouzaréa, just outside Algiers. There he gathered around him, not the bourgeois types one found in Ferhat Abbas's coterie, but rather, as Pierre Frédérix put it, "the lean Algerians, who, in France, worked for Doriot, the militia, the Communist party without discrimination: Jacks-of-all trades, the products of pauperism." [50] Part of Messali Hadj's strength arose from the numerical fact that in Algeria Muslim paupers far outnumbered Muslim business and professional people.

His return and immediate political activity weakened Muslim solidarity which sought an Algerian National Front through fusion of the U.D.M.A., the remnants of the old P.P.A., the Ulema, and Communists. The prophet-like Messali Hadj was back in circulation, insisting upon a leading political role outside the Algerian National Front. The M.T.L.D. won five of fifteen seats, a limited success at best. The successor of Dr. Bendjelloul's moderate *Fédération des Elus Musulmans* also known in the First Constituent as the *Union Démocratique,* the *Groupe Musulman Indépendent pour la Défense du Federalisme Algerien,* (called Muslim Independents) won eight seats. And the Communists claimed two.

Ferhat Abbas's U.D.M.A. took no part in the election, but its members were told to support the Communist list. Similar orders

65

went out from the Ulema. The U.D.M.A. leader probably reasoned that his recent failure to win the case for autonomy in Paris disqualified his program. Perhaps Messali Hadj's communists, advocates of independence, would awaken a dreaming French Assembly. Then, maybe the metropolitan politicians, the M.R.P. in particular, might listen to sweet reason. That the U.D.M.A. still influenced Algerian minds was obvious when it won four of the seven seats to the Council of the Republic, the Fourth Republic's equivalent of the Third's Senate. This victory was particularly sweet because these indirect elections were held in two stages, and in the proceedings of the second stage of electors (municipal councilmen, presidents of the *djemaa* in the case of mixed communes, general councilmen, and deputies), where French administrative influence did not prevail because of the secret ballot rule, the results reversed those of the first stage. This indicated that Muslims with some small political experience thought independently when protected by the secret ballot against reprisal and freed from the coercive force of the French bureaucracy and army. It also, once again, pointed up the means the French possessed to influence the less politically mature Muslims.[51]

Again the scene shifted to Paris where in August, 1947, another great debate on Algeria developed as the National Assembly strove to enact a governing statute. Four major points of view came to the surface. The Communist party put forward a plan which viewed Algeria as a territory associated with France with its own Assembly of 120 members empowered to decide all internal Algerian questions. The colonial executive, responsible to this Assembly, would function as the French council of ministers did, and would include representatives from the ministry in Paris. This plan called for suppression of the mixed communes, abolition of a separate administration in the Sahara, separation of church and state, and installation of French and Arabic as official languages. From the Socialist benches came the proposal for an Algerian Assembly of 120 members elected by the two colleges with powers to vote the budget and to apply the laws of the French Parliament in Algeria. An Algerian minister would remain responsible to the government in Paris and live in Algiers.

The Muslim Independents in the National Assembly and the U.D.M.A. delegates in the Council of the Republic sought an autonomous Algerian Republic joined to the French Union as an associated state. Legislative power would be entrusted to a parliament elected by universal manhood suffrage, and the executive would follow the Fourth Republic's example of a figurehead president, and a responsible ministry. A French delegate in Algiers and a representative of the Algerian Republic in Paris would effect liaison.

The fourth proposal, that of Ramadier's government which had barely three months to live, tried to compromise—to satisfy most Socialists, the M.R.P., and the Radicals. Algeria, a group of departments, would have its own civil personality and financial autonomy. Its Assembly of 120 members, divided equally between the two colleges, legislated on internal questions and voted the governor general's budget. That official represented France in Algeria and French sovereignty stood firmly entrenched. Finally, de Gaulle's Ordinance of March 7, 1944, was endorsed.

The government's burden was heavy. Four conflicting programs, not counting the solid *colon* opposition to all four or de Gaulle's statement from afar, complicated Ramadier's task. De Gaulle spoke in defense of the Ordinance of March 7, 1944, which the government supported. But then, he insisted upon full French sovereignty, association and balanced participation of Muslim and European in solely Algerian questions. More important, he demanded a two-thirds majority in plenary sessions of the two colleges. This gave the European community in the First College an automatic veto. "Today I tell you General de Gaulle . . . lost the confidence of nine million Muslims whether they be socialists or members of the M.R.P.," declared Lakhdar Bentaieb.[52] In contrast, the *colons,* who since 1943 considered de Gaulle a dangerous liberal who pampered the Muslims, now clutched him to their bosoms as the protector of "our patrimony."

It had been clear since his speeches at Bruneval and Strasbourg the previous March and April that de Gaulle was back in active politics. Had not Jacques Soustelle, the general-secretary of the

67

newly-formed Gaullist *Rassemblement du Peuple Français* (R.P.F.) counted more than 12,000 members in the department of Seine (April 14, 1947). The statement on Algeria, then, must be considered as part of a political campaign to win Overseas France to the R.P.F. banner. Overseas France had helped put de Gaulle over the top in 1944. Would it repeat this assistance? And it is interesting to note that the *colons* in Algeria endorsed his new viewpoint, which amounted to progressive assimilation but added a European veto on matters deemed important by the governor general.[53]

Mid-August is not the best of all times for debating, and the government's Algerian statute which reached the floor of the National Assembly in the third week of that summer month bothered both the French politicians and the Muslim representatives. Independent Muslims, such as Cadi Abdelkader, decried the sacrifice of the federalist solution. This group and such Muslims as Ben Taieb and Mohammed Smail who represented Algeria's first college endorsed Ferhat Abbas's viewpoint that autonomy within a French Union was infinitely preferable to the government's project. Division within Muslim ranks broke out when Lamine Debaghine of the M.T.L.D. demanded independence. "No solution can be accepted by the Algerian people, if it does not imply an absolute guarantee of a return to our national sovereignty." [54]

The most striking irreconcilable division within French ranks appeared when the requirements for Muslim members of the first college had to be defined. Upon this crucial issue depended the control of the Algerian Assembly because the second college was already entirely Muslim. The electoral law of October, 1946, opened the first college to Muslim veterans of World War I and to Muslim graduates of elementary schools—these two categories were added to those already made eligible by the Ordinance of March 7, 1944. The key issue involved the elementary school graduates who each year would surely increase in number, to a future point where they would offset European dominance. No one worried about the veterans of 1914-1918; they would die out. So the question was, would the National Assembly allow the

Muslim holders of elementary school diplomas to continue to vote in the first college? The answer was no, by the narrow margin of 316 to 286. In the debate Premier Paul Ramadier recognized that the time was not yet at hand when Muslims could dominate the advice offered the governor general; he stood against opening the floodgates. This particular measure worked toward the perpetuation of European control of Algeria, applied the brakes to home rule and the evolutionary increase of Muslim political responsibility. Likewise, it could be construed to deny the principles of assimilation, integration, or autonomy. It was strongly resented by Muslim moderates and nationalists alike.[55]

When the final text of the statute was voted on August 27, its opponents could muster no more than 89 votes while the Socialists, M.R.P., and Radical parties carried the measure with 322 votes. Against the statute stood deputies from the Algerian first college's extreme right who considered the measure too advanced, the Independent Muslims who wanted federalism, the M.T.L.D. members who sought independence, and a group of Overseas deputies most of whom favored a federal solution. The French Communists abstained.

Before the final vote, harsh statements passed back and forth. *Colon* spokesman Fernand Chevalier in effect threatened sabotage when he noted "The majority of Frenchmen [living in Algeria] would refuse to apply a statute which did not guarantee the security indispensable for the pursuit of their task."[56] Rather prophetic was the dignified statement of Félix Houphouet-Boigny, the highly educated chief of the Akive tribe, representing the Ivory Coast of West Africa.

> We have, in effect, two groups of Algerians. One [M.T.L.D.] no longer believes in the French Union and demands independence. Another, the *Amis du Manifeste* and the Independent Muslims, demands a statute for an Algerian state freely associated with France.
>
> Are you going to admit that the partisans of total independence are right by refusing the outstretched hands of the advocates of French Union?[57]

That the law of September 20, 1947, the so-called Algerian Statute of 1947, pleased neither the Muslim delegates in the National Assembly, thirteen of whom walked out, nor the *colons* must not obscure its importance. Together with the Ordinance of March 7, 1944, it represented the most serious effort to legislate a *modus vivendi* since 1919. The final text resembled closely the Ramadier government's proposal, but it contained compromises demanded by the M.R.P. in what that party believed to be the interests of the European community. On paper it discarded the assimilation policy and recognized that two separate communities lived together within the French Union. Yet the honest differences, which the debate brought to the surface, remained unresolved. Had the best will in the world prevailed on all sides, the future would have been uncertain. And that condition itself did not exist.

By the Statute, Algeria was defined as a group of overseas departments.[58] A governor general appointed by the French premier wielded executive power which he discharged with the help of a council of six. The French National Assembly retained the right to apply constitutional, civil, and criminal codes in Algeria. The Algerian Assembly of 120 members, 60 from each college, was basically an administrative institution charged with aiding the governor general to carry out policy. It voted his budgetary recommendations and, with his advice, adapted French laws to local conditions.[59] Its first college was elected by some 464,000 Europeans and 58,000 elite Muslims holding French civil status, while the second college represented 1,400,000 Muslim electors. Thus, while the Statute granted French citizenship to all inhabitants, clearly the elite Muslims possessed greater rights under that citizenship than their brothers in the second college. And Muslim women remained mute and shackled by tradition though the Statute granted them suffrage rights—rights which they first exercised in 1958. The Algerian Assembly convened three times each year, but the governor-general could, after twenty-four hours, demand a second vote on any measure, in which case a two-thirds majority was mandatory. In practice this

70

meant the European-dominated first college held an automatic veto.

In matters of local government the "fully organized communes" operated, as in France, with their own municipal councils. But for the "mixed communes," where administration was partly direct and partly elective, the Statute provided an evolution intended to eliminate this dichotomy and to give the Muslims greater political responsibility at the local level of government. Ultimately, all units were expected to be "fully organized communes." [60]

Under the Statute of 1947 each of the two Algerian colleges sent fifteen representatives to the National Assembly. These thirty representatives plus the fourteen senators in the Council of the Republic and the eighteen counsellors in the Assembly of the French Union completed Algeria's official delegation to Paris. Senators and counsellors were elected indirectly while direct universal suffrage named the thirty representatives.

Thirty deputies in a National Assembly of 618 men and women could scarcely dominate any question. Yet they could speak with some authority upon questions touching Algeria. The most optimistic supporters of the compromise Statute of 1947 hoped it would lead to mutual understanding between Muslim and European in Algeria and between inhabitants of Metropole and the colony. This did not come to pass. The Statute pleased neither Messali Hadj nor Ferhat Abbas. Nor could it be accepted by the *colons* who viewed it as an attenuation of French sovereignty which they in turn equated with their continued domination in Algeria. Still the Statute was the law, the governing principle.

THE BROKEN WORD

Two powerful forces emasculated that law both in spirit and in letter. In the first place the *colons* and governor-generals used their economic, administrative, and police influence to prevent its operation. Secondly, the intransigent Messali Hadj exhorted the Algerian masses, preaching eviction of the Europeans and independence. The economic and social soil was extremely receptive to these ideas. Real wages had declined compared to pre-war years since living costs mounted ten times above 1938 figures while wages increased in the order of six. On the average, Muslims got along on a maximum of 1500 calories per day. Hungry, badly clothed and housed, they flocked to the standard of the M.T.L.D. in the municipal elections of October, 1947, causing general alarm among the *colons* who traced this evil result to the Muslim-loving governor-general, Chataigneau.

Under the ground rules the premier appointed the governor-general, and since René Mayer of Constantine, once described as "colonialist" and "gravedigger of economic democracy," [61] served in Robert Schuman's cabinet as minister of finance, the liberal Chataigneau was recalled. This change almost blew the cabinet apart because Jules Moch, the strong-willed socialist, defended his partyman Chataigneau against Mayer's criticism. When the latter threatened to resign, a compromise, which replaced a socialist with a socialist, preserved peace. Chataigneau became ambassador to Moscow and Marcel-Edmond Naegelen, former minister of education, an Alsacian socialist who had fought the autonomist movement in that province, a remarkable administrator and tried patriot, came to Algiers in February, 1948. After sampling French opinion in the colony, the new governor-general reached the conclusion that a psychology of insecurity gripped the European inhabitants who took seriously the slogan-threat attributed to the P.P.A., "the suitcase or the coffin" (*la valise ou le cercueil*). Apparently Naegelen found quite a few settlers ready to dust off the suitcases. The villain, according to intelligence reports reaching the French civil authority, was none other than Messali Hadj's M.T.L.D. which reached into the remotest villages to spread the word that arms would soon arrive with which to drive the French into the sea. Messali Hadj's spokesmen promised Algerians an early opportunity to act against the French occupation. The M.T.L.D., thus reported, assumed the form of a well-knit revolutionary organization which collected funds from the loyal and intimidated the undecided or weak by threats of force or economic reprisals.

Governor General Naegelen's prefects warned, too, that, if

this nationalist propaganda circulated unchecked, the M.T.L.D. might control 90 per cent of the Muslim population. These reports emphasized the inroads made by the nationalists, sometimes through terror, upon Muslims loyal to France. Naegelen decided that the M.T.L.D. could not be allowed to dominate the Muslim vote in the forthcoming elections provided by the Statute of 1947. So, he used all his power to rig the elections in favor of the French presence. Pierre Frédérix, writing later in *Le Monde*, neatly described the governor-general's dilemma.

> With the end of winter [1947-1948] came the elections to the new assembly created by the Statute. The government feared this creation of the French Parliament. In our three Algerian departments the choice was not between free and falsified elections. It was rather between elections rigged by the agents of Messali Hadj and elections rigged by the French administration. We chose the latter.[62]

In this competition to "fix" elections in Algeria after 1947, the heavy advantage lay with the French who had not simply profited from studying various precedents in their own history which produced *assemblées introuvables,* but, more important, whose governors possessed better means for influencing voters and falsifying results than Messali Hadj. An administrative machine built carefully for more than a century could certainly outdistance untried Algerian nationalists in this gentle art.

The truth can best be seen in the results themselves. In the first college there was no problem; nearly one-half million registered European Frenchmen could safely dominate the 58,000 Muslim elite, most of whom thought like Frenchmen anyway or they could not have been considered elite. The Algerian Union, composed of the Gaullist R.P.F., the P.R.L. (*Parti Republicain de la Liberté*), "the authentic voice of the Right," the M.R.P., the Radicals, and Radical Socialists, obtained fifty-five seats. The Socialists got four and the Communists one. The margin of safety was great.[63]

In the elections to the second college, where roughly a million and a half Muslim electors voted, the "rig-work" became considerably more challenging. Even so, the French administration proved itself equal to the task. When the M.T.L.D. and U.D.M.A. parties were held to nine and eight seats, respectively, and forty-one independents—that is members independent of organized Muslim political parties but dependent upon French advice—were installed, the governor-general could fairly claim a good day's work. One independent federalist and one social independent rounded out the sixty men in the second college, the clear majority of which amounted to an official rubber stamp. Even the rather staid *L'Année politique* "suspected" irregularities.[64]

Though the margin of French dominance in the second college was also adequate, elections continued to be rigorously controlled by the government. In the partial renewal of the second college in 1951 the M.T.L.D. lost four of its nine seats, and the U.D.M.A. surrendered one seat. By this time five-sixths of the members were puppets placed in office by the French administration. The depth of official influence became ludicrous when in the elections of June, 1951, Ferhat Abbas could not win in his home town of Sétif. At Port-Gueydon, in the 1951 renewal election, of 23,676 registered voters, 23,671 voted. Of these, 23,645 endorsed the government's candidates and 9 voted for the communist. In the April, 1948, elections in Blida the M.T.L.D. candidate could obtain more than 10,000 votes on the first balloting, but in the run-off election scarcely 2,500. *Le Monde's* reporter at Rouget-de-l'Isle was told by Muslims sitting in a café near the polling place, "They vote for us, thus we don't have to inconvenience ourselves any more." Observers watching the voting places noticed, too, that at times, though no voters entered the booths, votes continued to be cast for official candidates. Other irregularities, such as voting without proper credentials, direct interference by officials, untimely closure of the polls, helped to pile up remarkable official majorities.

There is no point in multiplying examples of official intervention, chicanery, and downright fraud. These operations were witnessed by reliable reporters. In the French language the slang phrase "an Algerian election" came to mean a crooked election.

"In Algeria, electoral fraud is a state institution considered legitimate in order to defend French sovereignty." [65]

What all this meant was simply that the colonial regime of the nineteenth century returned to administer Algeria a century later. The emasculation of the Statute of 1947 brought tragic consequences to Algeria and France. The line runs straight between the inauguration of the policy of fraud and deception in 1948 to the outbreak of revolution in 1954.

In the feverish desire to save Algeria from the Algerian nationalists the French administration lost all contact with Muslim opinion. The high hopes for cooperation and progress of the believers in the Statute of 1947 splintered against *colon* intransigence which imposed an iron-fisted colonial administration. A far-sighted, generous spirit, Jacques Chevallier, deputy from Algiers in the National Assembly, could, in 1950, warn his readers that they had ignored the moral side of the question, that they misunderstood the evolution of Muslim hope. But his plea for dynamic Algeria, the Algeria between "the sectarianism of colonialism or separatism," fell upon deaf ears.

Many Muslim friends of France, such as those in the ranks of the U.D.M.A., felt betrayed, and so did some Frenchmen who protested the "Algerian Elections." Governor-general Naegelen lost his job over an election incident.[66] In March of 1951, after three years as governor-general, Naegelen had to go, but his replacement, Roger Léonard, a former Paris prefect of police, continued the ways of the iron fist and the fraudulent ballot.

These means mixed poorly with the rural amelioration projects begun in 1945 by Chataigneau. The bright hopes and plans for strengthening agriculture and rural communes, for stimulating industry, and, above all, for increasing Muslim educational facilities turned to despair. Somehow Algeria fell into the hand of forces whose interests were narrow and local. Here was a land on which ten million human beings depended. Surely the interests of seventy men who owned 200,000 hectares of the most fertile soil could not be considered paramount; the ten million down below counted for something. But when one examines the activity of this minority, its political objectives, which we have already seen turn Franco-Muslim relationships back a century, one does not hesitate to question this group's judgment. It seemed short-sighted in the mid-twentieth century where its interests were linked more closely than it realized to those of the whole population. When this minority could insist in Paris on parity prices for wine and wheat, and at the same time turn a deaf ear to questions of social security, it was, of course, seeking what it considered to be its own interests. It wanted for itself the best of Algeria *and* of France without paying the fair price in either market place. Put another way, and returning to the decade before World War II for the phrase, this *colon* minority thought "not in the French of France but rather in the French of Algeria." It spoke a language foreign to most Muslims and, perhaps worse, foreign to its own countrymen. But, as we have seen and are to see again and again, it spoke forcefully, and on the ground in Algeria it had a way of seducing governors and, after 1954, important army officers of the Fourth Republic.

Muslim reaction to the broken contract of 1947 and the accompanying backward-looking colonial attitude first took the form of disappointment, but was soon transformed to anger. Particularly violent was the language of the M.T.L.D. but Messali Hadj's followers scarcely stood alone in protest. On August 5, 1951, the Algerian Front for the Defense and Respect of Liberty took form with a broad Muslim base of support. Then the inconceivable happened. The U.D.M.A., the M.T.L.D., the Algerian Communist party, and the Ulema joined forces on broad issues, having found enough common ground in their opposition to French word and deed since 1947. Even so, this Algerian Front contained basic divisions. For example, the U.D.M.A.'s approach was laic while the Ulema always thought within the Islamic reference; the M.T.L.D. believed in direct action, the U.D.M.A. still preferred the "policy of dialogue" with the French. Also the M.T.L.D. and the Communists competed for the support of the masses.

Often the M.T.L.D. and the Algerian Communist party stood together. Yet they found it impossible to agree upon common objectives. The Algerian Communists, under the influence of their Paris comrades and the word from Moscow, had to concern themselves with the evils of capitalist imperialism—Soviet imperialism was fine—and the nefarious American military bases in North Africa. Likewise, they were expected to march in lock step behind the French Communists in defense of various uninteresting causes—for example, the Stockholm Oath or the liberation of Jacques Duclos, the sometimes arrested French Communist leader. The M.T.L.D., and even the Algerian Communists, could not always follow the Paris lead. They had noticed that the French Communists and the Communist-dominated C.G.T. (*Confédération Générale du Travail*) trade union showed no more than passing interest in Algerian problems. In the choice between the world and Algeria both the M.T.L.D. and the Algerian Communist party had to take the home team. The world could wait. Meanwhile, they competed for workers' support in the slums of Algeria and Paris.

Not content with this, Messali Hadj sought outside reinforcements for the cause of Algerian independence. In 1948 he appealed to the United Nations and following this he tried to whip up sympathy and aid from anti-colonialist groups in London and New Delhi. By May, 1952, after a demonstration by his supporters in Orléansville, Messali Hadj was expelled from Algeria and imprisoned at Niort in northwestern France.

BALANCE SHEET IN 1952

In assessing the situation as of 1952, it is painfully clear that the five year effort to strangle Algerian nationalism only strengthened it. The policy based upon the view that the Statute of 1947 must not be applied because it would lead to independence and the end of European dominance agitated the problem in several ways. It closed the door to conversations between almost all Muslims and Europeans, thus barring the way to an evolutionary solution. Worse, it resorted to police methods and fraud which in turn proved to be a long step toward a general violence on both sides. It surrendered the field of operation to the militants. Finally, the leaders of the European community of Algeria became

more and more a law unto themselves. They managed to emasculate the Statute of 1947, to influence Paris at the cabinet level
and thereby obtain governor-generals who would do their bidding.
What evolved was a kind of *colon* autonomist movement, which
respected neither the Muslim millions nor the Fourth Republic.

By 1952 violence struck in France's other North African
dependencies, Tunisia and Morocco, Muslim inhabited areas on
the east and west, respectively, of Algeria. Without discussing in
any depth these nationalist movements against the backdrop of
French policy, where conditions differ from those of Algeria, it
is important to note that in Tunisia and Morocco the French
found it necessary once more to use force to hold on. At the
beginning of the year the tough Resident-General of Tunisia, M.
de Hauteclocque, acting under Quai d'Orsay orders in which
colon influence (exerted by Senator Antoine Colonna and Puaux,
the younger, son of Senator Gabriel Puaux, himself a member
of the North African lobby) was obvious, arrested 150 members
of the nationalist Neo Destour. This led to rioting and additional
arrests, including that of the leader and future president of the
Tunisian Republic, Habib Bourguiba. In retort, the Tunisian
Trade Union Federation (U.G.T.T.) called a general strike.
Rioting culminated in the *ratissage* in Cap Bon where the Foreign
Legion sufficiently outdid itself to bring upon its head strong
protests from Frenchmen who decried the death, rape, and pillage. The Pinay government turned thumbs down on François
Mitterand's moderate proposal granting some internal autonomy
and proceeded under *colon* influence to a "get tough" policy.
Hauteclocque forced the Bey of Tunis to appoint M. Baccouche,
a *beni-oui-oui* said to be a large shareholder of Coca Cola Tunis,
as premier. This was followed in December, 1952, by the murder
of Ferhat Hashed, the leader of the U.G.T.T., who, journalist
Alexander Werth in Tunis in June, 1952, found to be "viciously"
accused by Hauteclocque's entourage for his "constant hob-
nobbing" with U. S. Consular officials.[67]

The murder of Ferhat Hashed, possibly by the *colon* Red Hand
organization, was bad enough, but when no one was arrested,
though it was said the Residence-General knew the identity of the

murderers, a wave of Muslim protest went up. A sympathy strike in Casablanca led to ruthless suppression and the death of perhaps "several hundred Moroccan workers." These proved to be opening events in a sequence which led straight to the independence in 1956 of Tunisia and Morocco.

Within a larger framework, 1952 must be remembered as the time of two unfinished wars in Asia—the Korean War was still a year away from the cease-fire and in Indo-China Dienbienphu was to surrender in May, 1954. Bright spots on the French 1952 horizon were the first signs of success in the seven year fight to stabilize prices and increase real wages.[68] This gain continued until 1955 when the costs of another colonial war—this time in Algeria—helped to dislocate the economy. In the years immediately following 1952 the studies on national income conducted by the National Accounts Commission, the National Statistical Institute, the Planning Commission, and Finance Ministry armed some of the brighter and younger spirits in the National Assemblies, such as Mendès-France, Edgar Faure, Pierre Pflimlin, and Christian Pineau, with facts upon which reasonably sound policies could be framed. The mysteries of economic theory, in which the French were somewhat backward, were about to be unveiled to the incredulous assembly. But before the experiment could go forward, a modicum of discipline and some continuity of leadership had to be found.[69] In the Faure and Pinay governments, which together lived twenty months, the recipes of the economic cooks varied, but there was relative continuity, and the statistics pointed toward price stabilization.

The return of France to economic good health in 1952 helped the country bear the heavy burden of war in Indo-China. So did American aid. At the same time this new found strength reflected itself in a more aggressive policy in North Africa—particularly in Tunisia and Morocco. In Algeria it would have been hard, short of complete suppression, to improve upon the French "get tough" policy begun in 1948 against the various Muslim groups which dared to hope for a freer status.

The momentum of this "die hard" attitude toward Algeria and the two North African protectorates was maintained by installing prominent members of the *colons'* North African lobby in the various cabinets. The extent and constancy of this influence is easily proved. Between November, 1947, Robert Schuman's government, and June, 1954, the beginning of Mendès-France's regime, the North African lobby placed a man in every cabinet. René Mayer kept the home fires burning in the cabinets of Schuman, Marie, Bidault, Pleven, Queuille's second cabinet, and Pleven's second. L. Martinaud-Déplat, known by some as "France's McCarthy," and his close political associate, C. Brune, carried on in the first Faure cabinet and in Pinay's; and they aided Mayer when he became premier in January, 1953. For the next four months three men in the lobby sat in the cabinet. Finally, Martinaud-Déplat served in the comfortable government of the bovine Laniel just preceding the Mendès-France period.[70] Need we say that no one served France's Muslim population at the cabinet level.

CHAPTER THREE

REBELLION

Violence broke out at approximately seventy widely separated points in Algeria on the night of October 31-November 1, 1954. Murderous outbreaks were not new in this land, and it was understandable that French authorities at first underestimated the potential of these. By 1958 these directed incidents had developed into a full-fledged revolution, tying up more than half a million French fighting men and creating an impasse which helped to destroy the Fourth Republic.

Nursed by nationalist frustration and pauperization, the rebellion began as the work of diligent, dedicated men who saw no possible middle solution between being French and being independent. The vision of an autonomous republic federated to France—once Ferhat Abbas's hope—collapsed before the events and broken promises of the post-war decade. Messali Hadj's M.T.L.D., for a time, reaped the reward of his moderate rival's failure. But his idea of a free Algerian parliament and government which might join any system it chose was impractical because it rested upon confidence in an electoral solution. Past elections had done the work of the *colons* not the Algerians. Besides, a free Algerian parliament and government could never, it was reasoned, attract enough French support to appear on any ballot. Thus, debate gave way to action, and leadership went to those resolute enough to kill for their cause.

If some leaders within the M.T.L.D. understood this, their personal rivalries and disagreement on tactics prevented them

81

from directing the rebellion. The split between Messali Hadj, the M.T.L.D.'s long-standing chief, almost a saint to his followers, and Hocine Lahouel, the secretary-general of the central committee was fundamental. It denied both the men and their party any decisive command of the forthcoming rebellion and opened the way to new faces uncommitted to the past and fiercely dedicated to the future.

Messali Hadj stood on his record. Leader of the *Etoile nord-africaine,* leader of the *Parti du peuple algérien* (P.P.A.), a worker in the Renault factory, friend of the Communists, and sufferer in French prisons for the Algerian cause, this authoritarian underwent, in the early 1950s, a metamorphosis and incurred a direct challenge from the central committee. Impressed by resurgent Pan-Arabism symbolized by the Heliopolis meeting and the Arab League (1945) as well as the later Bandung Conference (1955), Messali jettisoned Communist support. In basing his future upon an oriental, a Pan-Arab solution, in contrast to his earlier Leninism, he went all the way, even to the externals of wearing a beard, dressing in a black *djellabah* (robe), and outlawing the use of alcohol. By 1952, from Niort, in the department of Deux-Sèvres where French authorities placed him under a benevolent surveillance, he forced his will upon the M.T.L.D.

The Kabyle, Hocine Lahouel, looked upon the Pan-Arab idea as "an oriental mirage." To him the future of Algeria lay in hard work among the people of the cities, towns, and villages of Algeria. Aid from the Arab countries would always be welcome, but Algeria itself was the field of operation and any future plans and hopes had to be considered within the framework of cooperation with the other Maghrib areas, Tunisia and Morocco. Before Messali Hadj was shipped off to France in May, 1952, he and Lahouel worked together. Soon thereafter a brisk rivalry developed between the two men. Lahouel asked the first party congress of the M.T.L.D. to define the powers of the president. Since Messali had previously been a law unto himself, this request he correctly interpreted as a limitation upon his powers. Nor did Messali take kindly to Lahouel's decision to accept the offer of Mayor Jacques Chevallier of Algiers to collaborate in municipal affairs. Vitriol poured from Sables-d'Olonne. Messali wrote of "pashas of the party." Street fighting broke out between the two factions in Algeria. Then, Messali tried to obtain the power of the purse by ordering the party treasurers of the *kasmas* (cantons) to deposit their funds in an account which he controlled from France. Lahouel's central committee blocked this maneuver without trouble since the *kasmas* preferred to hold their own funds! [1]

The ultimate split between the central committee and Messali Hadj came in the summer of 1954. The former held a preparatory conference on July 10 in which it asked Messali Hadj to reconsider his position. A final congress was scheduled for mid-August. Meanwhile, July 14 to 16, Messali convoked a congress in the Star Cinema at Hornu, Belgium. One hundred fifty of his loyal men met for three solid days and nights during which no one left the hall. Their final resolution dissolved the central committee, promised to recover the party funds, supported the nationalist movement in Morocco and Tunisia, and named Messali Hadj president of the M.T.L.D. for life. In August the central committee repayed the president in kind by abolishing his office and excluding the *Messalistes*. This marked the end of unity within the M.T.L.D., and street fighting continued in the Algerian cities. Each faction had a newspaper: the central committee's *La Nation Algérienne* exchanged abuse with Messali's *L'Algérie Libre*. The rivals tried to sabotage circulation and destroy one another's presses.

By the summer of 1954 both wings of the M.T.L.D. endorsed a militant course of action. Even so, neither would set a deadline for organized rebellion, and their bickerings plus the moderate approach of Ferhat Abbas drove those Muslims dedicated to immediate resistance to organize themselves outside the framework of known political parties. Theirs was a protest against France, but it also involved opposition to the existing Algerian parties and hatred of the Muslim bourgeoisie upon whose support French rule depended through the *caïds*.

The organization which became known to the world as the F.L.N. in November, 1954, had a long and tortuous formation

83

which went back to the immediate post-war years. Its beginnings lay in the P.P.A. of 1947, which Michael Clark so picturesquely described as the submerged part of the revolutionary M.T.L.D. iceberg; its members worked day and night to organize the cities and countryside for a resistance which would lead to independence.

Already in 1947 Aït Ahmed, a Kabyle, dissatisfied with the rate of progress of the M.T.L.D.-P.P.A. operations formed the *Organisation Spéciale,* which came to be known as the O.S.[2] This small group of active militants endorsed immediate terror and proceeded to collect arms and to use them. For two years little was known of their guerrilla force which busily prepared itself throughout the countryside by founding cells, establishing a general staff, and amassing funds. A daring holdup of the Oran central postoffice in April, 1949, netted some $9000 for the cause. Later in that year Mohammed Ben Bella, a thirty-three year old Arab, born at Marnia near the Moroccan frontier who fought with sufficient valor with the French forces in Italy to be four times decorated, replaced Aït Ahmed as chief of the O.S. Liaison with the M.T.L.D. passed through the deputy to the French National Assembly, Mohammed Khider, former streetcar conductor and P.P.A. secretary in Algiers.

When French authorities happened upon this organization in 1950, many arrests took place, including that of Ben Bella. However, two places of refuge served to perpetuate the O.S.: the Kabylia Mountains, where local strong men, Belkacem Krim, Amar Ouamrane, Ali Rabia, and Amar Haddad held forth; and metropolitan France where members of the O.S. found jobs and continued their activities. In the Kabylia and in the Aurès Mountains, stronghold of Belkacem Grine, these men mediated tribal feuds, and raised funds through tribute which was the price of their justice. Here, too, in the absence of French administrative personnel these local strong men, reminiscent of the medieval baronage, almost assumed the status of governors. Considered by some observers to be no more than bandits, Algerian nationalists looked upon them as heroes, particularly when, once the rebellion began, they took command of the guerrilla bands of the Algerian Army of National Liberation.

In the early 1950's Cairo became the haven of Algerian revolutionaries. With a warrant out for his arrest as an accomplice in the Oran postoffice robbery and his tenure in the French National Assembly at an end in 1951, Khider went to Cairo. Ben Bella and Ahmed Mahsas sawed their way out of the Blida prison in March, 1952, and soon turned up in the same spot. Before this, a Maghrib Office had been created there to further, under the benevolent protection of the Arab League, the independent cause of Morocco and Tunisia. In this office, where acrimonious debates and personal rivalries flared up, the Algerians played third fiddle to Allal el Fassi of Morocco and Salah ben Youssef of Tunisia. Egyptian leaders thought the Algerians were not seriously enough engaged in the Pan-Arabic movement against colonialism. (By 1960 it would be difficult to find a nationalist movement which had fought more desperately, consistently, and against greater odds than the Algerian.) Besides, the vast majority of Algerians were of Berber, not Arabic, origin, but obviously this scarcely bothered the new leaders of Egypt in their desperation to reincarnate the "Arab nations from the Atlantic to the Persian Gulf." By 1952 Khider replaced Chadly Mekki as the Algerian spokesman in the Maghrib Office, and later, in 1954, when Gamal Abdel Nasser succeeded General Naguib, Ben Bella's stock rose. We know very little about the early relationship between Nasser and Ben Bella. "It is certain that the (Egyptian) dictator quickly saw the advantages of supporting this Muslim of Arab origin and military experience who did not hesitate before the idea of armed insurrection or an attack upon a postoffice." [3]

Whatever one may think of Nasser as an influence in recent international relations, Egypt under his leadership became a place to which Algerian nationalists could go, a place where the architects of rebellion could draft plans and start to build without fear of arrest. Further, the Special Service section of the Egyptian Army, in the persons of Major Fathi el Dib and Major Ezzat Soleiman, worked directly with Ben Bella in preparing the rebellion.

85

In Cairo, too, was Abd-el-Krim, the Riffian veteran and chief. Instrumental in recruiting young Algerians and sending them to "commando school" in Baghdad, this old war dog engaged in a private war with the Maghrib Office which led to his own withdrawal from its councils. Together with minority nationalist groups from Morocco and Tunisia he organized a North African Liberation Committee destined to be, as yet, stillborn.[4] And the graduates of "commando school" never did anything startling in the revolution, leading the French journalist, Bromberger, to reason that Cairo may be holding them in reserve for a later phase of the struggle.[5] Within the plotters' camp in Cairo frictions naturally arose. Another difficulty came from the fact that the Algerians labored under the close watch of Nasser's two majors.

Possibly it was to avoid this surveillance from a benevolent ally, whose judgment obviously contained much self-interest, that Ben Bella and his associates scheduled several meetings in neutral Switzerland between March and September, 1954. Another reason for selecting Switzerland was its proximity to France, allowing close liaison with O.S. workers hiding there. Four men dominated these meetings: Ben Bella, Belkacem Krim, the Kabylia chieftain whose job was to organize the inhabitants of those mountains, Mostefa Ben Boulaïd who performed similar work in the Aurès, and Mohammed Boudiaf, thirty-four year old O.S. fighter from the plateau area of South Constantine, "the brightest man" in the O.S., an educated tubercular who fled to Paris in 1950 and returned to Algeria to continue the work in 1953.[6] In March, 1954, the nucleus of four became "le club des neuf" who founded the Revolutionary Committee for Unity and Action (*Comité Révolutionnaire d'Unité d'Action*), C.R.U.A.[7] The nine were Ben Boulaïd, Didouche, Ben M'hidi, Boudiaf, Bitat, Krim in Algeria and Ben Bella, Aït Ahmed, and Khider in Cairo. All former members of the O.S., they agreed to put aside past rivalries and through the C.R.U.A. to organize an armed insurrection. Action, not politics, became the password, and the quadrilateral formed by Cairo, Algiers, Bern, and Paris hummed with revolutionary activity.[8] If we can say that the Algerian political parties were grandparents,

86

then the O.S. and the C.R.U.A. were father and mother to the F.L.N., National Liberation Front. The creative impulse, what some might call the challenge-response mechanism, motivating all these ancestors still remained a compound of pauperization and frustrated nationalist aspiration.

These four men, Ben Bella, Krim, Ben Boulaïd, and Boudiaf, took on important decision when they met in Switzerland in March, 1954. They ordered the O.S. refugees living in France to return to Algeria. Within a month some of them were seen back in their *douars*.[9] This aggressive action placed men loyal to violence and the Algerian nationalist movement in direct striking position to await the final order. And in Cairo on May 27 a Charter of Union of North African Commandos promised solidarity of action in the Maghrib.

At another meeting that spring in Switzerland the Arab League tried to conciliate the *Messalistes*, whose central committee was led by Lahouel, and to unite them with the Cairo group of Algerians pledged to action. Unity between these groups proved impossible, and the congress at Hornu and Algiers, mentioned earlier in this chapter, confirmed the split of the M.T.L.D. Nor did either wing join itself to the rebellion planners of Cairo, the O.S. or the C.R.U.A. organizations in Algeria itself. Both Messali Hadj and Lahouel adopted ambivalent postures vis-à-vis these movements. This disappointed the restless Algerian leaders in Cairo who were heartily weary of politicos who met, discussed Algerian problems, and finally cooperated with the French. In July, 1954, when another meeting of the Cairo group, O.S. and C.R.U.A. leaders in Switzerland broke up, the general staff—Ben Bella, Khider, Aït Ahmed—proceeded to Cairo while the future field commanders and organizers within Algeria itself—Belkacem Krim, Ben Boulaïd, and Boudiaf, and others returned to Algiers. Another stage in planning the rebellion had been reached.

April and May, 1954, were desperately important formative months for the Algeria rebellion. Yet in Paris, the French government under Laniel showed almost no awareness of the situation. The fall of Dienbienphu on May 7 preoccupied the political fathers with Indo-China. One man who saw the Algerian problem beyond the Far Eastern crisis was Pierre Mendès-France. He wrote Laniel:

> We deliberately close our eyes to the existence every-where in the world, and principally among people where we have introduced the taste for liberty, of deep national currents. We excuse the weakness of our politi-cal institutions with the most oppressive kind of police violence, the most odious, the most opposed to those liberal traditions which we have made respected the world over. The developments that France thinks it retards or checks altogether have actually been ac-celerated because among these peoples we transform their modest claims into rebellions. As for the masses of these areas, heretofore indifferent to the discomforts of the nation and to conflicts of a national character, we push them into action (against ourselves)! [10]

During the next three months the rebel organization took shape and the uprising was scheduled. Ben Boudiaf worked closely with the C.R.U.A. within Algeria, passing the word that financial aid from Egypt was certain. Independent Kabylia leaders, until this time skeptical and lukewarm to a full scale struggle, finally committed themselves. By September commands had been assigned. The rebellion adopted the same geographical divisions used earlier by the M.T.L.D. for political action. Algeria was divided into six zones (*wilaya*) which were further divided into sectors (*mintaqua*). *Wilaya* commands became known to a trusted few. They were:

Wilaya No. 1: the Aurès, Ben Boulaïd.
Wilaya No. 2: North Constantine Department, provi-sionally to Rabah Bitat.
Wilaya No. 3: Kabylia, Belkacem Krim aided by Amar Amrane, called Oumrane, both Kabyles.
Wilaya No. 4: Coastal Department of Algiers to depth

south on line Berrouaghia-Boughari-Boudeau, Mourad Didouche.

Wilaya No. 5: Entire Department of Oran, running west to Moroccan frontier, Ben M'Hidi.

Wilaya No. 6: Aumale-Sud, territory south of *wilayas* 3 and 4, including the Sahara where C.R.U.A. strength was thin and population sparse, unassigned.[11]

Didouche and Bitat soon swapped commands probably for tactical reasons. Didouche was killed early in action in the North Constantine area and Bitat fell into French hands in Algeria five months after hostilities began. Since then, he has been in prison in France. His replacement was the youthful Yacef Saadi, also arrested (September, 1957).

Early in October Boudiaf called a meeting of the *wilaya* commanders somewhere in Algeria. At this meeting these leaders were informed that the rebellion would begin at zero hour on November 1. Henceforth, too, the Algerian forces came to be known as the National Liberation Army, A.L.N., after *Armée de Libération Nationale*. It seems likely that *wilaya* commanders met for the last time before the uprising on October 25. In the interests of secrecy and surprise, local leaders received their orders as late as possible. Two days after this final staff conference Boudiaf, armed with a false passport under the name of Dridi left Algeria bound for Geneva. He reached Cairo on November 2. As late as the night of October 31 some local groups obtained assignments.

One of the last French official actions before the rebellion was the visit of François Mitterand, Mendès-France's minister of the interior to Algeria. This was the government's way of showing sympathy toward the Orléansville catastrophe when on September 9 a series of terrible earthquakes began which ultimately left 1400 dead and 60,000 homeless. Mitterand kissed babies, laid wreaths at monuments, and gave speeches. He promised to integrate the police of France and Algeria—a proposal which later produced a storm. At Oran on October 17 he was downright eloquent and many miles "off base." "In any case I can affirm that the French presence will be maintained in this country. We have no revolutionary plan: we have no intention to leap into the unknown." [12] No doubt the applause rang out.

In the early morning hours of November 1, 1954, at some seventy widely separated points, bombs exploded and isolated French posts fell under the attack of riflemen. These poorly equipped exploits of men lacking guerrilla-warfare training and unbaptized by fire yielded meager results. They took seven lives, wounded a few French, and damaged some property. Still the element of surprise and wide geographic zone of operations indicated considerable coordination and planning. This the French officials and residents could scarcely afford to ignore, and more was to come.

The uprising challenged both French authority and the Muslim bourgeoisie. One stood against Algerian independence; the other had long been the instrument through which the French maintained rural order. Tired of internal disputes within Algerian political parties, disillusioned with moderate statements, such as those of Ferhat Abbas, the leaders of the F.L.N. with Cairo as an unassailable headquarters and with a strong organization in the remote mountain villages, had finally begun the war of independence against the French and against the Muslim *caïds*, chiefs, whose existence perpetuated European dominance.

The men who planned and led the rebellion owed no political debts to pre-existing parties. Though Ferhat Abbas visited Cairo in July, 1954, he played no role in the events of November, and his U.D.M.A. had no influence. Nor did the fragmented M.T.L.D. thought by the French to be the culprit and therefore officially dissolved on November 5. Though Boudiaf, in Algeria, tried to interest Lahouel and the M.T.L.D. central committee in the new movement, these politicians knew nothing of the rebellion until their delegates reached Cairo after the November operation was scheduled. The rebels had wisely avoided the crossfire of the two M.T.L.D. factions and denied them confidence.[13] The best the Algerian Communist party could do in the months preceding the rebellion was to support its own Algerian Democratic Front

(F.N.D.A.) in which Lahouel's faction of the M.T.L.D. could come along for the ride to some unknown destination. The Algerian Communists missed the boat. Their "unifying program" as stated in January, 1954, looked fine on paper—a precise program conforming to the people's needs which would satisfy national anti-colonial forces without being exclusive; democratic organization of the masses on behalf of the common program; party components in this great unity to keep their independent organization, propaganda, and action.[14] This program failed to impress the revolution-makers in Cairo and in the mountains of Algeria. No, the rebels were not Communists. The *Alger Républicain,* whose editor was a Communist, could oppose the formula *"frapper a la tête,"* crack the rebels' heads, advocated by the other Algerian newspapers in the early days of November, 1954. But the sweet reasonableness of the Communist daily's observation, that force had failed in Viet Nam, Morocco, and Tunisia, that what was needed were democratic solutions, security, and fraternity of Algerians, came too late, lacked integrity, and was ignored by French and F.L.N. leadership.[15]

That Ferhat Abbas was himself surprised and that he underestimated the nature of Algerian resistance or its remarkable staying power, he proved in a telegram addressed to Premier Mendès-France and his minister of interior, François Mitterand.

> At a moment in which Algeria undergoes grave events, the U.D.M.A. in the name of the Muslim population confirms its will to combat the colonial regime by all legal means and in complete accord with democratic France. The current developments are the consequence of a do nothing (*immobilisme*) policy, of social conservatism, and of permanent sabotage of the will of the French legislature.[16]

And later in the Algerian Assembly (November 24, 1954), when speaker after speaker who had opposed the Statute of 1947 at the time of its passage and since helped to emasculate it, now extolled its virtues and pointed to its generosity, Ferhat Abbas delivered telling rebuttals.

91

M. Roux: "I love the Algerian Muslims. . . ."

Abbas: "Yes, like a beefsteak: bloody (*saignant*). . . ."[17]

Until the month of November in 1954 the topic of Algeria scarcely came to the surface of French political affairs. Cabinets, politicians, newspapers, and the public itself found the liquidation of the war in Indo-China and the debate on the European Defense Community more important. Save for a handful of colonial officers and those civilians whose stake was directly linked to North Africa, few prominent persons gave the Maghrib much attention. In Colombey-les-Deux-Eglises Charles de Gaulle worked on his memoirs, pondered the implications of a new German army in an atomic age, and related these new facts of political life to the French Empire. He looked upon the French Union as an important force in the containment of the expansionist Soviet Union. North Africa he considered indispensable as a link between the Metropole and French Africa.

> I envisage a combination in which defense and external affairs devolve upon France and consolidate with France the 100,000,000 inhabitants of the area, a combination whose positive actions are certainly in line with those of other Western systems, but for which its ministers and generals are responsible before our country. That is what should be created.[18]

Here in embryo were de Gaulle's thoughts on the Union, a preview of what was to come in the referendum of September, 1958. By that time, and later, conditions had changed and so had his thinking on Algeria.

THE FIRST TWENTY MONTHS

Looking back upon the rebellion six years after its beginning, the first twenty months, until the F.L.N.'s Congress in the Soummam Valley (August 20, 1956), appear to be a period of organization, some disunity, trial and error, a period of gathering momentum for the Algerian Front. For France it was a time of slowly dawning awareness that more than a sporadic protest was unfolding. Disunity prevailed, too, in the French ranks and three premiers, Mendès-France, Edgar Faure, and Guy Mollet faced the issue with no spectacular success. Algeria became, in fact, France's major problem and ministry-killer.

At the outset of the revolt French army forces numbered approximately 50,000 men, a force far too small to comb rebels out of the 850,000 square miles of Algeria. Adding local security units increased courage but scarcely touched the remote areas. Almost immediately Mendès-France announced that in accord with Jacques Chevallier, the Secretary of State for War (actually in Algeria) and François Mitterand, minister of interior, the government decided to send three parachutist battalions to Algeria. The flow of troops from France to the beleaguered colony began within a week. In May, 1955, French troops numbered 100,000 effectives. A year later 250,000 soldiers failed to halt an uprising which grew into a revolution and a full scale civil war.[19] Before the war reached its sixth year a half million troops were deployed by the French in Algeria. Three thousand casualties per month, one-tenth of which were French military personnel, the rest Muslim civilian and military, seemed like a fairly accurate estimate of the human cost as the revolution moved toward mid-1960.

As we have noted, the rebellion began modestly enough on Sunday night, October 31-Monday morning, November 1, 1954. Seven persons lost their lives in the south Constantine, in the Aurès region; Batna, Biskra, and Khenchela, foothill towns, fell under the heaviest pressure. The Kabylia area, too, took fire. In Algiers at 1 A.M. an explosion in the studios of Radio Algérie broke the early morning silence of rue Hoche. Quite a few low grade explosives were found by the French, some at the Billiard mole near 8,000 litres of stored gasoline. A 25,000,000 franc fire loss was reported at *Coopérative d'agrumes de Boufarik*. At 2 A.M. a paper factory at Baba-Ali took fire. Telephone wires at Tizi-Ouzou and Azazga were cut.[20]

The French riposte was not famous. It consisted largely, as Governor General Roger Léonard noted at his press conference, of picking up suspects and seizing such clandestine newspapers as *Liberté* and *La Nation Algérienne*. Arrests were made in

Algiers, Mostaganem, Batna, Blida, and Philippeville. "The most rewarding operation was the arrest of the chief members of a terrorist organization at Batna." Clearly the forces of law and order were a bit surprised. In Algiers they incarcerated Omar Lagha, president of the association of Algerian Muslim Boy Scouts, at 5 A.M. A Communist newspaper article three days later laconically added: "No one knows now where he is or what has become of him." [21] Moulay Merbah, the General Secretary of the M.T.L.D., found himself detained, although he had no connection with the events of November 1 or the F.L.N. The police struck out with blind abandon. M.T.L.D. officials telegraphed protests to Mendès-France and his minister of interior, François Mitterand.

By November 12 the government defined its policy which boiled down essentially to "firm sanctions but no reprisals." "Repression must be kept within bounds . . . it must fall only on those who are truly guilty and avoid the appearance of a reprisal which might hurt innocent people." [22] In the same debate Mme Alice Sportisse, the Communist deputy from Oran, saw the end of the colonial regime as the sole answer to the rebellion. To the view that Algeria was France, she raised several questions. Why was the country under a governor general, why were there two electoral colleges, why was Muslim representation inferior in numbers, and why was there a military regime in the territories in the south (Sahara)? [23]

In the early days of the revolution resistance centered in the Aurès mountains. Giving evidence, however, that this was no isolated movement, the North Constantine (*Wilaya* 2) and the Kabylia (*Wilaya* 3) fed fuel to the fires which fanned out by July, 1956. The French tried to weaken the hold of the F.L.N. in the Aurès, beginning November 20, by dropping 50,000 tracts, advising the sedentary population to part company with the rebels and come to security zones. "Agitators and strangers have brought bloodletting to our country and have settled in your territory. They live off you . . . exact tribute and take your men into criminal adventure. . . . Soon a terrible calamity will befall the rebels, after this French peace will again reign."

If the purpose of this maneuver was to place the regular inhabitants in French controlled zones in preparation for *ratissage* operations against the isolated rebels, then it failed utterly. After a week's time few families reported to the security zones. The Communist journal *Alger Républicain* counted 80 families while Michel Clark numbered 239 families at Touffana.[24] This meant perhaps 2000 persons of the Aurès' approximate quarter million regular inhabitants divorced themselves from their homes and villages in favor of French protection. The overwhelming majority remained stationary, either apathetic or evaluating the outcome in their own fashion and meanwhile exposing themselves to F.L.N. and French pressure. "Watchful waiting" was clearly the policy of the people of the Aurès.

The exact state of F.L.N. organization and its fighting potential, as of November, 1954, for the guerrilla war which ensued is hard to measure. By August, 1956, the time of the Congress in the Soummam Valley, an impressive and efficient structure emerged. An informed guess is that during these first twenty months the rebels learned quickly how to use their limited resources in the interests of making the enemy pay dearly for any encounter. One thing is certain: the F.L.N. did not start from scratch in organizing the Muslim population to cast its future with the revolution. The older P.P.A.-M.T.L.D. framework served a new master, and the work of the O.S. and C.R.U.A. helped make the transition. This early preparation proved to be a powerful advantage.

In the Aurès, where the hit and run tactics of the rebels proved effective enough to divert major French forces against them, Ben Boulaïd faced tough problems. His forces lacked arms and experience: local rivalries between the Auresi, Khenchelois, and Tebessi stymied cooperation; worse, his deputy Bachir Chihani proved ineffective, and finally lost a power struggle to Adjel Adjoul who was in charge of liaison.

Still some advantages favored the nationalist cause. The rough terrain with its jagged peaks and grottoes fitted guerilla needs perfectly. Few *colons* lived in the area, and this meant the F.L.N. competed on favorable terms with the French army and the very few administrators for local support. Nationalist propaganda therefore took the line with the Chaouïas that the Aurès had been abandoned by the French and the *caïds,* Muslim chiefs who co-operated with the European overlord in exploiting the people. Adjoul did a good job in bringing the *douars* into the rebel camp so that, despite heavy French military pressure, resistance was far from crushed. Rebel raids, while bothersome and costly of life, were not large or spectacular during these first twenty months. But they did disconcert the French, and by the summer of 1955 Chihani, who replaced Ben Boulaïd, controlled two-thirds of the Aurès area.[25]

Difficulties of command in *Wilaya* 1 stemmed from two sources. Ben Boulaïd, the excellent leader, was *hors de combat* during most of these months, and, second, rivalries among his lieutenants, plus localism within the population itself, prejudiced unity. Ben Boulaïd fell into French hands near Ben Gardane in southern Tunisia (February 11, 1955) on his way to keep a rendezvous with Ben Bella in Tripoli where they intended to buy weapons. On his person the French found a document indicating rebel combat strength in the Aurès at 359 men.[26] This left *Wilaya* 1 in the less capable hands of Chihani, native of Khenchela, a man more suited to the library than guerrilla warfare. Unable to impose unity among the eleven chiefs of *Wilaya* 1,—for one thing he was unacceptable to Auresi chiefs—he was also plagued with the vanity, ambition, and the incompetence of Ben Boulaïd's brother, Omar, who claimed nepotic leadership rights in the *Wilaya.*

Before Ben Boulaïd escaped from prison in Constantine in November, 1955, Chihani's leadership was repudiated by his lieutenants, and he had been executed (October 25, 1955).[27] Chihani's difficulties could scarcely be exaggerated, but basically they lay deep within himself. He failed at the staff level, and he failed with the people of the Aurès. When his supply section could not provide food for the fighters or itself, he decided to crack down on the impoverished population. When he prohibited smoking and punished infractions by cutting off lips and noses, he lost Adjoul's support. These mistakes compounded his problem of maintaining cooperation between the Auresi and Khenchelois. What finished Laghrour Abbès (one of Chihani's lieutenants),

96

a first class guerrilla leader whose authority carried to every man under him, was the indulgence of pederasty in Chihani's staff. These overtones dominated a crude trial in which Chihani's military judgment and loyalty also came under heavy challenge.

In January, 1956, Ben Boulaïd reached Attaf where he set about restoring unity and command. Later at his staff headquarters (*Idara*) of the Aurès the duties and rights of the freedom fighter (*Moujahid*) received precise definition and a military tribunal was created. Some executions followed, and the choice of life in the nationalist cause or death outside it was extended to the civilian population. On March 27, 1956, Ben Boulaïd lost his life to a booby-trapped radio in his command post.[28]

Wilaya 1 in the Aurès took the brunt of the early French pacification efforts without surrendering or dissolving. There was disunity and at times failure of command, but, considering all things, continued resistance and expanded nationalist territorial control indicated that the Algerian Liberation Army and its civilian sympathizers in the Aurès were a powerful and stubborn force still to be reckoned with.

In the early months of 1955 Algerian freedom fighters in the North Constantine (*Wilaya* 2) and Kabylia (*Wilaya* 3) stirred the pot of violence. This took some pressure off their brothers in the Aurès by forcing the French to thin out their pacification troops. In *Wilaya* 2 the blacksmith from Condé-Smendou, Youssef Zighout, rose quickly to leadership when Mourad Didouche was killed in combat in January, 1955. Although *Wilaya* 2 extended from Djidjelli to the Tunisian frontier, Zighout wisely reduced his control objective to the triangle Constantine-Phillippeville-El Milia. Between El Milia and Collo, the small Mediterranean port, lay the great cork (*chênes-lièges*) forest uncut by roads. In this isolated zone approximately 100,000 Algerians lived.

Zighout's strategy seemed based on the idea of lightning attacks upon French command posts, gendarmeries, official buildings, followed by quick withdrawal. If the French retaliated wildly in anger, they ran the risk of shooting down innocent Muslims who in protest against such injustice would join the F.L.N. As in the Aurès, resistance and recruitment marched together.

This overall objective would later be modified, and isolated attacks and sabotage kept the game going until large operations could be staged.

Take a tactical example carried out against the command post of French Colonel Ducourneau at El Arrouch. A seemingly undisciplined Muslim mob attacked the C.P. with cudgels and stones. When the parachutists filed out to disperse the mob, F.L.N. snipers on the roof-tops cut them down. A rapid F.L.N. withdrawal left the parachutists counting their own dead and facing a hostile mob. If they took reprisals against the mob, they lost the good will of the population. In this case French discipline held, and the bait was left in the trap.[29]

The most impressive operation in the North Constantine during the first twenty months of revolution took place on August 20, 1955. Although it is said Zighout commanded, at the most, five hundred *fellaghas,* on that day simultaneous attacks upon thirty-nine points (police headquarters, barracks, town halls) caused despair both in Algeria and Metropolitan France. It was apparent that these strikes depended in many cases upon the active support of Algerian peasants (*fellahs*), civils armed with knives and clubs and pulled out of the *mechtas* by the F.L.N. Some reporters say they were told the Egyptian army had landed at Philippeville to liberate them. In any case many centers in the north—Aïn Abid, Oued Zenati, Condé-Smendou, Collo, Jemmapes (!), El Milia, El Arrouch—plus larger cities such as Philippeville and Constantine felt the F.L.N.'s violence. In Constantine bombs exploded in a barracks and in a movie house. The nephew of Ferhat Abbas, Allaoua Abbas, also a pharmacist, was killed in his shop. In the pocket of the commando chief who carried out this assignment, and who was killed by French troops a few moments later, were orders for the execution of Ferhat Abbas and the Socialist deputy Benbahmed.[30]

Above all, this operation had a psychological objective. It was coordinated, not simply within *Wilaya* 2 but also with the massacre of d'Oued Zem in Morocco on the anniversary of the departure (kidnapping) of Mohammed V, that ill-advised French adventure which catalyzed Moroccan nationalism and independence. It was probably planned in Cairo. No important military objectives fell into F.L.N. hands. It was a straight guerrilla operation. French authorities claimed the rebels killed 71 Europeans plus 52 *beni-oui-ouis* and placed the number of rebels killed at 1273. It was noted that most of these were the *fellah* supporters not the actual F.L.N. troops. There could be no satisfaction for the European inhabitants or their troops in the calm after this battle. Hatred between Muslim and European increased as did fear in the European community where civilians in greater number began to carry small arms. Algeria was in the throes of civil war. Call it rebellion if you will or pacification; it was extremely unpleasant, and it had scarcely begun.

East of Algiers and stretching from the coast southward through the Kabylia Mountains lay *Wilaya* 3. Its chief or colonel was the remarkable Belkacem Krim, thirty-two years old the year the rebellion began, a former quartermaster in the French army with an excellent record as a fighting man. A militant of the P.P.A.-M.T.L.D., he began organizing the Kabylia in 1947.[31] Hero to the F.L.N. and bandit-murderer to the *colons*, he attracted an efficient staff. His first lieutenant, Amar Amrane, called Ouamrane, had served as a sergeant in the same French regiment as his chief. Born in Dra-el-Mizan, he took command of his natal sector, the western Kabylia. Krim's eastern zone commander was Moham'di Saïd, a four-year veteran of the French army, forty-five years of age, who once served in Jacques Doriot's French fascist group of collaborators. To this group of able and French-trained soldiers was added Ramdane Abane who served as secretary and political adviser to the *Wilaya* chief. The educated and politically astute Abane must be given heavy credit in representing Krim effectively with the Cairo group. Likewise his *savoir faire* tied tightly political and military resistance in the Kabylia making it one of the cornerstones of Algerian nationalist strength.

Though the population of both the Aurès and the Kabylia was Berber, special conditions in the latter area dictated a different, and more effective, resistance movement. Because population density was much greater in the Kabylia—130 inhabitants per square kilometer—and food supply low, many Kabyles sought work in the neighboring Algiers region. Perhaps 150,000 lived there permanently. Large numbers, too, went to metropolitan France. These migratory workers, exposed to the urban environment, returned to their villages with experience which broke down their provincialism. Indoctrinated with trade unionism, syndicalism, and Marxism, they formed a restless group of men who resented the *caïds* and Europeans alike.

These attitudes the men of Kabylia brought to the traditional democratic and elected Berber council, the *djemaa*. Try as they would to rule the Kabyles through *caïds* and French administrators, the French found that major decisions fell to the *djemaa*. This body, for example, designated the young men who would emigrate to French factories, and it chose those with large families in order to profit from the family allocations provided by French social security legislation. Once the rebellion began, the French found they administered an empty structure which the inhabitants ignored. Meanwhile Krim and Abane successfully organized a politico-administrative infrastructure in the two thousand Kabylia villages. Thus the area came to be saturated with F.L.N. cells, and Krim never overlooked the value of coordinating political and military action. Young sympathizers (*Moussebilines*) served an apprenticeship of sabotage and violence before entering the ranks of the F.L.N. fighters (*Moujahidines*).

Nor was Krim's leadership plagued with disunity and personal rivalries as was Ben Boulaïd's in the Aurès. A council of the *Wilaya* ratified the large decisions of the command. This close liaison between commander, political council, and troops carried down into the regional (*nahia*) and secteur (*kasma*) units.

Krim bided his time, making no spectacular military thrusts, concentrating instead upon gaining control over the population. He governed the Kabylia area before he undertook large scale operations. When he was ready, he levied taxes, imposed various services upon the population, and equipped and supplied his forces. His word was law—inhabitants who refused his demands often lost their lives. In the absence of French administration and serious military power Krim adapted Berber institutions to the

F.L.N. cause. From the point of view of the absent French state this was banditry, complete with murder, the torch, and assassination. It was equally an effective revolutionary organization in the hands of skilled leaders who understood guerrilla tactics very well.

During the spring of 1955 the powerful influence of Krim and Abane extended to Algiers, *Wilaya* 4. From the beginning of the rebellion Krim frequently visited, it was assumed, to plan in common with Rabah Bitat, who commanded there. When the French trapped Bitat in a café where he waited for Krim in February, 1955, *Wilaya* 4 fell under the nominal leadership of Ben Khedda and Yacef Saadi. These events coincided with increased French military pressure in the Kabylia. Krim counterbalanced this development by increasing the rebellion tempo in the western sector of his own *Wilaya,* the Tell Atlas area, where Ouamranc served, and by finding a *pied-à-terre* in the Algiers zone. Another reason for Krim's interest in the department of Algiers was the presence there of large numbers of Kabyles. His prestige stood high, then, in two of the five active *Wilayas*—the sixth in the south still lay in the blueprint stage.

The future of both Krim and Abane lay down the same road. This team, fighting as it was from the inside, needed liaison with the Cairo group for two reasons: (1) to wage war more effectively and (2) to attain personal influence at the staff level for their own advancement and that of the revolution. So in the first spring of rebellion Krim moved his headquarters to Algiers where he saw Ben Khedda and Yacef Saadi, while Abane, his political adviser, established direct contact with the Cairo leaders, becoming a kind of general secretary and communications chief between Cairo and all the *Wilayas.* That his stock rose became clear when he sat as a national political delegate to the Soummam Valley Congress held August 20, 1956.

During the first half of 1955 the revolution still found itself in process of basic organization. A start had been made. In order to hold on and gain ground, resources, planning, and devotion loomed as precious commodities, without which the movement would die. The National Liberation Front had to be broadened, to represent, as far as possible, every element of the Algerian nation. At the same time, leadership could not be allowed to dissolve in disunity that played into French hands waiting eagerly to exploit Berber barbarism and fratricide.

Given this situation, it was a moment of portent when "moderates" Ferhat Abbas, Dr. Lamine-Debaghine, and Dr. Ahmed Francis joined the "Front." Abbas needs no introduction. There is, however, some debate as to why he joined the F.L.N. One school holds he was frightened into the pilgrimage to Cairo after the rebels killed his pharmacist nephew and purportedly placed his own name on a death list.[32] This may or may not be true—no primary documents seem to be available to verify the opinion. Yet there is a document, which goes back to 1953, that leads one to believe that this moderate French-trained Algerian saw no future on the middle road between subjugation and rebellion for independence. He made his choice. This particular document takes us back to a meeting between Abbas and Alphonse Juin, distinguished marshal of France, the son of a policeman of Bône. The prefect of Constantine, an intelligent man, brought these leaders together for an open exchange of ideas. They met in the grand salon of the prefecture itself. At the end of the meeting the Algerian pharmacist sadly remarked, "I fear there is no other solution than resort to arms." [33] Here most likely is the reason Ferhat Abbas joined the F.L.N. in May, 1955, after having been earlier engaged in underground work. He reached Cairo on April 22, 1956, and since has held various responsible posts, finally being named President of the Provisional Government of the Algerian Republic in September, 1958. This was the man who hoped above all things for cooperation with France, and who for the first ten postwar years worked hard, but fruitlessly, to achieve it.

Dr. Mohammed Lamine-Debaghine joined the F.L.N. early enough to be arrested by the French in June, 1955. When he was released, and later confined to house arrest in the Constantine, he escaped to Paris en route to Cairo. Son of a restaurant owner, he was a scholarship medical student who joined the P.P.A. back in 1943. An early leader of the C.R.U.A. this doctor of medicine added luster to the ruling group, and in September, 1958, became foreign minister of the Algerian government.

Dr. Ahmed Francis, future minister of economics and finance, brother-in-law of Ferhat Abbas, graduated as a doctor from the medical faculty at the University of Paris. He followed Abbas to Cairo via the U.D.M.A., pausing to defend the revolution publicly in the Algerian Assembly.

These prominent Algerians were not the only ones to reach Cairo in 1955. Representatives of the Ulemas, some of the U.D.M.A. *élus* in the Algerian Assembly, and even some of Messali Hadj's representatives moved in for better or worse.

Behind the movement lay, in part at least, the clever hand of Abane who worked for Algeria, himself, and Krim—the exact order would be difficult to decide. Abane and Krim felt isolated on the front line, out of touch with the "historics," the founding fathers of rebellion, who sat in the relative safety of Cairo, trying to direct things without an efficient or rapid communication with the *Wilaya* chiefs. Involved here, then, was Krim's interest in sharing highest leadership with the "historics." He and Abane tried to dilute this bloc by helping to broaden its complement. They and certain followers flooded the ranks of the exterior command. The new men in Cairo soon came to be called "the parachuted." They dropped in to stay, and later their leaders were placed on the same footing as the "historics."

Meanwhile Messali Hadj tried to join the revolution by forming the Algerian National Movement (*Mouvement National Algérien*), M.N.A., early in 1955. He ordered his representatives in Cairo, Ahmed Mezerna and Chadly Mekki, to negotiate entrance of the M.N.A. into the "Front." Ben Bella insisted that this group recognize the primacy of the Army of National Liberation. This the M.N.A. agreed to do, but when Ben Bella discovered that these new partners tried to line up the Ulemas and some of the old U.D.M.A. in Cairo against the "historics," he had the Egyptian authorities imprison them.

In Algeria, too, M.N.A. men tried to join the Army of National Liberation. By mid-April, 1955, Abane wrote to Cairo, "We are resolved to crush the Messaliste chiefs." [34] Krim and Chihani, in their respective *Wilayas,* moved against the M.N.A. fighters. This explains in large part the Algerians in A.L.N. uniforms found dead at the hands of "their brothers." M.N.A. forces were driven southward toward the pre-Sahara area where they impinged upon *Wilaya* 6. The later Melouza massacre grew out of this struggle.

Resistance in *Wilaya* 5, which included the department of Oran west of Morocco and south to the undetermined frontier, centered in the Tlemçen zone. Two special conditions prevailed here: (1) the proximity of the Moroccan frontier where operations could be planned outside Algerian territory, and (2) the traditional opposition to Europeans in Tlemçen whose Muslim bourgeoisie never forgave the diversion of their commerce to the European city of Oran. As a result of these favorable circumstances revolutionary operations were quite audacious. Spectacular sabotage of the railroad line Oujda-Tlemçen, a trunk of the Casablanca-Tunis road, dramatized the rebellion. Broad daylight escapades against French military posts had the same result.

Ben M'Hidi commanded *Wilaya* 5 from the safety of Nador in Spanish Morocco. Actually operations did not start until September, 1955, when the return to Rabat of Sultan Mohammed V and the later proclamation of Moroccan independence spurred Algerian action. By December, Ben M'Hidi turned over his operation to Mohamed Boussouf and went to see Ben Bella in Cairo. A member of an influential Arab family with past Communist ties in the Mila region near Constantine, Mohamed Boussouf transferred his command post to Oujda and proceeded to equip and train two thousand *fellaghas.* With two automatic rifles per section and with each unit possessing a "walkie-talkie" transmitter-receiver set, this force became one of the best within the A.L.N. The French paid it a compliment when they constructed an electrified barbed wire barrier on the Moroccan frontier. A year later they built another on the Tunisian side. This did not prevent rebel access to the sea. In February, 1956, Ben M'Hidi returned to Morocco and proceeded to Algiers where he met the Kabyle leaders.

Between the F.L.N. and the Algerian Communist Party, P.C.A., there was no common ground at the rebellion's beginning. The

Communists, stunned at the prospect of seeing nationalists from outside the "party" lead an independence movement and torn by the presence in their ranks of Algerian rebels and European-oriented members who voted repressive laws against the revolt, stood in no man's land. At peak membership the P.C.A. counted twelve thousand loyal men, but 80 per cent were Europeans. Anxious to play some role in the growing rebellion, the party finally endorsed its activities. This brought dissolution in September, 1955, by the French authorities, suppression of *Alger Républicain,* and later the arrest of central committeeman Henri Alleg, the editor.

Apparently the illegal and clandestine party leadership, which operated after the suppression, hoped to penetrate the F.L.N. by offering arms and men to the Algerian nationalist cause. *Maquis Rouge,* or Fighters for Liberation as their guerrillas were called, performed some exploits, and once, in the spring of 1956 succeeded in delivering a truckload of French arms. The *Maquis Rouge* petered out before Dr. Saddok Hadjerès, the Jewish physician who headed the central committee of the party, made his bid for entry into the F.L.N.[35] Probably Moscow influence decided the choice of a Jew would be safest, in face of Muslim-Christian tensions.

During April and May, 1956, Hadjerès met Abane and Ouamrane, high ranking leaders of *Wilaya* 3 who also had a hand in *Wilaya* 4, in Algiers. The meetings took place in the home of Eliane Gautheron and her husband who served as liaison between the Communist organization and F.L.N. Hadjerès got nowhere with Abane by proposing an enlargement of the "Front" by bloc admission of the Communists. Abane insisted upon dissolution of the P.C.A. and admission of individual Communists upon profession of faith in Algerian independence and nothing more. At a later meeting, when Abane was absent, limited military cooperation between the two was agreed upon. Six small Communist action groups in Algeria came under Yacef Saadi's command as did the produce of Hadjères' little bomb laboratory. Some—probably less than a hundred—Communist *fellaghas* individually joined F.L.N. groups.

Before Yacef Saadi fell into French hands on September 10,

1957, he had used up the Communist groups placed under him and gotten rid of the remaining few. They mixed war and politics in such a disagreeable way that Saadi apparently got sick of them. A bitter exchange of invective and publication of documents ended the episode. Hadjères seemingly failed to penetrate the Algiers *Wilaya*. Saadi got some bombs, a few fighters, and a dull headache. Neither the M.N.A. of Messali Hadj nor the Algerian Communists succeeded in penetrating *en bloc* the F.L.N., though individuals from these groups who agreed to renounce previous affiliations and to dedicate themselves to independence were welcomed. By the spring of 1956 the F.L.N. needed to take stock of its situation. From Paris came the warning that eventually 400,000 French soldiers would reach Algeria, and by April effectives were placed at 250,000. Krim complained by letter to Boudiaf that the freedom fighters lacked proper arms. Meanwhile Abane demanded a meeting in which the Cairo men and the *Wilaya* chiefs could work out liaison, supply, and plan new tactics. The old decentralized, hit-or-miss, guerrilla warfare had to be reevaluated against the forthcoming French offensive.

THE SOUMMAM VALLEY CONGRESS

In the calling of the Soummam Valley Congress (August 20, 1956) Bromberger has seen the political ambition of Abane and the desire of the Kabyles to dominate the revolution from inside. It is true that eighteen months of struggle against fearful odds killed off all the original *Wilaya* leaders save two. Didouche and Ben Boulaïd were dead; Bitat fell into French hands. But let us not forget that these men were replaced; there was no vacuum of *Wilaya* leadership. Only Krim and Ben M'Hidi were still in business, and it was the latter who returned from Cairo in March, 1956, with word from Ben Bella. The word attempted to conciliate interior chiefs and their troops with the external leaders of rebellion. A congress would be held—and in Algeria at the scene of revolt, not in the relative security of Cairo or some other external point.

The Congress in the Soummam Valley began on August 20, 1956. Some two hundred delegates including security forces convened. Ben Bella and his exterior delegation never arrived. After waiting twenty days at San Remo for a green light to proceed, and after receiving a red light warning from Algiers that French authorities were alerted, Ben Bella's group proceeded to Tripoli. There they learned the congress had met. Likewise Omar Ben Boulaïd, the self-named chief of the Aurès after his brother's death, never turned up. This left the congress in the hands of Krim (Kabylia), Ben M'Hidi of the Oran *Wilaya*, Zighout, commander of the North Constantine *Wilaya*, Ouamrane, originally Krim's lieutenant in the Kabylia, by then ostensible leader in Algiers, plus Abane, political adviser who had become a liaison between the fighters of Algeria and Cairo.

A good deal has been made of the absence of Ben Bella or any representative from the Aurès. This is considered to be a planned effort of the Kabyle leaders present, Krim, Ouamrane, and Abane, to dominate the proceedings and the future revolution. In evaluating this interpretation,[36] it seems highly sensible not to forget the circumstances of any guerrilla operation. Liaison is always poor—a strength as well as a weakness. Personal rivalries exist in the best of military organizations, even the French. Difficulties between fighters on the line and staff outside the battle zone are always present in wars and revolutions. It is also important to remember that "divide and rule" is an old tactic. The differences between Arab, Berber, Kabyle, *et al* can be used as evidence of the conclusion that Algerians will be better off under the French —a people whose strength, too, has often been characterized by division and differences. Omar Ben Boulaïd was not much of a military leader, and it seems quite likely that Ben Bella's group were wise not to risk being picked up by the French, as they were the following October under rather surprising circumstances.

The importance of the Soummam Congress is that it went a long way toward organizing the F.L.N. and the A.L.N. It produced a statute, which may have been written up in advance by Abane, perhaps in consultation with the externals. It affirmed collective leadership, and brought some resolution to the problem of internal versus external control. Likewise the political-military relationship was refined.

From the Soummam Congress came the *Conseil nationale de la*

Révolution algérienne (C.N.R.A.), National Council of the Algerian Revolution composed of seventeen members and seventeen substitutes. The original seventeen included "historics," "parachuted," Cairo men, and inside *Wilaya* leaders: [37]

The Seventeen Members	*The Seventeen Substitutes*
Ait Ahmed Hocine	Aissa
(kidnapped October 22,	Ben Tobbal Lakhdar, Assist-
1956)	ant Commander of *Wi-*
Abane, Ramdane	*laya* 2
Abbas, Ferhat	Boussouf Abdil Hafid, Com-
Boudiaf, Mohamed	mander of *Wilaya* 5
(kidnapped October 22,	Ben Yahia Mohammed, for-
1956)	mer President of the
Ben Boulaïd, Mostepha	U.G.E.M.A. General
(killed, March 27, 1956)	Union Algerian Muslim
Belkacem	students.
Ben Bella, Ahmed	Dhiles Slimane, Assistant
(kidnapped October 22,	Commander of *Wilaya* 4
1956)	Francis, Ahmed
Ben M'Hidi, Larbi	Mohammedi Said, Com-
(arrested, February 25,	mander of *Wilaya* 3
1957 and died a few	Mezhoudi Brahim, Assistant
days later)	Commander of *Wilaya* 2
Bittat, Rabah	Mellah Ali, Commander of
(elsewhere spelled Bitat)	*Wilaya* 6
Khider, Mohamed	Mouloud
(kidnapped October 22,	Mourad
1956)	Massas, Ahmed
Krim, Belkacem	Mahri, Abdel Hamid
Lamine-Debaghine,	Said
Mohamed	Saddek
Mokrane	Thaalbi, Tayeb
Ouamrane, Amar	Zoubir
Tewfik, El Madani	
Yazid, M'Hamed	
Zirout, Youcef (killed)	

108

Belkacem, Mokrane, Aissa, Mouloud, Mourad, Said, Saddek, and Zoubir were unknown to the French police at the time this document appeared.

After the second congress held in August, 1957, a new National Council of the Algerian Revolution of fifty-four members was created. Members' names were not made public.

The published extracts from the Soummam Congress of August, 1956, note the creation of a Committee of Coordination and Execution, C.C.E., of five men elected from members of the C.N.R.A. inside Algeria. Though the names of members were secret, it can be guessed they were the *Wilaya* chiefs. Since some of these fell in battle and others became ministers, the C.C.E. composition was subject to change. Its creation represented an effort to co-ordinate the revolution from inside Algeria. Its job involved appointing committees in turn responsible to C.C.E. headquarters.

Several important policies were handed down at Soummam. Political matters received priority over military—"the political-military leader must strive to maintain a balance between all branches of the revolution." And in questions bearing upon internal and external activities the preference went to the internal. Was this such a triumph of the Kabyle influence, or was it rather a recognition of a fact of life and survival in a revolution? It may well have represented greater organization and solidarity rather than the triumph of Berber anarchy.[38] Looking back at these times from the observation post of 1960—viewing the continuing revolution, the debris of the Fourth Republic, the *colon*-army *putsch* of Algiers and France in January, 1960—and considering the constant and effective Algerian resistance, Berber anarchy does not loom as a dominant characteristic.

The organization of the Algerian Liberation Army, A.L.N., took final form and betrayed the influence of the earlier P.P.A.-M.T.L.D. structure. Six *Wilayas* were divided into zones (*mintaka*) which fell under orders of a captain. These in turn broke down into regions (*nahia*) under a sub-lieutenant. The smallest unit, the sector, was under a cadet. The post command at each echelon operated under the collective responsibility principle. In each post command a political-military representative of the

F.L.N. participated in decision. Promotions were made by "the organizational body immediately superior to that in which the man concerned belongs"—a system which might have been adopted from the American university if only it were more cumbersome. The whole game started with the staff, the colonels, and the chiefs of *Wilaya* who nominated officers.

Four colonels (Krim, Ben Tobbal, Boussouf, and Chérif) in time became ministers. When the staff headquarters moved to Tunis, Krim, for example, ceded his *Wilaya* command to Mohammedi Saïd who in turn gave way later to the famous Amirouche.

A pay scale was created, ranging from 1000 francs per month for a common soldier to 5000 francs for a colonel. No generals were to be named until after the liberation. Women soldiers received equal pay in rank with men. Nurses and doctors served as sergeants and lieutenants, respectively. Families of freedom fighters received monthly allowances. Rural dwellers could expect 2000 francs monthly basic plus 2000 francs per dependent member of the family. For urban dependents the basic came to 5000 francs plus 2000 francs per dependent.

Services of psychological warfare, widows and orphans, propaganda and information, and, of course, supply, were not beyond the scope of A.L.N. planning. In each *Wilaya* a popular consultative assembly of five elected by direct suffrage dealt with civil status, legal and Islamic affairs, financial and economic questions, and the police.[39]

Combatants in uniform, as earlier mentioned, were called *Moujahidines*. Aiding them to achieve various missions stood a vast army out of uniform, partisans, who served as guides, transporters of supplies and wounded, saboteurs. These *Moussebilines* often graduated to the uniform, but whether they wore military garb or not they served the nationalist cause efficiently. In villages the third level of resistants, the *Fidayines*, attacked the enemy, lit fires, and lobbed grenades.

The military statute of the Algerians, drafted in August, 1956, and made public later, raises the serious question as to whether it is a piece of paper or a realistic blueprint of the Algerian Liberation Army. It is easy enough to call the A.L.N. a gang of bandits—a reversion to the jungle—a different kind than the one imposed by thermonuclear weapons, nevertheless a jungle. Guerrilla warfare is no more a return to anarchy than the more sophisticated kind of twentieth-century means. Perhaps, because the F.L.N. leaders understood that guerrilla warfare alone could not bring victory, they joined political mission to it. And they began formally to organize.

> Guerrilla warfare is not a return to anarchy. It is a form of organized combat, although the organization is at the opposite extreme from nuclear war. In the latter, nothing is on the human scale: pilotless planes herald rockets carrying thermonuclear explosives hundreds if not thousands of miles. Guerrilla organization, on the other hand, depends constantly on individuals: the resolution of each man, the initiative of a few, the endurance of all, remain decisive. Ambushes which cost the lives of women and children, bombs which kill customers on café terraces, do not represent 'a fair fight' any more than saturation bombing. The discipline of clandestine war requires more brutality and terror than that of regular troops. There is always a danger that partisan warfare will degenerate into anarchy, and the revolutionary government, having triumphed through guerrilla methods, is condemned for a period to use violence to re-establish order and restore its troops to legality.[40]

During 1957 reliable eye-witness reporters assigned to the A.L.N. by their newspapers filed stories which indicated that the "rebels" had a substantially well organized army. Thomas Hodgkin wrote: "The Algerian National Army is now an efficient, disciplined force, with a unified command and strategy." [41] For a newspaper in the United States, Lee McCardell added, "Any doubts remaining in my mind as to whether the Algerian soldiers in the mountain camp belonged to an organized, disciplined army were resolved on the afternoon when the troops marched to attack the French. . . ." [42] Arnold Beichman of *Newsweek* agreed, "From what I saw, it had discipline, manpower, weapons, com-

111

mand and spirit. It is not a rabble." [43] Hodgkin, historian as well as journalist, caught one deeper implication. "Following the classic pattern of revolutionary wars, what has come into being during these last three years is not simply a new kind of army but also the rudiments of a new form of State—with its clandestine (or semi-clandestine) local authorities, courts of justice, police, schools, medical services, communications and taxation." [44]

For all the weaknesses of Berber anarchy and the alleged paucity of Algerian fighting power, the revolution, in its sixth year, holds its own against the half-million soldiers of the Fifth Republic. This is a fact, not French or Algerian wishful thinking. As late as the famous—or infamous—day of May 13, 1958, Pierre Clostermann, a French airforce major and a deputy in the moribund National Assembly, stood up in that windowless room in the Palais Bourbon and saluted the Algerian Liberation Army.

> I am neither a pessimist nor a defeatist, but I have made it a rule never to underestimate the adversary. Probably this explains why I am still alive. When I had to take risks and keep quiet about them I did this— nevertheless my plane was hit more often and more seriously on daily missions in Algeria than in four years of war against the *Luftwaffe*. In those days some believed the parliamentary investigation committees which reported that the *fellagha* had no anti-aircraft batteries. You will exact the truth when you will know that today, in Algeria, our troops fight on just about equal numerical terms with the *fellagha*. I will even say that in practice there are more *fellagha* first line troops than we have shock troops. On one side forty thousand *fellagha*, on our side scarcely twenty thousand men, always the poor paratroopers and the foreign legion, dead tired, mixed in all the sauces, dragged from one end of Algeria to the other to fill the holes or to mount the assault. . . . [45]

The Algerian Liberation Army proved to be considerably more than an army of bandits or a paper army.

Algerian nationalists understood the value, too, of sponsoring trade union activity. On this matter Messali Hadj's M.N.A. stole a march on the F.L.N. by organizing the *Union Syndicale des Travailleurs Algériens* (U.S.T.A.) in February, 1956. A month later the F.L.N. countered with the *Union Générale des Travailleurs Algériens* (U.G.T.A.).

Until July the two unions fought one another for recruits and for affiliation with the American influenced International Confederation of Trade Unions (I.C.F.T.U.). The M.N.A. originally claimed, and got, I.C.F.T.U. support, but by July the latter's executive board bowed to strength. It admitted the U.G.T.A. and forced out Messali's U.S.T.A. Pressure in favor of the F.L.N. union was apparently put by the *Union Générale Tunisienne du Travail*. In Algeria itself the U.G.T.A. commanded greater support among the working class largely because of its direct tie with the F.L.N. Among Algerian workers in metropolitan France, Messali Hadj's stock stood high. This led to violence in Paris and various French industrial centers between the two Algerian factions.

In Algeria the U.G.T.A. reduced to nothing the influence of the old, communist-dominated (since 1947) French *Confédération Générale du Travail* (C.G.T.). It likewise dealt an equally severe blow to the socialist *Force Ouvrière* (F.O.) and the Catholic trade union federation, the *Confédération Française de Travailleurs Chrétiens* (C.F.T.C.) whose penetration of the Muslim soul never went deep. "The F.L.N. greets the creation of the Algerian Trade Unions as the expression of a healthy reaction on the part of the workers against the paralyzing influence of the C.G.T., the F.O., and the C.F.T.C." [46] The old unions were out on the grounds of neocolonialism. An integral part of the nationalist movement, the U.G.T.A. leadership overlapped high-level F.L.N. personnel. This led the French authorities to arrest Idir Aïssat, the secretary general, in May, 1956, and later to treat him as a prisoner of war. U.G.T.A. members received written instructions outlining their duties—sabotage and recruitment (even of European workers).[47] "The spirit of combativity must be developed by organizing without delay military action of a supple and varied kind, in accordance with conditions of the moment (limited cessation of work, local strikes and the setting up of cooperatives for solidarity)." [48]

Late in 1956 the F.L.N. executed a series of local strikes,

practicing for a general insurrectionary strike scheduled for January, 1957, a time chosen to coincide with debate on the Algerian question in the United Nations. Finally, on January 28, the strike began. On the first day it caused serious problems in Algiers, Oran, and Constantine, but instead of gathering momentum for the eight day duration, it petered out.[49] To evaluate this gesture is difficult. The modest success or failure showed the French still controlled the major cities which was no secret. When paratroopers loaded Muslim workers into trucks, they went to their jobs despite strike orders. Paratroopers can be quite persuasive in a strike situation or in administering an "election." The F.L.N. did not execute a sustained eight day protest, and it is hard to see any positive gain to the nationalist cause resulting from it.

CHAPTER FOUR

FRENCH REACTION, 1954-1956

GOVERNOR GENERAL SOUSTELLE

Six French governments struggled with the Algerian revolution before the uprising of May 13, 1958 killed the Fourth Republic and placed future decisions in Charles de Gaulle's strong old hands. Generally speaking, each of the six, excepting Pflimlin's few trying days spent listening to the death rattle of the Fourth, tried seriously to end the revolution and hold Algeria. No government wished to exterminate the Muslim population, nor even all the rebels. Each tried to mix economic-social reform with pacification—tried in short to end the rebellion with force and kindness. This attitude reflected the ambivalent state of French public opinion. France was a proud and civilized nation. To lose Algeria after Indo-China and all the rest was demoralizing. The idea of withdrawal, after numerous humiliations since 1940, seemed hard to swallow. Yet the French stomach, or perhaps its conscience, could not tolerate a knock-down, drag-out war in Algeria.

In the beginning François Mitterand, Mendès-France's minister of interior, declared "Algeria is France." He went on to note that from Flanders to the Congo "one law, one nation, one parliament" prevailed. The sole means of negotiation, he thought, was war. Within two weeks after the rebellion of the F.L.N. French planes flew bombing missions in the Aurès and in January, 1955, armored troops moved toward that troubled area. Administrative reform—

115

joining the police force of Algeria with that of France, creating a civil service school in Algiers, reforming the Algerian section of the interior ministry—accompanied the early small-scale military operations. Appropriations for economic development were raised from $80,000,000 to $114,000,000 in keeping with Mendès-France's conviction that political reform and economic improvement must accompany pacification.

A new governor general, Jacques Soustelle, became the government's hope in Algeria. Appointed on January 26, 1955, this eminent anthropologist and Gaullist leader in the National Assembly replaced Roger Léonard on February 15. Ten days earlier Mendès-France's government had fallen under the blows of a jealous opposition which considered him the liquidator of Indo-China and the European Defense Community. The final torpedo was fired by his own Radical Socialist party colleague, René Mayer of Constantine, a *colon* representative who disagreed with the government's North African policy—"All these slow negotiations with Tunisia are having a very bad effect on Algeria. The atmosphere in Algeria is getting worse every day." [1] So Soustelle served Edgar Faure's government.

He worked hard and fast at his new job, trying to restore peace and to build hope for a French future. On February 23, the day Faure formed his cabinet, he told the Algerian Assembly "France will no more leave Algeria than Provence or Brittany. France has made its choice. It is called integration." [2] On June 28 over *Radio d'Alger* he defined again his kind of integration, a gradual process geared to the future of Algeria and France. "Integration is not assimilation; ethnic, linguistic, religious differences must be and will be respected, but they can not be allowed to prevent Algeria from becoming a truly French province in administrative, economic, social and political matters." [3]

Nimble-minded Raymond Aron later made an analysis of integration's implications and concluded that it was impossible. He did not believe Frenchmen would allow Muslims in Algeria to name approximately 25 per cent of the representatives to a French National Assembly, the logical outcome of political integration. Nor would he agree that France could sustain the monetary cost

116

of creating equal educational facilities for the Muslim youth. And the capital investment necessary to equalize the two economies and the attending social services reached an astronomical figure which, given national productivity figures and government investment commitments to the Metropole, made this aspect of integration a false promise.[4]

Jacques Soustelle had no reason to be deterred by this conclusion published in 1958. He pushed forward where Mitterand left off. The Soustelle Plan envisaged a large-scale agrarian, industrial, and social reform which someday would culminate in integration. The pauperized Algerian population had to be put to work on the land where it could support itself. Muslim landholding tradition allowed too many occupants under terms of collective ownership. This was a basic frustration of modern farming. These collectively held "arch" lands, in contrast to "melk" lands held by individuals, had to be broken down. Exchange, reparcelling, and reorganization procedures were therefore provided. Water had to be brought to parched land and used rationally. The *khamessa* tenant farmer system, which allowed the tenant one-fifth of produce, was altered to give him one-half. The tenants, *khames,* henceforth became eligible for workmen's compensation and social security, rights they previously lacked when classified as partners instead of wage earners.[5]

Industrialization lagged because raw materials, including low cost power, were either absent or undiscovered. In part, the shortage of capital explained this. The costs of two world wars ate up France's productivity and focused attention upon the Metropole. Soustelle advocated the equalization of power rates between these two parts of "France" and the diversion of some industry to Algeria. Using the Maspétiol report, he proposed large-scale capital investment to raise Algerian productivity. One impressive later result of this effort was the oil strike on June 12, 1956, in the first drilling at Hassi-Messaoud at a depth of 10,800 feet.[6] More of this later.

Integration meant bringing Muslims into the administration in increased numbers. The new governor general, therefore, immediately created an Administrative Training School for Muslims;

the long-range plan would be met by enlarging educational facilities. He succeeded in constructing 1200 new classrooms in his year of tenure and this doubled the original estimate. New departments and smaller units of government down to the "rural center," the size of a *douar*, took form in Soustelle's office. Finally, with the old Arab Bureaus as precedent, four hundred Specialized Administrative Sections (S.A.S.), *Sections Administratives Specialisées*, were planned. Algerian Affairs Officers, specially trained for the joint task of bringing French administrators into the most remote villages and at the same time engaging in all sorts of rehabilitation and construction projects, ran these sections.

At their levels, the S.A.S. and the sister Administrative and Economic Action services tried to kill the revolution with kindness. In the midst of blood-letting, carnage, school-burning, crop destruction, village bombing from the air, and torture of prisoners —neither side had a monopoly—some exceedingly devoted and courageous Frenchmen in Algeria were trying to build, preserve life, conquer disease. Obviously this effort was for France, but it was also for Algeria. Its overtone, too, was integration. Later these agencies, in particular the S.A.S., became paramilitary to the point where they sometimes placed their resources against decisions taken in Paris by the French state. On occasion they became a tool of the *gros colons*-army brass coalition—welfare storm troops of the "Algeria is France" school. But welfare troops nonetheless. They took form in September, 1955, operating in units in which an S.A.S. officer helped by a secretary and an interpreter commanded approximately thirty soldiers who protected him and performed good works—building schools, teaching classes, curing disease, and killing rebels. In time S.A.S. units tried to organize local groups to do this work.

By the end of May, 1955, Soustelle's plan, on paper, was ready for submission to Paris. Early the following month he explained it to a group of some thirty important people: cabinet ministers, generals, and bureaucrats assembled in the Hôtel Matignon.[7] Not until October 11 did the government's proposal reach the floor of the National Assembly.

Meanwhile in Algiers, Muslim political leaders still holding offices within the French framework, hence outside the F.L.N. orbit, met on September 26 to discuss the integration program. Sixty-one men agreed to Dr. Bendjelloul's demand for a meeting. Among the sixty-one were ten Muslim deputies to the National Assembly, five senators, four councilors of the French Union, and forty-two delegates to the second college of the Algerian Assembly. Not all of them turned up for the discussion, but the sixty-one had earlier agreed to support any decision reached by the majority of those present. After a wild eight-hour debate, twenty-five voted against integration and seventeen favored it.[8] Obviously the later published resolution did not represent even the majority of the sixty-one. Bendjelloul, aware of French plans for repression and pacification, declared integration inconsistent with the rapidly-developing nationalist movement. Abderrahmane Farès, former president of the Algerian Assembly, defended, unsuccessfully against Bendjelloul's maneuvers, the integration program. A year later Farès came full circle when, in an interview with *Le Monde,* he came out for negotiations with the F.L.N.

Soustelle cancelled the special session of the Algerian Assembly, thus frustrating the plan of the "sixty-one" to walk out, and tried to break down Muslim opposition to integration in a radio address. He spoke of his conferences with Muslim leaders who expressed keen displeasure and opposition to the resolution of the "sixty-one." "Without equivocation I declare that our objective remains the complete and rapid integration of Algeria; our goal: peace within justice." This opposition of some pro-French Muslims weakened in advance the cause of integration soon to be debated in Paris. So did the inclusion of the Algerian question on the agenda of the Tenth Session of the General Assembly of the United Nations on September 30, 1955. The vote went against France by 28 to 27, with the United States and the United Kingdom siding with their N.A.T.O. ally. The Soviet bloc, some Latin American states, the Arab states, India, the Philippines, and Greece voted to place the issue on the agenda.[9] The First Committee never considered the resolution which was post-

119

poned until the Eleventh Session. Still the General Assembly, over French opposition, had declared itself competent to consider the item.[10]

Soustelle considered the U.N. decision to be worth a shipment of arms to the Algerian revolutionaries. "It gave the *fellagha* hope of ultimate victory, if not by arms, by a political maneuver paired with external pressures." [11] He related U.N. action directly to new violence which broke out in the western zone of Oran department.

Before the National Assembly debated the Faure government's Algerian policy, several prominent Europeans in Algeria publicly opposed integration. The turbulent *Union française nord-africaine,* led by Louis Boyer-Banse and René Reygasse, wanted no discussion as long as terrorism continued. Actually this position stood, not against integration, but simply against any thought of reform in the midst of civil war. Not so with Jacques Chevallier, deputy in the National Assembly and mayor of Algiers, who earlier served as minister of war under Mendès-France. Interviewed by *Le Monde* on October 4, a week before the debate, he judged integration impossible because the *colons* would never accept it—never agree to standardize social services, wages, between the metropole and Algeria. He demanded instead hard and "profound" reforms to be undertaken without debate. This led Soustelle to observe that Chevallier, against integration because the *colons* did not want it, expected the government to impose even more revolutionary terms upon them.[12] Chevallier's inconsistency and confusion was scarcely unique, as the great debate soon proved.

For almost a week, beginning October 11, the National Assembly discussed the Algerian question. At the end, on the 18th, the Faure government won a narrow vote of confidence, 305 to 274, on a watered down resolution. To men like Soustelle, this failure to take a firm position and to create conditions for the fulfillment of integration proved keenly disappointing. Quite probably, the large problem of trying to cope with a growing rebellion, at the same time planning long term reform, was a

120

task too great for a National Assembly cut into six major parties and various splinter groups.

Bourgès-Maunoury, the forty-one year old minister of interior, former resistance leader and graduate of the Ecole Polytechnique, constructed boldly the broad outline of the government's program. He pushed Soustelle's reform program—agrarian reform, concessions to Islamic worship, instruction in Arabic, reorganization of certain aspects of local government. These had to be enacted quickly, with the concurrence of the Algerian Assembly scheduled to meet in November. Then he proceeded to the large issues of economic, social, and political reforms. Misunderstanding of integration, he warned, only brought about government disunity and strengthened Algerian dissent. The true application of the Statute of 1947 was the proper approach to integration. These important matters would be resolved after consultation with the two branches of the Algerian Assembly, but meanwhile the government would ask large sacrifices in order to restore peace.

So far so good, but this was only the curtain-raiser. The main event had still to be fought. Ali Cadi, deputy from Constantine, jumped into the ring with a loud blast against integration. "You have no right to integrate people who wish to keep their personality, traditions, religion, and language." That this utterance betrayed a misunderstanding of Soustelle's definition of integration, made no difference. Either Cadi did not understand or he lacked trust. He considered the policy a fiction. Alice Sportisse, the Communist deputy from Oran, fought integration because it "implied at least absolute equality of citizens" and "real equality between all the electors of Algeria," inconceivable suppositions.[13] René Moatti, Algerian born Independent deputy from Paris supported Bourgès-Maunoury's view that real integration would proceed from application of the Algerian statute.

By the third day of the debate, motions, orders of the day, and resolutions rained upon the chair. The situation was unusually healthy, spirited debate including those little intelligent French quips filled the room, and already there was a pretty good semblance of chaos. Jacques Chaban-Delmas, the Gaullist Social

121

Republican spokesman—this was Soustelle's party—could approve the integration of the two body politics, economics, and social sources, but he lacked confidence in the Faure government's strength of purpose. So most of the Social Republicans voted against the government and their own man, Governor General Soustelle. Speaking for the Socialists (S.F.I.O.), Alain Savary rejected integration and asked that the Algerian Assembly be dissolved and "free elections" held. Once the true Muslim delegates could be found, then discussions to plan the future might yield results. A "regime of association," a federal structure, or anything else might be the answer. Communist-mouthpiece Jacques Duclos blasted away at the fascist methods employed in Algeria by Soustelle. The Communists wanted negotiation with the "true representatives" of the Algerian people. Soustelle summarized this argument as one of abandonment.[14]

On and on went the debate. A Peasant party member, Paul Estèbe, decried the government's lack of power to guarantee property and life in the rebellious province. The government's motion presented by Radical deputy Roger Gaborit was less than brilliant. The motion shied from integration, mentioning it only indirectly. It spoke of dispositions tending "to integrate more intimately Algeria to the French Republic, always respecting its personality and originality." [15] Platitudes such as, "advancement of solidarity between Europeans and Muslims within a climate of economic progress and social justice which constitute the charter of Algeria," were sweet music in the midst of revolution.[16] But what could one expect? Premier Faure had to protect his political life. He included popular points in the government's motion—equal rights, continuation of the struggle against terror but no repression, land reform, true application of the 1947 Statute, no foreign intrusion into this French domestic matter, future reform of legislative and administrative institutions, and hooray for a loyal and constructive opposition.

Soustelle hoped for a giant and Faure spawned a mouse. The government's slender minority indicated quite clearly that large conception was not possible.

The basic difficulty stemmed from trying to reform and repress at the same time. Reform may be too weak a word and repress too strong, but this was the problem. And it was one which the Fourth Republic found very hard to solve. Frenchmen themselves stood in a dilemma as did, no doubt, quite a few Muslims. And the *colons* wanted to hang on and were about to convince the army of this wisdom.

It is easy enough, in 1960, to see these weaknesses and flaws. The rebellion persists—the Fourth Republic has fallen, even the Fifth has been groggy from blows struck in Algiers and Metropolitan France. There is no guarantee that even if the Soustelle Plan had been tried, it would have worked. Was integration honest or was it a smoke screen behind which French dominance could be perpetuated? Did the Muslims really favor integration of the kind Soustelle defined? It is certain that the word was bandied about recklessly, taken out of context, and misunderstood. But it is not certain that in October, 1955, as some men like Soustelle might accuse, the National Assembly had the correct formula in its hands and let it slip through greedy political fingers.

While the French government was trying to formulate a long-range program in 1955, the rebellion flourished. Take as witnesses the governor generals, first Soustelle and then Robert Lacoste who filled the Algiers spot on February 9, 1956. Writing in 1956 from notes and observations taken in February, 1955, Soustelle drew this picture of the military situation upon his arrival in Algiers.

> In February 1955 the resistance to terrorist aggression disposed of very feeble means: regular troops were few and poorly trained for the purpose; little or no extra means; practically no helicopters, few light aircraft, almost no radio equipment which was so necessary for providing warnings and communicating instructions rapidly; finally no legal means of dealing with the agents of rebellion.[17]

Soustelle's relief, Lacoste, in an interview given in his last days in office in 1958, explained the situation he encountered when he became governor general under Guy Mollet's government. "In February 1956, when I took over in Algeria, a reign of terror had been spreading over the land since November 4th, 1954." [18] Lacoste's problem was as difficult as Soustelle's. The rebellion had not been rolled back.

Yet Paris did increase its legal and military means during Soustelle's governor generalship. A "state of emergency," *loi d'urgence,* bill passed the Parliament on March 31, 1955, by a vote of 379 to 219. By its terms, prefects controlled movement of persons within designated areas. Also, protection and security zones could be created wherein special regulations could be imposed upon inhabitants. Authorities were given the right to expel troublesome persons from the area. Forced residences and authorized night searches became part of the final version of the law. The zone in which the "emergency" act could be applied was left to the governor general. Soustelle used it in Tizi Ouzou, Batna, and Tebessa, in the Kabylia as well as on the Tunisian frontier. Later, August 30, 1955, it was extended to cover all of Algeria.

Soustelle noted the shortage of troops. Many still served in Indo-China; no one wanted to weaken the N.A.T.O. shield. The Faure government (May 19) raised effectives in Algeria to 100,000 men, and on August 30, 1955, the draft class of 1954 learned its service period had been extended. These halting efforts failed to keep pace with the rate of rebel growth. Lacoste's analysis of the situation in February, 1956, was probably not far from correct.

On the world opinion front France also stood upon the defensive. In far away Bandung in Indonesia, for a week beginning April 18, 1955, delegates of the Afro-Asian world gathered together. Hocine Aït Ahmed and M'hamed Yazid, both to become members of the National Council of the Algerian Revolution, represented the F.L.N. Restless Tunisian nationalists sent Salah Ben Youssef of the Neo-Destour party, while his Moroccan equivalent, the Istiqlal party leader, Allal el-Fassi, carried his people's hopes for independence. A resolution, introduced by Egypt, supported the right of the three Maghrib peoples to self-

124

determination and independence. Passed unanimously by the political commission of the conference, it pressed France to seek an immediate and peaceful solution. In the corridors, Muslim delegates pledged financial support to the North African nationalist movements. At Bandung, and five months later in the United Nations, the Algerian revolutionaries put their case before the world. It was becoming increasingly difficult for France to avoid internationalization of this "domestic" issue.

At year's end in 1955 the F.L.N. stepped up the tempo of revolution, and France suffered one of its periodical political crises. This one was different because Premier Faure exercised his right to dissolve the National Assembly and called for new elections. Important repercussions took place in Algeria.

It came about this way. On November 29 Faure lost a vote of confidence by 318 to 218 with 20 abstentions. Article 51 of the Constitution allowed dissolution of the National Assembly if two ministerial crises occurred in which the government lost by an absolute majority within an eighteen-month period, except during the first eighteen months of any Assembly's life. This condition having been met, on December 2 the Assembly was dissolved and elections scheduled for January 2, 1956.

ELECTIONS, JANUARY, 1956

Dissolution and elections contained serious implications for Algeria. With dissolution the "state of emergency" law expired which meant that some twelve to fifteen hundred persons interned by French authorities could obtain their freedom, presumably to work again for the revolution. Night searches, control of the press, and special legal procedures against terroristic crimes likewise would discontinue if the emergency measures died out. Unable to gain any satisfaction from the caretaker government in Paris, Soustelle and his prefects took responsibility for maintaining "exceptional" procedures under the dead law. This brought upon the governor general a considerable invective from French defenders of civil liberties.

While the Republican Front in Paris campaigned for negotiation of the Algerian impasse, Muslims reacted to the political crisis. The F.L.N., "assuming its responsibilities before God, man, and history," issued stringent orders for abstention from elections. Loyal Algerian nationalists were urged to use violence on election day, to kill candidates and electoral officials. All Algerians holding office were ordered to resign by January 1 or face the consequences.[19] The Algerian Assembly, not wishing to risk more violence, postponed elections indefinitely. Ferhat Abbas' U.D.M.A. Algerians resigned from office in bloc. Meanwhile F.L.N. military activity increased in the east Constantine and Kabylia regions.

Soustelle approved the postponement of elections which, if held, might have increased the tempo of civil war. Committed to integration, he bitterly resented the Republican Front's formula, negotiation. "Negotiation," was the opposition's "cream tart" and "the atrocities of repression" its daily bread.[20] If there had been anything in common between the viewpoint of Soustelle and that of Mendès-France, who originally appointed him governor general in Algeria, the January 2 election killed it.

In his 1955 Christmas message to Christendom his Holiness Pius XII "alluded to centers of opposition in relationships between European peoples and peoples outside Europe seeking complete independence." This gentle, yet forceful, spokesman recognized one of the major issues of our time. Writing a year later, a Swedish social scientist put the issue strongly and reached his conclusion.

> In the era of awakened nationalism in the underdeveloped world the colonial system is now doomed, and its liquidation is one of the most important political avalanches taking place before our eyes. The remnants of the system are bound to disintegrate within a period of time which is very short in the annals of history.
>
> In the dependencies which still linger, the military and other expenses needed to maintain the régime, the costs and losses caused by popular revolts, and the financial burden of necessary social reforms and invest-

ments in economic development, take the profitability out of the colonial system and make it instead increasingly a liability to the metropolitan countries.[21]

From different walks of life, but joined by a common human sentiment, Pope Pius XII and Gunnar Myrdal did not underestimate the general problem they saw as crucial to their time. Both were involved, yet neither had direct responsibility. Centuries had passed since the Vatican or Sweden stood on the colonial firing-line. Applying this thinking to the specific case of Algeria and France on the eve of general elections—indeed to the revolution since 1954—one can afford charity both to the French and their Muslim opponents. Americans, aware of the vast difference between campaign promises and their fulfillment and concerned with unsolved racial questions and disarmament in a thermonuclear space age, can easily sympathize with other nations at grips with unyielding questions.

Undoubtedly the French electorate believed that the January 2, 1956, elections held some importance; otherwise 80 per cent of the registered voters would not have disrupted their important holiday to go to the polls. Civic interest was not lacking though it should not be confused with virtue. Algerian problems scarcely dominated the campaign, yet they were surely directly related to the outcome. In retrospect the postponement of elections in that rebellious province (or country) looms exceedingly important. This meant that instead of sending thirty men from Algeria to Paris, granted they would have been Frenchmen and *beni-oui-oui* Muslims, none came. Thus even official communication was blocked. Particularly did it reduce *colon* influence upon the Metropole. Lacking their own spokesmen in the National Assembly and given no decline in the revolution's tempo, the road was opened for direct action if the government's future program should be disapproved in European-*colon* circles. Even earlier, Soustelle found it difficult to prevent Europeans in Algeria from forming themselves into unofficial vigilante troops. After 1956, more than before, both clandestine and public opposition to the government thrived in Algeria.

127

Ordeal in Algeria

The quickest, possibly the surest, way to understand the 1956 elections is to study the official results. In Metropolitan France this was the distribution in votes in 1951 and again in 1956.

DISTRIBUTION OF POPULAR VOTE IN METROPOLITAN FRANCE [22]

	1951	%	1956	%	Gains or Losses Total % of Votes
Communists	5,056,605	26.4	5,492,326	25.5	—0.9
Socialists	2,732,969	14.2	3,187,890	14.8	+0.6
Radical Socialists & Left Rep. Rally	2,094,333	10.9	2,952,567	13.6	+2.7
M.R.P.	2,368,793	12.3	2,355,873	10.9	—1.4
Moderates	2,363,703	12.3	3,084,576	14.2	+1.9
Social Republicans formerly R.P.F. Gaullist Rally of French People	4,102,769	21.4	911,450	4.2	—17.2
Poujadists	Nil		2,608,481	12.0	+12.0
Miscellaneous	247,790		692,405		

Since the popular vote was heavier in 1956, parties could gain votes and still hold smaller percentages of the total vote.

SEAT DISTRIBUTION IN THE 1951 AND 1956 NATIONAL ASSEMBLIES [23]

1951		1956	
Communists	99	Communists	144
Union of Progressive Republicans (affiliated)	4	Union of Progressive Republicans (affiliated)	6
Socialists	107	Socialists	95
		U.D.S.R.-R.D.A.	19
U.D.S.R. (Democratic and Socialist Resistance Union	16	R.G.A. Left Republican Rally Split from Radical Socialists in 1956	14

R.D.A. African Democratic		M.R.P.	73
Rally	3	Radical Socialists	58
Radical Socialists	72	Overseas Independents	10
M.R.P. Popular Republican			
Movement	85	I.P.A.S. (Independents and	
Overseas Independents		Peasants for Social Ac-	
(affiliated)	9	tion, inc. some R.P.F. dis-	
Independent Republicans		sidents	83
for Peasant and Social			
Action	40	Peasants (affiliated)	12
Independent Republicans	51	Social Republicans	22
R.P.F. (Rally of the French		U.F.F. (Poujadists) French	
		Unity and Fraternity	
People) Gaullist	121	group	52
Unaffiliated	19	Unaffiliated	8
Total	626	Total	596

Le Monde's headline noted five tendencies: (1) rise of the Poujadist movement; (2) decline of the M.R.P. and foundering of the old R.P.F.; (3) Communist gain in seats; (4) decline of moderate strength; and (5) equilibrium in Socialist and Radical strength since 1951.[24] Genêt, the *New Yorker's* Paris correspondent drew a monstrous insect whose body, paralyzed in the middle, was unlikely to get off the ground because of its swollen, heavy wings on left and right.[25] The weighty question was, could a government be found between the Communist left and Poujadist right? The Poujade right, founded upon small shopkeeper discontent with the tax collection system, full of bullies and hecklers, led by Pierre Poujade who had a good war record, was destined to be no more than a passing fancy. The movement contained anti-semitic overtones and some observers saw fascism within it. Commenting on Poujadist sins, a former prefect wrote: "It seems their adversaries call them fascists in virtue of the old proverb, 'He who wishes to kill his dog calls him mad.'" [26]

Not until January 31 could Guy Mollet get the monstrous

insect into the air with a coalition government in which sat
Socialists, Radical Socialists of the Mendès-France stamp, and
one member of the U.D.S.R.-R.D.A., François Mitterand. This
was the Republican Front which Soustelle disliked intensely. The
National Assembly voted 420 to 71, with 83 abstentions, to seat
the ministry. Mollet, a fifty-one year old professor of French and
English literature, had served the Resistance movement during
the Occupation, and was Léon Blum's minister of state in 1946.
A confirmed Socialist, he brought Mendès-France into the government as second in command.

Mollet's thoughts on the Algerian question conformed to the
Socialist Party platform which had been published before the
election.[27] Resolution of colonial questions depended, according
to the platform, upon resolving the economic and social issues
jointly with those political. Since the Algerian Statute had not
been applied, the Socialists demanded a new Algerian Assembly
manned by an equal number of Europeans and Muslims. A single
electoral college (*collège unique*) using proportional representation would name representatives for both ethnic groups.
This approach was easier outlined than accomplished, and Mollet
soon ran up against the violent opposition of European mobs
in Algiers.

Those mobs were the instrument of *colon,* veteran, and student
organizations which reacted from frustrated efforts to crush the
rebellion—weak policy on the part of French government—and
from disappointment over the outcome of an election which
turned thumbs down on integration. European sensitivities were
rubbed raw by the departure of Soustelle whose term expired
on January 31, 1956. He had become the darling of the powerful
European leaders in Algiers, who gave him a royal send-off on
February 2. Worse, from the *colon* viewpoint than Soustelle's
leaving was the appointment, three days earlier, of General
Georges Catroux as minister-resident in Algiers—the post had
been raised to cabinet rank. His earlier associations with Lyautey
in Morocco and with de Gaulle in Algiers in 1943 stood as
nothing against his mission, taken a few months earlier, to

Antsirabé in Madagascar, where he secured the approval of exiled Sultan Mohammed Ben Youssef to France's withdrawal from the Moroccan protectorate. The word was out; Mollet would negotiate a peace. To these frenetic "Algeria is France" people, peace equaled capitulation. Algeria would go the way of Morocco and Tunisia—"down the river" to the independence "within interdependence" which came about in March, 1956.

In his investiture address Mollet recognized the "Algerian personality" and promised elections after a cease-fire. He spoke of the co-existence of Muslim and European, of *free* elections, and a permanent union between Algeria and France. Catroux on top of these possibilities was just too much. So, when Mollet arrived in Algiers on February 6, 1956, now famous date, various European organizations dedicated to protection of their "birthright" swung into action. The *Comité d'Entente des Anciens Combattants* advised a chilly-silent protest, but it could not contain the students and other activists—18,000 all told—who expressed displeasure with the government's proposals by pelting Mollet with stones and ripe vegetables. Mollet accepted Catroux's resignation and returned to Paris. While in Algiers, under the militant inspiration of Jean Biaggi, president of *Anciens Commandos de France*, a veteran group with no Algerian branch, a Committee of Public Safety took form. This Committee died a few days after birth; it was too extreme for the *Comité d'Entente*. Later, in May, 1958, the committee of public safety took new life. The residue of the Muslim "sixty-one," however, voiced approval of Mollet's plans.

MINISTER RESIDENT LACOSTE

The premier was not a man to surrender under a barrage of ripe vegetables, but he did require a minister to serve in Algeria. He chose Robert Lacoste, old-line socialist from Dordogne, not a pretty man—his contour resembled that of a wine barrel. No greenhorn in the deadly game of French politics, he came up via trade union activity through the Resistance to

131

the ministry of industry and commerce in four post-war cabinets. By February 10 he went to work in Algiers, having surrendered his post as minister of economic affairs. Mollet then left for Paris after making a cursory inspection of the eastern military zone.

Back in Paris, Mollet once more defined the principles upon which his Algerian policy rested. To the National Assembly, on February 16, he minimized military operations. "I have been told this by the military leaders themselves: the army can keep terrorism in check. But it cannot eliminate it if the terrorists have the support of a large section of the population." He promised security but he relied upon widespread economic and social reform to cut the grassroot support from under the F.L.N. Much of what he said jibed with Soustelle's earlier agricultural and industrial blueprint. Europeans and Muslims were told that France respected Algeria's personality. "One of the very first concerns of the Government is to hold free elections as soon as possible." He warned that special powers might be requested by the Government for swift forceful action against the terror, and France counted upon her friends among the nations to secure her Algerian policy.[28] Twelve days later he broadcast a similar message to the nation. To the Muslims he promised "free and fair" elections within three months after the guns cooled. At the conclusion a warning of "peace or else" crept in. To secure her vision of peace and justice France would mobilize her entire resources. France wanted "a free and fraternal Franco-Muslim community."[29] So much for principles; actions counted, too, and what was to be done?

On March 10 Lacoste pinpointed his own position. "Some people argue that the time for reform has passed. This is the excuse of those who wish to do nothing. What has passed is the time of promises. The time of firm and quick action is upon us." On the same day Mollet noted that one-fifth of the French army was stationed in Algeria. He expected obedience from every soldier and a speedy pacification.[30] Two days later broad special powers were voted by an impressive majority of the National

Assembly. This legislation gave the government a free hand in matters ranging from land reallocation to night searches and the control of travel between France and Algeria. In such questions as administrative reform and exploitation of the Sahara, Mollet was also given carte blanche. The procedure by which these special powers could be used was interesting. If a governmental decree, that is, an order issued without parliamentary consent, conflicted with pre-existing legislation, it could stand as law for one year. During that year the National Assembly had to ratify it to make it applicable beyond the year. The government, too, had the power to adapt Metropolitan French laws for application in Algeria. New and widespread powers over public order, security, and property were included, and Mollet's government, in this zone, could take almost any decision it wished. Military courts could try persons accused of terroristic action without prior examination of the case by a civil magistrate. All these powers lasted for the life of the Mollet government, and they could be (and were) extended by the National Assembly to succeeding governments.

In June, 1956, the first (two) Muslims were executed under this code. The F.L.N. retaliated by executing two French soldiers held prisoner by their forces. Rebel counteraction manifested itself through increased violence of all types, even against *fellahin* who showed an interest in participating in the land reform program.

The tempo of violence increased on both sides as more men were committed to the struggle. French army effectives reached 250,000 men in April. By August military, naval, and air force personnel in Algeria totaled more than 400,000 men with another force of approximately 150,000 standing by in independent Morocco and Tunisia. Against this impressive army, the A.L.N., according to French intelligence estimates of March, 1956, could muster 8,050 regulars and 21,000 auxiliaries.[31] Either this estimate was low or the freedom fighters were fantastically effective and had great local support. No one really knew the depth of A.L.N. manpower reserves.

By summer, 1956, Mollet's hope to obtain a cease-fire dwindled. Nor was there any point in talking about free elections; conditions did not permit this luxury. Instead, in April, the Algerian Assembly was dissolved and its powers assumed by Lacoste. There is evidence that the French Socialist party, not the government, tried to reach F.L.N. spokesmen, to test the possibilities of a cease-fire. According to a report carried in *L'Action* of Tunis, French Socialists Joseph Bégarra and Georges Goise met Mohammed Yazid in Cairo in April. Later in Belgrade, Pierre Commin and Pierre Herbaut, Socialist party officials, talked to Yazid. On September 2, in Rome, Commin met with Mohammed Khider of the C.N.R.A. plus Abderrahmane Kiouane and Yazid. The last meeting in this series fell on September 22 in Belgrade where Herbaut saw Lamine and Khider.[32] But nothing concrete came from these talks.

Meanwhile from the Socialist Party Congress, meeting in Lille in July, came different advice. The Mollet government was told to lead the struggle on both fronts—against the rebels and "the ultras of colonialism"—at the same time seeking a "cease-fire," a tough formula to fulfill.

Since "cease-fire," elections, and negotiations were obviously unattainable, the government climbed on the horse of reform. French administrative control was tightened by increasing Algerian departments from four to twelve and appointing superprefect trouble shooters, inspectors general of the administration on special mission, to oversee Algiers, Oran, and Constantine. The same decree transformed 79 mixed communes and 158 municipal centers into 1,071 self-governing communes. Provisions for self-government, with heavy Muslim participation, accompanied this policy. By April, 1957, some 442 "special delegations," 303 of which were presided over by Muslims, were in existence.[33] This replaced the old *caïd* system, and, of course, worked a hardship upon Muslim chiefs, *caïds*, who until then, served the French purpose, and who now found themselves in the no man's land between the French and the F.L.N.

In a different no man's land was Mendès-France who on May

134

23, 1956, resigned from the Mollet cabinet. The dynamic former premier and advocate of milk over wine accepted the military measures taken in Algeria, but he found the "concomitant" political and economic reforms to be sadly inadequate. His criticism fell particularly upon the agricultural policies. "They simply prove that M. de Sérigny continues to reign in Algiers."[34]

CHAPTER FIVE

ALGERIA IN THE WORLD 1956-1958

ALGERIAN REVOLUTION AND
AMERICAN CONSCIOUSNESS

Throughout 1956 the Algerian revolution had increasing influence upon international relationships; it attracted world-wide notice and broadened the base of revolutionary support. French orators in the United Nations or National Assembly could lose their voices proclaiming "Algeria is France," but in 1956 it became apparent that, even if that were true, France was still in the world. Algeria vitally concerned N.A.T.O. because beginning in 1955 the French detached the 2nd and 4th mechanized Divisions from the Atlantic force and sent them to Kabylia. In March, 1956, the Arab League denounced France's use of N.A.T.O. troops and equipment against the Algerian Liberation Army (A.L.N.). Mollet, in April, gratefully acknowledged this cooperation of the N.A.T.O. council, but later General Alfred M. Gruenther, Supreme Allied Commander, warned, "If the French problem became sort of permament, we would have to have a re-evaluation. We are assuming that French divisions in Algeria are in Germany." [1]

Meanwhile Morocco (March 2) and Tunisia (March 20) obtained independence. This facilitated the shipment of arms to the A.L.N. and provided a more satisfactory sanctuary for the freedom fighters. Tunis in particular, but also Rabat, became F.L.N. cities. Offices were rented; leaders conferred; and, above all, the newly-independent governments did everything within

136

their power to aid the revolutionaries. Some observers, Michael Clark for example, believe the rebellion would have been crushed in 1957 had Morocco and Tunisia not been given their independence.

Whether that guess is true or not, French authorities tried increasingly to cut the A.L.N.'s supply and to prevent the passage of freedom fighters across the Tunisian and Moroccan frontiers. But this was disheartening work. Not until September 15, 1957, was the "Morice Line" an electric barrier and warning system on the Tunisian frontier, completed. By this time many international incidents had come and gone and the A.L.N.'s equipment improved each day. Nor had rebel manpower declined.

Military equipment which ultimately reached Algerian hands sometimes originated in Yugoslavia, Czechoslovakia, or possibly West Germany. Various gun salesmen did their work and spot cash was paid. Egypt was an important point of assembly and served as a middleman in armaments trade. In an effort to detach Nasser from the F.L.N. foreign minister Christian Pineau made a pilgrimage to Cairo on March 14, 1956. Apparently he failed because everyday during the summer tension increased between France and Egypt. Even the friendly (to France) statement of American Ambassador Douglas Dillon that "Algeria was an integral part of French territory," given freely as a major State Department policy speech, on March 21 did little to prevent arms from reaching the A.L.N.

Pineau talked the French Algerian policy over with President Eisenhower beginning June 17, 1956. The day before the French foreign minister arrived, Ambassador Farid Zeineddine of Syria, representing the eight-nation Arab bloc, warned Deputy Under-Secretary of State Robert Murphy that "real and genuine coopera-tion" between the Arab states and the United States would be sorely prejudiced if the French continued to use American equip-ment against the Algerian Liberation Army. N.A.T.O., he insisted, had become a "direct means to support colonialism." [2] The later communiqué, issued jointly by Secretary of State John Foster Dulles and Pineau "expressed the hope of the United States Government" for a "liberal and just solution" in Algeria. Dillon's earlier policy speech in Paris thus received a toning down from Dulles who apparently argued that this would weaken the Arab claim in the U.N. that Algeria was an international issue.[3] Algeria may not have been an international issue—that depends upon the definition and the mind making the interpretation—but it certainly was being discussed at the international level. All the Arab states talked about it; the French needed the cooperation of their N.A.T.O. allies to prosecute the war; Nasser played big brother; Douglas Dillon made a speech; and Secretary Dulles retouched it.

From an unexpected sector of American opinion the F.L.N. received forceful support. When, on May 8, 1956, Robert Lacoste, the Socialist Minister Resident in Algeria, refused Irving Brown, AFL-CIO representative in Europe, admission to Algeria, he probably did not intend to unite the workers of two continents. When he accused Brown of "pursuing a reckless policy with dubious persons in utter contempt for the legitimate interests and incontestable positions of France in Algeria and North Africa," [4] he provoked a fight that he could not win and one which did France no service. Brown wanted to visit Algeria in order to study the application of the F.L.N.'s union, the U.G.T.A., for membership in the International Confederation of Trade Unions (I.C.F.T.U.). By July, the U.G.T.A., the "dubious persons," joined the I.C.F.T.U. George Meany, president of the AFL-CIO, spoke in September before the American Legion National Convention in plain words which challenged Lacoste, French policy, and put Washington on notice.

> We of the AFL-CIO protest vigorously against even a single American helicopter or any other military equipment designated for the North Atlantic Treaty Organization and the defense of free Europe being used against the Algerian national liberation forces. Instead, let our Government urge France to strengthen the cause of world peace and freedom by championing the establishment of a federation of democratic states of North Africa.[5]

138

Brown later demanded the rejection of the "Dillon Policy" which "tarnished us in the minds of the Arabs."

In some French circles these views simply proved that American trade unionists, like American businessmen, simply awaited the day of independence in Algeria in order to poach upon France's former preserves. The lunatic fringe, which often coincided with the extreme right, equated the origin of the Algerian rebellion with American policy. As though the Muslims needed word from the United States to verify their own position! Considering the dozens of nationalist movements which came to the surface after World War II, this compliment to American influence was too great—worse it was gratuitous and downright stupid. Neither American businessmen nor trade unionists have rushed into Morocco or Tunisia, nor have their Soviet counterparts. Both dollars and rubles seem quite scarce in the former French protectorates, nor are new francs raining down.

The game had gone full cycle. Way back on March 2, 1956, Pineau, speaking before the Anglo-American Press Association in Paris, had expressed his fears. "We have the impression that a game is being played between opposing powers, who ask themselves whether France can stay in North Africa, and who ask if, when France leaves, they can receive the inheritance.[6] Dillon's policy speech constituted a friendly reply. The American trade unions spoke out in favor of the nationalist aspirations of the peoples of the Maghrib and Secretary Dulles hoped for a liberal and just solution.

SUEZ AND A KIDNAPING

So far, so good, but now Nasser and the Suez Canal episode came on stage. France knew the Egyptian dictator as a crafty, unyielding opponent long before he nationalized the Suez Canal on July 26, 1956. Radio Cairo paid no compliments; Cairo gave refuge to the F.L.N.'s high exterior command; and, since Egypt's arms agreement with Czechoslovakia in September, 1955, Algerian freedom fighters seemed to be better equipped. It was more than a theory in Paris that if Nasser could be scotched the

Algerian rebellion would materially suffer. Anthony Eden's cabinet thought along similar lines for on July 27 Eden sent this message to President Eisenhower, "My colleagues and I are convinced that we must be ready, in the last resort, to use force to bring Nasser to his senses." [7] A military plan was ordered by the British cabinet. On August 1 President Eisenhower had not ruled out the use of force but he wished to exhaust all peaceful means of settlement. Secretary Dulles seemed to agree with his boss. "A way had to be found to make Nasser disgorge what he has swallowed." [8]

How to make Nasser disgorge, was the question. Both the French and British started out with considerable patience. But, then twenty-two powers meeting in London until mid-September failed to persuade him and the mission of Prime Minister Menzies of Australia to Cairo did no better. Secretary Dulles proposed a User's Club which would pay Canal usage dues to itself instead of to the Egyptian government. This concept finally became "a collection agency for Egypt." The Security Council of the U.N. took a hand, and, after three weeks, ran into the Russian veto. By mid-September Secretary Dulles, judging from a few statements made to the press, had shifted from contemplating the use of force to excluding it. He warned against "shooting our way through." By October 2 he found the soft middle ground.

> I suspect that the United States will find that its role, not only today but in the coming years, will be to try to aid that process [of self-determination], without identifying itself 100 per cent either with the so-called colonial powers or with the powers which are primarily and uniquely concerned with the problems of getting their independence as rapidly as possible.[9]

No ambivalence characterized the French official view of Nasser or the Suez issue. In the Egyptian dictator Mollet saw the reincarnation of Hitler; Nasser's *Philosophy of Revolution* recalled *Mein Kampf*. The Suez Canal to Egypt in 1956 was as Czechoslovakia to Germany in 1939. Pineau said Nasser had broken his word, and Lacoste believed the slightest weakness

140

vis-à-vis Egypt could bring disaster to Algeria. Even Gaston Defferre, Socialist minister of France Overseas, who had always favored negotiations with the F.L.N. against Soustelle's advice and Lacoste's judgment, favored intervention. Mendès-France, likewise, stood willing to call Nasser to account so long as peace was not jeopardized. Only Pinay and Pflimlin could see no reward in this line.[10]

On October 15 Major General Maurice Challe hurried to London with a top secret for Prime Minister Eden. The day before, the French had learned that Israel planned a raid into the Sinai Peninsula. Eden spent five hours in Paris on the 16th meeting with Mollet and Pineau. Franco-British intervention was agreed upon. From this point on, only a few highly placed persons knew the plan. On the French side, Mollet, his *chef de cabinet* Emile Noël, Bourgès-Maunoury, Defense Minister, and his *directeur de cabinet,* Abel Thomas, charged with liaison with Israel were the architects. Foreign Minister Pineau and Secretary of the Army and Algerian Affairs, Max Lejeune shared the intelligence.[11]

A few hours before Mollet and Eden put their heads together in Paris on October 16, French naval authorities stopped and searched the freighter "Athos," off Cap des Trois-Fourches, a point near the frontier between Morocco and Algeria. The ship's log placed Italy as the destination. Loaded at Alexandria on October 4-5, the "Athos" cruised an "irregular" course: toward Sicily, then leaving Sardinia on the starboard toward the Balearic Islands, thence toward Almeria on the Spanish coast, finally toward the small isle of Albboramm and Cap des Trois-Fourches. On board, according to the French, were six French nationals of Algeria—rebels—without papers, fresh from a course in terroristic tactics in Cairo. Below decks the search party found arms worth $5,700,000, enough to equip 1,500 men. The French claimed the arms were loaded by Egyptian soldiers and were destined for the freedom fighters of Algeria. This was probably true. It confirmed the necessity of dealing with Nasser. How else could the arms trade be checked?

A week later in Algiers another plot took form. It started at

8:30 A.M. when Pierre Chaussade, Lacoste's chief aide, reached his desk on the beautiful and rare morning of October 22. Chaussade, a prefect of many years, was an elegant and precise person. On the surface "very administrative"; underneath strong of will and with a reserve of cool energy—this was Lacoste's executive officer, and Lacoste was home in the Dordogne. That morning Chaussade's moment of reflection ended when Colonel Ducournau, Lacoste's military adviser, and his assistant Lieutenant-Colonel Branet burst into the office. Ducournau, a paratroop colonel (since promoted to general), a "go go" type, spoke with all his restless body.

"A tremendous operation, Monsieur. In a few minutes Ben Bella will pass over our heads in a plane. We ought to get him and all the *gaziers* (gas-fitters) with him."

"Not possible, Ben Bella. How so?"

"Here is how. The Sultan (Mohammed V of Morocco) will fly from Salé with Ben Bella and his group at 10:45. They will fly over Algeria en route to Tunis."

"It's impossible to watch those fellows pass over, noses in the air. However, the plane belongs to a foreign sovereign. Immunity applies." [12]

No French civil servant likes to make a large political decision. It is much better to have the approval of a cabinet minister who can either be made expendable or become famous, depending upon the results. So, that morning many telephone calls went out from Chaussade's office. General Frandon, commander of the Fifth Air Region, knew all about Ben Bella's trip. Colonel Germain, chief of counter-espionage in Algiers, had told him. The Tenth Military Region headquarters also knew, but felt this to be a civil question. Members of the Mollet cabinet were hard to find the morning of October 22. Lacoste could not be reached in the Dordogne; Henry Laforest, secretary of state for air, was in Lisbon. Bourgès-Maunoury, defense minister, left home at dawn, with Abel Thomas, for London where they were preparing the Suez expedition. At 7 A.M. Thomas, reached by telephone, gave an opinion, "It is the responsibility of the minister of Algeria." Finally General Lorillot reached Max Lejeune,

142

the Secretary of the Army and Algerian Affairs, who knew of the Suez project. Lejeune gave the green light and immediately reached General Cogny, commander of French troops in Morocco. *"Arraisonnez l'avion du sultan."*

The machine moved into action at 10 A.M. when the order to intercept the sultan's plane was issued. Half an hour later General Destaillac of Z.D.A. (*zone de défense aérienne*) received the official description of the plane: a Super-Constellation. Mistral fighters went on alert. At 11:30 A.M. the flight plan of the Super-Constellation was officially transmitted. This relieved the French interceptors. Radar tracking could handle this.

The trouble was that the Algerians were not on the Sultan's plane. They boarded a DC3, flight plan Casablanca-Salé-Oujda-Tunis. By 2 P.M. Algiers learned the flight plan had been modified. The DC3 would call at Palma. Riding with Ben Bella were Mohammed Khider, Hocine Aït Ahmed, Mohammed Boudiaf—all members of the original National Council of the Algerian Revolution as set forth at the Soummam Valley conference—and Mustafa Lacheraf, an F.L.N. information service officer, former professor at *lycée* Louis-le-Grand, who joined the group in Madrid.

By 3 P.M. all the French radar equipment was in use. An hour later Radio Oran spoke directly to the plane, "Pretend you have an equipment failure. Land at Oran."

DC3: "What's going on?"

Oran: "You have five *salopards* aboard. We want them."

DC3: "By whose order?"

Oran: "The Minister of National Defense."

A long pause, and finally at 4:30 P.M. the DC3 replied:

"Wait. I am landing at Palma."

At 6:30 P.M. the DC3 took off from Palma and signaled the airline Compagnie Chérifienne:

"Projected arrival time at Tunis 9:25 P.M."

The message worried the French who feared they had missed a great opportunity. So the control tower at Maison-Blanche took the relay from Oran and went to work on the French crew of the DC3 who were in the employ of Compagnie Chérifienne.

143

Algiers: "Come in, land in Algiers."

DC3: "For whom do you speak."

Algiers: "In the name of the French government, orders given by Lacoste, minister of Algeria."

DC3: "Repeat."

Algiers: "In the name of the French government, orders given by Lacoste, minister of Algeria."

DC3: "We work for a foreign company. Those orders do not concern us."

Algiers: "We must have the *fellouzes*."

At this point the commanding officer on the DC3 talked over the proposal with his crew and relayed the French request to the Moroccan authorities. The Moroccan ministry of transportation ordered the plane back to Palma. The French intercepted the message and blocked further communication between Rabat and the DC3. Finally at 7:00 P.M. the DC3 requested authorization from Algiers to return to Morocco. The answer was always the same. "Come to Algiers. . . . Come to Algiers. . . ." "Come to Algiers, governmental order to land in Algiers. Repeat: order given, order given."

At 7:30 P.M. the DC3 again requested permission to return to Morocco.

At 8:00 P.M. Algiers answered: "Negative for Morocco. Come and land in Algiers. You are covered by the minister."

DC3: "And what becomes of our families in Morocco?"

Algiers: "We'll take care of them at once. We'll put them in a safe place."

DC3: "But we have other passengers, particularly foreign journalists." (Thomas Brady, the excellent *New York Times* reporter was aboard.)

Algiers: "Don't worry about that."

DC3: "And if the rebels are armed?"

Algiers: "Make sure of it."

The stewardess went through the plane arranging the papers in the seat pockets. When she came to Ben Bella, he quickly deflected her.

144

"Don't bother with us, young lady."

Back in the pilot's compartment she passed the word. Ben Bella was a walking arsenal.

DC3: "What are we going to do if they find out we are over Algiers and then place a gun in the pilot's back?"

Algiers: "Our fighters will take off and you can argue that you are forced to land."

An Air France passenger plane cut in: "Bravo boys. Go to it. We're with you."

Meanwhile Lacoste's plane arrived at Algiers. The minister resident beamed when informed of the coup which was in the making. He wanted no shooting. The world must not think France would risk innocent passengers to capture the F.L.N. chiefs.

At 9:20 P.M. in clear moonlight the DC3 landed at Algiers. The F.L.N. chiefs still suspected nothing. Then abruptly the plane stopped and the lights were cut. Colonel Andres, air security chief, ordered all passengers, "Hands up." The handcuffs were brought out and identification and interrogation began.

"Ben Bella?"

The old military training sparked to life and the freedom fighter who held the Croix de Guerre and four citations, snapped, "present."

Later, under lengthy interrogation conducted by Rauzy, chief of the Security Police (*Direction de Surveillance Territoire*, D.S.T.) of Algiers, Ben Bella remarked, "You have well-equipped facilities. Later, we, too, will create a fine D.S.T." [13]

Meanwhile in Paris during the late afternoon Alain Savary, secretary of state for foreign affairs in charge of Moroccan and Tunisian affairs, heard from Boulabib, the Moroccan Ambassador, that the coup seemed likely. No one in Max Lejeune's office was giving out information since he had authorized the project. At the Hôtel Matignon Mollet was purported to have exclaimed, "It's not possible. It would be folly." By 10 P.M. Lacoste told of his catch. Mollet learned the news at a dinner, honoring General Gruenther. At 11 P.M. Mollet met with President René Coty who standing in his dressing robe told him, "We are dishonored."

Savary pleaded for the release of the prisoners; Lejeune argued against this.

From Morocco, Mohammed V interrupted his dinner to telephone President Coty. "The Algerians were under my protection. My hospitality has been violated. You know the Muslim tradition. It is a question of honor. The Koran says, 'Thy guest is more inviolable than thyself.' I am ready to give my sons as hostages." [14] The French ambassador in Tunis, de Leusse, agreed with the Sultan. De Leusse held a heated telephone conversation with Lacoste. Savary resigned his post in protest. But Ben Bella and his four associates went to Santé Prison.

The capture of Ben Bella's group was much more than an incident in the war. Its importance was not that it raised a question in international law [15] or that it awakened the Algerian cause or even that it drove Morocco and Tunisia into deeper sympathy with Algerian nationalism. It ended for the time being the possibility of some rapprochement between France and the F.L.N., and it once more dishonored the French word in Muslim eyes.

Mollet's government, involved in plans with Britain and Israel to crush Nasser and with that to deprive the F.L.N. of one external base of operations, at the same time had been seeking a dialogue with the F.L.N. leaders of the interior. Documents found on Mohammed Khider point to secret pourparlers between the F.L.N. and the French government.[16] Mollet had tried to reach the F.L.N. leaders through Moulay Hassan, the crown prince of Morocco. Two years before de Gaulle's "peace of the brave" offer Mollet gave this message to Moulay Hassan.

> We wish to end the war in Algeria. We have often tried to reach the F.L.N. chiefs in Cairo. But each time the fish seems inclined to take the bait, we end with the bare hook in our hands. At the end of the second day we can no longer hook anything. If the F.L.N. representatives in the interior [Algeria], those who fight us, wish to come to Paris, give me their names. On my word of honor I agree to bring them to

146

France, to meet with them, to guarantee their safe
return to Algeria.[17]

Mohammed V, meeting with Ben Bella in Rabat before the
ill-fated hop to Tunis, encouraged the F.L.N. to enter into a
dialogue with France. "The important thing is to get your foot
in the stirrup. Look at what happened in Tunisia where internal
autonomy lasted eight months or take the example of Morocco
where the Council to the Throne lasted six days!" [18] The Sultan
wanted the F.L.N. leaders to go to Tunis and join, as near equals,
since they did not represent an independent country, Morocco
and Tunisia in proclaiming the unity of the Maghrib. Such action
would have reduced Nasser's influence and to that extent played
the French game. Ben Bella, then, agreed to go to Tunis but
he seems not to have accepted the federal formula. An integral
nationalist, he demanded Algerian independence of France—
and of Morocco and Tunisia.

All these plans foundered when the DC3 was diverted to
Algiers. The larger French plan, the Suez expedition, to check
Nasser and thereby reduce external support to the F.L.N. also
broke upon the rock of American-Soviet opposition, and the
latter's threat of thermonuclear missiles. It seems likely—and
it has been said—that Eden and Mollet judged the Soviet
threat to be a bluff.[19] But what was of more importance, Douglas
Dillon carried a written note to Mollet—not an ultimatum but
une mise en garde. "If you persist in your culpable attitude, do
not count on the United States. . . . The U.N. is the only
admissible recourse. . . . Stop your troops . . . or count no
more on us. . . ." [20] President Eisenhower followed this with a
ten line note said to be "dry in tone" and "disagreeable to French
ears." The Anglo-French had sinned.

Eden, according to Tournoux, weakened first. On November 6
in a telephone conversation with Mollet in which Adenauer took
part the Prime Minister admitted he was beaten.

I am driven into a corner. I cannot hold out any
longer. Everyone is slipping away from me. My loyal

collaborator Nutting has resigned his ministry. I am not even able to count upon unanimous Conservative support. The Archbishop of Canterbury, the Church, the oil interests, the whole world is against me!

The Commonwealth threatens to explode. Nehru wishes to break ties. Canada and Australia will no longer follow our policy. I cannot be the gravedigger of the Crown.

Further, try to understand me, to understand me well, President Eisenhower telephoned me. I cannot play the lone horseman without the United States. That would be the first time in the history of England. . . . No, it's not possible. . . .[21]

After consultation with Pineau, Bourgés-Maunoury, and General Ely, Mollet gave the "cease-fire" order to French forces in the Suez area.

On the same day, November 7, 1956, Mollet spoke before the National Assembly. He tried hard to be optimistic, to put the best face on the Suez fiasco. But it was difficult to agree with him when he said:

> Our decision to continue and develop, in a climate of confidence, our friendly relations between France and an independent Tunisia and Morocco, our determination to reach a solution in Algeria which, at one and the same time, ensures the liberation of each of the inhabitants of Algeria, respect for Algeria's individuality and the permanence of the ties with France are both strengthened by what has occurred.[22]

The world had the opportunity to weight this careful statement against Ben Bella's defiant words at the moment of his arrest, "This is how you can trust the French."

The DC3 episode and the Suez fiasco placed any solution of Algerian questions at much greater distance. Morocco and Tunisia were offended; the F.L.N. lost further confidence in the Mollet government's word; Nasser rode high and could help the

Algerian nationalists with refuge, money, and arms; and the United States, by its Suez policy, indirectly encouraged internationalization of the Algerian issue. After the arrest of Ben Bella, Morocco called American attention to what would be the "grave consequences." The American Committee on Africa appealed to President Eisenhower on behalf of the kidnapped F.L.N. leaders.[23] An ugly rumor in Paris claimed that a document found on Ben Bella proved that two American oil companies had shipped a large quantity of arms to the Algerian freedom fighters. Ambassador Dillon had to deny this and the French government later agreed that the story had been false.[24]

Mollet spoke of friendly relations with Morocco and Tunisia. But in Meknès the kidnapping of Ben Bella led to retaliatory violence which took approximately fifty European lives. Two hundred farms were burned. Anti-European tension mounted in Casablanca, Rabat, and Tunis. As Alain Savary noted, when he resigned from the French government, a crisis in cooperation between Europeans still working in public services in Morocco and Tunisia and those newly-independent governments arose directly from the Ben Bella incident. Lacoste could boast of the importance of documents found on Ben Bella—a note showing that Prince Moulay Hassan proposed to give the Algerians arms, a report on F.L.N. strength in France, and the codes used by the F.L.N.—but the French position in November, 1956, was no better than it was a year earlier. In all probability it was a great deal worse, and the United Nations joined the act again.

The Algerian question, placed on the agenda of the Eleventh Session of the U.N. in September, 1956, reached the First Committee on February 4, 1957, and was discussed during seventeen meetings. Eighteen African and Asian countries introduced a draft resolution (Document A/C. I/L. 165) asking France to recognize the right of the Algerian people to self-determination and to negotiate with the Algerian nationalists. It failed on February 13 by a vote of 34 to 33 with 10 abstentions. A second draft (Document A/C. I/L. 166) sponsored by Japan, the Philippines, and Thailand simply expressed hope that France and the Algerians would end the war through negotiation. It passed 37 to 27 with 13 abstentions. The United States voted against both resolutions, thus supporting France. A third draft resolution (Document A/C. I/L. 167) put forth by five Latin American countries and Italy hoped for a peaceful democratic solution. It passed 41 to 33 with 3 abstentions. The United States and the United Kingdom voted yes. Since neither of these resolutions which were passed received a two-thirds majority, the various sponsors recommended to the General Assembly simply the hope that a "peaceful, democratic and just solution will be found." This passed unanimously 77 to 0 (Union of South Africa and Hungary absent).[25]

France abstained from the discussion and the vote but hailed the result as a great victory. The Algerian nationalists were cheered to know that their fight reached the United Nations. Washington, too, was probably glad the debate was over, and the Atlantic alliance intact for another year. It required clever footwork to support France as the N.A.T.O. bridgehead and to court Muslim friendship at the same time. These considerations plus American support of "peace," "justice," and the U.N. sometimes worked hardship on friends while the official American eyes remained closed to issues like the Hungarian massacres of 1956.

The French worked hard for the American vote. A full page advertisement in a New York newspaper under the banner "Americans, Your Voice Is Needed Now" was the work of a group of French and European publishers. If the United States deserted France, the Western alliance might dissolve.[26] French military men told their American equivalent in the Pentagon of Algeria's strategic importance. Albert Schweitzer urged President Eisenhower to support France in the U.N.[27] Against such an array of capital and distinction, hard realism and "justice," Bourguiba's appeal for Algerian independence lost out.[28]

In supporting the third draft resolution Henry Cabot Lodge, Jr. probably came close to expressing American policy. "It seems to us that the French program for a cease-fire, for elections, and for consultation with the elected representatives marks a significant and a hopeful forward step. . . . We must, at the very least, do nothing here at the United Nations which will interfere with that evolution." [29] Very fine, the only trouble was the cease-fire involved the French and the F.L.N. who scarcely communicated and who every day fired upon one another. Second, there had not been an honest election in Algeria in ten years; in fact the French could not risk an election in 1956 for fear of violence. So what hope was there that "elected" representatives would really represent anything or be free to evolve a philosophy?

THE FIRST HALF OF 1957

During the first six months of 1957 the Algerian wind carried new straws. The very nature of the nationalist rebellion and the French counteraction seemed to be undergoing change. Each side faced a new set of problems and the international community, more keenly aware of the issues, watched eagerly the unfolding of events, weighed interests, and sometimes offered comment and advice.

Both sides had increased the tempo of the war. All available estimates indicate that in 1957 the F.L.N. had more men and better equipment than a year earlier. So did the French. Germaine Tillion, a reliable witness and trained observer who left Algeria in April, 1956, and returned on June 18, 1957 as a member of the International Committee against the Regime of Concentration Camps, noted important changes.

> Since its origin I was a member of the committee and when the decision to investigate Algeria was taken, I was named along with M. Martin-Chauffier to serve with three foreign colleagues. These were the conditions under which we visited the major camps and prisons of Algeria. In the course of this trip I saw again many officer friends, civil servants or *colons,* and at the same time interned Muslims whom I knew personally or whose families I knew and who, for this reason, spoke to me as one speaks to someone who bears no ill-will.
>
> I must say that on the whole these conversations presented an extremely coherent picture of the situation.

151

The most striking aspect to me, having left Algeria in April, 1956, was the important development in one year's time of underground political construction [*structuration politique clandestine*]. Even more important and remarkable was what one might call the 'style' of the operation, of which its crushing speed was only one aspect.

I had always thought that in Algeria a [French] military victory was technically possible—one could neutralize a resistance by destroying all its resources, regardless of where or what circumstances, if one was willing to pay the price—but it now seemed to me that as soon as the [rebel] military machine would be reduced these underground political forms would reconstitute themselves.[30]

This analysis made the French future prospect in Algeria a part of a vicious circle. The F.L.N. had its problems, too. The capture of Ben Bella and the other leaders obviously did not finish Algerian resistance or even seriously weaken the external leadership. But it did raise questions. For the time being Ahmed Tewfik El Madani, secretary-general of the Association of Ulema and member of the National Council of the Algerian Revolution, replaced Ben Bella. From inside Algeria came word that the fight for independence went on.

In the Kabylia F.L.N. strength and unity held firm. There were, however, difficulties in the Aurès where Omar Ben Boulaïd could not bring command to bear in the style of his dead brother. Amirouche visited the *Wilaya* in an unsuccessful effort to re-establish unity.

With Tunisia F.L.N. relations had always been good, but by 1957 several issues rose to the surface. Tunisia not only served as a sanctuary and training ground for freedom fighters, it also became a haven for possibly as many as 200,000 Algerian refugees.[31] With F.L.N. troops and Algerian refugees on Tunisian soil, there arose a brisk trade in all sorts of military and civil necessities. And rumor had it that Algerian troops levied taxes upon Tunisian nationals. In short Bourguiba had a serious problem, that of an Algerian force operating in Tunisia. The transfer of F.L.N. external headquarters from Cairo to Tunis in April, 1957, bound more tightly these two sections of the Maghrib, but it also made imperative a clear definition of relationships.

The exact meaning of this transfer probably lay somewhere between a more convenient command location and a desire to reduce Cairo influences upon the F.L.N. external leaders. Tunisia was part of the Maghrib; Egypt was not. Belkacem Krim and Amar Ouamrane both left their *Wilaya* commands and went to Tunis. The former gave the Kabylia into the hands of Saïd Mohammedi while Ouamrane turned over the Algérois *Wilaya* 4 to Slimane Dehilès. From Tunis Krim served as liaison between the interior *Wilaya* commanders and the external authority. Ouamrane's job was to supply arms and equipment to the freedom fighters from Tunis.

Between the F.L.N. organization in Tunis and Bourguiba, a plan to preserve Tunisian sovereignty and at the same time help the Algerian nationalist cause was finally worked out. Bourguiba's Tunisian National Guard would carry supplies to frontier towns where Algerian freedom fighters would receive them. Various villages within Tunisia became exchange centers and safe points of haven for Algerians. Algerian wounded were to be freely admitted in Tunisian hospitals. Bourguiba also managed to put an end to the operations of Larbi Taleb, a free-lance rebel, who operated in southwestern Tunisia on the Saharan border without authorization of the F.L.N.'s Committee of Coordination and Execution. This cooperation between Bourguiba and the F.L.N. external leadership helped the latter keep its house in order.

In addition to the advantages already noted, it soon became possible to undercut Omar Ben Boulaïd in the Aurès and restore a semblance of unity. With Ouamrane in charge of supplies in Tunis, he easily brought Omar Ben Boulaïd to heel by depriving him of weapons and necessities. The latter finally turned against the F.L.N. but later made the pilgrimage to Cairo to explain his conduct. By June, 1957, Mahmoud Chérif, who once served as a lieutenant of *spahis* in the French army and who in the spring of 1957 turned up as a strong man in eastern Algeria, became the F.L.N. *Wilaya* commander in the Aurès. This holder of the Legion of Honor and the Croix de Guerre who had fought for France in Indo-China, gave excellent service in that difficult assignment.

Life was no easier for the French high command in early 1957. A suggestion of what could happen—and did happen in May, 1958—came up on January 6 when General Jacques Faure, second in command of the Algiers division, was placed under arrest for thirty days by Defense Minister Bourgès-Maunoury. Faure was charged with relations with an extremist committee. A week later an attempt was made to kill General Raoul Salan, French commander-in-chief in Algeria, with a bazooka. Salan escaped but Major Rodier was killed by European assassins or their hirelings. French chagrin was partly mitigated by the capture in Algiers of Larbi Ben M'Hidi (February 25, 1957), a member of the Committee of Coordination and Execution. A few days later guards reported finding him dead in his cell.

Whether Ben M'Hidi committed suicide or died under torture became a question in many minds because the use of torture had already become normal practice in the French Army and the Security Police. In protest against torture and terror General Paris de Bollardière on March 28, 1957, asked to be relieved of his command in the Atlas Mountains. He was given sixty days arrest.[32] Quite a large number of Frenchmen, some of them with international reputations, stood up publicly to protest the method of the "question" being used under the emergency laws. Three hundred fifty-seven eminent men addressed this appeal to President Coty.

> A large number of our young men, serving their terms in the Army or called back from the reserve, have received, in the name of the French people, the heavy and difficult task of participating in the war in Algeria. However, for over a year, we have collected a great number of concurring statements, based on testimony of

unquestionable validity, which affirms that these young soldiers have to participate, regardless of their desires, in actions which would arouse every human conscience. . . . It is not a question of facts, which, however numerous, can be qualified as isolated instances; rather, it concerns a widespread practice: we refer to the torture of prisoners, captured with their weapons in hand, but who, because they are 'rebels' are refused both the guarantees given by the Geneva Convention to enemy soldiers, and the rights which our law confers upon French citizens. We refer also to the summary execution of innocent hostages, to brutalities, pillage and the destruction of entire villages as measures of intimidation and reprisal.[33]

Among the signers were François Mauriac, Nobel Prize laureate in literature, André Philip, Socialist party leader and prominent political economist, and the reliable publisher, René Julliard. He published Jean Jacques Servan-Schreiber's book *Lieutenant en Algérie* for the edification of the French public, bringing upon himself and his author the undying hatred of the *gros colons,* the colonels who endorsed torture, and the extreme right. The basic fact was that the war was dirty—that F.L.N. terrorism brought French retaliation against villages and torture to prisoners.

Upon an important sector of the French public, probably a vast majority, torture "*à la Gestapo*" did not sit well at all. Someone remarked that after Algeria the French could no longer feel quite the same about Oradour—the French village where the Nazis ran amuck. Premier Mollet faced a difficult situation. The French were not making headway against Algerian nationalist forces; a "get tough" policy had been adopted, but Frenchmen recoiled at their own torture chambers. On April 5 the government announced the creation of a Committee to Safeguard Individual Rights and Liberties in Algeria. Its first meeting took place on May 10, and Pierre Beteille, a judge, was elected president. Maurice Garçon, a distinguished trial lawyer, and

Robert Delavignette, who wrote a model report on Algeria for the Economic Council in 1955, were also members of this twelve man committee. No doubt, the committee's creation lay in part to Mollet's desire to calm public reaction to torture. Yet apparently the committee looked into enough cases by October to arouse Delavignette, Garçon, and Pierret-Gérard, who resigned because no action had been taken.

By that time the responsibility was no longer Mollet's. His government fell, on a financial issue, on May 21. In a nutshell the commercial deficit, which ran 82 billion francs in 1955 and 413 billion in 1956, reached 221 billion for the first four months in 1957. This was too rich for the blood of the Independents and Moderates—and since the Communists had earlier withdrawn their support and the Gaullist Social Republicans never did support him—Mollet lost his grip. An Algerian war which cost roughly a million dollars, or 350,000,000 francs, a day surely related to the financial issue. "The triptyche, cease-fire, elections, negotiations, concealed badly the failure of the political solution" in Algeria. Tales of French-induced terror and torture did not help either.[34] After a three-week crisis Bourgès-Maunoury formed a government.

TWO AMERICAN CANDIDATES "LEND" A HAND

Back in November, 1956, just after the Suez expedition, Lacoste optimistically predicted, "We are in the last quarter hour: do not press us to propose political reform." Three months later the U.N. again discussed the Algerian question. By the end of that debate no striking signs of the end of hostilities could be seen. The revolution moved undiminished into its third year. The situation required close watching, and, as a sign of continuing interest in affairs African, Vice President Richard Nixon visited that troubled continent in March, 1957.

In Morocco and Tunisia, "the two wings of the Maghrib," the Vice President came face to face with the Algerian issue. The press reported that Nixon and the Sultan sought a peaceful solution. This report was not brilliant, but it showed concern, good will, and was uncontroversial. In Tunis, at the U. S. Information Agency Library, a Muslim woman grasped Nixon's hand and appealed in French, "Save Algeria! Be Humane! Algerians will fight to the death for liberty! End the war." [35] A Reuters account had Nixon replying, "We'll do our best." After talks with Nixon, Bourguiba explained that Americans stood for the liberty of peoples but that conditions sometimes prevented them from taking action. When the Vice President returned to the United States, Algeria was conspicuously absent from his public summary. President Eisenhower apparently received a secret evaluation.

After Nixon's return, Arab pressure upon the United States mounted. Reports on French atrocities prefaced by a letter from Messali Hadj reached the White House.[36] Eleven Arab states asked the United States to stop supplying France with economic and military aid which was being used to suppress Algerian liberty. France countered this Muslim effort to close off the American preserves by playing up the Melouza massacre, where on May 29, three hundred male Muslims fell, apparently victims of fratricide. President René Coty used the incident to divert attention from French methods of terror and torture. In a radio-TV broadcast, he asked friends of France not to listen "to the agitators and the agents of this horrible terrorism. . . ."

Neither side succeeded in winning over Washington. On June 28, 1957, the State Department rejected the Arab request that the United States terminate aid to France. Such action would negate American policy and "free world interests." The United States also condemned all atrocities and massacres.[37] A plague on both houses.

At this point, another hopeful candidate for the American presidency entered the act. On July 2 Democratic Senator John F. Kennedy of Massachusetts introduced a resolution asking the President and Secretary of State to use American influence, either through N.A.T.O. or through the good offices of Bourguiba and Mohammed V, "to achieve a solution which will recognize the independent personality of Algeria and establish the basis for a settlement interdependent with France and the neighboring na-

157

tions." Kennedy combined this light jab with a powerful uppercut. He further resolved that if "no substantial progress" could be measured by the next session of the United Nations General Assembly, the United States should "support an international effort to derive for Algeria the basis for an orderly achievement of independence." [38]

Kennedy and his staff had done a considerable amount of homework before introducing the resolution. His remarks bore the imprint of careful preparation. It was not hard to judge from internal evidence that the Massachusetts senator knew the studies of Raymond Aron, Servan-Schreiber, and had read the French press. The Senate spent the major portion of the day on Algeria and Kennedy spoke often and long.

> Mr. President, the most powerful single force in the world today is neither communism nor capitalism, neither the H-bomb nor the guided missile—it is man's eternal desire to be free and independent. . . . The war in Algeria confronts the United States with the most critical diplomatic impasse since the crisis in Indochina —and yet we have not only failed to meet the problem forthrightly and effectively, we have refused to even recognize that it is our problem at all. . . .[39]

The reasons why Kennedy considered Algeria such an important issue to the United States followed.

> The war in Algeria, engaging more than 400,000 French soldiers, has stripped the continental forces of NATO to the bone. It has dimmed Western hopes for a European common market, and seriously compromised the liberalization reforms of OEEC, by causing France to impose new import restrictions under a wartime economy. It has repeatedly been appealed for discussion to the United Nations, where our equivocal remarks and opposition to its consideration have damaged our leadership and prestige in that body. It has undermined

158

our relations with Tunisia and Morocco, who naturally have a sense of common cause with the aims of the Algerian leaders and who have felt proper grievance that our economic and military base settlements have heretofore required clearance with a French government now taking economic reprisal for their assistance to Algerian nationalism.

It has diluted the effective strength of the Eisenhower doctrine for the Middle East, and our foreign aid and information programs.[40]

Observing the three point French settlement program, based upon military reconquest or "pacification," socio-political reform, and ultimate political union with France, Kennedy was unimpressed. Citing General Wingate, "Given a population favorable to penetration, a thousand resolute and well-armed men can paralyze for an indefinite period the operation of a hundred thousand," the senator disposed of a military solution. As for social and political reform during a nationalist revolution, these Kennedy could not accept as substitutes for political freedom. "Most peoples . . . appear willing to pay a price in economic progress in order to achieve political independence."[41] And future political union between France and Algeria would have to bridge the gap between past French words and deeds which so seriously undermined Muslim confidence.

Kennedy's resolution kindled a friendly debate. Most Democratic senators drew him out in a favorable manner. Senator Chavez appreciated his colleague from Massachusetts. Referring to the pending Defense Appropriations Bill, which provided military aid for France, Chavez wanted "that aid to be used for the purposes it is supposed to serve, but not for the purpose of killing Algerians in North Africa."[42]

To the tired argument that the Algerians were not prepared to rule their own country since they lacked leaders and experts, Kennedy had only this to say. "But these obstacles come with ill grace from a French Government that has deliberately stifled

159

educational opportunities for Algerian natives, jailed, exiled or executed their leaders, and outlawed their political parties and activities." [43]

The old truism, that the American people make foreign policy, could perhaps be exposed by studying the case of Algeria. If the hypothesis that the people desired an American program of encouragement to the Algerian nationalists could be established, then it would be hard to show where that encouragement lay in actual American policy 1954-1957. Of course, no one knew what the American people wanted, and it was a safe bet that six out of ten "average" Americans did not know whether Algeria was in Africa or Asia. Kennedy surely knew his resolution would be stillborn; yet his speech raised questions, was in a sense an educational effort. The Vice President had gone to North Africa, shaken hands, smiled, said "We'll do our best." Then he came home and like a good G-2 officer reported to his chief. Kennedy was a Democratic senator; that made it different.

The reaction to the Kennedy resolution was quite enlightening. As was to be expected, the official French and the State Department found it ill-considered. Press opinion was mixed; various distinguished citizens gave their views; and organizations went "on record."

According to André Morice, Defense Minister in the Bourgès-Maunoury government, the senator's intervention would increase the number of victims and prolong the drama "that would have been long ended if so many of our unthinking friends had weighed their words or their acts." [44] It was hard to reconcile this old tune with frequent uprisings in Algeria during the nineteenth century, with revolution since 1954, and with the contention that Algerians lacked political maturity. The minister did the senator too much honor.

In Algiers a bomb exploded at the American consulate on July 4. It was probably placed there by a European extremist. Resident Minister Lacoste invited Kennedy, "a young, ambitious Senator," spokesman for "the old maids of the United States" to be his guest. "We will give him all the facilities to observe the situation so he will stop talking like a deaf and blind man." [45]

The Eisenhower administration found it necessary to defend itself. The senator had advocated a change in policy and had singled out Dulles, Dillon, and Lodge as guilty of error. Secretary Dulles, speaking to the press, considered Algeria to be primarily a French problem. The correct American posture lay in being willing to assist, not "trying ourselves to assume the responsibility for the solution of that extremely difficult problem. . . ." A later *State Department Bulletin* [46] suggested that Senator Kennedy might find better places to chase down colonialism than in Algeria. Hungary, maybe? Writing later, Dean Acheson, former Secretary of State under President Truman, criticized the senator and judged that France would ultimately lose Algeria.

> Nothing could be more injudicious than this proposal, except making it. The act has contributed to the difficulty of solution in Algeria. The Senator should have known that he was not telling intelligent Frenchmen anything they do not know. What he does not understand is the humiliating agony of the loss of power and position. One does not need a crystal ball, either in France or here, to foresee the outcome in Algeria; but the adjustment of a society to loss takes time. [47]

From Bonn, Adlai Stevenson feared that immediate independence for Algeria would lead to chaos and from Brooklyn Democratic Representative Emanuel Celler called the Kennedy resolution "immature" and "unfair."

Kennedy replied to his critics on July 8.

> No amount of hopeful assertions that France will handle the problem alone, no amount of cautious warnings that these are matters best left unmentioned in public, and no amount of charges against the motives or methods of those of us seeking a peaceful solution can obscure the fact that the Algerians will someday be free. Then, to whom will they turn—to the West, which has seemingly ignored their plea for independence; to

the Americans, whom they may feel have rejected the issue as none of our affair while at the same time furnishing arms that help crush them; or to Moscow, to Cairo, to Peiping, the pretended champions of nationalism and independence.[48]

Standing with Kennedy was Senator Hubert Humphrey of Minnesota who padded the punch with the observation, "We seek to cooperate not dominate. In the spirit of friendship to France we seek to advise not chastise." Reinhold Niebuhr and Norman Thomas were among the supporters of the Kennedy proposal.

Newspaper opinion varied. Editorial support came from a wide range of newspapers—*Boston Herald, Minneapolis Star, Birmingham News.* Often the larger dailies remained silent or were critical. The *New York Times* first spanked the brash senator. Then, some six weeks later, moved toward his position. Henri Pierre, Washington correspondent of *Le Monde,* paid Kennedy a high compliment when, while not always agreeing with him, believed he had said "much truth" and "opened the eyes of many Frenchmen." [49]

For a host of reasons anti-colonialism was much stronger in the United States than within Western Europe or the white British Dominions. An analysis of these reasons deserves separate study and could be exceedingly rewarding. One can conjecture, however, that such an attitude arose from the independent American experience; the road from British colony to the American nation seemed similar to that sought by peoples trying to exchange colonial for independent status. Also, in the twentieth century the evolution of the Philippine Islands, if not Puerto Rico, stood as an example. To many Americans the highest objective of colonial administration and policy was to raise the colony to a point where it stood, independent, upon its own feet. Some people just could not square their idea of human dignity with what they read about (or saw) in colonies. Others were idealist enough to wish to see the Atlantic Charter in operation. These people, in some cases, inclined to put the issue on a moral plane.

Liberty was a good thing—good for everyone in the world. American trade unionists, as we have seen, were very much interested in the working conditions of colonial man.

These were some of the reasons any American president was limited in peacetime, and even in war, in his ability to commit the United States to support the old colonial powers in Western Europe even though those powers were political allies. Also there was the Senate, standing watchdog, where treaties required a two-thirds majority.

> Were it not for all the complicated tactical interests involved in carrying on a cold war by means of a great number of diverse and often fragile alliances, the United States would come out even more often, and more bluntly, on the side of the poorer countries. In particular it would back liberation movements in the countries which are still political dependencies.[50]

The worn out analogy, which frequently came from Paris, that, after all, the Americans had practically exterminated the Indians, and should not complain about a few liquidated Muslims, lacked cogency. First, this was the mid-twentieth century, not the eighteenth or even the nineteenth. Second, there still were some Indians around, some even sitting on their oil wells. Third, two wrongs do not add up to a right. Too, there were at least nine million Muslims living with the one million Europeans in Algeria. By 1980 there might be twenty million Muslims and still one million Europeans. So, quantitatively the comparison did not hold either. Some die-hards argued that the reason the Muslim population increased so rapidly in the twentieth century was because the French treated them so much better than the British colonists and later Americans treated the Indians. Perhaps so; penicillin was unknown earlier. Nor did the United States require Indian manpower for wartime use in quite the same way the French needed Africans of all types in two world wars. The main point was, man having reached this stage, could not rationally turn back to the jungle, toward extermination of any subject people. Of course, no one on either side in his right mind advocated this. All the formulas worked toward a future progression of some kind: independence, autonomy, or integration.

BOURGÈS-MAUNOURY, FELIX GAILLARD, AND THE LOI CADRE

Some problems in human relationships seem to defy solution. Algeria was one of these. No quick answer came from the battle-front or from Paris. Nor did the United Nations, the Nixon mission, or the Kennedy Resolution provide much help. The revolution ground inexorably on during the second half of 1957.

In his policy statement before the National Assembly on June 12, Bourgès-Maunoury, the forty-three year old Radical Socialist Premier Designate who formed a three and one half month government, placed Algeria as his first concern.

> We do not have the choice today between two courses,
> one being the continuation at all costs of an unending
> and absurd struggle, and the other leading suddenly,
> as by a miracle, to peace and prosperity.
> We must wage the struggle as long as it is forced upon
> us, and at the same time, we must help millions of men
> to build together a new Algeria.[51]

Invested by the light vote of 240 to 194, the new premier carried on Mollet's policy in its essentials. Lacoste stayed on as proconsul in Algeria. After eighteen months in the "White City" his viewpoint came increasingly to resemble Soustelle's. A new Algeria had to take form. Negotiations with the F.L.N. were impossible as was a "cease-fire." France had to crush the rebellion. Should a withdrawal be attempted, Lacoste foresaw the French of Algeria rebelling against Paris and forming an Algerian Republic in "the manner of South Africa and the army would march with them." This possibility of an army rebellion against Paris was something Max Lejeune, Secretary of State for War

164

in 1957, often referred to. This was why the government said little about the repression and torture practiced by the army. Where was the army going? No one knew but Lejeune put it this way, the army "had learned politics: it had been humiliated; it wanted no more of that. To all its difficulties I did not wish to add a troubled conscience." [52]

Bourgès-Maunoury's government fell on September 30, 1957, when the National Assembly rejected the *Loi Cadre* for Algeria by a vote of 279 to 253. In defeat the premier received more votes than at the time of his investiture. The proposed *Loi Cadre* called for the creation of a Single Electoral College thereby abolishing, structurally at least, the political divisions between Muslim and European. In addition, Algeria would be divided into (eight) autonomous administrative districts and provision was made for a federal organ to tie these districts together. This proposal, though trimmed in a round table conference of the various French political parties, failed to withstand the developing opposition and the government fell. Among the opponents were Mendès-France, André Morice, minister of national defense, André Marie, Duchet, the Independent, Jacques Soustelle, and the Communists. For different reasons, these men and their followers refused the government's program.

The government's fall precipitated the eighteenth ministerial crisis of the Fourth Republic and one of the longest. Thirty-five days later Félix Gaillard, a thirty-eight year old Radical Socialist and financial expert, formed a government. In contrast to the ruling political alignment since January, 1956, the Republican Front which was left center, Gaillard found a working majority further to the right. The M.R.P. returned to the fold. The moderates were satisfied enough to favor investiture by a vote of 337 to 173.

In his address Gaillard called for early approval of a *loi cadre* which would guarantee a single electoral college in Algeria. At the same time he demanded and received the emergency powers necessary to wage the war of pacification. While the premier designate demanded suspension of the ordinary police rules and judicial procedures, thus allowing continuation of many abusive practices in the dirty war, he also asked for a miracle.

> Within the framework of indissoluble ties between Metropolitan France and this territory, the personality of Algeria must be able to develop fully. It will succeed in this only by respecting the ethnic communities of which it is composed and by ensuring equitable representation for all the human and economic components of its population on all the administrative bodies of the territory.[53]

Thus Gaillard promised a *loi cadre* and at the same time a new electoral law. He also appealed for a cease-fire. "My Government will be ready to make all the necessary contacts, at any time, with those who are fighting against us in order to bring about a cease-fire." So, what the new government wanted was to keep Algeria French, to reform political institutions in that hapless area, tending to equalize Muslim influence with European, and to further economic and social progress. All the Algerian nationalists had to do was to lay down their arms and be happy with a *loi cadre* and an electoral regime imposed by Paris. The obvious hitch was that the F.L.N. officers kept reaffirming, as for example, from Tunis on October 31, 1957, a week before Gaillard was invested, that all negotiations depended upon previous recognition of Algerian independence. Thus, as far as the F.L.N. was concerned, the *loi cadre* and all the predicted reforms counted for very little.

Before the National Assembly debated the new government's Algerian proposals in January, 1958, Gaillard faced another international complication directly related to the Algerian revolution, Bourguiba in Tunisia wanted arms to defend his country against French aggression. In September, 1957, he let it be known that he would find the guns "no matter what the price." If the United States and Britain would oblige, fine; if not, then Moscow could be approached. "Must a country be in desperate straits or rotten with communism before it can expect help?" he asked.[54] Washington stood once again on the spot. Bourguiba would go to Moscow if necessary, and the French ally claimed the equipment would certainly end in Algerian hands. On November 15, the United States and Britain began sending arms to Tunisia—500 rifles and 350 machine guns, including ammunition, composed the first delivery. French threats to withdraw from N.A.T.O. filled the air but finally Premier Gaillard, though deeply disturbed at this "unfriendly gesture," decided not to weaken further "what is left" of N.A.T.O. Secretary Dulles assured Foreign Minister Pineau that the arms would not reach the Algerian rebels.[55]

Events moved at an accelerated pace during the last months of 1957. After recalling his ambassador from Paris (October 7), in protest of a French communiqué authorizing planes to bomb Tunisia upon provocation, Bourguiba tried to end the war in Algeria before his country became more deeply involved. He and Mohammed V of Morocco, on November 22, offered their "good offices" to settle the Algerian problem. A week later the National Assembly approved the Gaillard government's *loi cadre* by 269 to 200 and the Algerian electoral law by 267 to 200. Not until the end of January were the final texts adopted. French reform activity, always strongest in the autumn of the year before the Algerian question might come under debate in the United Nations, was exceptional in 1957.

It had to be because there was evidence that John Kennedy's earlier proposed resolution in the Senate had made some imprint upon American policy. Also Canada entered the game more actively. To make a long and tortuous story short, the First Committee of the Twelfth Assembly heard the Algerian item fourteen times, beginning November 27, and the General Assembly finally passed a resolution suggesting France enter into pourparlers. The First Committee could not decide between two resolutions: one, supported by seventeen Asian and African states, applied the principle of self-determination for the Algerian people and called for negotiations; another, sponsored by Canada, Ireland, and Norway, reasoned "that the people of Algeria were entitled to work out their own future in a democratic way." The

167

Asian-African proposal demanded negotiations, the amendment of Canada, Ireland, and Norway asked for "effective discussion." No matter how you look at these resolutions, they both put pressure upon France.

But fortunately, perhaps, for that power, the lack of agreement within the first committee meant no motion would be recommended to the General Assembly. However, on December 10, 1957, a joint resolution submitted by Argentina, Brazil, Canada, Cuba, the Dominican Republic, India, Iran, Ireland, Italy, Japan, Mexico, Norway, Peru, Spain, and Thailand was approved unanimously (80 to 0) by the General Assembly. This resolution noted the good offices of Tunisia and Morocco and expressed hope that "pourparlers will be entered into and other appropriate means utilized, with a view to a solution in conformity with the purposes and principles of the Charter of the United Nations." France abstained; the United States did not.[56]

During the U.N. discussion, Henry Cabot Lodge, Jr. considered the proposed *loi cadre* a forward step as he did the offer of good offices from Morocco and Tunisia. All this proved to be wishful thinking because at this time the French rejected good offices, and the *loi cadre,* though adopted in final form on January 31, 1958, never was applied.

Still this new covenant marked an important evolution in French thinking though it failed to touch the F.L.N., dedicated as it was to independence. Algeria remained an integral part of the French Republic and all citizens, "male and female . . . without distinction as to race, religion, or origin," were guaranteed "equal enjoyment of all the freedoms and all the political, economic and social rights pertaining to the status of French citizen" and were subject to equal obligations. Algeria was divided into (five) self-governing territories (later defined as Oran, Chélif, Algiers, Kabylia, and Constantine). Each was to have a Territorial Assembly and a Territorial Council of Communities, the latter containing an equal number of citizens subject to the French Civil Code and citizens living under Koranic personal status. Where differences between the Territorial Assembly and Council of Communities arose, the Minister Resident had the option of accepting the version of the Territorial Assembly or allowing the Council of State to serve as arbiter.

After two years, the Territorial Assemblies might entrust some of their responsibilities to a Federal Assembly which would be made up of delegates, in equal number, from the Territorial Assemblies and the Territorial Councils of Communities. The French Parliament and Government reserved jurisdiction over the following matters: nationality, ordinary civil law, foreign affairs, national defense, elections, currency, foreign exchange, taxes, customs regulations, and state expenditure as well as criminal law, education, the public domain, mining and power resources. A Minister Resident appointed by Paris still directed the services of the state. Likewise, a Representative of the Republic appointed by Paris presided over the government of each territory.

Title VII of the *loi cadre* provided for evolution of Algerian institutions. "When, after consultation with the Territorial Councils of Communities, concurrent resolutions of the Territorial Assemblies and the Federative Assembly propose modification of the institutions provided for by the present law, the Government shall be compelled to place the matter before [the French] Parliament." Fair elections were guaranteed and a single electoral college would provide "true and obligatory representation of the various communities at all levels." Finally, the Statute of September 20, 1947, was set aside at all points where it conflicted with the *loi cadre* of 1958 and the Sahara Regions were specifically excluded from the 1958 covenant.

It is purely academic, but quite worthwhile, to speculate upon the intention and possible effects of this legislation since the fall of the Fourth Republic the following May ended any hope of applying it and brought forth still other formulas. The *loi cadre* increased tremendously Muslim participation, formulated a single electoral college guaranteed by a new electoral law of January 28, 1958, decentralized government at the same time it provided a federal structure tied directly to a France maintaining basic control over matters of common interest.[57] No wonder the European die-hards in Algeria disliked this newest Paris experiment.

169

Had it been activated, Muslim influence surely would, in time, have dominated local and provincial matters and sent more, and better, representatives to a future National Assembly in Paris.

Such an evolution was stymied by the unfolding of events in France and Algeria in early 1958. Even had these events been more favorable to settlement we must remember that the F.L.N., with at least 42,000 good fighting men, better armed than ever, stood firmly for independence.[58]

THE REBELLION AND THE LAST DAYS OF THE FOURTH REPUBLIC

The direct line between the fall of the Gaillard government on April 15, 1958, and the Algerian revolution began at 11 A.M. the previous February 8 when eleven French B-26 bombers and six escort planes bombed the Tunisian village of Sakiet Sidi Youssef, killing sixty-nine persons, twenty-one of whom were children. This brought to a violent head a series of border incidents along the Algerian-Tunisian line which Bourguiba had found serious enough to call a state of emergency back in September, 1957. A week after the bombing of Sakiet, France and Tunisia accepted the "good offices" of the United States and the United Kingdom. The good officers, Robert Murphy and Harold Beeley, worked some fifty days, trying to resolve the problems. Then, on April 15, the National Assembly voted 321 to 255 to abandon the "good offices" approach. This was not a vote of confidence, but, since it repudiated Gaillard's efforts to settle the dispute, he resigned.[59] Moderates and Communists had combined to kill the government with notable aid from the "four paragons of *Algérie française*," Soustelle, Duchet, Bidault, and Morice. A popular line of reasoning ran this way: today Washington and London intervene to settle the crisis with Tunisia, tomorrow they will impose their solution in Algeria and once more France will be sold out.

How "good offices" helped lead to the accession to power again of Charles de Gaulle is discussed in the next chapter. Before examining that question, a glance at the Algerian side of the

170

revolution before May, 1958, completes the picture in the last days of the Fourth Republic.

The Algerian nationalists tried to internationalize their cause to gain their independence, just as the French tried to keep the revolution a domestic matter to hold Algeria. The French blockade of arms and men flowing into the fighting zone forced the F.L.N. to find precious weapons any way it could and to risk men against the electric wire barriers. Increasingly, it seemed, weapons came from Yugoslavia via Morocco. The Yugoslavian ship *Sbrija* deposited seven tons of arms and seventy tons of ammunition in Casablanca on August 7, 1957. The bill of lading placed Saudi Arabia as the final destination. This was hard to believe. Six months later a French patrol intercepted the Yugoslavian ship *Slovenija* off Oran, carrying another arms shipment of German and Czechoslovakian manufacture. The Zurich import-export house Felix was involved.[60]

Arms procurement from Communist countries by the F.L.N. posed serious issues for Tunisia and Morocco. These states feared a preponderance of Cairo influence in Algerian nationalist high councils. In December, 1957, F.L.N. representatives sat in an Afro-Asian conference in Cairo in which Soviet delegates were present. What this added up to was possibly no more than the hard fact that the F.L.N. would take all the help anyone would give. But for Bourguiba and Morocco the solidarity of the Maghrib was exceedingly important. To prevent the further penetration of Cairo and Moscow into the Algerian nationalist command, a conference at Tangier met to define the common interest of Morocco, Tunisia, and Algeria.

From April 27-30, 1958, while France cast around for a new government to replace Gaillard's and a solution other than "good offices," representatives of the Istiqlal Party of Morocco, the Neo Destour Party of Tunisia, and F.L.N. delegates met in the Marshan Palace at Tangier. Representing the Algerians were Ferhat Abbas, Abdel Hamid Mahri, Mohamed Boumendjel, and Abdelhafid Boussouf. The latter, as *Wilaya* 5 (Oran) commander, promoted later to minister of communications, handled military questions. Apparently, earlier difficulties between the

F.L.N. and Morocco were patched up, and Morocco promised full cooperation. The three "states" present proclaimed "the right of the Algerian people to sovereignty and independence" as the only condition for peace. The conference recommended the creation of an Algerian government, which, joined with Tunis and Morocco, would form a Maghrib federation. Nor did the communiqué fail to denounce the aid the West contributed to maintain French colonialism.

Mahmoud Chérif, a member of the F.L.N.'s Committee of Coordination and Execution, considered the Tangier Conference to be a turning point in the war.

> France has always isolated Algeria in order to fight our Revolution effectively.
>
> For four years of struggle France's constant obsession has been the construction of a united North African front.
>
> This has now been realized, and we can say that one of the great achievements of the Conference of Tangier was to inaugurate this edifice.
>
> The aid that Morocco and Tunisia have continually extended to the Algerian people will increase in the weeks and months to come. All North Africa from Agadir to Sollum today lines up its power and throws out to colonialist France an ultimatum: give Algeria independence or see the war extended to the Maghrib.[61]

Another African conference, this one held at Accra in Ghana April 20-28, 1958, and attended by Morocco, Tunisia, Libya, Sudan, Liberia, Ghana, Ethiopia, and the United Arab Republic broke several lances for Algerian independence. These countries agreed to help the Algerian people materially and diplomatically. The conference asked the French to negotiate a political withdrawal from Algeria and to recognize the authority of the F.L.N. It also promised to explain the Algerian problem to the world through a permanent traveling commission.

That this promise of material aid was not made lightheartedly became clear on October 18, 1958, when the Arab League Council announced an assessment upon its ten members of $34,400,000 for support of the Algerian revolution. This help did not match the sum of $655,000,000 France obtained from the European Payments Union, International Monetary Fund, and the United States Government the previous January, but Algeria's needs were simple. France was trying to balance its budget at home, wage a war of pacification in Algeria while it increased its capital investment there and in the Sahara region. All the Algerian nationalists sought was independence.

The winds of change once again blew through Algeria and France in early 1958. Confidence characterized the nationalists in the fifth year of struggle. They had reached the United Nations forum, obtained a guarantee of solidarity from their brothers in the Maghrib, been offered help by eight Afro-Asian states, and even thought they detected a favorable evolution in the American press.[62] Morale seemed high and the Army of National Liberation had not weakened in the face of the French "get tough" policy. For these Algerian soldiers, whose equipment improved daily, there was perhaps more hope than in the hearts of the great Muslim masses who bore the brunt of both sides of the war. Yet the Army of National Liberation came from those masses, was largely sustained by them, and no doubt believed itself to be their shield and future hope.

In Paris things were different. A sign on the Palais Bourbon might have read "Government Wanted, Good Pay, Tenure Indefinite." And in Algiers, within the French community, there was uneasiness born of a distrust of the Muslim masses and the government in Paris.

CHAPTER SIX

"WHEELS WITHIN WHEELS," MAY 13, 1958

PREPARATION FOR MAY 13

Although the Gaullists were by no means the sole group responsible for bringing about the Revolution of May 13 in Algeria, early in the spring of 1958 they became the drive-wheel of its complicated mechanism. At the hub of the wheel was, of course, Charles de Gaulle, and his centripetal force pulled together critics and opponents of the Fourth Republic from within and without the army. As this chapter is being written it is indeed the Gaullist party, *Union pour la Nouvelle République* (U.N.R.), and a group of ministers tied in most cases by long and tested personal friendship with President de Gaulle, who are the direct political beneficiaries of the new regime. There are serious rumblings of discord in the alliance over the development of de Gaulle's Algerian policy away from the U.N.R.'s pet theme of integration, and the right wing Gaullists have suffered some decimation. After a serious strain in January, 1960, the surface allegiance of the French army, with few exceptions, is united behind the government of the Gaullist chief, a general who appears these days less frequently in uniform than in the frock coat of a diplomat or the full dress-with-decoration of the "gentleman" monarch of France. And the war in Algeria goes on.

After World War II, de Gaulle had hoped to use his authority in the Provisional Government to construct a new system for France. This was to be based on a renovated Constitution which would provide for an executive whose power could not be

174

emasculated by ceaseless ministerial crises nor molded by pressure groups. But a kind of revulsion from Vichy authoritarianism had seized the French people, and this oriented them toward a different kind of republicanism. Because of the strength that the Communists and Socialists had manifested in the Resistance Movement—some had been the strong men, the risk-taking men—and the utter collapse of the right, the immediate postwar period was one of well-earned influence for the left. Certainly patriots from the parties of the right and center, and men from no parties at all, had been active in the underground, but the left had earned the esteem of the nation. Post-war political currents ran towards a philosophy of checks and balances—a powerful legislative branch and a responsible, even vulnerable premier—rather than a strong executive. When de Gaulle's proposed Constitution was defeated, he went into partial retirement.

In the spring of 1947 he and his friends began to rally under the banner of the *Rassemblement du peuple Français* (R.P.F.). His motives were the same as they had been after the war, but his earlier partisans did not have the vital concern for politics that they had had for liberation. Indeed some of them had succeeded as politicians under the "system." The *Rassemblement,* therefore, brought together a motley crew, fringes from the left and the right with no solid core. De Gaulle was once more unable to unite sufficient strength behind his political program for France. So, again, after the disastrous municipal elections of April, 1953, he retreated to Colombey-les-Deux-Eglises. Although saddened and embittered, he managed, while playing the part of recluse, to remain one of the best-informed men in France. He has always been one of the men to love France best.

Over the years he has been deeply aware of French politics and cognizant of colonial problems. He had strong ties in the army high command and among the politicians friends like Jacques Soustelle who had survived the de Gaulle organization of World War II. With a feeling of deep humiliation he followed the course of world diplomacy, hating France's subservient status in a Western Europe dominated by two great powers. And all these phenomena he evaluated in an extremely personal style. With the dissolution of the R.P.F. his hopes to build a non-party, non-system government had vanished for a second time. He never let it leave his heart or mind.

At Colombey he continued the writing of his impressive *Memoirs* which proved to be important both as literature and history. This record of a great man's thoughts and deeds, instead of gracefully closing the brilliant active chapter of his life, has become instead the philosophical justification of his new career, and the charter for a very personal and powerful politique which has recently changed the face of western Europe.

The failure of the R.P.F. marked de Gaulle's second defeat at the hands of the Fourth Republic. With each defeat his will to power grew consciously or unconsciously stronger, more stubborn, and more convinced. So also grew his determination to destroy the Fourth. Over the years he had ceaselessly condemned its constitution as impractical because it arrogated too much power to a National Assembly riddled with numerous parties and the pressures of special interest groups. Above all, he had condemned the machinations of the party leaders who failed to place the welfare of France above their petty portfolios. He is said to have remarked after his first retirement: "I am worth more [to France] than all of them together." In his self-proclaimed isolation he clung to this thought; except for constitutional reform he advocated no special program, he espoused no cause, delegated for himself no spokesman, and allowed no doctrine to be uttered in his name:

"A *politique* cannot be defined by phrases. It is in contact with realities that I will make my own precise." [1]

There are unmistakable overtones in this statement that do not come from a man who has given up all thought of political power. And certainly his isolation was broken by weekly Wednesdays in Paris, which, if the atmosphere were exciting enough, sometimes spilled over into Thursdays. There in modest quarters in the rue de Solférino after his return from a triumphant tour in Africa in 1956, he found the spirit of the times had quickened, changed. Statesmen and ambassadors from many places were flocking to see the *"monument historique"* toward which power seemed to be returning. Moulay Hassan, the son of the Sultan of Morocco, came to see him, Adlai Stevenson, and Douglas Dillon. Soviet Ambassador Vinogradov was a visitor, and Félix Houphouet-Boigny from tumultuous Black Africa. Came whimpering ministers of the Fourth Republic, caught in the game of parliamentary Russian Roulette. Came generals, prefects, business men. Jacques Soustelle, both before and during his stint as Governor of Algeria, was a frequent caller; and certainly he gathered ammunition in the rue de Solférino for his harrying of the ministry of Félix Gaillard and the would-be ministry of René Pleven as these "princes" one after another stubbed their toes on the Algerian problem. Soustelle and Georges Bidault were largely responsible for the bulldozer tactics which wrecked Gaillard's government on April 15, 1958. The shrill cry of Pierre Mendès-France, de Gaulle's only rival of any stature, who maintained that French policy in Algeria could never make progress while it continued to offer, on one hand, bloody repression, and on the other hand, economic subsidies, hollow offers of autonomy at a local level, and hollower promises of integration, found no response.

Frequent visitors to the "Wednesdays" were Gaullists with a purpose: the new revolutionaries, Jacques Chaban-Delmas, Minister of Defense for the Fourth Republic, and Léon Delbecque whom Chaban-Delmas later made his Algerian arm for the purpose, not of defending the poor old *Quatrième,* but of making certain it collapsed under a Gaullist attack. As the tomtom beat increased, the man of Colombey-les-Deux-Eglises became the center of a dozen plots. The man who promised no one anything became the man who might deliver anything to anybody. He embodied the hopes of colonialists and anti-colonialists, of Communists and revived Pétainists. Vichy and the Liberation joined hands and danced a Spring dance of hope around this great Maypole of a man—the uncommitted, the undefiled, the cleanest hands in France. The faith of the Liberation long since tarnished by the self-interest of politicians rose again in the hearts of Frenchmen tired of seeing the remaining jewel in the French colonial crown bartered in the pawnshop of the Assembly. Hazy but still lively notions of a government of *Salut Public* ² rose and surfaced in many different waters. Soon plots were bubbling and boiling in the army high command, in a rejuvenated R.P.F., in certain ministerial circles, in the hearts of the colonials of Algeria who were exasperated by governmental indifference to the already long war waged by the F.L.N. for Algerian independence, in the camps of the ultras, Poujadists, old Vichyites, fascist organizations such as *Jeunesse Patriote* and the newer *Jeune Nation;* and, as we have seen, in the very ministry of National Defense. Certain old Resistance leaders, among them Michel Debré and Jacques Soustelle, had become vociferous champions of the integration of French Algeria, and their Gaullism channeled these views toward a government of *Salut Public* under the leadership of Charles de Gaulle. Out of these plots and their many divisions, out of the "spontaneous" revolution of May 13, 1958, came the ascent by way of his own system, the curious accession of the Gaullist chief.

In mid-April of 1957 Jacques Soustelle led the attack which sank the Gaillard ministry over the affair of Sakiet. The Sakiet bombings left a bad smell in nearly everybody's nostrils. Foreign journalists wrote indignant articles about French attacks upon "neutral" territory and unprotected villages. The French army which had been harried by F.L.N. bands appearing from across the Tunisian frontier and retreating there at will, felt much as General MacArthur did when he was unable to chase the North Korean troops over the Chinese border; here was a foreign power giving comfort and assistance to the enemy and there was no legal way to retaliate.

> The brutality of the attack, however, shocked the world. Sakiet was subjected to daylight bombing and strafing by three waves of planes, including United States-made B-26 bombers and Corsair fighters. According to official Tunisian figures, sixty-eight persons were killed in the raid, among them eleven women and twenty children; 100 persons were wounded. Although the identity of the male victims was not disclosed by the Tunisian

178

Government, Premier Félix Gaillard told the French National Assembly on February 12 that the 'majority of the victims were soldiers of the F.L.N.' This assertion cannot be checked, since to my knowledge, no newspaper correspondent on the spot made any effort to ascertain the identity of the male victims. . . .

For Tunisian Sakiet—as distinct from the parts of the village occupied by the Algerians—the raid was a catastrophe. Apart from the death . . . material damage was considerable. Visiting correspondents reported that private dwellings, a school, stores, and 'public buildings' had been hit.[3]

One of the worse aspects of the incident was that the French government let the army take public blame for the bombings when it was the government which ordered the retaliatory attack to convince Tunis that aid to the Algerian rebels was most unwise. Official statements laid blame on the private stupidity of a young French officer, and more bad will was generated between the government and the army.

Finally, in the National Assembly Gaillard was obliged to make the following defense of the bombings. The Tunisian Government, he said, had been warned to expect "retaliatory" action if it continued to harbor and aid Algerian rebels. Bourguiba could not accept this viewpoint and promptly replied that his sovereignty had been threatened. In return he demanded that French troops stationed in Tunis by order of a mutual defense agreement dating from the independence negotiations in 1956 be confined to their camps. The French naval yard at Bizerte was blockaded and France ordered to evacuate her garrison.

Both Tunisia and France filed complaints with the Security Council of the United Nations. Tunisia openly announced its hope that the incident would lead to UN debate and conciliation of the Algerian problem. However, neither party really wanted to await international settlement of the Franco-Tunisian dispute, so instead, the American offer of "good offices" was accepted. France, of course, although she allowed Deputy Under-Secretary of State Robert Murphy to discuss proposals for an agreement, would not allow the United States to arbitrate the Tunisian affair, and still less the Algerian question. Murphy, who had long since given sympathetic voice to the right of self-determination, and Harold Beeley of the Foreign Office, were chosen to negotiate with Bourguiba. To Paris on March 17, 1958, they returned with the following proposals.

1) Withdrawal of nearly all of the 22,000 French military personnel in Tunisia
2) Neutral surveillance of former French airports against the possibility of their acquisition by the F.L.N.
3) Tunisian sovereignty over Bizerte and negotiation of a new basis for French occupancy
4) Re-examination of cases of dispossessed French colonials in Tunisia
5) Reinstatement of French Consular officials.

With the exception of the Algerian-Tunisian frontier issue, the cause of the immediate dispute, France accepted the proposals but only as the basis on which direct negotiations might be opened. Rumors flew thick and fast and the *New York Times* ran articles suggesting that the Murphy-Beeley mission should seek to produce an environment in which the Algerian revolution could be halted. Upon this news the French exploded, and the government rejected, over the fallen Gaillard cabinet, the *"bons offices"* of that "villain" Murphy who was out to liquidate the French empire single-handed.

Both Bidault and René Pleven, whose conceptions of the Algerian problem were quite different, after weeks of fruitless debate, failed to form a ministry. Their attempts, from right and left alike, were scuttled by the insolubility of the Algerian war. As early as May 6 President Coty was so discouraged over the prospects of the Assembly reaching a working agreement that he sent word to General de Gaulle: would he be interested in trying to form a ministry? Earlier than this, during the cantonal elections in Lyon, Soustelle had appealed to de Gaulle in the name of the country at large. De Gaulle answered Coty by an intermediary on May 8. He stated the conditions under which he might serve the nation. They were, first, that he would expect a letter from President Coty formally asking him to constitute a government and dispensing with such conventions as the traditional visit to the President of the Republic and consultation with the party chiefs. Second, he wished to be allowed to form a cabinet without any discussion of the parties. Finally, his investiture would be voted in his absence and only then would he come to the Elysée palace. These arrogant demands invoked the haughty days of the provisional government. De Gaulle, in his reply to Coty, did not offer any indication of his own political program; he mentioned neither the Algerian problem nor a plan for constitutional reform. The inflexibility of the recluse of Colombey had something maddening in it and practical René Coty did not feel he wanted to push the matter any farther. Parliament was not yet ready to accept this particular kind of dictation. So negotiations broke down.

Apparently during the early days of May, 1958, Charles de Gaulle strongly doubted that the pressure of events would be great enough to push him into office through regular channels. In any case he despised the regular channels. Although he did not contemplate being president of a band of paratroopers nor of an Algerian Committee of Public Safety, he wanted to be something more durable and more representative of the will of France than a premier under the Fourth Republic. As the plots rolled on, his attitude made it very clear that he was in favor of a clean sweep and that he was not partial about brooms. Certainly, though, the turmoil of the army and its great despair at the vacillation of the government's Algerian policy must have been closer to his proud old heart, more understandable to his hierarchical spirit than the "clerk's treason" at the Palais-Bourbon. And so, perfectly informed and enigmatic as the Sphinx he watched the beginnings of the revolt in the army add fuel to the Gaullist fire.

Since February, when the Sakiet affair first made angry headlines, the Colonel's Club meeting in Paris under General Lecomte, Director of the *Ecole de Guerre*, had grown restless at the talk of negotiations which sprang up in the National Assembly at each new crisis. Lecomte had also approached de Gaulle to sound him out on the Algerian situation, but the general gave him no satisfaction. To Jacques Chaban-Delmas and Léon Delbecque, who had been working to reorganize the R.P.F., he also spoke in discouraging generalities. He would be willing to serve France if the people wanted him. It was Lucien Neuwirth, one of the instigators of the army plot in Algeria, who asked him if he would take power at the hands of the army. He drew from the general this interesting remark:

"In '47 I tried to save France by a 'cold' operation. Now doubtless I'll have to use a 'hot' operation!" [4]

Michel Debré, Soustelle, Oliver Guichard, the General's public relations man, and Roger Frey, the "pin-up boy of Gaullism," were actively pursuing a campaign for de Gaulle by means of petitions, speeches, newspaper articles, and letters to the press. Counsellor of State Maxime Blocq-Mascart, who believed in an authoritarian and federalist constitution, was working with the legal Gaullists but also rounding up conspirators of much different persuasions. General René Cogny, a tried veteran from the campaign in Indo-China, later to be connected with the famous affair of the bazooka, was one of his men, and in Algeria, he counted Jean Baptiste Biaggi, lawyer and revolutionary by nature. This old Resistance leader of the Fourth Commando was an expert, if extreme subversive, looking for a path to personal power in the "new" government. Cogny and Biaggi were birds of a feather, but it is surprising to find them nudging such a bird as syndicalist leader of the C.G.T., André Lafont.

In January, 1958, Biaggi had been one of the founders of the *Comité d'action des Associations Nationales des Anciens Combattants*, a veterans committee which came to be known as the C.A.N.A.C. His chief associates in this project were André Achiary and Mario Faivre of Algiers. The policy of this organization was obviously to keep Algeria French. About this time Biaggi decided that the policies of the ultras whose reactionary outlook and particular acts of violence (*ratissages*, and *ratonnades*—French colonial expressions made from the verb *ratisser*, to scrape or rake, or the noun *raton*, little rat, which denoted indiscriminate murder of Muslims) could not succeed, and he therefore threw his weight behind Soustelle's policy of pacification which had a constructive aim—the prosecution of the war against the rebels and a program of economic, social, and political reform for the Algerians.[5] Biaggi was able on one occasion to turn back a group of *colons* from a burning-out-the-Casbah party and lead them home chanting slogans of brotherly love and integration. This was quite a trick, and a man who could change a mass murder into an orderly demonstration has manifested considerable talent for organization. Therefore, if he was an activist, Biaggi was not of the worst brand. In defense of the activist position during revolution he stated, "From the moment a man is determined enough to gamble his life, his action weighs a thousand times more than the vote of a citizen. For me it is not the question of being one in a mass (of agitators) rather we activists are the crystals which precipitate the freezing when the critical temperature has been reached."[6]

In spite of his extremist philosophy, Biaggi was acceptable to the group of Gaullists working with Blocq-Mascart because of his attachment to the person of General de Gaulle, his theoretical acceptance of a Republican constitution, and a certain liberalism in his views concerning the Franco-Algerian future. It was rumored in the Biaggi camp that General Cogny was the prospective military arm of the Blocq-Mascart combination, but Cogny's power was temporarily eclipsed the moment the bazooka was aimed at General Salan. At this time Robert Lacoste, the minister resident, ordered Biaggi out of Algeria, but both Cogny and Biaggi were in evidence during the machinations of May 13. Michel Debré, later to be given the post of premier under de Gaulle, also worked through the Blocq-Mascart combination. All his efforts were, however, in the direction of legality. He believed that de Gaulle would not take power as the result of a military coup. Long a sincere integrationist, after the formation of the Fifth Republic he was to use that word concerning the government's policies while his chief never consented to do so. It was Debré who made the often quoted and much ridiculed statement (while de Gaulle was speaking cautiously of the Algerian personality) that there were nothing but Frenchmen on both sides of the Mediterranean, "from Dunkirk to Tamanr'aset."

THE ARMY IN POLITICS

Working sometimes in the same direction as the Gaullists and sometimes toward a military solution of the problems of the Fourth Republic, was the French army. During the bad years of the war in Indo-China, the loss of Tunisia and Morocco, the French army, although riddled with personal animosities and private wars between Gaullists, Giraudists, and Pétainists resulting from the Second World War, presented a solid front to the machinations of the politicians. Although the only hope of a solution in Indo-China would have been a political one, as indeed seems to be the only hope in Algeria, the army was far from appreciating the attempts the successive governments of the Fourth Republic had made in the direction of a political settlement. The military could agree on one thing, that the French government was weak and vacillating and engaged in a process of liquidating French overseas power faster than they could defend it. Fuming over the loss of Morocco and Tunisia, the recall of the Suez expedition was the last indignity the army intended to tolerate. So, at various levels and in many ways officers and soldiers entered the political conspiracy which was already complicated enough.

The entry of the army into the political arena had not come suddenly. Ever since 1940 army officers had been forced to make political decisions. They chose between Pétain and Giraud at first, and later between Giraud and de Gaulle in Algiers. In Indo-China in 1945 the army had to work with the Japanese, in Syria it wavered between generals Henri Dentz and Georges Catroux, and there are many other examples that could be listed. From the Vietminh, French officers had learned methods of subversive warfare and political tactics, and in Algeria, engaged as members of the *Sections Administratives Specialisées* (S.A.S.) (formed from the old Arab Bureaus) under Jacques Soustelle, they had put these methods into practice. Soustelle chose the S.A.S. from among the "enlightened" and "anti-subversive" military. Men of the S.A.S. did many kinds of work in all parts of Algeria, but particularly in the rural and impoverished areas where the French had not previously penetrated in force. The S.A.S. worked on roads, built schools, handled health problems and general hygiene, and in many ways came into intimate contact with the people. At first the S.A.S. was controlled by civil authority, but in areas where that authority was scattered or endangered by the F.L.N. the sections took over more general powers. Sometimes there was friction between the civil and military authorities, but as the guerrilla warfare of the rebels increased so did the army's popularity as protector and guarantor of the general welfare of both the native and the French populations. As an example of this growth of power of the army at the expense of the civil, there is the case of General Jean Gilles, who assumed both civil and military power in the Constantine, one of the worst areas of the rebellion.[7] During four years of "pacification" in which fighting and reconstruction went hand in hand, many officers of the army came to believe that only an enlightened and generous French policy could bring the *fellaghas* back to the fold. This element became progressively more alarmed at the government's too-little too-late policy. After the government's rejection of the *loi-cadre* in 1954, army sentiment ran high; Dienbienphu, the loss of Morocco and Tunisia, and the Suez fiasco, all had caused humiliation and great discontent, for the army believed in itself and blamed the politicians for its defeats. "*La Grande Muette*," scarcely mute these days, realized that it was one of the few cohesive forces in French life. So it entered the arena of active politics determined to make its influence felt. By and large the movement within the army in favor of integration had sincere motivation and those officers and men who espoused it were known as the *pur et dur*. The word "pure" separated these army integrationists from many of the colonials who gave the idea lip service and realized that they might have to accept it as a necessary fact of life, but neither believed in it or wanted it.

Alfred Fabre-Luce in his study *Gaulle Deux* [8] gives an explanation of the seemingly irrational switch of some of the non-military
Europeans of Algeria from unredeemed colonialism, a policy of
racialism and second-class citizenship for the Muslims, to that of
complete integration which means equality of rights and duties
between the two peoples, and even that elusive product of the
French Revolution, fraternity. This evolution in the thought of
people basically hostile to any change in the Muslim status was
accomplished quite apart from humanitarian considerations. It is
rather that the Europeans became certain that Algeria would be
lost to them without some significant amelioration of the governing policy. By the spring of 1958 they showed unmistakably the
wear and tear of more than four years of war, sporadic violence,
property damage, and general insecurity.

The *colons,* that tight little, but terribly influential, European
minority, have finally realized that if a progressive policy of
recognition of the rights of Muslims within an Algerian framework is offered to Algeria, the French will be outnumbered ten
to one. In a short time the Europeans would have no control
over the future of the country. On the other hand, if complete
integration with France is pursued, the Europeans will still out-
number the Muslims five to one for a number of years. There is
still another arithmetical consideration underlying integration.
That is a lesson the war has also taught these super-Frenchmen
in Algeria: that they are dependent on Metropolitan troops and
money. It is quite possible that the European Algerians themselves do not yet realize the enormity of the change in their
point of view but hold the false dream that integration might
become in the long run just a new form of the old French policy
of "assimilation." If real integration could be reached honestly
and quickly, it could possibly keep Algeria under the French flag
for a long time, but much more than good will would be
necessary—countless millions of francs and years of education and
building. And this kind of an Algeria would delegate privileges
and responsibilities to the Muslims that the *colons* of "Papa's
Algeria" would never have agreed to offer. It might even give the
Muslims more than a government of their own could afford to give

them for years to come. But it does not offer independence. In spite of U.N.R. support of integration in France and rightist sentiment in Algeria, de Gaulle himself has never thought integration was practicable and has favored an autonomous Algeria linked to France.

In his book *Problèmes stratégiques de la guerre révolutionnaire en Chine* Mao Tse Tung wrote: "The partisan characteristic is the essential trait in our army, it is an advantage which gives us the possibility of vanquishing the enemy. . . . The morale of the people is the morale of the nation in arms. That is precisely what the enemy fears." Or the primitive analogy, "The army should be within the people like a fish in water," which carried a powerful message.[9] If it is not surprising to find this kind of thinking basic to the structure and faith of the F.L.N., it is somewhat surprising to find it a motivating force of the French army in Algeria. Jacques Chaban-Delmas, Minister of Defense under the Gaillard government, was anxious to try out these theories of subversive warfare which the F.L.N. had applied so successfully against the French. At Paris he formed *ateliers* where officers could learn the arts of subversion. This war would be prosecuted by political commissars, by guerrilla and *maquis* action; powerful groups of veteran organizations would formulate its political goals; and the methods of the fifth column, of propaganda, of brain-washing, of the use of defeatists and traitors would make the reconquest of Algeria more likely. Chaban-Delmas, though a minister of the Fourth Republic, saw in the National Assembly the main enemy of military success. He recognized that the army was the one coherent element, except perhaps the Communist party (and that is doubtful), in French political life, and he hoped that an army revolt might ultimately bring about a military dictatorship or a strong government under the presidency of General de Gaulle. So in the very heart of its defense the Fourth Republic harbored an opponent of the regime. To pursue his psychological warfare in Algeria, Chaban-Delmas appointed Léon Delbecque chief of the Algerian branch of National Defense. Delbecque's organization was installed in villa El Biar, later to become notorious in investigations of the practice of the "Question" (interrogation by torture) by French soldiers and police. Henri Alleg, a member of the Algerian Communist Party and the editor of *Alger Républicain,* a leftist Algerian paper from 1950-1955, was arrested in June, 1957 by paratroops of the 10th Division Parachutists who kept him for a month at El Biar. Of the practice of the "Question" he reports on one occasion:

Suddenly S— pulled me up. He was beside himself. This was going on too long. 'Listen, you scum! You're finished! You're going to talk! Do you hear, you're going to talk!' He brought his face up close until it was almost touching mine and shouted: 'You're going to talk! Everybody talks here! We fought the war in Indo-China—that was enough to know your type. This is the Gestapo here! You know the Gestapo?' Then, with irony: 'So you wrote articles about torture, did you, you bastard! Very well! Now it's the Tenth Paratroop Division who are doing it to you.'

I heard the whole band of torturers laughing behind me. S— hammered my face with blows and jabbed my stomach with his knee. 'What we are doing here, we will do in France. We will do it to your Duclos and your Mitterand, we will do to them what we are doing to you. And your whore of a Republic, we will blow it up into the air, too! You're going to talk, I tell you.'

On the table was a piece of cardboard. He picked it up and used it to beat me. Each blow stupefied me a little more, but at the same time confirmed me in my decision not to give way to these brutes who flattered themselves they were like the Gestapo.

'All right,' said C—. 'You've asked for it! We're going to throw you to the lions.' The 'lions' were those whose acquaintance I had already made, but they were going to exercise their talents still further.

S— dragged me back into the first room, the one with the plank and the magneto. I had just had time to see a naked Moslem being kicked and shoved into the

188

corridor. While S—, C— and the others were 'looking after' me, the rest of the group were continuing their 'work' using the same plank and the magneto. They had been 'questioning' a suspect in order not to lose any time.

L— fastened me down to the plank: a new session of electrical torture began.

'This time, it's the real thing,' he said.

In my torturer's hands I saw a different machine, larger than the first, and even in my agony I felt a difference in quality. Instead of the sharp and rapid spasms that seemed to tear my body in two, a greater pain now stretched all my muscles and racked them for a longer time. I was taut in my bonds. I tightened my teeth on the gag with all my might and kept my eyes closed. They stopped but I continued to shake with nervous convulsions.[10]

Another branch of subversive warfare was the notorious *Ecole Jeanne D'Arc*. Colonel Marcel Bigeard, Commander of the famous 3rd Regiment of *Para-Casquettes*, the so-called *"bande à Bigeard"* had been instructed to form a training school through which would pass all officers arriving in Algeria. They spent two months in this atmosphere of intense propaganda, called by many the school of the coup d'état, and here they were taught administrative practices and how to direct a subversive war.

Soon El Biar became aware of the machinations of Colonel Jean Thomazo "Nez de Cuir" (Leather Nose). "Let us say at once that he is the apostle of the revolution in Algiers, the revolution whatever it will be, which will sweep away the regime ready to abandon French Algeria." [11] Delbecque and Thomazo, working together in the very shadow of Minister Resident Robert Lacoste, planned to mount a military revolt in Algeria during August, 1958. By this date Bigeard hoped to have trained sufficient officers to carry out the administrative detail, El Biar would have silenced liberal opposition, and the disaffection of the *colons*, already meeting clandestinely in Committees of *Salut Public*, would be channeled behind the army. Delbecque believed that neither General Raoul Salan, Supreme Commander of the Inter-Armies in Algeria, nor General Jacques Massu, the popular paratroop leader, a *"pur et dur"* (pure and hard) of Algiers, could be counted on to take over the army when the revolution began. General Cogny was his candidate for military dictator. Loyal to the Cogny coup were, of course, General Bigeard, Colonel Thomazo, General Jean Gilles of the air command and Colonel Crespin, Commander of the Helicopters. It has been stated that Generals Paul Allard, Paul Ely, and Maurice Challe and his deputy Lieutenant Martin were also heavily involved. But the infamous affair of the Bazooka (January 16, 1957) brought about by activists who would not wait for the "legal" appointment of Cogny over Salan spoiled the timing of the army plot. On this lamentable occasion two shots were fired from a roughly constructed Bazooka gun set up across the court from the window of General Salan's G.H.Q. At the moment of the attempted assassination, Salan was out of the office, but one of the junior officers was killed. When the guilty men were arrested they mentioned General Cogny as one of the instigators of the plot. This quite naturally put him on the black list of the metropolitan government and in Salan's file of unsavory characters. Even Chaban-Delmas, who narrated the affair to a skeptical de Gaulle, was not able to arrange the nomination of this particular anti-parliamentarian general. But there were others, and in the meantime Salan hung on.

The hope, not of the army coup but of the activists, was soon to become Lieutenant Colonel Trinquier, who had already displayed certain fascist tendencies in Indo-China. Salan appointed him to replace Bigeard as head of the famous band of paras. Almost immediately Trinquier found himself in deep sympathy with the cause of the *colons* and the ultras. Hoping to suppress both the F.L.N. attacks in metropolitan France and the murderous counter-terrorism of the ultras, he formed groups of local patrols, home guardsmen—the *Unités Territoriales Blindées,* (U.T.B.)—from colonials and reserve army personnel, and these became almost like his private army—a group of mercenaries at his beck and call. Neither the revolutionary colonels nor the

Gaullists could count on him as their man, and actually he was partially responsible for the defeat of the Delbecque forces and the premature activist coup of May 13.

General Jacques Massu whose popularity in Algiers allowed him to direct the first few hours of the May 13 coup was one of the most inspired revolutionary warriors. Paul Gerin quotes the following excerpts from one of Massu's orientation notes having to do with the special problems of the Casbah of Algiers. He mentions that "the reading of this text gives an idea of the intelligence, the imagination, and the conscience actually demanded of the subaltern offices in an elite unit" (a far cry from the tactics of El Biar).

> Each captain should have the responsibility of a given area for several months, where research and exploitation of information will be his proper function. . . .
>
> It is necessary for the captain and his men to have not only legs, but also heart and head.
>
> 1) heart because without 'the burden of love' of Lyautey they will obtain no results in African territory or anywhere else.
>
> The qualities of heart demand the protection of the European colonials who have worked for fruitfulness in these formerly uncultivated regions, and also aid for the misery of the Muslims, too often without work, under-nourished and despised.
>
> The habit of fraternity developed during the war among all the troops of the French Union will be pursued on this terrain in the hope of repairing contacts with the Muslims, veterans, and otherwise, among whom we can expiate our neglect and injustice.
>
> Meals in common as well as games, sports, contacts with the young, the cultivation of *healthy* reading (the italics are the authors'), medical assistance, generosity in all its forms, these constitute certainly the most powerful means of action, with the help of God, never invoked in vain.

191

2) Head. We must be astute enough to separate the cluster of influences at work upon the Arabs and the Kabyles and distinguish those which can be used for the profit of the Franco-Muslim entente.

We must learn their language, study their mores, their customs, and to do that we must, as we once did, live close to them, adroitly, patiently.

Since the territorial command now speaks of 'nomadization' we must apply the principles of life in the Sahara and rejoin Psichari and Foucauld.

The purely military processes of counter-guerrilla, security, ambuscades, attack, choice of camp installation, clandestine life, etc., *necessary weapons* to defeat the irreducible rebels, also demand study, adaptation and training.

Both imagination and a sense of métier are necessary for the efficient handling of this enthralling politico-military action.[12]

These are very great demands to place upon ordinary soldiers and draftees, and it is doubtful that many young Frenchmen performing their military service in Algeria were as deeply involved in the philosophy of revolutionary warfare as Massu and his band of elite.

Certainly dissatisfaction with the government was widespread. In southwest France, for example, the revolution was much farther advanced than it was in Paris. During the last ten years this territory had become the land of repatriated colonials—those Europeans who had taken seriously Messali Hadj's threat "the suitcase or the coffin," and had fled there to start a new life. In flight from Tunisia, Morocco, and finally Algeria, they had done a magnificent job of turning vast acres of mediocre land into a domain of flourishing farms. Here the philosophy of French Algeria had followed them. "Toulouse is also the capital of the paras whose berets bloom in the streets. They spread out over the surrounding area, at Castres, at Montauban (old stronghold of the counter-revolution in 1790), at Perpignan, at Pau, at Tarbes and at Bayonne." [13] Here also the old *maquisards* had kept close contact with each other. In the southwest and in other parts of France Michel Debré and Soustelle won over a secondary administrative service, at once Gaullist and secret. (Soustelle's training in World War II as de Gaulle's Commissioner of Information made such activity very natural to him.) These groups, sometimes comprised of dissatisfied Fourth Republic officials, were prepared to move into power at the time of the coup. According to the Brombergers, five thousand men were ready for mobilization in the southwest, as many as in all the rest of France together.[14] General Roger Miquel, a Moroccan veteran of twenty-five years and anti-system to the teeth, disposed of all the shock troops in that area, and he enjoyed the friendship and esteem of General Descours [15] commanding the Lyon region and General Lecoq commanding in Bordeaux. Miquel was to be chosen from Algeria to head military operations in France after May 13, operation "Resurrection," so-called.

To Jacques Soustelle goes the honor of uniting the rebellious army and the rebellious civilians. Much has been written of this strong, controversial man. After a phenomenal record at the *Ecole Normale Supérieure,* he rose to prominence as de Gaulle's General Director of Special Services in Algiers during World War II. Here he helped the general in his fight to supplant Giraud, the choice of President Roosevelt's war counsellors, and to attain his position as the embodiment of the Fighting French. Soustelle had always idolized de Gaulle, but his story is important in more than its Gaullist aspects. Before 1940 he pursued a notable personal career as an anthropologist in Mexico and had written scholarly books on Aztec civilization, which earned him the nickname, "Jacques the Aztec." At the age of twenty-five he was appointed Under Director of the *Musée de l'Homme* in Paris. In 1948 Soustelle had been the Secretary of the R.P.F. when de Gaulle tried his come-back. As a member of the R.P.F. he was elected deputy from Rhône in 1951 and continued to sit in the National Assembly even when the Gaullist movement failed. Although most of Soustelle's early thinking had been oriented to the left, after the defeat of the R.P.F. he became an inveterate

193

harrier of the policies of the various moderate governments. He disputed the policy of European Defense Community, E.D.C., which was so long pondered by the French Assembly before it was rejected in 1954, and he vigorously fought any policy of "abandon" in the affairs of Morocco and Tunisia. In 1955, Mendès-France, in a move which alienated some of his own party, named Soustelle Governor General of Algeria. At this time Mendès-France's government was involved in negotiations with Tunisia for independence and was considering discussing the Algerian situation in a conciliatory framework.

While the government that he would officially represent was granting important concessions to the North African states, Soustelle was thinking in terms of a French federation of North Africa. He conceived of Algiers as the second capital of France, since it was there that the French government had returned to dignity and responsibility under Charles de Gaulle in 1943. He realized, particularly with the beginning of the revolt in the Aurès Mountains in November, 1954, that the Algerian revolutionaries had synchronized their rebellion with the Moroccan movement for independence and that the French could only defeat this impetus in a framework of great concessions of local autonomy and industrial and educational aid for Algeria. He began then to formulate an advanced policy of integration. Taking a firm stand against the terrorism of the F.L.N., he refused to envisage Algeria, all the while thinking of that country in most generous terms, as anything but a part of the French nation.

Mendès-France's government was defeated by a vote of 273-319 with 27 abstentions on February 5, 1955, after a two-day debate on North Africa, ten days before Jacques Soustelle officially took up his duties as Governor.[16] However, Edgar Faure's newly formed government—farther to the right than Mendès'—renewed Soustelle's appointment. For the first year or so the new governor was not at all popular in Algeria. Strangely enough he was remembered as a Mendès man (one of the *"bradeurs"* of empire) rather than as a man whose appointment had contributed strongly to Mendès' defeat. Perhaps he was unpopular because of his ubiquitous Gaullism, for the man of

194

Brazzaville had not been loved there as the man of Vichy had, and certainly the ultras felt that he was inclined to give too many concessions to the Muslims. At the beginning of his tenure in Algiers he still favored a federal solution, to the great distaste of the ultras. In any case, for a long while he was one of Alain de Sérigny's favorite targets in the very colonialist *Echo d'Alger*. By the time 1956 had rolled around, the war of the F.L.N. had gathered momentum and support in many quarters. The Muslims elected to the National Assembly had placed themselves officially on record as demanding recognition of an Algerian nation, and, failing to obtain any consideration for their demand, had resigned in a body. A certain amount of foreign concern had been demonstated regarding the French policies of "pacification," and the rebels, with support from their brother Moroccans and Tunisians, proved to be far stronger and more enduring than the French believed possible: all this in spite of increasing French army strength in Algeria and a greater war budget.

Gradually the ultras came to the conclusion that it would be well, either honestly or hypocritically, to change their point of view. As we have remarked, "integration" became their byword and suddenly they recognized that Soustelle was a very valuable champion of the cause of French Algeria. Soustelle himself severely altered his thinking by 1956. After witnessing the massacres of August, 1955, and seeing French policy in Morocco fail utterly, he forgot about federalism, pushed for integration and war to the finish against Islam and the Arab League. The *Echo d'Alger*, recognizing its new champion, changed its tune over night. It was recalled that Soustelle, far from being a Mendès man, had helped overthrow his government at the time of the North African debate.

The integration policies of the French army on whom the ultras depended also helped modify colonial thinking. The *gros colons* were forced to admit, in the face of continuous Muslim rebellion and the beginnings of terrorism in the city of Algiers, that only a very magnificent and heart-felt gesture of Frenchmen toward Muslims had even the slightest chance of bringing back the peace. Promises broken to second class citizens must be re-

deemed to first class citizens. The French must voluntarily abandon their privileged positions and their feelings about the in-
equality of cultures to build a new country with the talent of
both races. Sweeping reforms had to be made in face of the relatively few colonial barons who lived a life reminiscent of the
old South of the United States. These people must invite, as it
were, their slaves to table, permit an equitable redivision of the
best land, change the system of management and the allocation
of profits in industry, and, above all, educate the Muslims in many
fields, not the least being the area of local self-government. Once
forced to accept these conclusions, the *colons* were quick to see
that they had two champions of stature, the French army and
Jacques Soustelle. Soustelle was even able to make these people
understand the wisdom of the *collège unique* which would in
time permit the Algerians to run their own National Assembly.
This was a great stride for people who in 1954 would not even
admit the necessity of the Algerian Statute of 1947, the so-called
loi cadre, which they vitiated in the application.

Soustelle's Algerian policy took shape in the Four Year Plan
which envisaged:

1. The immediate execution of many small or medium sized
public works.
2. Completion of all partially finished projects abandoned for
lack of funds.
3. Important increases in wages.
4. Immediate attention to be given to areas where conditions
were critical.

The Four Year Plan constituted Soustelle's first attempt to
ameliorate the lot of the Muslims in a framework of what he
called "the community of interests of the two populations." These
projects and the money to guarantee them were part of an overall policy whose most important aspect was pacification and an
affirmation of France's decision to remain in Algeria. Of the pacification Soustelle said in his first speech to the Algerian Assembly:
"The simple duty of all democratic authority is to put an end to
the murders, attacks, and acts of pillage and of vandalism. No

one has anything to fear except those who are guilty of these crimes. It is pacification and not a blind repression that the government of the Republic plans to wage to good ends."

With some difficulty Soustelle was able to exact the terms promised him by the government of Mèndes-France from his successor, Edgar Faure—these were to raise the 28 billion francs allocated for Algerian economic and social reforms to 40 billion ($100,000,000). Of this amount 5 billion francs was immediately to go toward the rural amelioration foreseen in the Four Year Plan—wells, roads, and a planned doubling of the scholarization from 600 classes in 1954 to 1200 in 1955-1956.[17] Soustelle also created a general staff composed of both civil and military personnel. General Paul Cherrière was his close associate in this effort to face the reality of the war in the Kabylia and the Aurès, and the staff decided upon the most urgent needs of men and matériel as they planned the French war strategy. The existence of this civil and military body working for coordinated aims deepened the army's interest in politics and increased its control over local civil authority in Algeria.

Soustelle also decided that he would begin to implement the Statute of 1947 which even at this late date was little more than a piece of paper. This Statute, as we have seen, created an Algerian Assembly of 120 members (sixty members from each college) whose duties were for the most part financial and administrative. "Algeria constitutes a group of departments endowed with a civil personality, financial autonomy and a particular organization defined by the following articles." [18] Among the articles of the Statute were certain ones charging the Assembly—and only the second college, the Algerian branch, would have sufficient interest to formulate these laws—to make laws guaranteeing the independence of the Muslim cult vis-à-vis the state, and to organize Muslim instruction in terms of its own language and culture. The Statute was also supposed to suppress the existence of mixed communes, but in 1955 this provision had not yet been put into effect.

This brief outline of Soustelle's Algerian policy does not begin to indicate his activity in other directions. Hand in hand with his plans to change the face of Algeria went his conviction that the heart of the problem lay in the Fourth Republic. His battle against the system took the form of Gaullist regroupment in an organization called the Union for the Safety and Renewal of French Algeria (*Union pour le Salut et le Renouveau de l'Algérie française*), the U.S.R.A.F. By 1957 he had taken a position way beyond the Statute of 1947 and in favor of a single college because he realized that the only possibility of continued French sovereignty lay in sweeping reforms which would win over the neutral or apathetic Muslims by their very shock value. Before the end of 1958 this man, known variously by friends and enemies as "a born secret policeman," "the most dangerous man in France," and "the Molotov of Gaullism," had not only helped to produce another Gaullist play but had secured a lead for himself.

OPERATION SEDITION

Under the benediction of the U.S.R.A.F., Committees of Public Safety took shape in French cities and in Algeria. Remnants of the old *maquis* assembled, as we have already remarked, and early in 1958 these committees made liaison with dissident groups in the army. Meanwhile, by March of 1958, Blocq-Mascart's C.A.N.A.C. was said to control 2,000,000 veterans in metropolitan France ready to demonstrate against the government of the Fourth Republic.

It was when the forces of Delbecque and Soustelle recognized each other's value that the revolution really began to move. Soustelle, long since replaced in Algeria by Robert Lacoste, had fathered the formation of the U.S.R.A.F. in Algiers and had participated in the Gaullist meetings presided over by Chaban-Delmas and Frey. It was to be his task to persuade the Algerians, both Muslim and European with whom he had earned a great popularity by the end of 1955, when Edgar Faure dissolved the National Assembly, that they were Gaullists as well as integrationists. Then of course there was the little miracle of making de Gaulle believe, temporarily at least, that he was an integrationist, or at least a Gaullist. But that was to take a year longer.

"Wheels Within Wheels," May 13, 1958

Robert Lacoste as governor of Algeria was a strange backdrop for the kind of plotting that was going on around him. He had been sent to Algeria after the Mollet-Catroux fiasco on February 6, 1956, and supposedly he carried with him a number of staunch S.F.I.O. (Socialist Party) notions about the Algerian problem. His notions regarding colonial policy had been close to those of Mendès-France, for example. But once in the febrile atmosphere of the White City he became nearly as rabid an integrationist as Soustelle. Though he quit Algiers just before the May 13 uprising, there was no doubt that his sympathies lay with the rightist revolutionaries. With Lacoste's change of heart the city was left open to the machinations of the various plotters.

By April, 1958, events had moved fast enough in Algeria to permit such a disparate group of individuals as Michel Debré, Jacques Soustelle, J.-B. Biaggi, Blocq-Mascart, Léon Delbecque, Pascal Arrighi, a Corsican deputy to the National Assembly, and General Cogny to act together in a kind of fugal arrangement and risk the main chance—which was in most of their minds the success of the chief candidate of the *Rassemblement*—Charles de Gaulle. In April, too, the F.L.N. managed to bring acts of terrorism into the very heart of Algiers in spite of the exceptional clean-up job which Massu and his paratroops had done late in 1957. A state of hysterical anxiety pervaded the White City. Terrorists brought counter-terrorists into the capital with arms and plans, too often carried out, of non-selective vengeance. By this time the shameful period of Alleg's *Question* was in full swing. It was the period of *ratissages* and the torturing of suspects among the native population. The U.T.B., a local force of reservists and public spirited citizens who voluntarily served three days a week in a sort of citizen army or Home Guard, patrolled the city in small tanks and "halftracks." They broke up suspicious gatherings, picked up loitering Muslims, and generally constituted a kind of law unto themselves reminiscent of the vigilantes of the Far West. Their sympathies were far more partisan, their emotions more embroiled than the average draftee from Paris or metropolitan France, and they were feared by the non-European population of Algiers. At times they even caused

199

trouble for the army and in general added to the atmosphere of tension and overt violence.

Among the army chiefs who thrived in this melodramatic milieu was General Jacques Faure, Commander of the First Regiment of the paras (*Berets Bleus*). Faure had lost a son in Algeria and was a desperate enemy of the Fourth Republic. He had been anti-E.D.C., anti-Gaullist and a personal friend of the Poujadist deputy, Jean Le Pen. For months he talked openly of a military *putsch* which was to take place simultaneously in Algiers and in Paris, and the blue berets were much in evidence at El Biar. He found his natural allies among the activists of the city and was particularly in sympathy with the adventurer, the athletic Dr. René Kovacs, immortalized by the affair of the Bazooka. The Bazooka episode was not the first of its kind to shine in the career of Kovacs. He had been engaged in counter-terrorism since 1956. In 1957 his men planted explosives in the confessionals of the Algiers churches on Saint Sylvester night, hoping to murder Bishop Duval, a liberal clergyman of the city.

In January, 1958, the attempt on the life of General Salan removed both Kovacs and General Cogny from the list of active conspirators and drove Minister Resident Robert Lacoste at long last into admitting in Paris the serious nature of the bubbling revolution. At his request the *Sûreté Nationale* of Paris conducted a government investigation. On the outskirts of Algiers they discovered the headquarters of this band of brigands ("Villa les Sources") composed of civils like Kovacs and "adventuring" officers of the army. There were arrayed the ghastly instruments for torture, the *"baignoires"* and the electric devices that had become a commonplace in the hands of ultras among the police, military, and civilians. Cached in the villa's basement were supplies of food and arms and a loud speaker. All this interesting equipment was available to the paras when they needed it and to other groups in foment, such as Robert Martel's (*Union Française Nord-Africaine*, formerly directed by the *colon* Louis Boyer-Banse), and various clandestine groups dedicated to the preservation of European dominance. Upon the arrest of Robert Martel the government agents discovered that he was also connected

200

with the new *Cagoule* in Paris. Kovacs' testimony gave the *Sûreté* lurid evidence of the revolutionary plans of the so-called "Committee of Six." According to him this committee included Soustelle, Michel Debré, Pascal Arrighi, General Cogny, and a hyphenated name which could have been Blocq-Mascart. The sixth identity was not disclosed but rumor had it to be the Prince Napoléon.[19] Alan Griotteray, one of General Cogny's staff, was accused of master-minding the plan to kill Salan. Although he and two other intermediaries of the "Committee of Six" were arrested, strangely enough the principals were not brought to justice until after de Gaulle's government was in power.

To imagine the Algerian state of mind, which could greet quietly and even suppress the news of an attack upon the commander in chief of the armed forces, is to envisage a fantastic vacuum of both civil and government morale. It also reveals the depth of involvement of serious people in the plots and counterplots. This entire incident seems to have been invented as a kind of prelude to the main Algerian extravaganza (whose script was written and acted by a crew of lucid madmen), whose curtain went up on May 13. Certainly General Salan had reason to believe that he was the intended victim of more than just a handful of ultras when none of the Committee of Six were pursued at law. Though fusses were made by a few *Mendésistes* (and they *were* few at this time) and some Communists over the parliamentary immunity of Soustelle, Debré, and Arrighi, it was not until these men were firmly entrenched in power in the regime *à* de Gaulle that the affair of the Bazooka was brought out in open court. And even then, the lawyers for the accused (Biaggi, of all people, and the anti-Gaullist Tixier-Vignancour) refused to release all the evidence to the public on the grounds that an army at war might be dishonored in the world's eyes. It seems certain, Committee of Six or no, that the basic facts of Kovacs' testimony regarding the Gaullist plot were true. It seems equally certain that this group did fear that Salan might prove a stumbling block to their plans.

And, then, ever since the days of the French Committee of National Liberation in Algiers during the Second World War there had been a dangerous precedent for military assassinations.

201

The army still remembered the mysterious killing of Admiral Darlan, the star chamber proceedings and the quick execution of the guilty student, and the "stray" bullet that landed in General Giraud's jaw.[20] On the other hand it is probably absurd to think that men like Soustelle and Debré would stoop to machinations of this sort. But there was enough truth in Kovacs' charges to make them feel very uncomfortable and none of them could afford to admit the existence of a serious plot before the plot had succeeded.

It is interesting at this time to try to imagine the state of mind of General de Gaulle when his chief advocates were implicated in such unsavory affairs. Such Machiavellian intrigue sat queerly beside his high moral preoccupations.

Certainly he knew much better than the pallbearers of the Fourth Republic what was going on among the conspirators, but he gave no sign of being ashamed of his cohorts. Apparently he neither directed nor advised. He accepted and waited. Sometimes his attitude is hard to understand, but it had something God-like and fatalistic about it. Both good and evil were to be allowed to serve indiscriminately the prescribed destiny of Charles de Gaulle, coming president of the Fifth Republic.

According to the brothers Bromberger, between December, 1957, and the beginning of May, 1958, Léon Delbecque took twenty-eight trips to Algeria on behalf of Minister of Defense Chaban-Delmas. He made numerous contacts with the remains of the old Resistance, but in spite of a great personal belief in Gaullism and his own strong magnetism, he realized that it was only in the person of Jacques Soustelle that Gaullism could be made acceptable to the *colons*. Gaullists *per se* were as few in Algeria as they seemed to be in the National Assembly. Therefore Delbecque joined hands with Soustelle and with Alain de Sérigny, publisher of the *Echo d'Alger,* and associated himself with the U.S.R.A.F. From the various groups of plotters he formed a Committee of Vigilance and he was not at all discriminating. The Committee included Poujadists under Dr. Bernard Lefevre, veterans from the C.A.N.A.C., and a new group of student agitators under their association president, the young Pierre Lagaillarde.

"Wheels Within Wheels," May 13, 1958

Delbecque did not spurn politicos either. Gaullists, M.R.P.'s, and Independents all were rallied. In the person of Colonel Thomazo, "*Nez de Cuire*," the army liaison was secured. The vigilantes also claimed the participation of Martel's supposedly outlawed group (U.F.N.A.) which had direct connections with the "Grand O" of Paris. This hodge-podge of active dissatisfaction was led by the Group of Seven, and they represented a formidable welding job for Mr. Delbecque. According to the Brombergers, the seven leaders were as follows: Lagaillarde, former para and schoolteacher, Robert Martel of the U.F.N.A., his chief aid, Crespin of the C.R.F., Dr. Lefevre, the Poujadist and old Pétainist, his accomplice, restaurant owner Goutallier, Ortiz, a quasi-Poujadist café owner, and M. Baille, a lawyer and the "theoretician of the coup d'état." The Committee of Seven were not Gaullists, and they entertained many ideas hostile to the Delbecque group. It is claimed that they hoped to bring the army to power in the person of General Salan; in this they shared the sentiment of the "Grand O" in Paris. So, if officially, they followed the policy of Delbecque, they intended to take the revolution in their own hands when the time was ripe. Actually in large measure they did direct the events of May 13. It was General Salan's delaying action and his pronunciamento in favor of de Gaulle that upset their plans. In many ways the part Salan played in all this confusion is somewhat obscure, but his reluctant Gaullism was the price exacted for army unity.

When the Gaillard government fell on April 15, 1958, Delbecque swung into action and incited a great demonstration of all the anti-system people in Algiers to be held on April 26. Governor Lacoste became worried that such a gathering might degenerate into a *ratissage* and he formally forbade the demonstration, which he had at first condoned. He managed at the last minute to impose censorship on Algiers' newspapers, but in the spots where the announcements were to have appeared were empty boxes more provocative than the original exhortations. In the end Lacoste only succeeded in keeping the veterans at home. The French army was prepared to march, and the police and the C.R.S. (Republican guards) were ordered not to interfere with what had been planned as a peaceful demonstration. Even if he had ordered the police to intervene, it is doubtful that they would have. Colonel Godard, working with the *colons,* had strong control of the police, and Lieutenant-Colonel Trinquier was the real leader—the grass-roots boss—of Massu's paratroopers. In the meantime, General Salan, called to Paris because of the government crisis, left General Paul Allard in command of Algiers. The demonstration turned out to be both calm and impressive. Even the fire-eating *colons* of the U.F.N.A. were persuaded to keep the peace, perhaps because police and army units stopped and searched cars from neighboring points, and all arms were taken away from demonstrators. The unknowing gave Thomazo and the army credit for the orderly parade of some 30,000 citizens, but actually it was Léon Delbecque who could rightfully remark on the eve of the 26th: "I now have Algeria in hand!" [21]

After this audacious display of anti-governmental power, Robert Lacoste realized that his days as Minister Resident in Algeria were numbered unless he could make some kind of a compromise with his former politics. After two years in Algeria he was strongly infected by the French-Algerian virus. He believed with the conspirators that the system was guilty of a weak and vacillating policy and that it was ready to abandon Algeria as it had given up Tunisia and Morocco.[22] His own work as governor had given him a feeling of great hope, and he stated his sentiments about the Algerian situation in this fashion: We must not fail "this population which asks nothing but to believe in us, this army which has done its duty, these six thousand Muslims who, at my call, in spite of the menaces of the F.L.N., had accepted positions in the special delegations to administer, in the name of France, the towns, communes and the *douars* of our Algeria." [23]

On May 8, 1958, the thirteenth anniversary of V-E Day, Lacoste was honored by the presentation of a medal, the Cross of Military Valor, and a citation from the Algerian High Command. The citation applauded him for twenty-seven months of "patriotism, courage, and abnegation." [24] Lacoste's parting speech was far from echoing Socialist party sentiments, but instead underlined the need for a government of national union or a revolutionary government of Public Safety.

In January, 1958, the National Assembly had at long last ratified the *loi-cadre* which, while declaring Algeria to be an integral part of the French Republic, stated it was composed of federated territories which would freely and democratically administer their own affairs. Above all, the *loi-cadre* guaranteed the one-college assembly which would lead inevitably to a preponderance of Muslim control in the development of the country at a local level even while it guaranteed French governmental control from above. Lacoste felt bitterly that all these gains were to be sacrificed by the stupidity of the present metropolitan government, and he was greatly tempted to throw in his lot with the French army and the integrationists. He was not, of course, in favor of the ultra branch of the revolution. Personal disappointment entered in, too, during the first week in May, when his party refused to form a government with the M.R.P., Radicals, and Independents thus terminating his incumbency as Minister Resident to Algeria. Earlier he had spent some time with de Gaulle. It seems certain that if the sphinx of Colombey had given him an indication that the problem would eventually be solved in a manner which Lacoste could approve (i.e. Republican legitimacy) he would have stayed on in Algeria. Delbecque, Alain de Sérigny, and Colonel Thomazo begged him to resign from the Socialist party and hold the civil power in Algeria until a government of Public Safety was formed in Paris. The Group of Seven under Dr. Martin also approached him and asked him to opt in their favor, but in this latter delegation he felt a note of menace, a "be with us or else" undercurrent. If they succeeded in pulling off the revolution, he would be little better than a hostage to a band of desperate power-seeking men.

While Delbecque was working on Lacoste, Alain de Sérigny went to Paris (during the first week in May) to persuade Jacques Soustelle to declare himself in favor of a government of *Salut Public*. It seems certain that if Lacoste or Soustelle had received a green light from Colombey, they would have felt free to organize a holding action in Algeria. But neither of them was prepared to go out on the precarious and illegal limb alone. About this time de Gaulle answered a probing letter from Soustelle in this fashion (the statement is paraphrased from a letter of Soustelle's): "On [the subject of] integration he [de Gaulle] remains reserved because he is not certain that the Muslims would accept it willingly. On the other hand he estimates that pacification should be energetically continued and accompanied by a great social, educational, psychological, and political effort. . . ." [25] Soustelle also tried to extract a positive statement from de Gaulle regarding the ambiguity of Lacoste's position. But the General did not give either Lacoste or Soustelle any encouragement.

By May 10 an angry Robert Lacoste, having accepted a military decoration at the hands of General Salan, left Algeria for Paris. There he announced: "I warned Gaillard long ago. He did not even answer my telegrams. Now Pflimlin and Duchet want me to go back there and preach calm, so that the (May 13) day will pass without trouble. Me, I say there is nothing left to do but pray. The train is on the rails." [26]

At the same time, General Salan, after a personal conference with Pleven in Paris, returned to Algiers and sent the Chief of Staff, General Paul Ely, in Paris, a telegram, which he in turn delivered to President Coty. It was a strong and dignified statement reminding the civil powers of the temper of the army in face of the proposed cease-fire offer to the F.L.N. It was a long telegram and had somewhat the feeling of a pronunciamento. It said:

> The present crisis shows that the political parties are profoundly divided on the Algerian question. Press reports suggest that the abandonment of Algeria may be contemplated by means of a diplomatic process that could begin with negotiations toward a 'cease-fire.' I take the liberty of reminding you of my conversation with M. Pleven, in the course of which I stated categorically that the sole clauses of a 'cease-fire' could not be other than these: 'France, confirming her appeal for a

"cease-fire," invites the rebels in Algeria to turn over their arms as soon as possible and guarantees, with a large amnesty, their return to the bosom of a reinvigorated Franco-Moslem community.'

The Army in Algeria is disturbed by the sense of its responsibility:

—toward the men who are fighting and who risk a useless sacrifice if the national representation is not determined to maintain French Algeria, as stipulated in the preamble of the *Loi Cadre;*

—toward the French population of the interior, which feels abandoned; and

—toward the Moslem French, who, in greater numbers each day, have again placed their reliance in France, confident that our reiterated promises never to abandon them will be kept.

The French Army in its entirety would feel the abandonment of this national patrimony to be an outrage; ITS REACTION OF DESPAIR COULD NOT BE FORETOLD.

I ask you kindly to call our anguish to the attention of the President of the Republic; it can be dispelled only by a government resolutely determined to maintain our flag in Algeria.[27]

This telegram had been drafted by Generals Salan, Jouhaud, Allard and Massu, and Admiral Auboyneau. It was also intended to instruct Pierre Pflimlin, who was trying to form a government. Informed observers believe it was this text, widely dissimulated, which helped save the unity of the army threatened by the rebellious attitude of the younger officers and the fire-eating colonels. In keeping the army together it prevented the activists from taking power once the explosion came.

By May 10 everyone was ready for his own revolution. It was only de Gaulle who had not definitely committed himself to action. Now an excuse had to be invented for the insurrection itself. Since Pflimlin hoped to achieve investiture on May 14,

May 13 was a strategic date. And the F.L.N. presented the colonial super-French their cause. Three French soldiers who had been prisoners of the rebel forces for some eighteen months had been accused, according to the F.L.N. press bureau in Tunis, of torture, rape, and murder and sentenced to death by a special tribunal of the A.L.N. (Algerian Army of National Liberation). *El Moudjahid* had notified the French, who were executing Muslim rebels as common criminals, that: "The blade of the guillotine must stop. Let French opinion be warned. Beginning tomorrow, each Algerian patriot to mount the scaffold signifies one French prisoner before the firing squad." [28] On April 24, the day before the three French soldiers were allegedly sentenced, three terrorists had been guillotined in Algiers.

Thereupon the seething town decided upon a ceremony to honor the three French dead to be held on the afternoon of May 13. The stage was now set. A worried Léon Delbecque who had his plans set for May 26 was forced to agree to the earlier date. But the departure of Lacoste left a power vacancy in Algiers which, while it pleased the activists, was embarrassing to Delbecque's Gaullists and to the French army. General André Petit was sent on urgent mission to bring back Soustelle if possible, for he was the link needed to channel the army's very un-Gaullist sentiments in the right direction. But Soustelle was not able to obtain a straightforward answer from General de Gaulle and was loathe to leave the National Assembly before the vote of investiture took place. Rumors filtered through that Soustelle might be called upon to form a government of Public Safety in Paris. Meanwhile the country tottered on the brink of civil war.

In Algeria the high command faced a dilemma. The question was: to fire or not to fire upon the mob that would surely develop out of the demonstration of May 13. A failure to fire upon the insurrectionists would indicate complicity, and yet it was unthinkable for the army to shoot down Frenchmen supporting their cause. When the time came, the metropolitan government simplified the problem by ordering the army not to fire upon the rioters. The high command was also aware that Algiers in revolt could be neatly cut off from the Metropole, and so General Edmond Jouhaud recommended that Major-General Maurice Challe, Ely's closest collaborator, put at his disposition 60 Nord 2,501's (transport planes destined to carry paratroops and a "certain number of large civil airplanes—Bréguet-Deux-Ponts or D. C. 4's)." These would be sufficient to transport two regiments and their arms should they be needed, as was claimed, by the encircled French garrisons in Tunisia or, to take the city of Paris! "A well-filled day, that of May 10: the insurrection fixed for the 13th; the power vacuum left in Algiers; the union of Gaullists around Soustelle; the rallying of the Algerian conservatives to the General; salute of Soustelle by the high command; the planes promised for the paras. Only de Gaulle had spent a very tranquil day, apart from all these preparations, anxious only for the future of his country under a regime which was impotent to solve its dramatic problems." [29]

On May 11 the newly rallied Gaullist Alain de Sérigny published his appeal to de Gaulle in the *Echo d'Alger*. Beginning "Parlez, parlez, mon général . . ." it was further to mobilize public opinion in Algiers for the Gaullist camp. And Lieutenant-Colonel Trinquier brought his 3rd R.P.C. (the old *"bande à Bigeard"*) back from the Tunisian frontier. These graduates of the famous *Ecole Jeanne d'Arc* could be counted on for their loyalty to the rebel stand. General Salan's orders regarding the procession of May 13 were issued to the army and the people; both were to parade in dignity and order. The army counted on Soustelle. Such was the picture in Algiers.

Meanwhile, back in the jungle of the National Assembly Pierre Pflimlin asked General Cogny, of all people, if he would take over the Algerian army! Soustelle, torn between his duty as a deputy and the hope that he might influence parliament to act either for himself or de Gaulle, sent word by Oliver Guichard, de Gaulle's public relations expert, to ask for advice. De Gaulle's laconic answer is not very helpful. "Let Soustelle do what he believes he ought to do." [30] So Soustelle stayed in Paris, sending word to Algiers through Léon Delbecque to keep the insurrection alive until May 14 by which time the investiture would either have succeeded or failed. An airplane was kept in readiness for him and he expected to fly to Algeria disguised as an orderly of Colonel Guille as soon as the vote on Pflimlin's investiture was held. The army was preparing to land paratroops in Paris six hours after the formation of the hoped-for government of *Salut Public,* and in that city, Biaggi, General Cogny, and Colonel Griotteray were coordinating the C.A.N.A.C. and the various activist associations. Biaggi planned to arm his gangsters and dress them as paras for the assault upon the Palais Bourbon.

In spite of all these revolutionary preparations, the position of Pierre Pflimlin at this moment was not determined by the Algerian situation, or so he felt. It is for this reason that he was unable to form a compromise government including Soustelle or Bidault or Morice. Concerning his views at the crucial moment he said:

> It [a compromise government] would have been exactly contrary to the intentions which were directing my action. You must remember that at this period it was not the destiny more or less removed of Algeria which was in question, but the attitude of France vis-à-vis Tunisia. We had just had Sakiet, the French garrisons besieged by Tunisian barrages, the 'good offices.' Other more serious battles were being prepared. Soustelle had just overthrown the Gaillard government on a project of accord with Bourguiba. They [the opposition] had invented, to defeat it [the Gaillard government], the false problem of the French airports abandoned to the Tunisians. General Pinsard had been sent to me by General Gambiez to expose the perilous position of the French army in Tunisia. The soldiers were ready to do whatever the government wanted: peace or war. But a choice had to be made. . . . General Gambiez estimated that it would be better to make peace. The Saraha units, tied down at Remada and at Gafsa, were needed in Algeria. The accord with Bourguiba would permit us to reinforce the essential base at Bizerte.[31]

And a little later Pflimlin guessed correctly: "When de Gaulle takes power he will immediately activate the accord virtually concluded with Bourguiba. He will not take M. Bidault into his cabinet. . . ." [32]

On May 12 General de Gaulle received a very persuasive letter from General Ely, and he finally decided to act. On that day in Algiers the Group of Seven hoped to steal a march on the Delbecque group and the army, and to start the uprising during the morning of May 13. Trusting neither Soustelle nor de Gaulle, they planned to establish an army dictatorship which would prosecute the Algerian war with more vigor.

"DAY OF THE DUPES"

Tuesday, May 13, I arrived in Algiers in the dawn of a day which was to become historic not only for Algeria but for the whole of France. The sky was radiant, and as soon as the sun rose one could feel its heat, but without excess as it generally is during the admirable Algerian springtime.

During the morning the atmosphere of the city was quite normal—like that of any other day. The order to strike had been given for one o'clock but in awaiting this hour the stores were open, offices and administrative employees were working. If one could sense a feeling of anticipation in the air, it was anticipation without anguish, serene even, almost joyous, and that up until the time when everyone returned home for the midday meal.[33]

The military had taken certain precautions. General Massu ordered three companies of paratroopers of the 3rd Regiment to guard the Leclerc Stadium, and the rest of the regiment stayed at nearby Sidi-Ferruch under Lieutenant-Colonel Trinquier. These dispositions supplemented the normal protective measures of the army and police in the city of Algiers and its outskirts.

Shortly after 2 P. M. (the secondary schools and University being closed) groups of students, boys and girls, began to form in the streets. First they threw rocks through the windows of the American Cultural Center in protest against the Murphy mission, and then they tried to pillage the American Information Library on rue Michelet. Paratroopers from the Third Colonial Parachute Regiment protected the office of the *Journal d'Alger* from the crowd, and then Lieutenant-Colonel Trinquier's troops were ordered back to the center of the city. The mob swelled larger and larger. To parades of students and professors carrying signs of French Algeria (*Algérie Française*) were added local U.S.R.A.F. groups from nearby Coléa, Rivet and Blida. Placards reading "Soustelle with us" and "Bourguiba to the stake" added variety, and cars whose horns sounded "French Algeria" in code—three shorts and two longs—milled among the excited demonstrators, repeating over and over the noisy form of "dot, dot, dot, dash, dash."

By 4 P. M. the student mob reached the steps of the Forum, the place where for the next ten days the whole population of Algiers would gather to hear announcements, greet newly rallied patriots, acclaim General Massu and the formation of the Committee of Public Safety, finally cheer Salan, scream for a returned Soustelle, and ultimately rally to the cry of *"Vive Général de Gaulle."* In the square in front of the ministry, the Government General, "G.G." of Algiers, the C.R.S. (Republican Security Guard) was mobilized in five jeeps and fifteen autos. A detachment of these troops took a stand on the highest stairs of the G.G. between the mob and the offices of the now absent resident minister and his staff. The government employees were perhaps the only people in the city still at work. As these clerks and stenographers appeared timorously at the windows they were hissed and booed. Stones hurtled toward the office façade.

In another part of the city, at the *Monument Aux Morts, Place des Glières*, the ceremony honoring the three French soldiers had begun. Delegations of Muslim veterans were pouring in carrying their banners and singing *La Marseillaise*. According to Sérigny, by 4:30 in the afternoon some 100,000 people were gathered in the vicinity of the square. As the veterans placed their wreaths for the three French victims of the F.L.N.—Sergeant Richomme, and Privates Decourteix and Feuillebois, loudspeakers began suddenly to proclaim the formation of a government of *Salut Public*. Speakers vilified the "system" and its cohorts and tried to whip the volatile crowd into a revolutionary mood. "They treat us as ultras" boomed the sound tracks, "Ultras, yes, of patriotism."

Now the Republican Guards were forced to use tear gas to effect a passage for Generals Salan, Allard, Jouhaud, Massu, Admiral Auboyneau, and Serge Baret, the Prefect of the *Igame* of Algiers. The French military hierarchy placed a wreath on the monument and forced its way back through the wildly excited crowd. As the "big brass" left the square, the loudspeakers blared that the C.R.S. tear-bombs were acts of "unprovoked violence" on the part of the hated government, and finally came the long-awaited cry, "Everyone to the Government General. We'll find *them* there."

Actually it was only about a hundred students, led by Pierre Lagaillarde, President of the General Association of Students of Algeria, in an old para uniform he had no right to be wearing—in great annoyance Massu referred to it as a "disguise"—that swarmed against the grilled gates of the ministry and forced back a C.R.S. contingent which had been ordered to hold fire. A few more tear bombs slowed the assault for a while, but no resolute defense was maintained against the young rebels. Soon they rushed into the building and government dossiers began floating like ticker-tape from the windows; they started a fire in the ministry library which was promptly extinguished by the local fire department, which did not have much difficulty in getting through the "revolt." By this time it was nearly seven o'clock in the evening, and the rioters were badly out of hand. Nearly sixty automobiles in the courtyard were seriously damaged—their tires cut, windows broken, bodies staved in, and the square was littered with glass from the windows of the Government General. Overhead army helicopters circled the city.

Standing on the balcony of the first floor, Colonel Paul Ducournau, Lacoste's head of Algerian Defense, impotently tried to restore order. Since his voice was drowned in the general roar he wrote in great letters on a blackboard: "I have just telephoned Paris. We have demanded a Government of Public Safety . . ." and then on the other side of the blackboard: "The army is the guarantor of French Algeria." [34]

By 7:00 P.M. General Salan, who had returned to 10th Army Headquarters at the Place D'Isly after the commemorative ceremony, was receiving urgent calls concerning the disorder in the city. Mob violence, although it had not been fratricidal, had already cost too much in property damage and there was no point in allowing it to continue. Realizing the possible political implications of any army action at this moment, General Salan took the underground route from headquarters to the G.G. He arrived with General Jouhaud shortly after General Massu had reached the Forum. Massu, the popular "cleaner" of the Casbah and disciplinarian of the European ultras, was triumphantly hailed by the crowd and allowed to pass through in his jeep. General Allard who by this time was also hurrying to the ministry gates was literally carried on the shoulders of a delirious crowd shouting "the army to power."

According to the various reports of the night of May 13, there were at least seven men in the G.G. who represented the government in Paris and as many more representing the nucleus of the Committee of Public Safety which would be formed in a few hours. Spirited arguments engaged the two groups. Besides this discord there was trouble between the Chaban-Delmas men and the activists who had jumped the gun on Delbecque. While Delbecque and Lagaillarde discussed the day's events with asperity, the crowd below the window clamored for action. Colonel Ducournau begged Massu to direct the riot into peaceful channels. Journalist Paul Gerin, an eye witness, says of the moment:

> Massu is an idol of the Algerians [meaning the French Algerians]. Since he has been responsible for the order of Algiers there have been no more bombs exploding in the cafés (*sic*). And then, Massu, in his camouflaged

uniforms, is a little bit like Tarzan. The hour is pathetic. 'Massu to power! Massu to power!' screams the mob in the Forum. Massu is displeased and turns his back on the crowd making a gesture of repudiation with his arms. He says to his neighbor but the crowd does not hear him: 'They are making a c. . . . Today it was to be a manifestation honoring the three French soldiers shot by the F.L.N.' [35]

While Thomazo and Ducournau, colonels on different sides of the fence, said unkind things to each other in the background, Salan stepped out on the balcony to quiet the crowd. But the target of the "Bazookists" was no popular hero at the moment. He was hissed and booed. Like all the crowds in the forums of history this one, too, wanted its sacrifices as well as its heroes. Testily Salan stepped back into the room and said to Massu: "Go on. Go on." And Massu makes the historic announcement: "The army is with you wholeheartedly . . . but you will serve the cause of French Algeria by remaining calm and disciplined. We are agreed vigilantly to await the news that we hope to hear from Paris." [36] Acclamations of the crowd. Massu then ordered Lagaillarde to take his excited schoolboys home and keep them out of further trouble. But Lagaillarde insisted that his "men" would not leave the Forum until a government of Public Safety had been formed. If Pflimlin is elected, they will continue the riot. If he is not, they will go home.

At 8:45 P.M. a Committee of Public Safety was formed under the presidency of the heavily pressured Massu, and an hour or so later, with Salan's tacit approval, the following message was sent to President Coty. "Wish to inform you of the creation of a Committee of Public Safety, civil and military, in Algiers, presided over by *me, General Massu* [the italics are the authors']. Because of the gravity of the situation and the absolute necessity to maintain order and avoid bloodshed the Committee anxiously awaits the creation at Paris of a government of Public Safety. Only a government of Public Safety is capable of preserving Algeria as an integral part of the metropole." [37] The *moi, Massu*

215

so reminiscent of the *moi, de Gaulle* from the period of the Committee of National Liberation during World War II was to resound ominously from the Paris newspapers. It was the particular tone of this telegram that led Pflimlin in Paris to assume that Massu was one of the instigators of the coup and to name him prominently among the "factious generals." This was an honor he did not deserve.

Before Massu could order two battalions of paras to clear the tag-ends of the mob out of the G.G., he was obliged to satisfy the activists and ebullient youths who had forced their way into the building. They wanted a Committee of Public Safety before they would leave and before they would cooperate in dispersing the crowd outside. A decision had to be made. Salan remained mute, and Massu tells us he had forty seconds to decide to create a Committee of Public Safety. The alternative was to use the military against the crowd, and this, too, was risky since no order to fire had been issued by the civil authority in Paris. Besides it is doubtful that the army would have obeyed. Massu took a sheet of paper and wrote some names on it. He placed his own name at the top of the list, designated Colonels Thomazo, Trinquier, and Ducasse as aides, and then added seven names of persons in the room: Lagaillarde; Paul Moreau, a film distributor who had been in the building by coincidence; Gabriel Montigny, a cash register company employee; Joseph Jolivet, a foreman; André Baudier, a tall, young, bespectacled clerk in the housing administration; Rodolphe Parachini, a Shell company employee and Armand Perroud, a salesman who arrived in Algiers from Morocco eight days earlier to visit friends. These seven, together with Massu, appeared on the balcony and told the crowd to go home.

The telephone rang, and it was Lacoste in Paris asking for Massu. "Yes, that is correct, we have named a committee. . . . It is not a coup d'état. . . . It is simply to impress upon the National Assembly the demand of Algeria to remain French. . . . I could not do otherwise. I would have to open fire upon the crowd. Are you giving the order to fire? No! Then, all I can do is to talk!" [38]

Not a single known Gaullist was on the original list of seven

216

civilians, but this was no more than a beginning. Later in the evening four Muslims and various Europeans became members of the Committee of Public Safety. It grew until, by May 14, it totaled seventy-two persons. The Muslims were all *beni-oui-oui's:* Saci Mahdi, a retired major; Saïd Mohand Madani, trade unionist employed in a chemical plant; Mohammed Berkani, an accountant; and Taieb Chikh, landowner and member of the Vigilance Committee. Gaullist Delbecque soon arrived and got himself named vice-president. Various activists, some of the violent type, became members: airline pilot Auguste Arnould; Robert Martel of the U.F.N.A. with Cagoule connections; engineer Merlo; and the indefatigable Dr. Lefevre. Inevitably, too, Alain de Sérigny joined the adventure.

Little by little the members of Lacoste's staff sneak from the G.G. via the secret passage. It is well that they disappear for at 3 A.M. on May 14 came the news that Pflimlin, directly as a result of the Algerian revolt, had attained his investiture by a solid majority which included the Communists. Was a different kind of Committee of Public Safety, one more analagous to the "Twelve Who Ruled" in 1793-1794, being composed in Paris, or were Frenchmen witnessing the reincarnation of the Popular Front against the menacing right?

In Alain de Sérigny's narrative of the "historic day" in Algiers, we find an account from Lagaillarde of his attack on the G.G.

"On the 13th of May I had stirred up about five thousand persons from inside the schools to follow me. At 4:30 P.M. I set out in parachutist uniform [Lagaillarde was a second lieutenant in the para reserves] in a [Peugeot] '403' preceded by a personal guard of four armed *harkis.* I went to the *Monument Aux Morts* where I was 'cut off from my troops' by the crowd.

"Then I climbed up on the monument so that my people could see me and it is at this moment that I took the oath to go *Jusqu'au bout* [to the bitter end].

"At 5:40 I began to send elements to the upper part of the Forum to begin a mass agitation near that objective.

"I wanted to wait for the moment when the generals arrived and I didn't want the manifestation to lose sight of the goal.

"When they [the generals] did arrive at 6:00 o'clock there

was a moment of silence and it was in seeing Salan turn away that I cried, 'Let's go. Everyone who is against the rotten regime to the G.G.' " [39]

It was at this moment that the *bagarre* (street fight) between the Republican Guards and the mob began. The use of tear gas seemed to clinch the matter. However, at no time was there any danger that either the C.R.S. or the French army would fire upon the crowd. Both sides were sure of that. From Paris had come much earlier the order to "hold fire" and the French army in general was so much at one with the revolt that there was small chance of bloodshed. In fact one cannot escape the thought that the whole affair resembled nothing so much as a farce put on by a bunch of amateurs. There was something of the circus about it, too, and something of a child's fairy tale, fantastic and unreal. Just as children took over the G.G. so their elders seemed to be involved in some huge production of an inferior "Midsummer Night's Dream," but in this script no one seemed to come out of the spell. The night has by now stretched into more than two years and yet what the atmosphere of Algiers does to seemingly rational men still remains inexplicable. Lacoste only just escaped. Soustelle is a victim of the enchantment. The real question is yet to be answered, and that is: have enough Muslims fallen under the spell? Has de Gaulle?

The Brombergers add these interesting details to our knowledge of the night of May 13 in Algiers. "Another fact was manifest. The paras from every echelon obeyed [the government at G.G.] with a sluggishness and a softness that was evident. Only part of a company arrived at the Forum and they were late. They were quickly submerged. 'The *hommes peints* [a familiar name of the Algerians for the camouflaged uniforms of the Paras] pushed us [forward] while pretending to hold us back,' said one of the rioters." [40] In another place we are told that the crowd which until nightfall had been made up of many sober family elements, lost them at dinner time to the needs of the children and the hearth. After dinner a whole new group of agitators arrived. ". . . Warned by the radio and the rumors, the Algerians came running. They went to the revolution as if to a formidable spectacle of '*Son et Lumière*'—more sound than light besides."

During that strange night when it seemed that everything had transpired so well for the revolutionaries—after all, the minister resident and his staff had been ushered out the door, the army under the darling Massu had rallied in time to form a C.P.S.— something secret and in the end devastating had also transpired. It came in the form of a telegram from Félix Gaillard, whose caretaker government functioned until Pflimlin's investiture, and it gave General Salan "Superior Command in Algeria to take all necessary measures for the maintenance of peace, the protection of persons and property until further orders." It was by this cable that the "system" slipped into the revolution by the back door, and Salan who had already been forced to delegate at least temporary authority to Massu found himself playing the game, both sides against the middle. He alone among the military personnel involved in the coup of May 13 was acting in perfect legality; he risked no trial for treason if the coup failed. One can understand why this old war dog did not court any more unpopularity with the mob by avowing the receipt of the government telegram. Witness to the confusion in Paris came in the form of a second telegram, which Salan conveniently lost, that limited his powers of command to Algiers. Apparently Paris trusted him, but not as much as it trusted the generals in Oran and the Constantine where rebellion had not yet broken out. Pflimlin did finally unfreeze 80 million francs for Algerian military expenditures that had been curtailed by the government of Gaillard.

Soon other orders followed from the central government which put Salan in a most equivocal position. While Paris gave lip service to his loyalty, it cut off from him and the army, ships, planes, food, arms, gasoline and oil, and it intercepted all communications. For a few days Paris tried to play it both ways— to conciliate the high command, and arrest treasonable officers, ministers, and rightists. This, as Jules Moch was to find out, would only push the rebellion further. One thing that the double game achieved was the temporary sequestering of Jacques Soustelle who, on May 14, had, along with Morice, Bidault, Duchet, and, of course, Delbecque, publicly commended the Algerian rebellion. By the time he escaped house arrest and found a plane to bring him to Algiers, his arrival was an anti-climax. Among all the events of the day and night of May 13 one thing is conspicuous by its absence, and that is a single reference to the name of Charles de Gaulle, who was to become the heir of the revolution.

When Brigadier General André Petit, General Ely's right-hand man in Paris, arrived in Algeria without Soustelle whom he had promised to deliver (and with him the Gaullist cause), the C.P.S. reacted somewhat like a rudderless boat. And the Algerian generals and colonels, except for Salan with that telegram in his pocket, wondered who they could invest with the civil power, for the army dearly loves a proconsul. On the other hand, the activists who feared Soustelle's liberalism and wanted an out-and-out army dictatorship were very happy. How long the old germs of Vichy had stayed alive in that atmosphere of maddening sun and brilliant light, of army hierarchy, racism, and the way of a privileged class. Not only did Petit fail to bring back Soustelle, but he brought news of the stiffening of the governmental backbone in Paris. Had the breath of the Algiers revolution blown life back into the moribund Fourth Republic?

When from the G.G. General Petit drafted a message to de Gaulle asking him to assume civil power while the army "held on" for him in Algeria, a stiff-necked Salan at first refused to send it over his name. This general, republican though he may have appeared, was no man of Brazzaville. Enigmatically he pocketed the document and said: "I am preparing my files for the High Court." But Massu, the adaptable Massu, finally persuaded Salan to allow the message to be sent. At about this time the news of Pflimlin's statement regarding the pourparlers offered by Morocco and Tunisia reached Salan. Interestingly enough, the statement was couched in nearly the same words de Gaulle had used in an earlier discussion of the same problem: "The government does not reject *a priori* the idea that our neighbors [Morocco and Tunisia] might one day use their weight and aid toward bringing

220

our adversary [F.L.N.] toward a pourparler with us in the hope of a cease-fire." [41] Such an attitude was, of course, unacceptable to an army which believed that the government must not talk negotiation when its soldiers were fighting and dying. As a result of this news from Paris, Salan decided to consolidate his position with the inhabitants of Algiers. He therefore published the following proclamation, "Algerians, having the mission to protect you, I take provisorily in hand the destiny of French Algeria. I ask you to have confidence in the Army and in its chiefs, to prove your determination by your calm." It was enough to turn the hisses of the volatile crowd into cheers and so the astute Salan moved into his proper place as head of the army, and Massu moved strategically to the background, good soldier that he was. Incidentally, in all this mess of plot and counterplot, Massu, although he played quite happily into the hands of the revolution of May 13, seems to be uninvolved in the early conspiracy. He was neither a Gaullist nor an activist, but a *"pur et dur."* Salan, with his connection to the "Grand 'O'" in Paris and his affiliation with the veterans of Indo-China must have been very much aware of what was transpiring. So also were generals Ely, Petit, Allard and many others. It is perhaps for this reason that, while good republicans in Paris were using Massu's name as a swear word, General de Gaulle was able to shake his hand after the coup and say: "I understand you."

Paul Gerin says that he heard officers remark that Massu was perhaps the last to be aware of what was going on in Algiers. If this clears him of the charge of being among the "factious," it does not overpraise the powers of his observation. [42] Probably without too much critical analysis he had been very deeply involved in the double policies of pacification—the proposed reforms on one hand and the electrodes of El Biar on the other. Massu was a perfect product of the school of subversive warfare, and apparently he had managed to brain-wash himself considerably. It was his great popularity with the Algerian citizenry that placed power in his hands on the night of May 13, and not any covert treason. There is no reason to believe that he was not content, and perhaps a little bit relieved, to step back into a

221

position of subordination to Salan. Actually the politics of the latter are much more equivocal and it is interesting to note that de Gaulle, upon his accession to power, promoted Salan to the same office, that of Inspector General of the French Army, which he earlier gave to General Giraud, his power rival in 1943. While Giraud, who had been actively supported by Franklin Roosevelt in the period of our "Vichy Gamble," retired from active service and refused to accept another post at de Gaulle's hands, Salan accepted his "promotion." The Algerian command has since been given to General Massu who, until January, 1960, remained a strong figure on the Algerian scene. It was difficult to know whether Salan's changed status is due to excessive loyalty to the Fourth Republic or to Gaullism that came a little late.

CHAPTER SEVEN

DE GAULLE TO POWER

THE NEW FRATERNITY

During the night of May 13, 1958, and the early morning of May 14 events moved as fast in Paris as they did in Algeria. As we have mentioned, Pflimlin insured his investiture and quickly began to take vigorous counter-measures against the rebels. Although Oran was still loyal to the central government and Constantine cut off from Algiers, word had come in from the Sahara that Fort Flatters, Laghouat, El Goléa and Hassi Messaoud (the oil communities) had rallied to the Committee of Public Safety. No planes were permitted to fly between Paris and Algiers, and telephonic communication with the Metropole was broken. The situation was very confused. On one hand the C.P.S. had sworn disloyalty to any ministry selected by Pierre Pflimlin. On the other hand, the army which supported and shared in the membership of the C.P.S. was publicly committed to the central government as well as to French Algeria. Salan's control was vested in him by the Metropole. But what, really, did Salan's control mean if the army was to be blockaded from Paris? With no food, no fuel and no money, the army would be forced to take action against the Metropole to find a source of supply. There were almost no regular troops left in France and these were tied up in the N.A.T.O. command. Even if the Metropole called them into service, it was highly unlikely that they would fire against their brother soldiers in the Algerian theater.

To add to the confusion, different statements were emanating

223

from Salan at the G.G. and Massu at 10th Army Headquarters. Massu declared that the C.P.S. would relinquish control in Algiers when a new Resident Minister took over in Algeria. Delbecque, on the other hand, said that the C.P.S. would remain in power until Pflimlin's government resigned in favor of General de Gaulle. The third power rival, the activist group, had thrown out Salan's minister of information, and Lieutenant Neuwirth of the C.P.S. had taken over the vital post of information. During the day General Gilles in the Constantine and Prefect Jean Chapel sent word that they supported the new regime in Algeria. The prefect at Bône admitted that his sympathies were with the army and the *colons,* but he felt obliged to maintain his functions and keep his subordinates working until a change of power was duly delegated or at least became *de facto.* In the heart of the C.P.S. the important development was a negative one—the absence of Jacques Soustelle. Learning of his house arrest in Paris and that Salan was still working in liaison with the central government, some of the original rebels began to wonder if they had been had.

By May 15 running to the Forum had become a regular morning exercise for the volatile residents of Algiers. Here on this day was to transpire the next important step in the revolution. A reluctant Salan persuaded by Delbecque, who was becoming more and more nervous at the absence of Soustelle, launched the crowd into a movement for de Gaulle. Turning away after a short and enthusiastically received address in which he claimed to be one of theirs because his son lay buried in *clos Salambier,* Salan suddenly faced the microphone on the balcony where most of the comedy had been played and shouted—or did he *ad lib*— this phrase: "*Vive le général de Gaulle.*" [1]

Each day since May 13 a few more Muslims had mingled with the Europeans in the public square. The army had spread rumors of a new fraternity, and its proof had come in an amnesty given to thousands of political prisoners. Native charwomen who worked in the homes of *colons* were told to spread the word in the Casbah, and women from the brothels were advised to swell the crowds. The word passed to the natives was that a true equality

224

with the French was soon to be accorded the Muslim brothers. The bad times of the *ratissages* and the indiscriminate arrests were over. Of course in some circles this news evoked a natural cynicism but, on the other hand, it was apparent that the long-hostile attitude of the colonials had undergone a subtle change. In spite of all the opportunity for violence in the crowded streets there had been no militia activity directed against the native population. In fact it was the Europeans who were fighting Europeans ("The Roumis are fighting the Roumis") in the name of French Algeria. So the persuasion of the French army at whose beck and call they had been for a long time, curiosity, and a sudden realization that racial tension had for some reason decreased, brought hordes of Muslims out of the Casbah. The name of de Gaulle probably had some magic significance, too, since, as we have seen, in 1944 he had been responsible for giving full French citizenship to certain categories of Muslim elite. Since the beginning of the rebellion in 1954, the F.L.N. radio had often broadcast the thought that it was only with de Gaulle that an honest peace could be made. What he had done for the Muslims was not such a great thing, but he had given them exactly what he had promised them, and this was a unique occurrence in Franco-Algerian relations during the last twenty years.

Whatever the explanation for it, and certainly it was contrived to a large degree, there was still something mysterious in the great day of "Fraternization," May 16. It astonished journalists and army men alike and gave renewed hope to the possibility of a settlement of the Algerian problem within the framework of French Algeria. It was one more testimony to the fact that, given half a chance, many of the Muslims would have worked with the French. The actual story of the manifestation is simple enough. Supplied with headbands and armbands saying *"Algérie Française"* and marching behind banners of the Committee of Public Safety of the Casbah, the Muslims swarmed out of their stronghold to embrace the Europeans. Some had been invited by the city notables, some had been "invited" by officers of the S.A.S. The Europeans counted on a demonstration of 4,000 to

5,000 people—in fact the plans had been laid for several months.[2]
An astonishing thing, the so-called *Miracle Passionnel* was that
some 25,000 Muslims, mostly young people, flooded the main
streets and the Forum of Algiers. All the long years of promises
broken, of chicanery over the *loi-cadre,* of battle and suffering, of
torture and imprisonment, of a terrible and always decreasing
standard of living seem to have been forgotten in the one gesture
of *"Français à part entière."* People tired of the war and the
terrorism in the cities, people tired of being squeezed between
the authoritarian tactics of the F.L.N., and the French army and
colons took a walk in the spring sunshine, smiled beatifically,
held hands, Muslim and Christian together, and for a brief
moment acted as brothers should. According to witnesses, old
soldiers wept, tough "moi Massu" had tears in his eyes, and
journalists wrote stories that trembled over the wires. Even the
correspondent of *Le Monde* was shaken! What they had witnessed
was more than a trumpery performance even though the Algiers
C.P.S. had manufactured its beginnings. C.P.S. organizers drew
crowds to the Forum taking care to vary the composition. Inhabitants of the Casbah dominated the people who chanted slogans
and followed the orchestra leaders on the balcony on May 16.
The following day the Haïks performed; on May 19 demonstrations from Saint-Eugène, Bouzarea, and El Biar, all suburbs, had
their day. But despite this partly synthetic fraternity there is
reason to believe that what observers saw in Algiers on May 16
might have been honest emotion given expression—a sample of
what the French might have had if they had practiced a different
policy fifteen years earlier, if, for example, the 1947 Statute had
been honestly administered as a point of departure toward a
future evolution.

Somewhere between the orders given by the French masters
and accepted by the Algerian slaves, between truth and the hope
for a different kind of a truth, there fell the shadow of real
fraternity. The shadow of a cease-fire and peaceful cohabitation.
But soon again the specter of the two absolutes reared its head,
the no-compromise of the F.L.N. on the subject of independence
and the refusal of the French to think of Algeria outside of the

French "empire." The few veils hastily torn off were probably replaced by irate husbands on the evening of the glorious day, and soon bombs thrown by the violent of both persuasions made red blossoms in the cafés. The grueling war became bloodier. The dream of de Gaulle, that the Muslims would believe his word, accept his amnesty, lay down arms and begin life under an ameliorated French order did not materialize. There was only this brief, pleasant, local and only partly real pageant of fellowship, this pathetic demonstration of loyalty and devotion to a hope invested with the name de Gaulle.

What seems saddest of all is that under an enlightened French community, the kind that de Gaulle himself seems at last determined to build, these Algerians could no doubt more quickly achieve the increased standard of living through technical training and educational advancement, material growth of industry and agrarian reform, and cultivate the art of self-government, than they could under an independent but struggling Algerian state. But the French vision of history, though glorious, has seemed in our time to be half a century behind realities; the Algerian people are no longer thinking primarily in terms of material things but of the idea of equality, the dignity of independence.

STILLBORN MINISTRY

Meanwhile back in Paris on May 14 the moribund Assembly was rallying to the sincere Republican efforts of Pierre Pflimlin even though the cause was already lost. Only one trump card was still in his hand. In spite of the work of Biaggi and the Indo-Chinese veterans, Paris was not mobilized for a revolution. On that day some several thousand veterans and *Biaggistes* were massed around the *Etoile* with a plan to invade the National Assembly. Fortunately they did not have the news from Algeria to spur them on or the manifestation might have turned into a serious offensive. "A captain of the paras with 200 men could have taken Paris to the sound of applause." [3] In the Assembly Bourgès-Maunoury gave orders to arrest certain known conspirators. Out of a list of twenty-two guilty persons only four were arrested by a very uncooperative police force. Generals Cherrières and Chassin, both connected with the "Grand O," were the first to be picked up. Chassin spent fifteen days at the Santé and at Fresnes prisons in the cell of North African political prisoners. A raid was made at 45 rue de Naples, the seat of the Veterans of Indo-China. There the police found a plan to take over the public buildings of Paris, the Palais Bourbon, Matignon, the Elysée and the prefecture of police. A raid was also made on the headquarters of the *Jeune Nation* and eighty people were arrested there.

Of greater importance to the security of the state was the destination of Chaban-Delmas, whose job was now filled by the strongly republican Bourgès-Maunoury, and, of course, Jacques Soustelle. Bourgès-Maunoury put a C.R.S. guard around all planes at Villacoublay in case either of them should think of joining the forces of the coup d'état. Apparently even Robert Lacoste was much tempted to cross the Mediterranean once more, but both Gaillard and Pflimlin convinced him that until a new government was stabilized or de Gaulle came to power he would be no more than a hostage in the hands of the army and the activists.

After much talk of a Ministry of Public Safety comprised of Lacoste, Soustelle, Bidault, Morice, and Duchet or a government of National Union headed by Mollet and Pinay (which would have been much less favorable to the events transpiring in Algeria), Pflimlin had finally been invested at 2:45 A.M., May 14.

By 4 A.M. the reaction of Algiers, through Communiqué No. 1 of the Committee of Public Safety, approved by Salan and read from the balcony of the G.G. by Massu, stood as a threat to the new government.

> We inform the population of Algiers that Pflimlin's government of surrender has just been invested . . . as a result of complicity of the Communists.
>
> We express our gratitude to those of the population who, as a result of the announcement made earlier,

have stayed up to greet M. Jacques Soustelle. M. Jacques
Soustelle has twice been prevented from coming to join
us. . . .

The Committee of Public Safety earnestly begs General de Gaulle to break his silence by speaking to the
country in the interest of forming a government of
public safety, which alone can save Algeria from abandonment and . . . from the 'diplomatic Dien Bien Phu'
spoken of on several occasions by M. Robert Lacoste.[4]

At 5:30 A.M. on May 14, after approving Gaillard's measures
of the night and day before, Pflimlin's team began to try to cope
with the revolt in Algeria. A special telephonic communication
was set up with General Salan who maintained that he had the
army under control "to keep Algeria French." All planes were
forbidden to take off or land in Algeria, and maritime cargoes en
route to North Africa were ordered back to the Metropole. On
one occasion Admiral Auboyneau, who was under Salan's authority, resorted to piracy. He seized two oil tankers which had
turned back towards France when nearly in Algiers' harbor and
ordered his men to unload the oil which the French rebels
desperately needed.

Pflimlin's government had five objectives at this moment. They
were, in the order of importance, to maintain union between
Algeria and the Metropole, to see that the army kept its unity
beneath a general who was "loyal" to the government, to avoid at
all cost a recourse to de Gaulle who had refused to denounce
the army plots or state that he would only take power under a
system of republican government, to consolidate his own ministry, and to avoid civil war. The basic confusion in this program
was that there was still much false information at large regarding
the nature of the coup in Algeria. At first the government judged
it to be a revolt arranged by Massu and Trinquier to which Salan
had later given his support hoping he could control and contain
it. It was this belief that motivated the government to arrest
certain generals, blockade matériel, and to try to cut off Algiers
from the hinterland of Algeria, and these orders certainly contra-

dicted Gaillard's early telegram to Salan. It was a consciousness of this double game which finally reconciled Salan to step beyond the limits of legality and put his weight behind the coup of Corsica, and even behind the proposed para-landings in Paris.[5] Since by this time, however, Salan had already given his nominal support to de Gaulle who represented the unifying element between the discontented politicos and the dissenting army, his actions cannot be considered as a bid for personal power under a military dictatorship.

What irritated Salan most was the change in orders from Paris. At first, on May 13, he was given command of all Algeria, and then of the Algiers areas only. The prefect of the Kabylia was ordered to set up a barricade between himself and Salan's "loyal" troops. The Kabylia had been for several years a strong bailiwick of the F.L.N. and nearly denuded of European population. To set up a barricade of a few Republican Guards on the road to Tizi-Ouzou against the whole of the French army was not so much annoying as laughable; it exemplified the helplessness and the foolishness of the central government, which apparently did not even know that most police and security forces were by this time in a state of questionable loyalty. In fact government control of Salan and the army was strictly imaginary. In spite of these difficulties once Salan had spoken, reluctantly or not, for de Gaulle, the main objectives of the rebellion were clinched. They had been the legitimation of the coup, which Pflimlin had unwittingly facilitated, intensification and spread of the revolutionary spirit, and army control, at least until a government of Public Safety intent on keeping Algeria French, could be established.

OPERATION SEDUCTION

De Gaulle had been ready to take power as early as May 12 if it had been offered to him. Between that day and May 15 it was only a question of means.[6] Apparently Salan's somewhat reluctant declaration of that date answered this problem for him and on May 16 he uttered the marvelously enigmatic

statement which nearly drove Guy Mollet and the other politicians of the system who were looking for a legal way to bring
him to power, quite, quite mad. The declaration read as follows:

> The disintegration of the state infallibly entrains the
> separation of associated peoples, anguish among the
> army in combat, national dislocation, the loss of
> independence.
>
> For twelve years, France, in the grip of problems too
> difficult for the party regime, has been engaged in a
> disastrous process.
>
> Formerly, the country in the depths of misfortune,
> had confidence that I could lead it back to health.
>
> Today, before the trials which once more increase
> around it . . . I hold myself ready to assume the powers
> of the Republic.[7]

And that was that. Parliamentarians gasped. The powers of
the Republic included the powers of the President, of the legislature, and of the Council of Ministers. The Communists sniffed
dictatorship on every breeze from the Mediterranean. The Socialists were indignant. Did the old Pétainist Radicals feel more at
home? Next came the overwhelming shock that General of
Aviation Challe, Ely's right-hand man on the general staff,
was heavily immersed in the troubled waters of the military plot
and that Paris was therefore in imminent danger. When questioned by Guy Mollet, General Challe declared that the army had
no real desire to take over the state, but that it could no longer
put up with the parliamentary stalemate of the last few years.
It would prefer an assault on Paris to the Pflimlin government,
and furthermore it was capable of occupying Paris in forty-eight
hours. This was straight talk.

Ely also claimed that it was not the officers of the general staff
who were primarily to blame for this state of affairs, but the
young colonels and lieutenants who were ready to revolt against
their senior officers if these remained loyal to the central government. It was Challe, of course, who had furnished the insurrection with enough planes to undertake the landings in France. He

had requisitioned them on the pretext that they were needed to protect and aid the beleaguered French garrisons in Tunisia in case that situation deteriorated farther. M. de Chévigné, minister of national defense under Pflimlin, upon hearing this report, sent Challe off to Brest and refused to allow him further communication with General Ely.

In the Assembly on May 16 Guy Mollet took a public step toward de Gaulle, and this against the wishes of his party. He asked de Gaulle to clear up three points: 1) did he recognize the actual government as the sole legitimate one, 2) did he disavow the C.P.S., and 3) was he ready to constitute a government in the traditional manner—that is, present himself to the Assembly and retire if he was not invested. De Gaulle of course did not bother to answer these questions. He said instead, "No . . . I will not enter into their games. I will not submit to their timetable. I have things to say. I will say them in my own time. . . ." Still, on the evening of the 16th de Gaulle declared that he would make another public announcement on May 19. Also in the Assembly on May 16 the government passed the special powers reserved for a state of emergency by 462 votes to 112. The Communists voted with the government. And in Algiers, as we know, had transpired the famous *"miracle passionnel."*

On May 17 came the resignation of General Ely, protesting M. de Chévigné's treatment of General Challe and his deputy, General Martin. Apparently, Ely's resignation was an important factor in keeping the army together. Ely, while he remained a government appointee, had far less control over the men of the line than he had in open disagreement with the Fourth Republic. It was unofficially and in secret that he was able to forestall an immediate coup against Paris and to work for General de Gaulle. Ely had support in General Faure, a strong Gaullist with the N.A.T.O. forces in Germany, he had support in Lyon, in Dijon, in Toulouse and with Admiral Barjot in Toulon. On the Côte d'Azur and in Bordeaux, whose deputy was Chaban-Delmas, Gaullism was strong in the army hierarchy. In the Metropole, then, seven generals immediately declared themselves in favor of the Algiers coup. They were Miquel in Toulouse, General

Cogny, late of Algiers, Descours of Lyon, Lecoq of Bordeaux, Manceaux-Desmiaux in Rennes, and, of course, Faure and Ely. Even some of the atomic divisions dismounted their equipment in order to transport it to Algeria. On the other hand, Jacquot, Commander in Chief of the French Forces in Germany was loyal to the central government and far from representing the viewpoint of the ultras in Algeria. In Paris General Morlière was a strong government man. Here the rebels were counting on the task force of Patton tanks under Colonel Gribius at Rambouillet and Saint-Germain-en-Laye. With all this open adherence to illegality there was of course much concern for the ultimate outcome of the rebellion. Would the revolting generals be heroes or face a firing squad? The longer de Gaulle waited to announce his intentions and Salan played a temporizing game, the more anxious all these committed ones became. Something had to give.

With the long and awkward shadow of de Gaulle hanging over the Algerian coup, the question in that capital of what to do with Soustelle should he evade house arrest became a bit grotesque. It is said that Biaggi, upon his gentle eviction from Algeria, was told to forewarn Soustelle that all might be better arranged without him. Not only had the army rallied directly to de Gaulle, but it seemed more than likely that Pflimlin's government would soon come to the same solution. Forewarned or not, Soustelle, with the help of friends and possibly his guards, was finally able to escape from Paris. In a relay of waiting automobiles he was driven swiftly to Geneva, and there met four of his closest friends and collaborators. Among them were Charles Béraudier, deputy to the mayor of Lyon, René Dumont, industrialist. Posing as newspapermen, after some difficulty they found a plane and a pilot—a Viking de la Balair bound for Tunis. This, so the story goes, they sequestered in air at pistol point and directed toward Algiers.

The arrival of Soustelle in the White City put Salan in a very awkward position. He was already somewhat suspect to the disgruntled activists who felt that he had come to terms with Pflimlin and the system. If Soustelle were not extremely tactful,

233

a new wave of revolt might sweep the lower cadres of the army and the *colon* extremists and force him into power in spite of his Gaullist preoccupation. Salan also had personal misgivings on the subject of Soustelle. There were rumors that this *Robespierre de l'insurrection* had been connected with the affair of the Bazooka. Salan had been the target. Curiously, or not so curiously, no one informed the High Command of Algiers that Soustelle was on the way until he was circling the airstrip of Maison-Blanche. Even as the plane landed the message was sent from General Bénouville to General Massu. It was, of course, intercepted by Salan and General Petit, whom Salan had kept beside him since May 13 as the symbol of the authority of the General Staff. These two rushed to the airport and managed to intercept Soustelle before he made a triumphal entry into the city which had been anticipating him, calling his name, for three days. Massu, also making tracks for the landing field, joined Salan in persuading Soustelle that precipitate action on his part might upset the resignation of Pflimlin, which they expected within forty-eight hours, and also the appeal to de Gaulle.

A somewhat chastened Soustelle agreed that he did not want to upset so remarkable an apple-cart, and he offered to leave Algiers or at least to remain incognito as long as the army wished him to. But it was impossible to hide the fact of his presence in Algiers. Almost immediately Delbecque was notified and he alerted the Committee of Public Safety. Quickly the partisans rushed about town with the familiar rallying slogan. "Everyone to the Forum. Soustelle is here." Delbecque then hurried to join the group at the airport, and so did Alain de Sérigny. Meanwhile units of the U.T.B., the *Unités Territoriales Blindées*, that military organization composed of colonials and army reservists, which had been mobilized permanently since May 13 to stand guard over the Committee of Public Safety in Algiers, and the reserves, rolled out to meet Soustelle. Salan, with his immediate perspicacity again phoned Pflimlin and reported that the Fourth Republic's wandering boy had turned up. He explained he realized that his duty toward the central government indicated the arrest of Soustelle, but he knew such action would touch off further revolt. Pflimlin exhorted Salan to do his duty and promised neither to resign nor to forgive Soustelle's action. Situation stalemate.

Then, later in the afternoon of his arrival (May 17) Soustelle made a creditable public statement to the people and the press of Algiers which somewhat cleared the air. Denying all interest in personal power he said, "I have no other ambition than to reaffirm the national unity between two sides of the Mediterranean." And again, "There are only 9,000,000 Frenchmen here." And finally, "There are differences [of opinion] between Algeria and the government," he said, simply, during the course of his press conference, "The arbitrator of it will be General de Gaulle. As for me, I do not yet know how I can be useful." [8] It was the performance of a wary statesman. He refused the proffered presidency of the C.P.S. and suggested that Muslim Sid Cara was the logical candidate for this post. It seems apparent that Salan, upon hearing this measured statement, made a decision to conciliate Soustelle. A strong pro-Soustelle line might have brought on a military coup resulting in a triumvirate of Soustelle, Sid Cara, and perhaps the popular Massu. A strong stand against Soustelle risked dividing the army, and this neither he, Massu, nor de Gaulle wanted. Even so, Salan was no doubt glad to know that Soustelle, during his first night in Algeria, wrote a letter to Colombey urging de Gaulle to act quickly.

Charles de Gaulle had promised a new communication to the country on May 19. Either with or without his knowledge there was an abortive attempt made to promote a May 13 in Paris on that day. Of course most of the Gaullists were unwilling to subscribe to it because of numerous reports that de Gaulle preferred to take power in strict "legality." Nevertheless Massu had sent officers from Algeria to the Metropole to test the revolutionary spirit of the army there; and the activists had plans to stir up the Indo-Chinese veterans, the *Jeune Nation,* the student groups, and any *canaille* that could be induced to follow in the wake of the excitement. Jules Moch, aware of the proceedings, had mobilized the available C.R.S. and had taken provisions against police arms falling into the hands of the army. During the

235

morning of that day patrol cars broke up gatherings of people in the street. The proposed Communist strike, protesting the revolutionary movement, did not mobilize in any great strength. At 3 P.M., with both sides relatively lethargic, de Gaulle appeared at the Palais d'Orsay in a peaceful Paris to give a speech before the assembled radio and television networks. The Brombergers give a moving description of the reaction some million Frenchmen might have had before the screen portrait of Gaulle II. "The de Gaulle in gray suit (civilian) and pearl gray cravat is no longer exactly the General of 1944. He weighs more. He is thicker. His hair has thinned out. His voice is less resonant, duller. He wears glasses with double lens. His features, somewhat coarsened, have taken on a mildly unctious expression. He seems a little more human also. One does not find in his present attitude the iron disdain (*mepris de fer*) of which so much has been said. But in aging he has become bigger than ever. His presence is crushing. His great nose, his long arms demolish the little screen." [9] De Gaulle said:

> What is happening at this moment in Algeria with regard to Metropolitan France and in Metropolitan France with regard to Algeria could lead to an extremely serious national crisis. But it could also be the beginning of a kind of resurrection. This is why the moment seemed to me to have come when it would be possible for me once again to be directly useful to France. . . .
>
> When someone assumes the powers of the Republic, it can only be because the Republic will itself have delegated them. . . .
>
> In Algeria there is a population that for years has had to face war, murders, attacks. This population has found that the system established in Paris is unable to solve its problems. Worse still! It has seen this system turn recently to the good offices of foreigners. It has heard a man, who, moreover is my friend and who happened to be Minister of Algeria at the time, declare publicly, 'We are heading toward a diplomatic Dien

236

Bien Phu.' It has seen crisis follow crisis in Paris, impotence added to impotence, the same representatives of
the same parties substituting themselves for each other
ad infinitum in the same ministerial positions without
ever coming up with anything clear, precise, and effective. How could this population not be expected to
revolt in the end? How could it not seek recourse for
its misfortunes elsewhere than in parliamentary combinations? This is inevitably what has occurred. . . .

In these circumstances, the Army, observing the
immense popular emotion, concluded that its duty was
to prevent a reign of disorder. This is what it has done
and done well. Besides, the Army is itself profoundly
affected by the tragedy resulting from the bankruptcy
of the public powers and inflicted on the country the
Army serves with great merit and sacrifice. . . .

I therefore fully understand the attitude and the
action of the military command in Algeria and I hope,
in the national interest, that the Army will remain
coherent and united, an example at a time when
examples are so few. . . . [The italics are the authors'.] [10]

When de Gaulle was asked by a distinguished assembly of
French and foreign journalists, who should have known the
answer from his speech, if he condemned the army uprising in
Algeria, he remarked that the army had been the object of
no sanction of public powers; that they had in fact been
delegated the powers they now exercised by the Fourth Republic.
When asked if his tolerant attitude toward the revolt would
result in a diminution of traditional Republican liberties, he
answered in this vein: "What makes you think that at sixty-seven
years of age I would commence a career as dictator?" But one
French political commentator replied: "Some men, like Molière's
M. Jourdain, who spoke prose without knowing it, speak dictatorship without knowing it either." [11]

In Algiers the news of this conference, in which de Gaulle
congratulated the army for keeping the peace and acting in the

237

national interest against a stagnating government, was read with some dismay. There was in it no word mentioning the formation of the C.P.S. or the pet theme of integration; therefore Lieutenant Neuwirth and Soustelle were obliged to rephrase the general's words on the balcony of the Forum. On the same day General Salan further upset ultra opinion by offering the rebels a new *Aman* or pardon. They were asked voluntarily to surrender their weapons and take part in the "new French Algeria."

OPERATION CORSICA

In the midst of this confusion, Pascal Arrighi, the Corsican delegate and accused Bazookist landed in Algeria. While Salan would probably have liked to see him behind bars, Massu wanted him for the forthcoming Corsican coup. Therefore the paras allowed him to sneak in. Unlike certain other ministers who were caught in the revolution, arrested, or placed in forced residence in or out of the country, he survived in freedom to help plan the next step and write a little book about it called *La Corse atout décisif.*

Since no one, either on the side of the Fourth Republic or the insurrection, was really sure where Salan's heart lay, the colonials planning the Corsican coup had not at first taken him into their confidence. Massu, on the other hand, had been aware of it for some days. Salan's position of authority, in the face of Massu's popularity with the army and Soustelle's influence with the Europeans of Algiers, was difficult to sustain throughout the effervescence of the early days. Upon learning of the Corsican coup, he had at first some doubts about its value. De Gaulle's speech of the 19th must have cleared his mind of worry as to the legality of the army's activities, and the feeling grew in him that a seven-league boot step onto the historic island of Corsica would finally arouse spring-fevered Paris to the gravity of the situation, convince Pflimlin of the necessity to resign, and galvanize de Gaulle into action before the less desirable elements of the revolution took over. So it was that Salan finally acted on the far side of caution. On May 21 he made his shortest and most popular speech which ended with these words: "Thank you for these complimentary words—'The Army to power.' But you must know that we are all united and that thus we shall march together up the Champs-Elysées, and we shall be covered with flowers."

The island of Corsica, having furnished more than 100,000 of its children to the European population in Algeria, had naturally been in a state of great excitement since May 13. Henri Maillot, a cousin of Charles de Gaulle and a Resistance leader who had helped prepare the North African landings in 1943, had done his part to stir up and renew Gaullist sympathy in Corsica.[12] General Massu had sent his Corsican brother-para officers pamphlets explaining the revolution of May 13. He urged the Corsican army to declare themselves with the French troops in Algeria and set up their own C.P.S.

By May 21 news reached the White City of the unanimous motion of the Pflimlin government thanking the army in Algiers for its loyalty to the central government! What this particularly unwanted gratitude aroused, in fact, was sufficient indignation in the "loyal" army to push it to even more unequivocal action. A para-landing at Ajaccio could not possibly be misconstrued as loyalty to Pflimlin's home team. It was the young Corsican deputy Pascal Arrighi who exhorted his people over the clandestine radio circuits now connecting the Algerian High Command, Corsica, and General Miquel at Toulouse, to set an example for the other departments of France by declaring themselves in revolt against the *Quatrième*. Pressure from activist centers in Algiers upon the C.P.S. to declare a directory under Soustelle increased this agitation. This became so strong and articulate that Massu himself was obliged to warn the Algerians against counterplots which might divert valuable energy from the main objective. On May 24 Corsica "revolted." "Were there any deaths?" journalists asked Pascal Arrighi on the day after the revolt in Corsica.

"Eh, no," replied the deputy from Ajaccio, "This was a revolution not an election." [13]

And once again the observer notes the not quite real, the comic-opera effect of this Twentieth Century French Revolution,

239

stage all carefully set, players well-rehearsed, and the main character all the while pretending, as he walked the gardens of Colombey and offered tea to friends—the desperate delegates of the Fourth Republic, Pinay and Mollet sent by Pflimlin and Coty—to be a detached member of the audience.

Henri Maillot had arranged for the meeting of some forty-three World War II Resistance groups at a certain café in the heart of Ajaccio on the afternoon of May 24; these men were to take over the prefecture which had already been warned it was to be taken over. A division of the First Battalion of shock troops under Captain Ignace Mantei supported the bloodless operation. Certain other troops on Corsica under Colonel Prigent of the IX Region of Marseille felt at first that they could not obey orders from the X Region of Algiers but were finally persuaded to go on with the show. The paras along with a mission from Algeria planned to meet and sustain the group of civil activists toward 6 P.M. While they were enroute to Ajaccio, came word that two airplanes full of C.R.S. sent by the Pflimlin government from Nice were arriving to forestall the revolution. But when these troops landed they joined forces with the paras, declaring that, *après tout,* they *had* been sent to maintain order. The local gendarmery formed a symbolic barricade before the prefecture, but when Maillot's men brushed past them their colonel cried to him "Vive de Gaulle, monsieur." In Corte the under-prefect greeted the C.P.S. with wine and little cakes; at Bastia there was a formality of resistance by the mayor's deputy, Sébastien de Casalta. Phoning Jules Moch, he explained to Pflimlin's tough minister of interior, that he had nothing or no one with which to resist the rebellion, and the story goes that Jules Moch recommended that he rely upon the old maquis! By evening of Sunday, May 25, Algiers sent its emissaries to coordinate the new revolution with the parent one in North Africa. Delbecque, Frey, de Sérigny, Vinciguerra, and Colonel Thomazo with accompanying journalists arrived personally to join Arrighi and expel the lone hold-out, Casalta. Although he begged them to put him out by force and save his face, they refused to do so. He became convinced of the need to surrender only when Thomazo

240

waved a telegram from Salan to prove that he, old *nez de cuire,* has been designated the new civil and military governor of Corsica.

When, a few days later, the news of de Gaulle's accession reached the island, the natives had a wild celebration lasting from Thursday, May 27, until the following Sunday. Everyone with a gun fired it wildly into the air. The paras were disarmed by the Corsican civilians, and tommygun volleys added to the confusion. It took Colonel Thomazo, who was an old fire-eater himself, several days to quell the spirit of mob celebration before too many accidents involuntarily quieted the people. But we go ahead of our story.

THE INVASION OF PARIS

In Algiers the original plan for the invasion of Paris was set for the night of May 24, the same day that the original C.P.S. in Algiers was expanded to take in the delegates of the Sahara. General Salan and Muslim Sid Cara headed the new committee as co-presidents, and Delbecque, General Jouhaud and Azem Ouali became vice-presidents. The policies announced earlier by Massu are here underlined: that is the necessity for every C.P.S. to be made up of army personnel and Muslims as well as *colons.* However, as news of the Corsican coup reached him, de Gaulle went into action, and so forestalled the first plan for the landings in Paris. By this time the government is in *extremis.* A frantic Jules Moch realizes that his forces could not withstand even a handful of paras if they arrived with the necessary bravado. A worried de Gaulle, even though he has reached no agreement with the central government, began to form his cabinet by telephone. Of course no one except the army leaders really can estimate how much of pure bluff and how much of actual threat there was in the para operation. Certainly the air-waves were kept buzzing with mysterious messages about "Puss-in-Boots" and "Ernestine is in the Kettle" which brought the sweat out on many a republican brow.

As a last resort Jules Moch appealed to the navy, but he had

241

no luck with the admirals afloat. Auboyneau, directly under Salan's authority, had earlier made it clear that he stood beside the insurrection. Other admirals felt that they had ties to N.A.T.O. which they could not summarily disregard, and, although they would not officially rally to the revolution, neither would they ferry Moch's strong-arms across the sea to pit against the army.

On May 25 two decisive letters reached Charles de Gaulle who had been trying unsuccessfully to arrange an interview with Pflimlin by means of Oliver Guichard. One, from the generals in Algiers informed him that they felt they could wait no longer than the evening of May 27 for the para landings in the Metropole. Furthermore, it advised de Gaulle that unless he represented the government—was, in fact, the new government—he could exercise no pertinent pressure against the coup as it was now planned. The other letter was from Guy Mollet who had disregarded Socialist party policy to make a personal appeal to the general. (The authentic version of this letter, which caused much animosity between Mollet and the Socialist party was published in *Le Monde* months later when Mollet withdrew his support from the government over the issue of Pinay's financial policy.)

Upon receipt of Mollet's letter, General de Gaulle took a step which must have greatly troubled his pride. He sent a message in his own handwriting to Pflimlin requesting a meeting in the shortest possible delay—a secret meeting. Apparently the proud man who had promised to wait until "they" came to him considered the situation to be desperate. Pflimlin who was still concerned with the M. R. P.'s judgment upon him for taking this step was relieved to hear of Mollet's letter. He also hoped to have his vice-president appear with him at St. Cloud to share the anti-party and extra-curricular political activity necessitated by the government's inability to function in the crisis.

Both Pflimlin and Mollet were agreed that de Gaulle should accede on two points before they could come to terms with him. One was that he must openly denounce the illegality in both the Algerian and the Corsican coup, and the second was that he must accept investiture under the terms of the Constitution of the Republic. At the last minute vice-president Mollet was not able to persuade his party of his personal point of view regarding de Gaulle. Instead of going to St. Cloud he was forced to hold a meeting with the Socialists urging them to boycott the Syndicalist-Communist proposed general strike which would only increase the difficulty of an impossible situation. Jules Moch militantly tried to refute Mollet's reasoning; he was strongly opposed to the party's participation in any appeal to de Gaulle. Once more Mollet found himself in a very uncomfortable situation. But his willingness at that moment to act outside of the framework of his party made the meeting between de Gaulle and Pflimlin possible. It is not certain that Pflimlin alone would have taken such an unpopular responsibility on his shoulders.

De Gaulle believed that the Fourth Republic, in accepting the St. Cloud meeting, was prepared to admit its complete incapacity to deal with the crisis and that Pflimlin would simply ask him to form a government, trusting in the Gaullist honor that this would be done astutely and in legality. He was surprised and offended to learn that there were still misgivings on Pflimlin's part, and strings attached to the offer. De Gaulle once more reaffirmed that he could not denounce the seditious in Algiers and Corsica until he possessed governmental authority. Thinking of Algiers' state of mind and the waiting paras, he became impatient and angry. Premier Pierre Pflimlin, on the other hand, thought in terms of the National Assembly and was fearful that de Gaulle could not win a vote of confidence before he had denounced the rebellion. The meeting was scarcely a success. It ended with the prospect of a meeting with the party chiefs at which de Gaulle could explain his point of view and perhaps win the support he needed for the vote of investiture. This, de Gaulle had promised himself he would not do.

But events were moving fast. Five hours later, although de Gaulle did not make a public statement condemning the army plans, he did make one which tended to delay the landing in Paris. It was another of his very personal and enigmatic pronunciamentos and it enraged Pflimlin, who had reported to the party that there had been no agreement at the meeting of the previous night. For de Gaulle now let the people assume, and most particularly the army, that a satisfactory solution had been reached between himself and the government. It was a devious and adroit maneuver, a coup of pure genius. It read:

> Today I have taken the first step in the regular *processus* [strange word with dramatic and religious connotations] necessary to the establishment of a republican government. In these circumstances any and all action from any source whatsoever endangers public peace, risks grave consequences.
>
> While understanding the provocation of circumstances I would not be able to approve such action. I expect that the land, naval, and air forces in Algeria will remain exemplary under the orders of their chiefs General Salan, Admiral Auboyneau, General Jouhaud.
>
> To these chiefs I extend my confidence and my intention to remain in constant contact with them.[14]

This message was carried to Pflimlin by Oliver Guichard, and General Salan received an even more explicit order, "Action foreseen is no longer envisaged for the moment." [15] De Gaulle was astute enough to send this wire to Salan through official channels via General Lorillot, the government's successor to General Ely, and one of the chief thorns in the side of the rebellious army.

After de Gaulle's paradoxical announcement there seemed to be a great relaxation of tension in Paris. The atmosphere which, as the French put it, "smelled of the paras," was suddenly clear of everything but tufts of spring clouds. Only in the National Assembly were there Frenchmen unable to face what was in verity a *fait accompli*. Once again, with the sustenance of the Communist vote, poor Pflimlin, who was himself ready to capitulate but unwilling to allow a power vacancy to develop, maintained a strong majority of 405 to 165. The M. R. P. refused to let its president resign. Neither Guy Mollet nor Jules Moch, although this latter had been considerably mollified by the attitude of de Gaulle toward the embarkation of the paras, was willing to follow his reasoning to its logical conclusion. It was the old story of the chicken and the egg. De Gaulle did not want to come to Elysée until invited by Coty (which would presume the resignation of Pflimlin) and Pflimlin was unwilling to resign unless de Gaulle was waiting in the wings.

Finally, after a moving and honest speech by René Pleven in which he somewhat brutally reminded parliament that the government, although it was legal, had neither army, police, or airforce with it; although it had a minister of Algeria and one to the Sahara these ministers were unable to reach their posts; although there was a minister of interior his sole remaining strength was one of censure, Pflimlin changed his course of action. Pleven's speech apparently was the last argument he could withstand. He turned then to President Coty and the old search for power in legality evolved a step further.

While Pflimlin went home for a long-deferred sleep, Coty continued to wrestle with the problem, his good sense and his conscience not always working together. This old man of seventy-six had for two weeks lived almost without repose, fulfilling his regular functions with a great deal of dignity and *sangfroid*. He realized that in Paris the game was not yet won for the Gaullists. In spite of Mollet's appeal, the diehard Socialists and the troublesome Communists had staged a massive rally on May 28 on behalf of the Republic. Depending on whether one read *Figaro* or *l'Humanité* there were 120,000 or 500,000 manifestants. The Popular Front, stagnant for so many years, was moving again, though not very fast. Very few ministers marched in the parade from Nation to République. Of course there were Mendès-France, Gazier, Daladier, Duclos, and Mitterand, who hoped to be the next premier. Eyewitnesses remarked that although the crowd was bursting with republican sentiment there was nothing do or die about it. The three powerful trade unions, the Communist-dominated C.G.T., the Socialist F.O. and the Catholic C.F.T.C. opposed the Algerian plot and de Gaulle's candidacy, but they lacked unity. The F.O. and the C.F.T.C. feared the Communist C.G.T. more than possible fascism. Thus no joint and concerted action came from the Fourth Republic's loyal strongest line of defense within the nation. No general strike took place, and a pale parade, with Communists bringing up the rear under orders to keep quiet and not show Communist placards, was the last feeble gesture. Not many of these leftists would be prepared to man the barricades against a military coup should it come. Mollet is conspicuously absent. He is negotiating with the great de Gaulle. Or at least, along with Pinay and Teitgen, conferring with President Coty about the power vacuum.

Coty had received another ultimatum from the colonels. The embarkation was now ready for May 30 at 1 P.M. The final moment of recall was set at 3 P.M. on May 29.[16] The key words to forestall the landings were "De Gaulle in power." For the previous forty-eight hours hundreds of officers in Paris had been mobilized and the activists had occupied key positions. Lagaillarde was in the city under an assumed name. Nascent Committees of Public Safety had been set up in the revolting prefectures; secure in their backing of local police, they awaited the signal to take over authority. Under this pressure a new mission toward de Gaulle was undertaken by President of the National Assembly, André le Troquer and M. Monnerville, the president of the Senate, who met the general at St. Cloud. While the parliamentarians spoke of the vote of investiture, de Gaulle offered a referendum and a two year vacation for the National Assembly. Once again there was no meeting of the minds and de Gaulle returned to Colombey in rigid disapproval.

DE GAULLE TO POWER

At eleven o'clock on the morning of May 30 President Coty took matters in his own hands. He read a letter to his colleagues of the National Assembly in which he offered his resignation against their acceptance of the leader of his choice, General Charles de Gaulle. Once again the colonels preparing operation "Resurrection" heard the news and stayed their hands to await further bulletins from Paris. Publication in the morning press of letters written by de Gaulle to Vincent Auriol removed many of the Socialist doubts, and President Coty's statement was not without its effect. Once again de Gaulle and Coty met, and this time de Gaulle came all the way to the Elysée. He avoided the crowd of spectators and journalists and entered a private door of the porte-cochère. Here, at last, progress was made. Charles de Gaulle made certain concessions. He agreed to limit the "vacation" of the National Assembly to six months and to meet with Socialist party heads, Auriol and Mollet. In a day or so de Gaulle will move even closer to parliament's conception of legality and offer to read his plan for the new government at the Palais Bourbon. But he refused to await the formal vote of investiture—and the deputies were obliged to address their questions to an empty chair.

Then the public was finally rewarded with the news of de Gaulle's accession to power. For the most part Paris was delirious with joy. Only the activists, the plotters, and the waiting paras are a little deceived, a little let-down. They wonder after all if de Gaulle has become the prisoner of the system rather than the figurehead of complete renovation. They brood on the near-miss of a chance for glory. Not until 10 P.M. come the orders to the straggling revolutionaries in the cafés surrounding the Hôtel-de-Ville to withhold their attack on that edifice. But the plot is only in disgruntled abeyance. As a delegation of Socialists headed by Auriol sounds out de Gaulle's thinking, an edgy army simply postpones the date of the tentative landings to May 31, then June 1, and then perhaps to a future time dictated by events.

Meanwhile de Gaulle completely wins over Guy Mollet and many of the Socialist leaders by explaining to them his liberal plans for the colonies of North Africa. If there was then some talk of the future political status of Algeria, it was not given prominent billing. This has leaked out slowly and over a period of time as de Gaulle felt he was able or forced to handle the situation. And then General de Gaulle took the one step farther he had promised never to take. After explaining his colonial program at length to the S.F.I.O., the most hated of parties in *colon* circles of Algeria, he asked Pflimlin to become one of his ministers, and Guy Mollet, the tomato-martyr, to be his vice-president. His projects appeared so liberal that a restless Right became angry and the Communists began to rally round. It is obvious that

247

de Gaulle forced himself to hold these party caucuses because he had to be sure of the vote of investiture. Once gaining enough Socialist votes, he knew he had sufficient support from the other parties to win the election. Even so, the investiture vote was only 329 to 224. Eighty-three of the negative votes were non-Communist. The speaker for this negative group was Mitterand, and he compared his followers to the famous 80 resistants of Vichy.

The Revolution was over, at least for awhile. With the exception of the chronic bloodshed in Algeria, it terminated without violence. Mendès-France justly complained that the Assembly had been forced to vote with a pistol at its temple, and certainly one wonders how successful de Gaulle's maneuvers would have been without the "Resurrection" waiting at his back. As the Brombergers say on the last page of their book; "For the first time also, a [French] revolution had been nursed by the regime it abolished and celebrated by the Chief of State who was retiring."

The people of France heaved a great, and for a change, nearly unanimous sigh of relief, and Algiers viewed with dismay and wonder, but still hopefully, this lofty repercussion of the coup of Lagaillarde and his school-boys on May 13, 1958. What now, it asked itself, would become of the Government of *Salut Public*, what reorganization would the French army undergo, and above all, what was to be Charles de Gaulle's Algerian policy? In any case, it was not on *their* shoulders anymore. It was for the "Grand Charlie" to worry about.

There were very few people who mourned the passing of the Fourth Republic, so glad are human beings to bury the scapegoat of their own error. Except for a few articulate men like Mendès-France and Jean-Paul Sartre, who wrote some brilliant articles in *Express*, everyone seemed metamorphosed into a happy, confident Gaullist. And yet the Fourth Republic was an honest government in that it sensitively and faithfully expressed the deep division of the French nation over the Algerian question. A chronic doubt, a moral schism gripped the country and its symptoms were evident in the plague of ministerial crises.

Although the impression the *Quatriéme* made outside of France was one of complete impotence, it had certain achievements to its credit. It had commenced the overdue modernization of French industry and economy, and made noticeable increases in industrial production. Social reform legislation was passed and certain steps to solve the critical housing problem were undertaken even though they did not go far enough. The beginnings of French integration with a European, even a world-wide economy were made. Though the cost of living was high, France's standard of living rose steadily, as did the long-stable French birthrate. And under Lacoste an application of the *loi-cadre* in Algeria had been attempted. What the French chose to do, or perhaps let the army do for them, was to relinquish responsibility, to renounce an honest failure, a democratic one, for a policy of unity of action in the hands of a strong man. That the strong man had a character of great patriotism and integrity somehow camouflaged the real nature of the French nation's renunciatory act upon which true judgment cannot be made for some time to come.

CHAPTER EIGHT

DE GAULLE'S MISE EN SCENE

THE CONSTITUTION OF THE FIFTH

Even before the French people had time to absorb their amazement over de Gaulle's coming to power, his government committed its first significant act. It demanded and received a mandate from the National Assembly by a vote of 350 to 161, and from the Council of the Republic by a vote of 256 to 30, to draft a new constitution for the French people. This constitution was to be prepared by a Consultative Constitutional Committee working with General de Gaulle, and to be presented to the French people on September 28, 1958, in the form of a referendum—a simple yes or no. Between June and the end of September, 1958, de Gaulle held what was in reality a blanket authorization from the parliament of the defunct Fourth Republic to act for all branches of the government and the French Overseas Community.

It would be interesting but beside the point of this study to recapitulate the last thirteen years of de Gaulle's views on the French Constitution as it existed under the Fourth Republic. Suffice it to say that he believed it to be the chief source of governmental instability. That many people agreed with him was also apparent, for at the outset, in October, 1946, the constitution was adopted by a vote of only 35 per cent of the eligible electorate. Thirty-one per cent of the electorate voted against it and 32 per cent abstained. Since that time almost every government had discussed the problem of ministerial instability which was directly connected with the division of powers under the constitution.

On August 27, 1946, de Gaulle made a statement to the press concerning this problem: This draft (1946) "denies the government the maximum independence and cohesion, without which it would be merely an organism divided against itself."

In their efforts to form governments, Edgar Faure (1952), Antoine Pinay (1952), Paul Reynaud (1953), Pierre Mendès-France (1953), and Georges Bidault (1955), had all asked parliament to consider this pressing problem. Back in 1953 Mendès-France put the matter in these words:

> The repetition of political crises is only the deep-seated sign of the malady from which the country is suffering . . . I do not conceal from myself and I do not conceal from you the difficulty of effecting these reforms . . . I shall ask Parliament, *the only judge in the matter*, to examine very soon the extensive constitutional amendment, so often announced, so often promised and so often postponed. . . . [In this statement the italics are the authors'. It is interesting that Mendès, unlike de Gaulle, intended to place the matter before parliament rather than before the people of France.] [1]

Although certain small amendments were made in 1950, and in 1955 there was a discussion regarding the duration of parliamentary sessions, expenditures, and proposed changes on the vote of confidence—the heart of the matter—in June 1958 these amendments were still not laws. It would seem that parliament preferred to keep its control over the executive.

The constitution which de Gaulle finally submitted to the people of France and the Overseas Community was much the same as that which he had envisaged after World War II. At that earlier time his concept of a strong executive gave a nation recently liberated from authoritarian Vichy a shudder of bad memories. Turning down de Gaulle's suggestions, a guilt-ridden and civil-warring nation took on its shoulders what seemed the least centralized authority it could find. Drafted by the Constituent Assembly, the Fourth Republic's constitution concentrated power in the legislature, the National Assembly, where the political parties enjoyed a thirteen year picnic. By 1958 the picnic ground was littered with paper and debris and the caretaker tried to give it some order.

De Gaulle's Constitution of 1958 was based on the following five principles:

1. Universal suffrage is the source of power. Both legislative and executive power are derived from it.
2. The powers of the legislature and the executive must be separate.
3. Government is ultimately responsible to parliament.
4. The government may ask the people to vote on the text of a law, or in new elections after the dissolution of the National Assembly. [This statement proves the degree of responsibility the government has to parliament, since the president has taken upon himself the ultimate right to dissolve parliament.]
5. Special powers in time of emergency accrue to the president at his discretion.
6. The President of France is also the President of the Overseas Community.

The president receives his authority from an enlarged electoral college comprising the members of parliament, the General Councils of the Overseas Territories, the mayors of France, and presidential electors of large cities chosen on a representative basis.

Parliament is composed of two houses: the National Assembly, elected by direct, and the Senate by indirect universal suffrage. The territorial units are represented in the Senate. Parliament will enact the laws; Article 48 provides that on the agenda of both houses government-introduced bills shall be given priority. If bills considered urgent or important by the government are not passed by one or the other houses after two readings, a committee representing both houses is formed to agree on a text. If this text still fails of passage, the Assembly is required to choose and pass one of the government's texts—the committee's, or the latest version agreeable to the Senate, or the Assembly's bill.

Of key importance in legislative-executive relations are motions of censure and confidence. The new constitution follows past proposals in placing on the Assembly the responsibility for overthrowing a government, not on the government for winning a vote of confidence. If the government chooses to stake its life on a particular text, that text will be considered adopted unless a motion of censure is filed within twenty-four hours. Motions of censure are difficult to enter—they require the signature of at least one-tenth of the Assembly's membership—and are even harder to pass. A delay of forty-eight hours must intervene before the voting. Then, when the votes are tabulated, only those favoring censure [no abstention is permitted] are tallied, and the motion loses unless it receives an absolute majority of the Assembly's membership. . . . The same members may not introduce a second during the same sessions, if the first has failed, unless the government decides to ask for a vote of confidence on a particular measure.[2]

Sessions of parliament were shortened to approximately two three-month periods a year, beginning respectively in October and April. Extraordinary sessions could be called at the request of the premier or the majority of members of the National Assembly. The tools of dissolution and referendum were also put in the hands of the executive further to delimit the powers of parliament. De Gaulle and his constitutional advisers decided that dissolution was the sole prerogative of the president in consultation with the premier and the presidents of the legislative branches. He could not use this right more than once a year but he could use it, by calling new elections, to strengthen the government in power, "to change the political complexion of the Assembly, and to bring important issues before the people." Parliament maintained the power to regulate civil rights and the fundamental liberties of French citizens, save in a period of exceptional presidential powers such as under the *loi d'urgence* now in effect.

The Government determines and carries out the policy of the nation and has at its disposal the administration and the army, navy, and air forces. It may not declare war without the authorization of Parliament. An important new regulation, providing that the office of minister in the government is incompatible with that of deputy or of senator, was written into the constitution.

The Constitution of September, 1958, instituted the "Community" between metropolitan France and the Overseas Territories. From the bulletin of the French Embassy comes this statement concerning the organization of the Community:

> The Community is founded on the principle of the self-determination of peoples. [Except for Algeria; that state was not given this opportunity]. Equality of rights among its members is ensured. The Community is consulted at the time of referendums. There is only one common citizenship. The members of the Community are represented in the common institutions.
>
> The institutions of the Community comprise: A President of the Community who is the President of the Republic;
> An executive body of the Community, composed of the Ministers of all the Governments;
> A Senate of the Community, composed of delegates from the Assemblies of the member countries;
> A Court of Arbitration charged with seeing that the common institutions function properly.[3]

There are many more provisions of the Constitution which might be mentioned, but these concerning the relative powers of the branches of the Government and the special powers of the President and the powers of the Community are most interesting for the purpose of our discussion.

On September 28, 1958, and the following weekend, the constitution was put to a referendum vote. 47,249,142 registered voters of metropolitan France, Algeria, the Overseas Departments and Territories, and French nationals abroad returned a total of 38,097,854 votes. 79.8 per cent of the French people had voted and over 80 per cent of them had voted *yes*. This was an amazing, a spectacular endorsement of the policies of General de Gaulle and the confidence of the French in them. (Of all the Overseas possessions only Guinea voted the *no* which guaranteed its independence of the Community.) The unanimity of the general vote contrasted greatly with the constitutional vote of 1946 which, we mentioned, only attained some 35 per cent of the electorate, and it augured victory over the parliamentary haggling which had split the people's representatives in parliament for more than ten years. Also, in a certain sense, it legalized de Gaulle's means of taking power, since it demonstrated the electorate's overwhelming approval of the man and his aspirations, perhaps even excused that part of his behavior which it could not understand. With such a mandate a government had no excuse for inaction. While the greater part of metropolitan France breathed a sigh of relief and shifted its pressing problems on what it hoped were omniscient shoulders, certain liberals, and, of course, the Communists, wailed fascism and dictatorship.

On September 25, for example, there appeared in *Express* an article by Jean-Paul Sartre explaining his *no*. He called it "Les Grenouilles qui demandent un Roi," alluding to the voracious stork king of Aesop's fables and the foolish frogs he gobbles up. Speaking of the various Gaullist points of view in France, he reproached both the "de Gaulle is the only man who can . . ." attitude equally with the "de Gaulle is the least bad choice among evils . . ." attitude, saying:

> They are mistaken. This vote of confidence in de Gaulle represents not power but impotency. A political leader has force when he is supported by his peers who have confidence in his *program* and will press him to carry it out. But the man elected by impotence, willful impotence, must refuse his electorate or become impo-

tent himself. This one wants to be the elect, the chosen one of everybody: among those who have given him their vote there are those who avowedly wish to use him to cover their fascism, and others, the left-wing Gaullists, who ask him to adopt, if not a completely leftist program, at least a liberal and social one.

Who will win? I am going to tell you. If one admits for an instant that there are fascists—and if one supposes which I consider very probable—that de Gaulle disapproves this brutal and vulgar form of authoritarianism, can one hope that he will find support against them from these neutral electors, among these 'yesses' for the least evil? Not for an instant. These people have taken an oath to find good in advance in all he undertakes and then have gone back to sleep. Fascism? Anti-fascism? They have no opinion and nobody has asked them to have one. They would softly answer: 'Oh fascism *with de Gaulle,* is the least bad.' And they'll go very far in this direction: whether it is their massacre, or a St. Bartholomew organized by the *commandos,* one can always say that it would have been worse without de Gaulle.

In the same article Sartre mentioned the Algerian war in this fashion:

But . . . things have been going very badly: Since the month of June de Gaulle has gone from concession to concession. Now the French government is entirely in the hands of the army. Scarcely several days ago the President of the Council announced this significant phrase: 'There is no dissimulating that the Algerian war will go on for a long time.'

And then Sartre inferred that de Gaulle must follow a prescribed course vis-à-vis Algeria whether he wanted to or not because he was virtually a prisoner of the army. The article ended with this strong statement:

256

Understand, one does not pull a country out of impotency by confiding its affairs to the omnipotence of one man. The only way to avoid these sweet-tasting but empty monarchical forms or the *coup-de-main* of the Algerian commandos is to pull ourselves out of impotency, to conceive our own program, an alliance of parties, a defensive and offensive tactic against all those who want to attack the French people. *Yes* is the dream. *No* is the awakening. It is time to know if we want to wake up or lie down.[4]

The Communist newspaper *Humanité* ran headlines saying THE CONSTITUTIONAL MONARCHY IS ADOPTED and sub-headings recalling that millions of Frenchmen said *no*. But actually the referendum was a large, if temporary, defeat for the Communist party. At least one out of every four or five communists left the party line to support de Gaulle. Considering the amalgam of communists with other parties during the Resistance, and the hope among all Frenchmen that de Gaulle might be able to stop the Algerian war, the shift in their vote is understandable. Indeed de Gaulle's referendum momentarily united parties of the right and the left; it was the beginning of new alignments. If it can be said to have achieved as unanimous a vote as can be imagined in a democratic election, it must also be admitted that the French people had left themselves small alternative to a *yes* vote.

The conservative *Figaro* on September 29, 1958, gave the largest part of its front page to a description of the Algerian referendum. Of the some 400,000 votes tallied, there was recorded an unprecedented 97 per cent of *yeses*. In Algeria and the Sahara there were 4,694,270 registered voters, of whom 3,751,522 or 79 per cent participated in the election. French governmental sources assumed that this resounding affirmative was a rebuke to the leaders of the four-year-old rebellion. It was cited as a great vote of confidence, not only for de Gaulle, but for the French presence in Algeria, and since the F.L.N. had maintained a rigorous boycott of the elections and resorted to both physical and moral intimidation, the large turnout at the polls was considered a psychological defeat for the rebellion. In areas of rebel strength, armed bands did try to keep remote Algerians from reaching the polling places, and it is a demonstrable fact that in the Kabylia, for example, the vote was less than in other parts of Algeria. The French government also made a point of the fact that this election initiated the participation of Muslim women in political affairs; they had been urged to vote by "progressive" and pro-French religious leaders, and by the administrative services of the French army.

Against the optimistic French viewpoint must be ranged the fact of the "civil supervision" of the French army. If, for the first time, and even now we cannot be sure that this is true, the ballot boxes were not actually stuffed in Algeria, it was also true that the activity of the army's branch of psychological warfare had never been so strongly motivated. The polling places were under heavy guard during the voting hours and tanks with loudspeakers toured the villages urging the Muslims to vote their *yes*. A report from Associated Press ran as follows: "The voting proceeds under the protection of the army, which, in numerous cases, transported the Muslims in trucks to the polling place."

The observers were not, during the first day, witness to any physical pressure. However, the presence of armed soldiers at the doors of the polls and the intense official propaganda in favor of *yes* did not create a democratic climate. "But," answers the military, "you must remember that we are in a country at war." And that is just the point all commentators make. How foolish can an election be?

The British *Observer* remarked:

> As the principal organizers of the vote, the officers of the French army were very much in evidence. They assembled the electors and stuffed them into cattle cars for civilians for a part of their voyage to the urns. When the mountain roads were too rough, it was in army vehicles that they were taken.
>
> Each elector who lived at a distance too far to walk

to the polls was conducted by the *harkis* [Algerian] military auxiliaries of the French army. At the voting place itself the soldiers stood guard and contrary to former instructions, several soldiers manned the registration bureau [where at many places the Muslims were forced to identify themselves] and the officers freely circulated in the electoral tents.

ALGERIA AND THE NEW POLITICS

And that is one story of the touted free Algerian elections of 1958. On the other hand, it was probably the freest Algerians had in a decade, and they stood to gain more from it, one way or another, than they have during all of French occupation. This cannot be denied. How much faith the name and program of de Gaulle resuscitated in the Algerian setting can only be guessed. One expects that a large and generally apolitical population like the Algerian Muslim will react in the direction of the greatest pressure. If the F.L.N. had been manning the polls, it is quite possible, even probable, that an almost complete reversal of the vote would have taken place. And that is why the whole idea of a free election in a country torn by war and pushed from each side by intransigent groups is ludicrous. Therefore, it is hard to believe that the French, in spite of glowing press releases, took much authentic pleasure or even consolation in the Referendum vote in Algeria, 1958.

One of the greatest feathers in de Gaulle's cap was the birth of the French Community. In this election the French Overseas possessions, with the exception of Algeria which has "special" category, were given the opportunity to vote *yes* for the Constitution and, bilaterally, for membership, temporary or permanent, in a French Community of self-governing peoples, or *no* for full and immediate independence. "This option was designed to place France's relations with her former Overseas Territories squarely on the principle of their consent to association with Metropolitan France in a new Community whose members will have equal rights and duties, France herself relinquishing part of her sovereignty to the Community." [5] In September, 1958, only Guinea chose independence, the other Overseas possessions voting heavily in favor of remaining within the new Community.

Before we leave a discussion of de Gaulle's Constitution which shadows the form of the new government and its policies, it might be well to mention once more the enormous powers of the president. In any time of crisis he is able to take over the full authority of the state. In normal times he is elected for a seven-year term by an electoral college with a conservative bias. The president appoints the premier, who is supposedly responsible to parliament, but ultimately parliament is responsible to the chief executive. The president can dissolve the National Assembly and call for referendums on special issues. The National Assembly *can* overthrow the government but only by means of an absolute majority vote against it. The power of the Assembly is reduced considerably by an article which states that a bill relating to a motion of confidence becomes law even if rejected by the Assembly, unless the Assembly succeeds in passing the necessary vote of censure.

So much for the framework. The actual running apparatus is also very interesting. The de Gaulle government of June 9, 1958, headed by the general himself, in charge of national defense and Algerian affairs, included both Guy Mollet, S.F.I.O., and Pierre Pflimlin, M.R.P., as ministers of state. West African Félix Houphouet-Boigny of the *Rassemblement Démocratique Africain* and Louis Jacquinot, an Independent for Social Action, were the two other ministers in the interim cabinet. André Malraux, the famous novelist and aesthetician, served as minister delegate to the presidency, and Michel Debré, to become premier after the elections, began as minister of justice. Max Lejeune, Socialist and old Resistance man, was appointed minister of the Sahara, Pinay, of finances, and Couve de Murville, minister of foreign affairs. This first cabinet showed little influence of the Algerian ultras. Indeed, the inclusion of Mollet and Pflimlin was considered an affront to the *colons*, and certainly neither Houphouet-Boigny nor Jacquinot were rightists in their politics. Debré and Malraux were the sole R.P.F. men to be given power at this time, and the

260

M.R.P. and S.F.I.O. members were in a majority; there were two Republican Socialist and one Radical Socialist ministers.

The elections of November, 1958, gave de Gaulle a slightly different mandate on which to form his new cabinet. Generally speaking, the same ministers were kept at their old jobs, but there were a few changes. With the elevation of Michel Debré, U.N.R., to premier and the appointment of Jacques Soustelle as minister delegate to the premier there was an obvious swing toward right-wing Gaullism. Among twenty-one ministers there were at least seven U.N.R. or old R.P.F. people, and a number of men formerly serving in overseas positions. For example, Jean Berthoin, minister of the interior, had been a director of the *Sûreté Nationale* in Algeria, André Boulloche, minister of national education, had had a post in the 1957 organization of the Sahara region, and Robert Buron, minister of public works and transportation, was a former minister of France Overseas. This right-wing and Algerian bias to the government was somewhat balanced by Houphouet-Boigny, Jacquinot, the enigmatic Malraux, who seems, if rightist, inconsistently so, and by one or two Independents like Antoine Pinay and Roger Houdet. The dominant Socialist influence quickly passed from the picture. Algeria was very definitely in the scene in the person of Mlle Néfissa Sid Cara, the new secretary of state for social affairs, elected on November 30, 1958, as a Muslim deputy from one of the suburbs of Algiers on the French Algeria ticket. Of the twenty-seven ministers in the government, sixteen were elected to the present Parliament, eleven of them as deputies and five as senators. "The following occupations are represented in the Cabinet: 9 high-ranking government officials; 4 industrialists; 3 professors; 2 ambassadors; 2 lawyers; 1 doctor; 1 writer; 1 broker; 1 journalist; 1 labor leader; 1 agricultural expert; 1 business man." [6]

De Gaulle, after the encouraging statistics of the Algerian referendum, had hoped for a widely representative vote in the election of Algerian Deputies which was also held on November 30, 1958. At this election for the first time in history, seventy-one deputies to a single college were to be elected by direct universal suffrage. The historical end of the "Jim Crow" assembly was here marked.

Four of the seventy-one deputies were to represent Sahara and the Oases and Saoura, and the rest the eighteen electoral districts which have been set up in Algeria. The voting procedure of this election was the same as for the referendum. Two-thirds of the representatives chosen had to be Muslims, and there could be no voting on a split ticket, so a vote for one man meant selection of the whole ballot. Civil servants and soldiers serving in Africa were not eligible to run for office, and in spite of the guarantee of "free" elections, no candidate to the left of the *Algérie Française* platform was allowed to run according to the French rules of eligibility. So, although the election was universal in character, and controlled by a commission set up by de Gaulle, no campaigning nor any right of assembly was permitted to Muslims who thought outside the French context. As in the September elections, the army was much in evidence, the *fellaghas* presented their own physical and psychological boycott, and the voting could only be called "free" by a great stretch of imagination. The results, a collection of French colonial *beni-oui-ouis,* proved to be a heavy disappointment to de Gaulle. One wonders that he could have expected anything different.

Although the elections both in France and in Algeria were hailed by Gaullist newspapers as great defeats for the Communist party, it was in fact, the Communists who gathered the highest return for a single party. In the first vote they defeated the U.N.R. by 1.3 per cent. (Communists 18.9 per cent, U.N.R., 17.6 per cent, and the runner-up, S.F.I.O., 15.5 per cent.) This Communist showing did however fall short of the elections of 1956 and 1951, at which times the party was pulling in a neat quarter of all the votes. What the vote proved was not alone an enormous tidal wave of opinion for de Gaulle, but also the crumbling of the left. Any coalition of the S.F.I.O. and the M.R.P. for example, could have easily polled more votes than the Gaullist or Communist bloc. The extreme right, in the Metropole at least, showed an encouragingly small 3.3 per cent of votes. It is interesting to see how, out of this percentage of party votes, the seats were later apportioned in the Assembly.

The first vote, which was conducted on the basis of absolute majority (over 51 per cent) for any single candidate in his constituency, only provided thirty-nine seats for the Assembly. Four hundred and twenty-six had to be appealed to the second voting which was decided by a relative majority. It was in the second voting that the alliances between parties were made, and candidates of several parties could pool their votes to defeat a candidate with a simple majority. The second-vote candidates were those remaining after the realignments had been made. Between the first and the second vote many socialists and some communists faded from the picture. The center and non-communist left, particularly, bore the brunt of the country's disgruntlement with the party regime of the last ten years. Le Troquer, Bourgès-Maunoury, Daladier, and P. H. Teitgen retired from the lists. Replacing some of these old hands were two generals, to wit, Generals Bourgund and Noiret, and three colonels. The name of Lucien Neuwirth rang harmoniously with those of Biaggi and Péretti. Defeated in the election were such anchors of the old regime as Faure, Lacoste, Pinay, Mitterand, Duclos and Morice. The most important missing person was, perhaps, Pierre Mendès-France.

In the second voting a wave of Gaullism swamped the center and left. The U.N.R. came out of this contest with 189 seats in the Assembly, to which can be added the 71 seats of the right-wing Algerian deputies. The Gaullists, with only 17 per cent of the first vote, therefore racked up a neat score of 260 seats. The Communists, on the other hand, who had 19 per cent of the popular vote, were reduced to 10 seats after the combinations which produced the second ballot. The Socialists, who had received the third highest original vote, lost support to the U.N.R., but still controlled a sizable block of 40 seats. Together the Moderates and Independents won 132, the M.R.P. and Christian Democrats, D.C., combined 57 seats, the Radicals and center left 35 and the extreme right 1. Whatever the titles of the parties, the elections in fact showed a considerable turn to the right, although one not sufficiently ultra to quiet the diehards of the Algerian Committee of Public Safety. From the Algerian elections things were even worse. Lagaillarde came over to liven things up for his May 13 comrades, Le Pen and Demarquet, and to besiege Paris with the French Algerian point of view. In the eighteen electoral districts of Algeria only three slightly "dissident" candidates were in the running. In most cases the Committee of Public Safety ticket prevailed without question, without even an opposing choice. No socialist candidates were elected even in the areas of Bône, Oran, Tlemçen or Constantine where they were known to have some following.

In the week before the Algerian election some 800 rebels were placed *'hors de combat'* by the French Army. Though the Gaullist wave certainly sunk the old National Assembly—only 131 out of 537 incumbents were reelected—it had not stopped the war nor softened rebel hearts. A statement of Jacques Soustelle, however, proclaimed the Algerian mandate as one of continuing support of the French Algerian policy.

> The country wished for a renewal and it is certainly not to be doubted that the Algerian problem has weighed very heavily on these elections. In a general fashion the electors have voted for the deputies who have promised to keep Algeria French, and have voted against the presence in parliament of those deputies which they felt rightly or wrongly, signified a relaxation of the bonds between France and Algeria.[7]

Meanwhile the work begun by de Gaulle for the French Community was beginning to bear fruit. Madagascar, the Sudan, and Senegal declared themselves in favor of becoming Republics in the heart of the Community, and Gabon and Mauritania opted for the same choice. The one French colony which voted for independence during the referendum, Guinea, under Sekou Touré, and Ghana (formerly British) under Nkrumah, have laid down the framework for the United States of Africa, in spite of the disapproval of both French and British statesmen. According to Sekou Touré, this action put into question "neither the relations between Ghana and the Commonwealth nor those of Guinea with the French ensemble." [8]

THE PROVISIONAL GOVERNMENT OF THE ALGERIAN REPUBLIC AND MORE TERROR

Perhaps it was the Gaullist revolution in France which goaded the F.L.N. to make a concrete and formal statement of its beliefs and to set up a framework which would deal more effectively with the renewed government of the opposition. Certainly the tempo of the Algerian war had not slowed between June and September of 1958 in spite of French faith in the miracle-working of Charles de Gaulle. In any case on September 19, 1958, the Algerian National Liberation Front proclaimed a free Provisional Government of the Algerian Republic (G.P.R.A.) to conduct the fight for independence from France. A cabinet headed by fifty-nine-year-old Ferhat Abbas as premier was announced at news conferences in Cairo, in Tunis, and in Morocco.

The cabinet list included five Algerian rebel leaders still held by the French.

Mr. Abbas read the following statement:

> I have the honor to make this declaration which has been made in Algeria and communicated to all the population on Algerian soil.
>
> In the name of the Algerian people the National Algerian Revolutionary Committee [C.N.R.A.] decided to form a provisional government representing the Republic of Algeria.

The new Algerian government is responsible to the C.N.R.A., which is the high authority of the Algerian revolution representing all classes of Algerians.[9]

> The composition of the Government is as follows:
> Prime Minister—Ferhat Abbas
> 1st Deputy Prime Minister—Ahmed Ben Bella
> Minister of Defense and Deputy Prime Minister—Krim Belkacem

Secretaries of State—Lamine Khan, Omar Ouseddik, Mustafa Stambouli

Ministers of State—Hussein Ait Ahmed, Rabah Bitat, Mohamed Boudhiaf, Mohammed Khider

Minister of Foreign Affairs—Mohammed Lamine Debaghine

Minister of Internal Affairs—Lakhdar Ben Tobbal

Minister of Armament and Supply—Mahmoud Chérif

Minister of Communications—Abdel Hafid Boussouf

Minister of North African Affairs—Abdel Hamid Mehri

Minister of Economy and Finance—Ahmed Francis

Minister of Information—M'hammed Yazid

Minister of Social Affairs—Ben Youssef Benkhedda

Minister of Cultural Affairs—Tewfik-el-Madani [10]

The First Deputy and the four Ministers of State are all in French prisons. At the time of Ferhat Abbas' announcement, it was of course well-known that the rebels had been pinning down a French army force of some 500,000 soldiers. Besides, the rebellion was complicating French relations with the newly-independent and pro-Algerian states of Tunisia and Morocco. Particularly was this true in the case of Tunisia, which harbored, willy-nilly, F.L.N. troops on her soil—a convenient spot for raiding the border areas. Not only the United Arab Republic, but Tunisia and Morocco recognized the legality of the newly-formed Algerian government, risking grave repercussions from the French with whom they were engaged in various negotiations concerning property and capital. Also, the states of Iraq, Libya, and Yemen recognized the new Algerian government almost at once.

France's reaction to the declaration of the Algerian nationalists was quick and sharp. A French government spokesman warned that it would consider any state which recognized the Algerian Provisional Government guilty of an unfriendly act. France denied that the Algerian government had any real sovereignty or representative value except on the basis of terrorism and assassination. A foreign ministry official said that France's reaction to outside recognition of the coup of Ferhat Abbas would be, possibly, the withdrawing of French ambassadors or the breaking-off of diplomatic relations. Whether or not France's reactions were correct or logical is a separate question. After all, the F.L.N. had for some four years managed to sustain a war which, during the later months, kept a half a million Frenchmen tied up in Algeria. They must, therefore, represent some segment of men, ideals, money, and psychological support. If France did not hesitate to think of the French army as a representative body—certainly it is so representative that it has practically formed the politics of France in recent years—why should not the F.L.N. as it culminated in the Provisional Government of the Algerian Republic, consider itself representative of its nationals? Certainly, under the formal leadership of Ferhat Abbas, the rebel movement acquired status which it had not previously had. In September, 1958, the French themselves could see in black and white how far they had pushed their ancient pro-French following, to what extremes the battle had now gone. Certainly the statement of Abbas on September 19 would not make de Gaulle's task any easier.

If the formation of the new government, which French newspapers and certain other publications refer to in quotation marks, was the high point of political activity of the season, a great wave of terrorism in the Metropole was making the French aware of the F.L.N. Striking strongly and in many different places on August 25, 1958, the rebels brought the war back across the Mediterranean. For the first time, except in individual family losses, the vision of France at war was sharply evoked for the summering country. On the same day the G.P.R.A. was announced, Algerian Liberation Front frogmen attempted to sink two French warships in Toulon. Though the men were caught and arrested, this exploit, and a bomb placed high in the Eiffel Tower (discovered by a summer tourist before it exploded) were perhaps the most imagination-catching if not the most successful F.L.N. effort to bring the war to the continent of Europe.

Damaging attacks were made against oil refineries, television

267

stations, aviation hangars, railway and shipping facilities, and particularly against the gendarmeries, prefectures, and *surêté* offices in various parts of France. Paris began to look like an occupied city. Gangs of police in squad cars or motorcycle troops moved in the areas surrounding *"bidonville"*—the tin-can village of Algerian workers in the fifteenth *arrondissement* near the abbatoirs, and D.S.T. in twos and threes stalked Notre Dame and Place St. Michel. At night they roared around in squad cars. Policemen holding tommy-guns in readiness stood behind concrete blocks at the doors of the prefecture at rue de Lutèce, only steps away from the offices issuing authorizations for visits to Algeria—very scarce at that time. Algeria was France but one needed an authorization to visit that province!

What the *Echo d'Alger* of August 29, 1958, calls *Rafles Monstres* in the "medina" of Paris—round-up for questioning of some three thousand North Africans in twenty-fours—took place. The *Vélodrome d'Hiver,* a Parisian sports arena, became an enormous internment camp. The trigger-happy police, victims of potshots from terrorist cars and home-made bombs thrown by Algerians, became less than careful with their bullets. They shot first and asked questions later. So it was that various nationals, some Portuguese, some Italian, and more than a few Moroccans and Tunisians were struck down innocently in the game of terror and counter-terror. Even American tourists took chances if, approaching from the back, after dark, they tapped a gendarme on the shoulder. Chases went on in the *métro* (subway), corridors, and bombs were set off in corner cafés. Saboteurs from Rouen to Marseilles, at Mourépiane, Toulouse, Narbonne, and Petit-Quévilly destroyed 10,000,000 cubic meters of gas and high test gasoline—two days consumption for the whole of France. At Rouen the damage amounted to 50 million francs.[11]

Dernière Heure, an Algier's newspaper of August 29, covering de Gaulle's few days in the White City where he was sojourning just before the referendum vote, "taking the pulse" of the second city of France, mentioned also the renewal of terrorist activity in Algiers. On that day a train full of French soldiers and munitions,

268

had been blown up between El-Kantara and El-Outaya. The night before, two grenades exploded in the heart of Algiers. In Grand-Kabylia were discovered four hundred Muslim corpses, men supposedly executed by the famous rebel chief Amirouche, head of *Wilaya* III, commander of some four thousand men of the regular (*Moujahidine*) army. General Faure, commanding that sector of the Kabylia, with an equal number of French troops while looking for the headquarters of the redoubtable Amirouche, who has since been killed, came upon the carnage of Akfadou. According to the French, the massacre followed a military trial under the orders of Amirouche, for defection from the F.L.N., the summary execution of some traitors, and a horrible death by mutilation and torture for others. On the back of one corpse was found carved the Cross of Lorraine, symbol of the nature of the defection.

Since the question of French torture has been earlier explored, it is only fair to add a description of Algerian torture. "Near the potholes was abandoned a cross tied with cords, clubs, and rudimentary '*casse-têtes*,' sticks covered with cloth (*étoupe*) which had been soaked in gasoline and lighted in order to burn certain parts of the body during the interrogation, finally, a basin filled with water to use in the 'question.'" It seems all bully boys have practically the same ideas, though the invention of electricity perhaps makes the French method a little more subtle.

In the midst of this renewed F.L.N. activity in Metropolitan France and in Algeria, de Gaulle chose to make his impressive tour of Black Africa, ending his pilgrimage in Algiers. There for nearly three days, which except for a policy speech delivered just before his return to Paris, he filled almost entirely with private audiences with people of "all tendencies" in the gamut of Algerian political beliefs. Or so the *Journal de Alger*, August 29, 1958, claimed. De Gaulle's spokesman did not divulge the names of those who had appointments with de Gaulle, but he did say that the majority were Muslim. We do know, however, that the list of people who informed and advised de Gaulle on that day was compiled by General Salan and his aides. If there were any F.L.N. delegates among them, no publicity was given to the fact. Indeed Algeria looked even more like an occupied city, which of course it is, than did Paris.

DE GAULLE IN ALGIERS (AUGUST 27, 1958)

The authors, eyewitnesses to de Gaulle's arrival in Algiers on August 27, entered this account into their notes that day.

Algiers, August 27, 1958

This afternoon at three o'clock on a sweltering August day in Algiers, General de Gaulle and his entourage arrived in the "Super-Starliner" of Air France (a Lockheed Constellation) at Maison-Blanche airport. Algiers was the last stop in a 10,000-mile junket which began in Madagascar and continued through the French African colonies, an exhausting trip undertaken by de Gaulle to whip up enthusiasm for his constitution which will be submitted next month to a referendum in France and the empire.

Earlier today the French Army in Algeria turned out in force to greet the Chief and to provide prudent security measures against the possibility of a National Liberation Front (F.L.N.) attack. At the airport, thirteen miles outside the city, a detachment of zouaves, of the notorious paras (the *"berets verts"*), and a guard of navy and airforce riflemen presented arms to the new French Chief of Government.

A group of city notables, both army and civil, many of whose names recall the "historic" coup of May 13, the generals Salan, Jouhaud, Allard, Massu, Dulac, Admiral Auboyneau and Barat, secretary general of the government, greeted de Gaulle in the broiling sun. A small group of hand-picked citizens from the French community managed to penetrate the formidable military cordon at the airport. The Muslim representation was almost nil.

Some hours before the General's plane landed, a strong force of French soldiers was deployed along the road to the city from the airport. On each side of the road, at fifty-foot intervals stood a soldier armed with tommy-gun or rifle. Troops were concentrated even more heavily in courtyards and fields where rebels might take cover, and at each crossroad were stationed

270

armed jeeps, small tanks, and hospital units. Along the road there were few civilians, either French or Muslim. There were sparse contingents of Muslim veterans and Algerian children obviously entranced by the military display, the flags, the posters, the air of fête. To a neutral observer the holiday atmosphere seemed far from spontaneous. Was this the coming of the conqueror or the conquered? Certainly, as one Algerian porter put it with a big grin, "they must be afraid."

In Algiers itself the French troops were only a little less obvious, and still heavily armed. Dressed in their Sunday clothes, the French population lined the streets, shouting encouragement to the man they hope can keep Algeria French. Dominating with his height and bulk the Citröen D.S. 19 (a black convertible), came the man himself, with his familiar and solemn greeting of the upraised arms, the "moi, de Gaulle." The tricolor hung from many apartments and public buildings and the new symbol of the Algero-Gaullists, made up of the old V for victory and the Cross of Lorraine was scribbled on walls along with "*Vive Salan*" and "*Vive de Gaulle*." Posters of de Gaulle's face appeared everywhere, a number of them defaced or destroyed.

Next to the display of the troops of "pacification," the most striking thing in Algiers this afternoon was the absence of Algerian Muslims. In the quarter of the Hotel Aletti there were only Europeans to be seen. The city itself, with the exception of the main post office, looked like Paris, 1890, and the cafés and restaurants, shops and cinemas seem all transplanted direct from the Metropole. There were fewer Muslims on the streets here than in most of the working class sections of Paris, and it was hard to believe that the French represented less than one-ninth of the population of Algeria. If Algeria is not France and probably never will be integrated, certainly Algiers is not Muslim, and the French population is not about to give up its beautiful city and *la belle vie* without a terrible civil struggle.

During the afternoon there was no evident F.L.N. activity in the city. At 8:30 this evening a grenade was thrown at the Bar de l'Opera (the third at this spot), wounding two Frenchmen. In the departments of Oran, Constantine, and in the city of Tizi-

271

Ouzou, there were skirmishes between the F.L.N. and civilians, and between the French Army and F.L.N. bands. Apparently, however, the organized sabotage upon gasoline storage facilities in metropolitan France on August 25 represent the F.L.N.'s main effort for the moment. But Ferhat Abbas, speaking from Cairo yesterday, promised that the F.L.N. would continue its rebellion in France, thus putting pressure on the de Gaulle government on the eve of the referendum.

The General seems to be attempting the solution of the Algerian problem within the framework of a large package deal. His new constitution will include a strong executive, division of powers between the executive and legislative branches, and a revised imperial structure based on the idea of strong local autonomy within a French "Community", or Independence. The special place of Algeria in this framework is not yet precise. There is first the obvious need to avoid another civil war between the Europeans of Algeria, supported by the recalcitrant colonels, and the civil authority of France, to prevent, in short, another military insurrection of May 13. Second, French Algerians (but interestingly enough, not de Gaulle) speak of the future "integration" between the inhabitants here (9,000,000 Muslims and 1,200,000 Europeans). This latter point will not be directly considered in the September 28 referendum, and taken at face value it does not seem attainable at all. Against integration stand not simply the National Liberation Front (F.L.N.) in Algeria which demands independence, but also the governments and people of neighboring Tunisia and Morocco, newly created independent states. Likewise from Cairo comes the cry for freedom. These currents, which daily reveal themselves here and in France through public and private forms of propaganda are re-enforced by the inability of France to meet the financial demands of integration. Would it not be easier, say the F.L.N., to make 1,000,000 Frenchmen Algerians than to make 9,000,000 Algerians French?

True integration is no more than a myth, perhaps it is the myth upon which de Gaulle's followers rely to pacify the European militants in Algeria. Politically it is doomed to failure because no

272

French Assembly can 'accept the presence of some one hundred Muslim deputies from Algeria. Economically France cannot sustain the necessary capital investment required to provide equal social services for the Muslim population, to say nothing of capital for industrial development and the training of a professional class. This is particularly impossible when the present costs of the rebellion in Algeria have to be projected into the future in the face of F.L.N. intransigence. Finally, the Muslim population in Algeria increases so rapidly—it is expected to double in twenty years while the European remains generally static—that the present political and economic objections to integration will be critically amplified rather than reduced.

The obvious alternatives are independence or autonomy negotiated as a prelude to independence, with the Algerian nationalists. It is unlikely that the F.L.N. 'would accept anything except independence. Short of conceding to the F.L.N., de Gaulle must expect to continue the war here, a condition which not only makes any negotiation impossible but one which also pushes France itself toward an authoritarian form of government and drains the nation's already strained resources.

In the forthcoming referendum de Gaulle no doubt hopes the 3,500,000 (round number) registered voters in Algeria will overwhelmingly endorse the constitution. This result, it is reasoned, would publicly expose the F.L.N. as a terroristic minority and weaken their support. It is unlikely that the F.L.N. will fold up after the voting regardless of the outcome, particularly when support from the independent Muslim states of North Africa is guaranteed. Then, too, there is the fact that the French army will administer elections in the village areas and free Muslim opinion could not be expected to fare any better than it did under the *loi cadre* of 1947 where the French presence, it was reliably observed, favored decisions the French could accept.

The heart of the matter is that a population of 1,200,000 European Algerians assumes that it is able to keep a population of 9,000,000 Muslims in a status of second-class citizenship. The question is not whether the Muslims are ready to assume the burden of independence but that they will no longer tolerate an inferior status vis-à-vis the French.

Even the conservative newspaper of Alain de Sérigny, *L'Echo d'Alger* devotes an article to the shortage of skilled technicians available in the city. In an earlier article in *Le Monde* the fact that three hundred schools have been destroyed by the F.L.N. in Algeria and four hundred closed for reasons of security is cited. The French army acting under the *Sections Administratives Specialisées* (S.A.S.) has now reopened three hundred fifty schools in which army personnel are teaching. Government projects of building and road maintenance employ 11,734 workers, but a force of 10,493 soldiers is required to protect these workers because it is these "collaborators," above all, who are the butt of the F.L.N. attacks.

What becomes apparent is that this handsome and prosperous appearing Franco-Algerian structure is held up at great expense by metropolitan France and by the often unwilling arms and backs of the 'draftees,' not to mention the tougher backs of the regular army. If we are witnessing what has been called the "Miracle of Algeria," this miracle has certainly come armed with tommy-guns.

THE CONSTANTINE PLAN

Early in October de Gaulle returned to Algeria, and this time, speaking in Constantine, brought home the point in this troublesome and "liberal" region, that Algiers was not Algeria. Both his plan itself and the choice of Constantine for the address were certainly rebuffs to the ebullient chauvinism of the ultras of Algiers.

At that city on October 3, 1958, General de Gaulle expressed his conviction, "that all Algeria must have her share in what modern civilization can and must bring to men in terms of well-being and dignity. But the loftiest plans call for practical measures." He then proceeded to outline a number of political, economic, and cultural reforms which he considered essential and which would be put into effect within the next five years. Among other things, he called for:

Salaries and wages in Algeria to be raised to a level comparable to that in Metropolitan France;

617,500 acres of land to go to Moslem farmers, and other measures of agricultural development;

the oil and gas of the Sahara to be tapped and distributed;

the creation of great metallurgical and chemical complexes;

housing for a million people;

regular employment for 400,000 additional workers; this goal to be attained through a public works program and the employment of Algerian Moslems in the civil service in Metropolitan France and Algeria as well as through industrial expansion;

enrollment of two thirds of the children of school age (more recent estimates indicate that three quarters of the school age population, or 2 million children, will be enrolled by the end of the next 5 years).[12]

Following the first meeting of the High Council in Algeria, M. Paul Delouvrier, appointed by President de Gaulle as Delegate General of the French Government in Algeria, and an expert in economics, gave the press a broad outline of the conclusions reached by the council in its first session, February, 1959. They were, in brief, to make Algeria part of the French Plan, which has been adapted to the Common Market. But unlike the plan for metropolitan France, the Constantine Plan was to be one of development rather than of modernizing or re-equipping. Great industrial complexes and modest industries became future targets and agricultural development was to be pursued simultaneously. Certain advantages have been offered to enterprises wishing to

275

found businesses in Algeria in the form of equipment, subsidies ranging up to 40 per cent, tax exemptions, and reduced interest rates on loans. All these benefits accrue to new businesses whether they be French, Algerian, or foreign. These advantages, in some minimum form, were immediately defined by broad groups of industries, and new enterprises no longer had to await complicated priority ratings and other governmental red tape which has slowed them up in the past. Also 18 per cent of the industrialists' payroll for social services was assumed by the state.

To create new jobs, residents of Algeria with capital and French entrepreneurs were encouraged to set up small businesses and factories in rural areas to help employ the farm population which at present work only a few days a week. "Textiles, leather, and food products will be suitable for this purpose." Irrigation projects, land reclamation, building of houses, schools, roads, dams, irrigation canals are all part of the projected work in the next few years. "The present yearly average of 20,000 new housing units will be increased fourfold to furnish housing for a million Moslems during the next five years."

The modernization of agriculture was perhaps one of the basic aims of the Constantine Plan. During the five years, 1959-1963, if the objectives are attained, more than 600,000 acres of land will be distributed to the Muslims, and enlarged efforts will be made toward protecting, reclaiming, and developing the land by soil conservation and restoration projects, irrigation and tree-planting. Local workers will be employed wherever possible on these projects to alleviate the heavy unemployment. Specialized committees were set up to carry out the plan, a committee for total development, committees for industrial, agricultural and rural, social and cultural efforts, and then a crew of local and regional bodies to help the superprefects activate the work decided upon by the superior councils.

The goal of development set by President de Gaulle involved a heavy financial responsibility. "Financial experts estimate that approximately 2,000 billion 1958 francs, $4.8 billion would have to be invested in Algeria during 1959-63 in order to achieve the goals set in General de Gaulle's Constantine speech." Private investment of *Algerian* money was expected to account for half of this sum. Certain moneys would be taken also from the Algerian budget and the budgets of local communities. "About one third of France's share of the financing will come from private investors, with the remaining two thirds being supplied out of the public moneys. Loans from semi-private corporations will account for 5 per cent of the total." [13]

A NEW PRESIDENT AND OLD PROBLEMS

On January 8, 1959, in the presence of M. René Coty who officially transferred his presidential powers to de Gaulle, the newly-inaugurated President of the Fifth Republic had this to say on the question of the Community and Algeria:

> The destiny of the Community: it is a question of giving life to this magnificent institution, which by virtue of a contract entered into in complete independence, unites on the one hand, Metropolitan France, together with the Overseas Departments and Territories, and on the other, the Republics born in the lands of Africa where liberty, equality and fraternity have flourished under the tricolor flag. *In the union thus formed, a special place is destined for the Algeria of tomorrow, an Algeria that will be pacified and transformed, developing her personality herself and closely associated with France. . . .* (The italics are the authors'.) [14]

The final figures of the presidential election of December 21, 1958, gave General de Gaulle 62,394 votes out of the 81,290 votes cast by the 81,764 grand electors officially registered. The Communist party candidate, M. Georges Marane, received 10,355 votes, and the Union of Democratic Forces' choice, M. Albert Chatelet, polled the merest whisper of support, 6,721 votes.

De Gaulle's remarks about the separate Algerian personality were pounced upon by both houses. The ultras claimed treason once more, and the liberals gave a sign of renewed hope. But soon came the fuzzy words of Michel Debré—a policy statement on Algeria full of patriotic phrases and duties on a "high plane" toward the Muslim brothers. Beginning with an evoked vision of the great economic and human potentialities of Algeria, particularly now with the great *trouvaille* in the Sahara, and touching upon France's absolute duty to remain the bulwark of the western world in the troubled Mediterranean through her "incontrovertible presence and . . . undisputed authority," Debré goes on to place the moral issue before the French nation. He says, "there can be no enrichment and social betterment [in Algeria] tomorrow except through the effort of France—France's legitimate presence, I say, is fundamentally established in relation to eternal values, because it is the only one inspired by a desire for human brotherhood. . . ." Now this is quite a statement even for a premier under Charles de Gaulle. It did nothing to attract the F.L.N. to de Gaulle's proffered "peace of the brave," but it certainly placated the ultras of Algiers and no doubt the French army, of whom it said, in spite of France's legitimate presence in Algeria, "there would be no security if the Army were not there—the Army of the Republic, the Army of France. . . ."

After several paragraphs devoted to the government's plan for economic development of Algeria-Sahara and French duty to lead the social evolution in that country—the education of children, the emancipation of women and the training of men for higher positions in the social and political scale, Debré had these remarks to make about the rebellion of the Provisional Government of the Algerian Republic.

> An armed organization—the leaders of which have taken refuge abroad, and who receive from abroad, along with gold and weapons, orders to kill without letup—has fought against us for four years. Who gains by this struggle? Let us say it aloud so that all can hear: it is to the advantage of all the subversive forces of terrorism and of racism, at the expense of law and order, of peace, of brotherhood. Does the September Referendum mean nothing? Does this great mass of people reaching out to

278

General de Gaulle mean nothing? Algeria has spoken from the bottom of her heart, and she has not spoken for those who have chosen the side of the rebellion, that is to say the side of hatred.[15]

The new governmental policy in Algeria was, of course, closely related to the new budget. The continued war going hand in hand with the government's great plan to invest almost five billion dollars in the construction of an economically new Algeria was, certainly, the most pressing reason for a new financial policy. But there were other reasons, not new ones, which made the government's action essential. For years there had been an increasing deficit in the balance of payments between imports and exports, and foreign loans were almost exhausted. Prices continued to rise while salaries were unable to follow in an equivalent fashion. Production had been lagging behind, and signs of a general recession were apparent. One of the economic problems which had been with the French since the end of World War II was the instability of currency, an inflationary situation which encouraged at that time and ever since, the activity of a strong black market and the hoarding of illicit fortunes. Mendès-France, when de Gaulle called him from the "Lorraine" Air Force and made him Commissioner of Finance in 1943, advised a so called "Crippsian" policy of austerity and stable currency.[16] Werth writes of it as follows:

> Little or nothing, in his [Mendès'] view, could be done about the black market and the 'illicit profits' accumulated during the war years without a drastic monetary reform. Only a few weeks later, Belgium carried out a monetary reform rather on the lines of the Mendès Plan, complete with the exchange of notes, the freezing of accounts and an instructive, if not perfect, inventory of wartime profits. One of Mendès-France's principal ideas was that the black markets would necessarily be paralysed, if not come to a complete standstill, if the mountains of currency in the possession of the *trafiquants* were frozen, or exchanged for new notes, only

279

progressively, and subject to various controls and checks, as in Belgium. This monetary reform should, in Mendès's view, be accompanied by appropriate measures to balance the budget and to draw goods on to the official, instead of the black market. But monetary reform was the cornerstone of the whole structure.[17]

In 1944 de Gaulle decided against Mendès's ideas. Writing long after this decision, de Gaulle explained, "The country was sick and hurt. I therefore felt it was preferable not to press its subsistence. . . . As for the experiment which the Brussels government had conducted so successfully, I did not believe it would work in France." [18] He found France exhausted from occupation; there had been no Vichy regime in Belgium, nor did he find such a powerful communist movement there to endanger democratic government.

By 1959 Antoine Pinay was to administer a financial policy which had as its heartbeat the idea of the exchange of notes and the "hard franc." The salient features of the Pinay Plan, which tried to take into consideration France's new position in regards to the Community, her membership in the European Common Market, her policies of "pacification" and expansion in Algeria, were as follows:

1. An increase of taxes on corporative profits (from 42 to 50 per cent), high incomes, wine, liquor and tobacco by between 20 and 100 per cent, and exterior signs of wealth.
2. Withdrawal of government subsidies on many articles of consumer goods such as household appliances, bread, rice, chocolate, preserves.
3. Reduction of government subsidies which financed many nationalized enterprises such as railroads, *métro* of Paris, coal, electricity, etc.
4. Change in the operation of social insurance for war veterans not in need, etc., to make up the deficit in pensions to needy widows, orphans, disabled service-

men, etc. A cut in free medicine and medical insurance.

5. The abolition of escalator clauses which lead to inflation of the currency.
6. Increase of 25 per cent in investments, the source of future wealth and opportunities for the youth of France.

Certain ameliorations in other areas of financial life, it was hoped, would make palatable these harsh measures of austerity. The minimum guaranteed wage was increased, and a 5,200 (1958) franc raise in old age pension accorded. State personnel were given a 4 per cent salary raise and a special fund was set up whereby a combination of state and private funds insured the future of possible unemployed persons.

All of these separate clauses were based on the theory of hard currency. Therefore, de Gaulle, lowering the rate of the old franc so that it was convertible on the common market with the pound, lira, florin, etc., issued a new franc worth one hundred 1958 francs. Hand in hand with the new franc went the opening of foreign trade, "thus emphatically restoring France to her international rank in the economic domain." Quantitative restrictions were removed on 90 per cent of French imports from O.E.E.C. countries (based on 1948 levels). "In this manner 250 billion francs were cut from the budget. The saving, however, was offset by an increase of 245 billions in state investments." [19]

The Rueff report, which de Gaulle had ordered prepared in secrecy and then submitted to the government, was the source of France's new financial policy. In February, 1959, the ordinances were loosed in a torrent upon a protesting public, which answered its disapproval of many of the two hundred and fifty measures, and complained it had not even had time to read them.

While it was true that the minimum wage was raised a few per cent, the general outcry was that the new financial program hit the pocket of the small-salaried consumer and relieved the tax burden on corporate profits of industrialists. On the other

281

hand, farmers, having lost government protection, had to pay an extra 30 to 100 billion francs in taxes. "Consumers' incomes, it was estimated, would be reduced by 95 billion francs, and retail prices would rise by about 265 billion. These changes, taken together, implied a reduction in all-over consumption by about 2.3 per cent." [20] New charges for postal rates, transportation, social welfare, and imports raised production costs by nearly 2 per cent. The left bellowed that austerity should not be reserved for the poor, and Mendès-France declared de Gaulle's financial measures to be the most reactionary the French people had suffered since 1935.

De Gaulle's concept of austerity clashed with Mollet's buried Socialist principles, and that unnatural alignment was finally broken when the latter resigned from the government on December 27, 1959, but agreed to keep the news from the press until the new government had designated a premier. By this act the President's loyal opposition was further diminished, and, in consequence, rightist elements were strengthened. A divided left and security-minded workers were content with making disapproving noises regarding the budget. They did not act. Neither of the non-Communist trade unions wanted an alliance with the C.G.T., and therefore no concerted action was taken by the unions. At a political level, the parties of the right and center were too strong. As a result of the new financial policy, a price rise of 4 per cent was felt by the middle of 1959, but currency was stabilized and the foreign trade deficit had been ameliorated.

A new Economic and Social Council was formed to insure economic coordination among private and regional groups in order to support the Gaullist economic policy. This council was to direct employer-employee relations and make certain of political control of the economic sphere toward the desired goals of expansion. In February, 1959, state investment was blueprinted when the Third Four Year Plan of Modernization and Equipment (1958-1961) was approved. The Plan of Constantine was integrated with this all-over state corporate venture.

The Third Plan hoped to insure an increase in national production of 25 per cent (above 1956 levels) by 1961—30 to 35 per cent in industry and 20 per cent in agriculture. Some 17,000 billion francs would be invested over the four year period; over 3,000 billions for housing, approximately 2,500 billions to develop sources of energy, nearly 2,000 billion to agriculture and fishing and about 1,500 billion to processing industries. Insufficient, perhaps, but sturdy plans to increase production of energy, oil, gas, and electricity were also formulated.[21]

But all of the investment depended on de Gaulle's ability to sell his idea of French rejuvenation and "grandeur" to investors at home, abroad, and in the Overseas dominions. It also depended on a belief that the Algerian war, with its draining expenditures, would some day end. Meanwhile, though serious plans to ameliorate the terrible French housing problem were projected, and the Assembly voted a somewhat illusory reform to French education, it was the low income families and their children who footed the bill for "grandeur." It is their sons who are soldiers.

The government's education program will extend compulsory education two years (until the age of sixteen) and provided aptitude tests for children between eleven and thirteen. At thirteen years a child must decide between higher education and a terminal course. But the program did not ameliorate the crisis of teachers, institutions, and equipment, all of which are in great shortage. Professor Furniss says:

> Higher education in France has failed to provide the amount and range of scientific and technical training needed in a modernized, industrial economy. . . . 'Scientific research in France,' wrote Henri Langier, one-time director of the *Centre National de la Recherche Scientifique,* 'suffers from two maladies: an insufficiency of available funds . . . and a complete anarchy of structures.'
>
> Remedies for high costs and backward methods can be found if the central government will relax its paralyzing hold on education. While continuing to set national standards for educational performance and assum-

ing the major financial burden, Paris might still permit more initiative and entrust more responsibility to local authorities and directly to the educational institutions.[22]

The concept of "grandeur," however, is perhaps not compatible with democratization of educational opportunities. The long-established hierarchical system in France, which practically precludes the entrance of working-class children to the few great schools, has not yet been overhauled. Has de Gaulle asked himself how, then, to rejuvenate a country if one does not educate its youth according to its capacities?

CHAPTER NINE

THE ELUSIVE PEACE (1959)

DE GAULLE APPROACHES THE ALGERIAN PROBLEM

During the month of June, 1958, de Gaulle began the delicate process of separating the French army from the ultras of Algeria, a process which has had many set-backs and is doubtful of achievement. In June the intemperate C.P.S. of Algiers, presided over by General Massau and Sid Cara, sent him a telegram putting words in his mouth, words which aligned him with the integrationists of May 13. Baldly it stated that the C.P.S. had been able to obtain from the government "the promise of total, unreserved integration of Algeria with the *Métropole*." The telegram also demanded that the *loi cadre* of 1958 which had mentioned the "Algerian personality" in contradistinction to French Algeria, be repealed and a "Jim Crow" electoral system restored in place of the "radical" single electoral college which had been agreed upon at long last. The telegram contained a further blast against the regime of parties at the moment when de Gaulle had succeeded with great difficulty in persuading representatives of nearly all political segments in France to join his cabinet.[1]

De Gaulle replied in no uncertain terms.

> On the subject of the offensive and untimely incident caused by the peremptory motion of the Algiers Committee of Public Safety, I remind you [Salan] that this Committee has no other right and no other role than to express under your control the opinion of its members.

285

The regular authority, and first of all yourself, should not be a party to any matter which this Committee or any other political organization may express or demand. Moreover, there is reason to make interested persons understand that the national task I have undertaken with my government demands calmness of spirit and open and reasoned support of all those who wish to aid me in preserving national unity, integrity, and independence.[2]

The happy news of the referendum gave indisputable evidence that the Metropole and the Overseas Territories overflowed with an enormous confidence in de Gaulle's ability to work out the difficult future of France. The French army had organized the referendum vote in Algeria, and the C.P.S. temporarily subsided under army influence. Until the address of Constantine all Algeria seemed to be wearing a Gaullist mask. Certain chiefs, active in the rebellion of May 13 were reshuffled; Jouhaud and Salan were soon brought back from Algeria. The latter, as we have already mentioned, was at first given the innocuous job of Inspector-General of the Armed Forces. General Ely, still enjoying enormous prestige in the French army, was persuaded to return to the post of Chief of Staff. Thus the man who would *not* keep a position under the Fourth Republic gave evidence of his confidence in the Fifth Republic and de Gaulle. In October Premier de Gaulle issued an order for all army personnel to resign from the various political committees in which the exceptional circumstances of May, 1958, he said, had unwisely involved them. "Henceforth, nothing can justify their membership in such formations. I order that they withdraw without delay." [3]

In spite of the general aura of good will during de Gaulle's tour of the Community, his appearance at Constantine, where he once again mentioned the "Algerian Personality" had been received with great coolness. It was remarked in many news reports that he sang the *Marseillaise* almost alone in his strong, reedy voice, before a mute and grim audience. Because the C.P.S.'s were technically dissolved and the French army ordered out of politics, it did not mean that hearts or wills or long-time political philosophies were changed. Obedience was obtained by de Gaulle, but the schism between the integrationists and the people who believed in the necessity of Algerian self-determination grew in depth. The attempted coup of January, 1960, almost two years later, in which the French army and the original ultras were heavily involved gave tragic proof of that.

For a year after the referendum, de Gaulle and his government seemed to be pulled backwards and forwards over the possibilities of Algerian integration. For many months de Gaulle refused to utter the word in his public discourses; on the other hand the speeches of Premier Debré, ostensibly in the name of the government, frequently used this term to describe the policy of the Fifth Republic toward "French Algeria." In the referendum the people of Algeria had voted as a single electoral college in spite of the outspoken attitude of the C.P.S. toward such a policy. In the Constantine address, October 3, 1958, de Gaulle had once more emphasized the Algerian personality and indicated that a certain amount of autonomy must be projected for the future Algeria. These were ideas that seemed disconcertingly liberal to some Europeans of Algiers. About the political future of the country he made two comments, neither of them mentioning integration, and both of them leaving him much room in which to maneuver. "To what political statute will this profound evolution in Algeria lead us? I believe that it is entirely useless to freeze in advance by words that which, in any case, action will little by little delineate." [4] And later: "The future of Algeria, in any case, because it is the nature of things, will be built on a double base, its personality and its solidarity with the French Metropole." Here, of course, was a promise to both houses, an attempt to please everybody except, perhaps, the Provisional Government of the Algerian Republic.

Soon afterwards, on October 23, 1958, he made his attempt to

287

reach the Algerian rebels. At the "peace of the brave" offer made in a press conference, de Gaulle stated:

> As to the exterior organization which we were speaking of a little while ago (the F.L.N.) which from outside attempts to direct the battle, I strongly repeat what I have already made known. If delegates are designated to come and regulate the end of hostilities with the authority, they have only to address themselves to the embassy of France at Tunis or at Rabat. The one or the other will assure their transport to the Metropole [remember Ben Bella!]. Their entire security will be assured them and I guarantee them their freedom of departure.
>
> Certain people say: But what will be the political conditions upon which the government will accept debate? I answer: the politique of Algeria is in Algeria itself. It is not because one fires a gun that one has the right to dispose of it. When the democratic route is opened, when the citizens have the possibility of expressing their will, there is nothing else that can be acceptable. Besides, that route is now open in Algeria. The referendum was held. In November there will be legislative elections. In March there will be elections of the Municipal Councils. In April there will be senatorial elections.
>
> What will come afterwards? It's an evolutionary affair. Above all, an immense material (and moral) transformation has been commenced in Algeria. France, because it is her duty and because she is the only one able to do it, has started the work of this transformation. As the situation develops, political solutions will become more precise.
>
> I believe, as I have already said, that the future solutions will have as a base, it is the nature of things, the courageous personality of Algeria and its close union

288

with the French Metropole. I believe also that this ensemble completed by the Sahara will be allied for the common progress with the free states of Morocco and Tunis. Sufficient unto the day is the evil thereof. But who will finally win? You will see that it will be the fraternal civilization. . . .[5]

The era of Constantine and the referendum marked the high point of de Gaulle's hope for a quick and early settlement of the Algerian problem. His offer of the "peace of the brave" was angrily refused by Ferhat Abbas, who until this moment had been making the most hopeful and moderate kind of statements from Cairo. *Le Monde* quotes him, just before the resumption of the "hard" approach as saying this of de Gaulle.

I know de Gaulle. . . . I know he is a great patriot and a man of good will. . . . He has promised independence to the Africans. For what reason should the Algerian population be treated worse? We are not the enemies of France. We wish, on the contrary, to cooperate with the French on the basis of new relations when we have obtained independence.[6]

De Gaulle's attempt to separate the "external organization" of the F.L.N. from the Algerian nation, and his assumption that the war could only be terminated if the Army of National Liberation would lay down its arms and submit to the electoral procedure which he had outlined for Algeria sent the delegates of the G.P.R.A. into another bout of angry declarations. From an attitude of compromise, they returned to the position that they could not enter into pourparlers unless the whole political status of Algeria was to be considered. Abbas declared that the "Algerian ministers will not journey to Paris with a rope around their necks. The army of liberation is not ready to hoist the white flag."

Six months later, after the discouraging November elections, President de Gaulle answered questions of M. Laffont, Deputy from Oran, in these words which seem to mark a return, either real or tactical toward the line of the integrationists. Upon being reminded by M. Laffont that he (de Gaulle) had not once pronounced the word integration in relation to his Algerian policy, de Gaulle replied:

> [I have not done so] first because they tried to impose it upon me. But what have I done since I have been in power and even before? In 1943 it was I who gave the right to vote to the Muslims. Is not that integration?
> But those who today cry 'integration' in the loudest voices are the same who were then against this measure. What they want is that we give them back 'Papa's Algeria' but Papa's Algeria is dead and if they do not understand that they will die with it. And since I have been head of the state what have I done if not assure the respect of all in the equality of rights, create the single college, proceed to elections which permit the Muslims to represent their province, open different public functions to the Muslims, not only in Algeria but even in the Metropole: Finally to begin the Constantine Plan which is the most important of all, to begin a vast employment (*'déclochardisation'*) program for Algeria. Is not this true integration?
> As to the political significance of the word what does it mean? That Algeria is French? It is useless to say that since it is true.[7]

On June 24, 1959, speaking to a different audience, this time an international one, de Gaulle extolled the French tradition of self-determination, stating that "the organization of the world can have no other base, unless man finally is delivered into the hands of totalitarian dictators." Perhaps in face of a world audience de Gaulle was forced to take a wider view of the problem. After all, during five years of war, according to French figures, approximately 100,000 Muslims have been killed bearing arms against France. How many more will die, or live, to achieve independence even de Gaulle cannot estimate. But surely this is already a sizable group, a group of élite. If pacification, as the French call it, is attained, and this seems to become more and more unlikely, then there will be at least one very important and devoted group who will have no right to help decide the destiny of their people. "In terms of a war waged to the finish, the right of option [promised by de Gaulle to all Algerians] will be nothing but a malhonest and hypocritical caricature of the right of self-determination." [8]

Alain Savary finds, in an analysis of the Constitution of the Fifth Republic against that of the Statute of 1947, a net decline in the concept of the Algerian "personality" and a retreat into the policy of integration. The Statute of 1947 stated not that Algeria is France, but "Algeria, though it is French territory, constitutes the sole part of this territory endowed with an elected assembly capable of legislating upon limited matters. . . ." Also under this statute the Algerian Assembly drew up and voted the budget for Algeria. It had the right to take certain decisions which adapted metropolitan law to Algeria in realms that were not specifically limited, under Articles 8 to 13, to the French Assembly.

In the new Constitution Articles 72 and 73 redefine the territorial collectivities of the Republic as communes, departments, and overseas territories. "All other territorial collectivity must be created by law." Algeria is given, therefore, no regular status and is dependent upon a special law which must be passed before that country has the right to an elected Council. Article 34 stipulates that the French Parliament handles all financial decisions. In restraining Algeria to this particular budgetary framework, the new Constitution, whether or not such was de Gaulle's intent, leaned toward the integrationist tendency rather than toward that of the Algerian personality which incorporated a high degree of local autonomy. [9]

Hidden in the Constantine Plan were, on the other hand, implications that de Gaulle thought in terms, not of a country colonized, but of a country learning to stand on its own two feet.

For example, in promising to allot 250,000 hectares of land in five years to Muslin farmers, de Gaulle obviously was thinking in terms of agrarian reform at the expense of the *colons* for there is simply not that much free cultivable land in Algeria. In promising to construct metallurgical and chemical plants and combines in Algeria, de Gaulle risked competing with the investments of French *colons* and Frenchmen of the Metropole. If these were interesting premises, the accomplishments, after a year under the plan, were not at all impressive. For example, only one-tenth of the promised land has been delivered into Muslim hands. At Bône a large steel mill, capable of producing 480,000 tons of raw steel a year was projected. But in spite of government subventions, direct and indirect, in the amount of 42 billion francs, the equal investment left to outside financiers has not been grabbed up because of the riskiness of capital investments in wartime. Very little progress has been made toward the promised employment of 80,000 more Muslim a year.[10] What has become apparent in the sluggish application of the Constantine Plan is that an underdeveloped country cannot be hauled into the twentieth-century by a so-called "modern" country unless the huge masses of the people are working for this end. The divided state of mind of the Algerian masses, not to omit differences within the French camp in Algeria and the Metropole, and the long war have made impossible any such effort in Algeria at present.

There are other signs of integrationist tendencies of the Fifth Republic in certain legislation relating to the departments of Algeria and the Sahara. Among these are laws proclaiming that the Algerian budget is a part of the French budget and must be voted upon by parliament; and that the currency of France and Algeria and the Sahara are one and interchangeable. "Also, the suppression of Algerian stamps and their replacement by French stamps gave a symbolic satisfaction to the partisans of integration."

In an analysis in *France Observateur,* July 16, 1959, Mr. Alfred Sauvy pointed out another important sign of the theory of *de facto* integration. He stated that efforts to augment metropolitan production of energy have been deliberately slowed down to keep France dependent on Algerian oil production. He suggested that this is also true in atomic energy.

> The end of the operation is to chain France to Algeria in such fashion that another politique in regard to that country would prove to be too onerous and full of risk. If the immense sums consecrated to that war had been used to obtain national energy (atomic, tidal energy, metropolitan oil wells), the energy problem would have been resolved today for France on the triple grounds of quantities, price and security.[11]

Savary adds that under the pretext of assuring the interdependence of the French-Algerian bloc, the government is tending to sacrifice the real needs of French independence.

The delicate problems with Tunisia and Morocco which have been occasioned by the Algerian war remain one of de Gaulle's most insoluble difficulties. When he took office in June, 1958, he hastened to settle the affair of Sakiet in a manner advantageous to Bourguiba—in fact his offer to the Tunisians was more favorable than that which the Anglo-American "Good Offices" missions had tried to obtain. France agreed to withdraw its garrisons from all parts of Tunisia except Bizerte by October 1, 1958. De Gaulle's government recognized the sovereignty of Tunis over Bizerte. In return, Tunis removed its barricades from around French soldiers and civilians isolated since the Sakiet bombing, and gave the Fifth Republic the right to build a pipeline from the oil field of Edjelé to El Skhira, near Gabès.[12] De Gaulle, giving more concessions than the poor old Fourth Republic had even tried to offer, gambled that he would thus woo Bourguiba from the Algerian nationalist cause. But this was only one, and a serious example, of the border issues that continually plague Franco-Tunisian relations.

Generally speaking, Tunis and Morocco have been obliged to walk a difficult tight-rope since the beginning of the Algerian war. Because they are both going through a crucial time in their development as young independent states, they need the help and support of French money and technical ability. The French try to force them into an unnatural neutrality and continually accuse them of too much complacency toward the F.L.N. The F.L.N., on the other hand, have been difficult guests using their terrain for many purposes in their war for independence. The Algerians throw religious, ethnic, and linguistic bonds of the Maghrib in their faces, and claim they have not done enough for a brother state, a Maghrib neighbor which is only seeking the same independence they have already achieved. Both Bourguiba and Mohammed V realize, also, that in some measure the freedom they won from France, which had in general allowed them, as protectorates, a much more liberal evolution than it gave Algeria, was, in part, due to the distracting action of the Algerian rebels. Even the most pro-colonial French army officer, after the defeat in Indochina could not argue the advisability of fighting on the whole Maghrib front at one and the same time. Therefore Algeria was chosen, for all the obvious reasons of deep French penetration over a long period of time, as the scene of the last-ditch stand, and Tunisia and Morocco were reluctantly given freedom.

Tunisia and Morocco cannot help but be miserably torn by the sight of their beleaguered neighbor. Perhaps if an honest policy of integration had proved workable, the brother states would not have felt the same kind of guilt. But the attempt at integration has in reality been the most schismatic element in the whole picture. If it should have, by some miracle, been acceptable as a policy to the Muslims of Algeria as well as to the Europeans, the other states of the Maghrib would have been torn for a different reason. Their geographical unity would have been split by a state whose economic development, pushed by heroic efforts of the colonizing modern power, might have rushed far ahead of their painfully struggling economies, thus throwing general doubt on the wisdom of the course of independence. So, in spite of all the French can do, both Tunisia and Morocco are

294

openly supporting their Muslim brothers with bases, with supplies, probably with soldiers, and most important of all, with propaganda offensives in the United Nations. On April 7, 1960, from Tunis came a resolution of the National Assembly denouncing "the aggressive intentions of French leaders toward Tunisia" and affirming the Tunisians' will to defend their country. Bourguiba accused the French once more of reviving the "right of pursuit" in connection with rebel attacks of French posts along the Tunis-Algerian border. A press release in the *New York Times* on April 17, 1960, mentioned still another bombing incident, still another protest note from Tunisia to France, and gave the official figure of fifty-four French border violations. Morocco's radio is continually agitating for the withdrawal of some 12,000 French troops left over from the French protectorate which ended in 1956. From Algeria itself came rumors that the French are expecting heavy rebel attacks along the Tunisian border as a result of the April speeches of both de Gaulle and Debré.[13]

When General de Gaulle first came to power, however, the states of the Maghrib and most of the states of the new Community went a period of great hope that the Algerian question would be settled. If de Gaulle offered the right of self-determination, secession, and independence to all the other Overseas Territories, by what logic could he refuse it to the Algerians, those favorite children of the French colonial effort? But until the declaration of the President of the French Republic on September 16, 1959, there had been little evidence of such an evolution.

DE GAULLE AGAINST THE GAULLISTS

Before a discussion of the statement of September 16, 1959, it is important to consider de Gaulle's views on the status of Algeria as declared at Algiers on October 12, 1947. They are particularly significant in the light of the evolution of his thinking. Here there is already evidence that he was, in general, favorable to the independent development of Morocco and Tunisia in tight alignment with France and her protectorates. After a paragraph devoted to the strategic importance of North Africa, he went on to say:

> But the well-being of Algeria lies in this, that France continues and develops there the admirable work that she has undertaken during one hundred and seventeen years. This work has been accomplished under her authority by virtue of her sons from the Metropole and by the work of others.
>
> These are the three elements which have made Algeria what she is. If France ever tolerates the destruction of one of the three, there is not the least doubt that the whole edifice will crumple and that Algeria will be quickly plunged in a confusion from which no one will benefit except the universal trouble-makers.
>
> The authority of France must therefore be affirmed here as clearly and strongly as on any other French territory. The Algerians of Metropolitan origin should continue with confidence all that they have undertaken without having to fear that they will ever be submerged. The French Muslims of Algeria should find in the esteem of our people, in the frame of French sovereignty and with their personal statute all possibilities of ameliorating their destiny in the degree that their country progresses and of exercising their capacities in the degree that they develop them. . . .[14]

This, of course, while never an ultra viewpoint, was decidedly integrationist, since it stressed the development of the Muslims within the French framework. But it is much different from de Gaulle's painfully acquired logic of September 16, 1959.

By the autumn of 1959 de Gaulle had experienced the disillusion of the November, 1958, elections of Algerian deputies to the French National Assembly. He should have been warned by certain symptoms apparent in the referendum, but circumstance forced him to consider this vote in its most optimistic light. The unhappy side was that, although an almost totality of yes votes was balloted in the referendum, the voting had been limited to less than three-fifths of the eligible population. The reasons for this were manifold. First, the F.L.N. had boycotted the elections with threats of reprisal. Second, there were rumors, after de Gaulle's "peace of the brave" speech, that the French government was engaged in some sort of negotiations with the Algerian nationalist leaders. These conflicting facts, along with the very real apparition of the army and the Europeans encouraging the integrationist or *beni-oui-oui* candidates, were sufficient to drive moderate Algerian candidates from the lists. For, how would pro-French Muslims fare after a settlement with the nationalists? And how would any 'liberal' Muslims fare with the ultra organizations of Algiers?

So, in spite of de Gaulle's promise that Muslims would constitute two-thirds of the Algerian representation in the National Assembly,—a milestone in historic evolution—the election was a dismal failure. It simply did not provide de Gaulle with a moderate or evolutionary element with which he could ultimately negotiate. Was it perhaps at this time that his thinking was forced into different channels? It must be admitted, that, given the situation of a country at war, de Gaulle did as much as possible to secure the honesty of the elections. He forbade all employees of the government, both civilian or military, to run for office, and thus several army officers, notably Thomazo, returned to France to run in the metropolitan race. He ordered freedom of expression for all candidates except those who supported an Algeria independent from France. But what he got back from the election was a large group, sixty-seven to be precise, ultras, and a few tired straggling Socialists from outside of Algiers. Furniss says of the election "French conservatives like Duchet were regarded as dangerous leftists in Algeria; Algerian candidates called 'moderates' would have been on the extreme Right in France proper. De Gaulle's efforts had not ended the isolation of Moslems from Europeans, or of Algeria from the Métropole." [15] So de Gaulle garnered for the National Assembly a hardy group of trouble-makers who were to intensify the integrationist stand of most of the U.N.R.

Meanwhile, as de Gaulle watched anxiously for the sign of moderate evolution, of confidence in him, to become apparent in the "free" elections of Algeria, Premier Michel Debré was expounding his particular view of the Algerian problem before the National Assembly. On January 17, 1959, he stated not without incredible ego:

> France is in Algeria by virtue of a fundamental necessity that our ancestors knew and that we cannot misunderstand without betraying. . . . French legitimacy in Algeria is truth beyond the fact that Algeria is a common creation of diverse elements which were soldered and founded by the action of France, beyond that other fact that tomorrow there can only be an enriching and an amelioration (social) by the effort of France; French legitimacy I say is fundamentally established in regard to the eternal values because it is the sole which is inspired by the will toward human fraternity.[16]

Speaking of the rebel government of the Algerian Nationalists, whom even de Gaulle declared had lost 100,000 fighting men in the struggle, he made this rather stupid statement before the Senate on June 24, 1959.

> Negotiate? but with whom? a pseudo-government which does not represent Algeria, is made up only of prisoners, prisoners of themselves—prisoners of the rebels. Its members have not come forward to negotiate because they represent nothing and cannot present themselves before us at the hour when Algeria forges an élite and affirms her faith.[17]

Algeria has indeed forged an élite, and she affirms her faith. But this élite is not made up of integrationist ultras, fascist-minded army colonels, and *beni-oui-ouis*. One cannot help pitying de Gaulle whenever this man speaks in such a vein for the government. It is fortunate that the President's faith resides in the sovereignty of the people of France and not in their justly elected delegates.

In May, 1959, the Senatorial elections were held and oddly enough, most ultras of the secessionist or fascist kind were defeated. But this one happy straw in the wind did not markedly alter the picture which had by then taken shape. President de Gaulle, with the best will in the world, much strength and subtlety, was not going to end the Algerian war in the near future.

With his Premier running off at the mouth in favor of an integration he had never formally espoused, what was de Gaulle's army, the army subservient to the will of the French state, doing these days? It was, it appeared, doing the same old thing. Having brought de Gaulle to power on the theme of integration and French Algeria, it would have been strange if it had not gone quietly on its subversive way in spite of the official banning of army men from political activities. Before the referendum vote in Algeria, Salan, who still held both civil and military power in Algiers, sent out the following directive:

> This campaign will unfold in three phases.
> First phase: Phase of psychological shock for mass inscription on the electoral lists.
> Second phase: Phase of putting in condition and maintaining the integration of spirits which will permit General de Gaulle to decide upon the integration of institutions.

and farther on:

> Integration de Gaulle; integration peace refound; integration country rediscovered, integration *"Français à part entière."* . . .[18]

After the referendum de Gaulle's prestige was at an all-time high, and the French army could afford to sit for awhile and await possible developments. The formation of the Provisional Government of the Algerian Republic announced on September 19, 1958, under the presidency of 'moderate' Ferhat Abbas, and the subsequent statement from Cairo on September 26, 1958, that the Algerians were "ready to negotiate" with France, and that "the independence of Algeria is in no way an obstacle to the

establishment of new relations between France and Algeria"
were straws in a wind which might blow toward a cease-fire. De
Gaulle's settlement of the Sakiet affair with Tunisia, had certainly
been as liberal an action as the Maghrib could hope for. Compromise was in the air. When de Gaulle ordered all French
officers to resign from the Committee of Public Safety in Algiers,
therefore, Major-General Jacques Massu and eleven other officers
complied. In October, too, the All-Algeria C.P.S. dissolved, but
it regrouped to form the Organization of Public Safety Committees.

But in October came de Gaulle's first set-back. The Provisional Government of the Algerian Republic turned down his
"peace of the brave" offer and the Algerian war returned to
status quo. This meant, unfortunately, a renewal of the army's
activity in the old pattern. By December, 1958, General Salan,
soon to be replaced, published a directive which demanded of
the army that all élites unite in order to participate in the realization of the government's plan.

> It is indispensable that associations, circles, reunions of
> the French of Algeria, of all origins and of all conditions,
> be multiplied . . . so that they can discover together,
> strong in their unity, the solutions to the problems posed
> by the evolution of Algeria and its definitive accession to
> the rank of French province (*à part entière*).[19]

We were later to know of the activity and the multiplicity of
these French reunions officially sponsored by an army directive
soon after de Gaulle had ordered the army to return to its non-
political role.

By this time it had become apparent on both sides that there
was no turning back. In November, 1958, the election of ultra
and *beni-oui-oui* deputies from Algeria once more increased the
army's responsibility to protect and foster that part of the Algerian community which had committed itself to France. As
political and social integration proceeded, the devotion of the
army became even more unequivocal. New army spokesman in

300

Algeria, General Challe, who had on December 12, 1958, replaced Salan, made statements to the press insisting that the French government had gone as far as it could vis-à-vis the F.L.N. in the October offer. By April 22, 1959, he cautiously ventured in *Le Monde:* "I estimate that there is a possible military solution to the Algerian affair, because the barricades [of electrified wire] at the frontiers are fulfilling their role and it is possible to get rid of the adversary quite rapidly." But he also said that if the war should be won, the mission that General de Gaulle had confided to the army would be of long duration. It is true that while de Gaulle was, during the course of the year 1958-1959, evolving towards the policy of September 16—the offer of self-determination—he was also reassuring the army that there would be no vote on this question until pacification was complete—namely, a conclusive military victory. And the army was matching the new intransigence of the F.L.N. with its own resolution. The Challe Plan became the military answer to the rebels, and the continuous plots in which the army mixed were evidence of its refusal to abstain from politics or to accept the self-determination formula.

Early in 1959 it was apparent that a kind of military stalemate was reached. If the French penetrated an area in numbers, regrouped the inhabitants and chased out the F.L.N. (the application of the Challe Plan), they could hold on to that area just as long as they did not reduce their effectives. But the moment they moved on, the F.L.N. crept back and reinhabited the "pacified" area. If, as a result of the new electric frontier barriers and the increased French offensive, the Army of National Liberation did not make the sizable sorties against the French in 1959 that it made in 1957, it continued to make numerous guerrilla raids. If its numbers were seriously depleted in these raids, the next guerrilla band had garnered replacements from somewhere. Perhaps the new men were younger and less trained, but the F.L.N. seemed to be able to recruit an endless number of young Muslims to its banners. If, apparently in the cities, terrorism declined for awhile, if life seemed normal, even burgeoning with reconstruction and "business as usual," beneath the surface of Algerian life festered enormous numbers of Muslim arrests and persecutions, and the unhealthy swelling of the camps of *hébergement*.

THE POSITION OF THE ALGERIAN REBELS
VIS-A-VIS DE GAULLE

When de Gaulle became President of France in January, 1959, he offered clemency to thousands of political prisoners who were held without specific charges. A number of unexpiated death penalties were also revoked by him. If at this time the F.L.N. had any hopes of a cease-fire, they were closely and uniquely connected to de Gaulle, the one Frenchman who had kept his word in North African dealings in the last two decades. But under de Gaulle there was still the French army to deal with, and many proofs that the leader and his military were often working at cross purposes. Although it is recorded that de Gaulle has freed some one thousand Algerian suspects per month from camps of interrogation and internment, the French army and the French police managed to find a new thousand each month to put in their place. In sum total there were in 1960 more Algerians in prisons and places of forced residence than there have been at any time since the start of the revolution. If there is one certain fact about the Algerian problem, it is that it does not get simpler, or better.

In January, 1959, Mohammed Yazid, Information Minister of the G.P.R.A., announced that it had become evident that "Debré's government"—in spite of certain befogging subtleties of General de Gaulle—was supporting the position of French Algeria. By this statement he ignored de Gaulle's new offer of cease-fire on January 30. Other press stories questioned the possibility of an open rupture between de Gaulle and his government over Algerian policy. The Lauriol Report, with its integrationist measures, emphasized the right-wing stance of the Debré forces, and rumors of an open schism between the premier and de Gaulle, who was tentatively offering hope of a more moderate solution, were rife. That government tensions were unresolved was apparent in the speech of January 30, 1959, in which de Gaulle made his first reference to a political solution of the Algerian problem.

Jean Daniel of the *Express*, in a long interview with four of the principal members of the Algerian Provisional Government, which by this date had established headquarters in Tunis and Rabat, had these points to make on February 5 on the "Case of de Gaulle" and the rebels.

> In the discourses and proclamations [of de Gaulle] . . . the word integration was in effect absent, but the actuality of integration is more concrete than ever. With the Sahara enterprise France in Algeria becomes spectacularly enracinated; with the Constantine Plan they are drowning the political solution. The Socialists, they wanted a cease-fire before elections. De Gaulle held elections without a cease-fire and he allowed integrationist deputies to be elected with the help of the army.[20]

The same spokesman also said that there had been no direct envoys sent from the French government under de Gaulle. M. Pompidou from the French side and certain members of the F.L.N. address letters through channels to moderate Algerians of "good will." France uses the embassies of Morocco and Tunis to forward information to the G.P.R.A. This procedure contrasted strongly with that of the Government of the Fourth Republic under Guy Mollet and was less satisfactory since it made chances of agreement that much more remote. By February, 1959, the Algerian rebels had concluded that de Gaulle would continue to fight, not with a belief in total military victory, but because he still hoped for a mysterious and miraculous *ralliement* of the Muslims in his name. This meant that the rebels would continue to fight. They were not deluding themselves, either, that they

303

could decisively defeat a French Army of 500,000 men, but time and public opinion and, they thought, justice, was on their side.

> This [de Gaulle's] idea that one could demand of them to wipe away all they had accomplished and to recommence, simply because France has a prestidigious President, is an idea that seemed unbelievable. . . .
> Even if to make an absurd supposition, we would decide to put our faith in the hands of de Gaulle, thinking that he alone would be able to lead us toward constructive independence, economic and all; even if this treason towards our *maquisards* should be committed, we cannot forget that de Gaulle is not God, that he is not eternal, that we read the French newspapers, that we see those who prepare to succeed him: our worse enemies, and if to achieve the little that he has done actually in the good direction, he is constrained to make so many compromises and disagreeable maneuvers, then one sees very well what will, without him, become of the situation.
>
> However, one has at times the impression that he would be really disposed to recognize the North African complex, this complex which would at least permit one thing. We are disposed to make more concessions to the trio Tunis, Morocco, France. It is for that reason that we have installed ourselves in North Africa and no other place. It is because if there is even a small chance to advance things politically, we will not let it pass, and contrary to what has been said, we want to do everything to stop this war which provokes so many misfortunes.[21]

On February 12, 1959, Jean Daniel wrote to the *Express* from Algiers:

> All this is very fine [possibility of a politique of peace] but we [the Algerian citizens] have the most precise

kind of disquiet. We have not yet finished with plots, agitation, factious groups. The flux of the new politique plunges certain military circles in confusion and gives courage to the agitators.

And,

> The latest terrorist attempts in the Algerian capital are the work of Europeans belonging to ultra groups. . . . In brief, in the fifth year of the war, we must restate the simple fact that any political beginning in any sense of the word, cannot be attempted until the problem of Algiers—and the power it represents—is resolved.[22]

In the same month General Challe announced these figures on war casualties: January 1-February 12, 1959—the French killed 2,500 rebels and captured 900. No figures were given for French casualties. Certainly the war was continuing at its pre-de Gaulle rate of mortality.

In France itself, municipal elections also showed an infection from the "flux" of the government's Algerian policy and unpopular financial decrees. Although the fact was temporarily obfuscated by government spokesmen, the communists regained their former electoral strength. Total communist vote increased by 300,000 and their percentage rose as high as 27.2 per cent. *Le Monde's* comment was: "After three days of reflection the Interior Minister discovers that the comeback of the extreme Left is, after all, a setback. He cites figures which, we have to regret, we believe to be false." [23]

Government censorship of an article in the *Express* by rebel leader Si Azzedine, describing the failure of a French attempt to negotiate a cease-fire with him, raised a tempest with more than teapot implications. The government was under severe pressure from the Left, the Right, and almost everyone else before its first six months of life were spent.[24]

The municipal election for Algeria, delayed until April, 1959, because of the Ramadan religious holidays in March, was received with tremendous apathy. Once again men standing for municipal council (from which the mayors and their assistants are elected) were threatened from both sides, the F.L.N. if they ran, and the ultras if they did not. Four days before the election not one list of candidates had been received. Then the army and the U.N.R. went to work. The latter, under Jacques Soustelle finally backed a list of right-wing candidates, and the army rounded up some *beni-oui-ouis*. No inclination to run was shown on the part of any non-integrationists. The election returns indicated 56 per cent abstentions in Algiers—abstentions heavier among the Europeans than among the Muslims, interestingly enough. The F.N.F. (*Front National Français*), Orthiz's group, under a slogan "*S'abstenir = F.L.N. — Voter = F.N.[I.]F.*" and the U.N.R. delegations each received fourteen of the possible seventy-five seats, and most of the rest went to incumbents who represented the *status quo* of French Algeria. Certainly their election gave weight to the French presence.

Voting figures for such embattled areas as Sétif were as low as 37 per cent, and those of Kerraba, Djidjelli and Azaga about the same. At Oran the figure rose to 65 per cent; at Constantine 55 per cent, and at Biskra (all areas where de Gaulle's preeminence was indisputable) 80 per cent of the vote came out, or was brought out in army trucks.[25] If Algiers showed anti-Gaullist or pro-F.L.N. tendencies, or both, at least there were some areas which seemed to give evidence of a gradual working out of the President's plan of the evolution of democratic electoral procedure. Or perhaps this was a measure of the French army's discipline over the people. Certain liberal-minded mayors were re-elected over candidates of the C.P.S. movements in Blida, at Bougie, and Philippeville. The elections brought about a heavy recrudescence of terror in Algiers and Constantine, while in the *bléd* the F.L.N. took reprisals against several Algerians who had joined the French electoral lists.[26]

A dispatch from Algiers in *France-Presse* gave (at approximately the same date in April), this glamorous picture of an *hébergement* (regroupment) center under the French army.

Threats, rackets in money or food, misdeeds of all kinds, and often crimes of the rebels inflicted on the population of isolated *douars,* especially in the mountains, have caused the military authorities to order regroupment of population in several regions of Algeria in centers or in villages which can be more easily protected either by the army or by the inhabitants themselves.

This solution at the same time has the advantage of depriving the rebels of resources—freely given or not—which they preempt from the meager goods of the peasants in order to assure their subsistence.

Criticism has been formulated—and notably in a report that has no official character but from which certain passages have just been published—on the execution of this measure in itself explicable and justifiable.

A visit made yesterday to several of these centers permits better judgment than second hand accounts of the difficulties of the operation which involves at times several thousand people. Inevitable errors have been committed, but also a number of very real successes are enregistered.

From the *djebels* where they were living in conditions of continual insecurity, we have brought families and cattle in places summarily prepared and where, before everything, it is a question of sufficient water and enough land.

A temporary installation is arranged under army tents, then houses of bricks mixed with straw are started, then in stone and cement.

The material means of the army and the financial resources of the administration permit a rapid progress in the work. In the region of Blida, for example, several of these 'villages' are complete. One of them, Sidi-Madani,

counts eight hundred and fifty-two inhabitants, all shel-
tered in simple but sufficient houses, covered with tile.
In a few days water will run from four fountains and in
the basins of a laundry tub.

A school of prefabricated elements is already built and
functions under the authority of an instructor, actually
an adjutant of the artillery who teaches one hundred and
twenty-six boys and girls. . . .[27]

Other less complimentary versions of the regroupment operations will be discussed later. At this time suffice it to say that
the regroupment effort was a concomitant of the Challe Plan,
which according to its mentor in April, 1959, was working out
its double object of breaking up rebel strongholds and clearing
out zones of refuge for the F.L.N. General Challe described it
himself:

I put reserves in the *djebels* to break up the rebel structure, and behind them commando groups who take
turns harrying the fight until the adversary is dispersed.
These [commandos] are not alone. They are the most
dynamic [element of the plan]. But there are other
tasks to accomplish in the sectors . . . which constitute
the points of a center of pacification. We have broken
the rebel structure. . . .[28]

Alain Jacob in *Le Monde*, May 20, 1959, listed these four indispensable elements of the French offensive.

1. Assure the frontiers.
2. Destroy the A.L.N. regulars.
3. Annihilate the politico-administrative organization
   of the rebels.
4. Substitute a French and loyal native structure which
   will have Algerian support.

The most difficult areas to subdue, he added, are the Ouarsenis,
Kabylia, the surrounding country near Algiers, and the North
and South Constantine.

That the rebels were defeated was, of course, only a hopeful statement. That casualties were higher than ever was evidenced by these figures which the F.L.N. presented to the January, 1959, meeting of the United Nations in New York. Mr. A. K. Chanderli, for the twelve day period, January 5 to January 18, cited casualty figures of 1500 dead and wounded. He said that the war had cost 3800 Algerian lives since December 13, 1958.[29]

A new clemency act of de Gaulle on behalf of Algerians condemned to death added to the grace accorded 184 Algerians and one European in January, 1959, unleashed a series of anti-Gaullist activities in an Algiers which had been completely apathetic during the municipal elections. Already that city was beginning ruefully to think in terms of the first anniversary of the May 13, 1958, uprising. Should the second May 13 be a day of celebration or a day of mourning? The French government undertook to direct the festivities by publishing a prescribed commemorative manifestation—parades, delegations, and finally a banquet to be offered to the organization of the *arrondissements* of Algiers.

From Algiers an eyewitness report of preparation for the second May 13 was published in *El Moujahid,* May 25, 1959.

> For three days Algiers has been inundated with tracts; the newspapers are filled with motions and declarations. On one side Lagaillarde refused to participate in the manifestations, the CSP, the University Movement, Boyer-Banse and the students concede a [day of] mourning by denouncing the 'inadmissible pressures of a government which betrays the ideas of May 13 and a politics which opens the door to abandon.'

Of the Casbah he reports:

> For us, the participation has been planned for a long time. Our local head received the order from Captain Bapst of the SAU of Basse Casbah, order transmitted by the 'blues' (*bérets bleus*), with the usual threats, to have to present 30 persons at the rendez-vous of the military

trucks: There, as usual, they take our identity cards and give us arm-bands. I got up to go out earlier. I won't be taken in the group from the quarter.

Although three thousand soldiers and veterans, including Muslim soldiers, marched in the demonstration, there were few if any French flags in the windows and confetti made from black bits of paper was dropped along the route of the parade. Some Europeans, mostly mothers with children, came out to watch the troops go by, but applause was minimal and this day had little or no relation to the hysterical period of a year ago. The European Algerians were quiet and disillusioned, and the Muslims no longer had much faith in the miracle of de Gaulle. The next day both sides could take pleasure in the manifestation. There were, after all, no incidents, and the army kept both sides well under control. In truth, it sounded like a "celebration" in any occupied city.

During the third week in May, violent battles were reported on the outskirts of Algiers—the F.L.N. answer to a heightened French offensive. De Gaulle accorded clemency to eight more Algerians under sentence of death and the F.L.N. returned his largesse by liberating fifteen French prisoners—nine soldiers and six European civilians—in Tizi-Ouzou. In the same week Mohammed V of Morocco reaffirmed his solidarity with the Algerian rebels to certain ministers of the G.P.R.A., Belkacem, Krim, Mehri, and Boussouf. Mohammed V made it plain that he hoped to be the agency, along with de Gaulle, to bring about peace in Algeria and to strengthen the unity of the Maghrib.

As we have mentioned, a more hopeful sign of de Gaulle's policy might be read in the Senatorial elections, held also in the third week of May. These Algerian lists showed more liberal tendencies than in previous campaigns; more Muslims allowed themselves to be candidates, and certain ultras were defeated. On May 26 a nasty story of counter-terror appeared in *Le Monde*. It was an account of the assassination of Ould Audia, Kabyle lawyer who had defended fifteen Algerian students involved in the reconstitution of U.G.E.M.A. (*Union Général des*

310

Etudiants Musulmans Algériens), an organization working for Algerian independence which had been outlawed by the French government. There was a second news report stating that other lawyers involved in the case had received numerous threats and telephone calls from right-wing terrorists.

Early in June the episode of the government *vs* the book *La Gangrène* left a bad taste in many mouths. An old press of the Resistance, *Editions de Minuit* brought out the controversial book only to have it confiscated by the minister of the interior on June 20, 1959. Parts of the story had already been published in *Le Monde's* documentary section, and it told of the imprisonment and torture of five of the students who had been defended by the murdered Ould Audia, believed to be a victim of the Red Hand (French counter-revolutionary terrorists). The students, Béchir Boumaza, Mustapha Francis (brother of Ahmed Francis in the G.P.R.A.), Benaissa Souami, from *Ecole de Science Politique*, Moussa Khebaili, and Abd el Kader Belhadj, each told his separate story of the torture of the D.S.T. At the end of the book these accounts were corroborated by an Algerian newspaper correspondent and some medical personnel in Paris. This book was a thunderous echo of Jean-Jacques Servan-Schreiber's *Lieutenant in Algeria* and Henri Alleg's *The Question* and aroused metropolitan anger hugely. André Malraux, who had made formal statements to the French people asserting that there had been no torture since the *régime à de Gaulle*, was put on the spot and the government's entire Algerian policy was once more opened to wide criticism.[30]

DEGAULLE'S OFFER OF SEPTEMBER 16, 1959: SELF DETERMINATION—ALMOST

On August 16, after a half-year in which the Algerian war grew in scope and international importance, after a half-year or more of de Gaulle's inconclusive efforts, sixteen members of the United States Congress signed a declaration supporting the right of the Algerian people to independence.[31] They asked that the United States' Government take the lead in the U.N. General

Assembly to *demand* negotiations. They wanted no more namby-pamby abstentions. But before that session, the Fourteenth Session of the U.N., could convene, President Charles de Gaulle made his first important speech concerning the Algerian question, September 16, 1959. Here he declared that his Algerian policy rested ultimately on a theory of self-determination.

This statement was hailed everywhere as historic because it marked the first time a French government dared publicly to offer self-determination to the Algerian against the wishes of the *colons* and the army. However, the offer was carefully hedged in many ways. It looked wonderful from the headlines. But it was not easy to accept from the Algerian nationalist point of view.

De Gaulle first declared that "pacification," although not yet achieved, was greatly advanced. His statement was "that there is no comparison in terms of the safety of goods and persons, between the situation which prevailed two or three years ago and that which prevails today." He pointed out that although elections held during troublous times were not the most representative, still a long step had been made toward giving the Muslim Algerians a voice in their own development. Then he sketched the outline of France's social program for Algeria, without which any political settlement had very little meaning. He mentioned the following achievements of France in Algeria during the "last ten months."

> Ten industrial plants have applied for permission to settle. Twenty thousand acres of fertile soil are being allocated to Moslem land workers. The number of Algerians working in Metropolitan France has increased by 50,000.

> The numbers of Moslems in public employment has increased by 5,000. At the beginning of the coming school year schools in Algeria will be receiving some 860,000 children as against 700,000 at the corresponding time last year and 560,000 the year before.[32]

312

Next de Gaulle lauded the development of the oil communities in the Sahara. "In six weeks the oil at Hassi Messaoud will be arriving on the coastline at Bougie. In another year, the oil at Edjelé will be reaching the Gulf of Gabès. In 1960 the gas from Hassi R'mel will begin to be distributed in Algiers and Oran, later at Bône." The pith of the speech was this:

> Taking into account all these factors—those of the Algerian situation, those inherent in the national and the international situation—I deem it necessary that recourse to self-determination be here and now proclaimed. . . . I pledge myself to ask the Algerians on the one hand, in their twelve departments, what, . . . they wish to be; and, on the other hand, all Frenchmen to endorse that choice.

> The question, obviously, will be put to the Algerians as individuals. For since the beginning of the world there has never been any Algerian unity, far less any Algerian sovereignty. . . . As for the time of the elections, I will decide upon it in due course, at the latest, four years after the actual restoration of peace; that is to say, once a situation has been established whereby not more than 200 persons a year will lose their lives, either in ambushes or isolated attacks.

> The ensuing period of time will be devoted to resuming normal existence, to emptying the camps and prisons, to permitting the return of exiles, to restoring the free play of individual and public liberties, and to enabling the population to be fully aware of what is at stake.

As to the political destiny of the Algerians de Gaulle had this to say.

> Everyone knows that in theory it is possible to imagine three solutions [which will be] . . . put to a vote.

313

Either—secession, where some believe independence would be found. France would then leave the Algerians who had expressed their wish to become separated from her. They would organize, without her, the territory in which they live, the resources which they have at their disposal, the government which they desire. I am convinced personally that such an outcome would be incredible and disastrous. Algeria being what it is at the present time, and the world what we know it to be, secession would carry in its wake the most appalling poverty, frightful political chaos, widespread slaughter, and soon after, the warlike dictatorship of the Communists. But this demon must be exorcised by the Algerians themselves. If it should appear through some inconceivable misfortune, that such is indeed their will, France would undoubtedly stop devoting so much of value and so many billions of francs to a cause shorn of any hope. It goes without saying that, on this assumption, those Algerians regardless of origin, who might wish to remain French would do so in any case, and that France would arrange, if need be, for their regrouping and resettlement. On the other hand, everything would be arranged so that the operation of oil wells, the handling and shipping of Saharan oil—which is the result of French efforts and which is of interest to the whole western world—would be ensured in any event.

Or—out-and-out identification with France, such as implied in equality of rights: Algerians can accede to all political, administrative and judicial functions of the state and have free access to the public service. They would benefit, as regards salaries, wages, social security, education and vocational training, from all measures provided for in Metropolitan France; they would live and work wherever they saw fit, throughout the territory of the Republic; in other words, they would be

314

living, from every point of view, regardless of their religion or the community to which they belonged, by and
large on the same footing and at the same level as other
citizens, and become part and parcel of the French people who would then, in effect, spread from Dunkirk to
Tamanrasset.

Or—the government of Algerians by the Algerians,
backed up by French help and in close relationship with
her, as regards the economy, education, defense and foreign relations. In that case, the internal regime of Algeria
should be of the federal type, so that the various communities—French, Arab, Kabyle, Mozabite—who live
together in the country would find guarantees for their
own way of life and a framework for cooperation.

But since for a year now it has been settled that—
through the institution of equal voting rights, the single
college and the emergence of a majority of Moslem representatives—the political future of Algerians is to de-
pend on Algerians; since it has been officially and solemnly emphasized that, once peace has been restored,
the Algerians will let it be known what fate they want
for themselves, to the exclusion of any other, and that all
of them, whatever their program may be, whatever
they might have done, wherever they come from, will
take part, if they wish to do so, in this vote: what then
could be the meaning of rebellion? [33]

These were the parts of the de Gaulle offer which were memorable and hopeful. But, having offered Algerian self-determination, he then qualified it in many ways. Quite understandably
he underscored that, should the Algerians choose independence,
French capital investments would be reduced. This was the
procedure followed in Guinea when that area voted for independence in the 1958 Referendum. But de Gaulle went way
beyond this condition to promise regroupment and resettlement

315

of "those Algerians, regardless of origin, who might wish to remain French." Was this not a threat of partition which sat oddly beside the idea of an independent Algeria which could evolve legally and logically from the offer of self-determination? To this condition, he added insurance of the operation of the Saharan oil wells and the flow of the oil through Algeria toward France.

Algeria independent would not be, apparently, the same Algeria for which the F.L.N. was fighting. The fact that the French nation would have to ratify an Algerian vote for independence was a thought that could not please nationalist patriots. Also, the rebels eyed with skepticism, the emphasis on the duration of "pacification" and the four-year waiting period. Certainly a time to cool passions and bring about rehabilitation was a logical suggestion, but insistence that the rebellion first be formally brought to knee was another question, and one that was impossible for them to accept.[34]

So, although the American and European press lauded de Gaulle's offer and predicted that peace talks were in the offing, the Algerians and the friends of Algeria in Tunis and Morocco reacted cooly to the conditions of the offer of self-determination. One nationalist leader stated of the September 16 speech, "The mountain has labored and brought forth a mouse." [35] From Algeria itself came rumors that the Muslim citizens were disappointed that de Gaulle had not made any definite offer of a cease-fire. From the right-wing Algerians came angry reproaches of de Gaulle's liberalism. More important, from the Provisional Government of the Algerian Republic there was silence for nearly two weeks, until September 28. On that day a communiqué from Tunis stated that the G.P.R.A. accepted de Gaulle's principle of self-determination for the Algerian people. It also remarked that the Provisional Government was ready to engage in pourparlers to discuss the political and military aspects of a cease-fire. In contra-distinction to de Gaulle's cautious four-year wait and peace-after-pacification idea, the rebels in upper case letters informed the world that (PEACE) CAN BE IMMEDIATE. They qualified their own position in this fashion. The

Provisional Government is "the depository and guarantee of the interests of the Algerian people until they have freely pronounced themselves." Peace therefore must be negotiated through this channel.[36]

The G.P.R.A. Response

The text of the answering declaration of the G.P.R.A. contained some telling points. It reminded the world that the right of people to self-determination was included in the United Nations' Charter. It also proclaimed the national entity of Algeria, recalled the intangible principle of the integrity of national territory and expressed "the unshakable determination of the Algerian people to oppose any attempt at partition."

> As for the riches of the Sahara, prospecting and exploitation of these cannot in any way be changed into right of ownership. In the general interest these riches, a source of human progress first of all for Algeria and North Africa, can only give rise to wide and fruitful cooperation.
>
> On another plane, to subordinate the free choice of the Algerian people to the consultation of the French people would be the very negation of self-determination and democracy.[37]

The Algerians also attacked the French concept of "pacification." A war, they said, continuing in a murderous fashion was not likely to bring peace to Algeria. Free choice meant nothing when the army of occupation counted 500,000 soldiers and "almost as many gendarmes, police and militia." Nor does it have any meaning while a quarter of the population is detained in prisons, camps, or forced into exile. "It cannot be exercised under the pressure of airplanes, tanks and cannon, under the pressure of an administrative structure whose traditions of electoral frauds is known." [38]

317

But in spite of large differences separating the two adversaries, neutral observers were happy to note that some closing of the gap had been achieved. De Gaulle's principle of self-determination had been accepted by the G.P.R.A. as a "democratic and peaceful means by which the Algerian people can achieve national independence." Up until this time the G.P.R.A. had demanded outright independence as the price of peace. This was a major step toward de Gaulle's position. Also, the nationalist communiqué was careful to use the word *pourparlers* instead of negotiations in the hopes it would ease de Gaulle's promise to the army that he would never *negotiate* with the F.L.N.

Officially France, which does not recognize the existence of the G.P.R.A., took no notice of Ferhat Abbas' statement which answered with great political acumen, de Gaulle's memorable speech of September 16. French diplomats simply indicated that de Gaulle would not invite the F.L.N. envoys to Paris on the basis of the Tunis proposals.[39] Therefore, the further concessions of the nationalists—that they would come to Paris rather than insist on negotiations in neutral territory, and that they would not insist on U.N. observers to watch elections for self-determination—were useless in face of French intransigency. De Gaulle had gone as far as he dared go, or as far as he wanted to go. No one could be sure, at the moment, which.

The Algerian rebels addressed several pleas to the United States, asking that country to press the French toward peace talks and to take a pro-Algerian stand in the forthcoming United Nations debates. The United States remained over the barrel since it had already expressed sympathy for de Gaulle's offer of September 16, which had been so well-timed and so tightly hedged that one wonders if it had much more meaning than to bolster France's fight for a hands-off Algeria policy in the United Nations General Assembly.[40]

On Tuesday, October 13, 1959, just before the opening of the Algerian debates in the French National Assembly, Ferhat Abbas made a conciliatory statement to the rightist weekly *Jours de France,* lauding de Gaulle as a great leader and a prophet. In

318

this interview he declared his willingness to come to Paris to discuss a cease-fire with de Gaulle, but he also said he would ask to have as part of his delegation three members of the G.P.R.A. who were still detained in Paris jails. Once again he returned to the position, which he had given up a few weeks earlier, of internationally supervised elections for Algeria.

From Algiers, itself, a city living somewhere between war and peace, Henry Tanner (*New York Times,* October 25, 1959) wrote this:

> Daily (the citizens of Algiers) submit absent-mindedly to the ritual of a search at the door of the building where they work, of the store where they buy their clothes, of the restaurant where they dine, the cinema, the dance hall. Women automatically open their bags. Men stop and lift their arms as the watchmen's hands slowly feel along their sides.

> Driving to and from the city, *Algérois*—Algiers' residents—slow down patiently for the Army's many, constantly shifting roadblocks. Coasting slowly, they wait for the soldiers to recognize their white skin and proper clothes, and to wave them on as harmless Europeans. Suspect-looking Moslem cars, usually battered and coughing, are motioned to the curb for a thorough search, often with mine detectors. Most of the bombs that have been exploded in Algiers were brought in from the country.

> The army is everywhere in the city. Slow-moving patrols, in single file and fully armed, thread unobtrusively among the shoppers. Soldiers shepherd the children when school lets out. They pounce on a group of back-country Moslems to see if they have the required passes for a visit to the city. Some of the loveliest views of the bay and the city are through rolls of barbed wire.

> European *Algérois* pay little attention to the war as long as their part of the city is free of violence. They know,

of course, that the roads a few miles away cease to be safe for travel in the late afternoon, and that curfew in the surrounding villages begins at nightfall. They read in their papers that grenades explode three or four times a week in the cafés and on the streets of the Moslem neighborhoods. They have come to take it for granted that soldiers and Moslems are getting killed. Few noticed that each of three army trucks which ploughed through downtown traffic the other day carried eight coffins, or that those other trucks, on another day, were taking huddled groups of Moslem prisoners to a camp on the edge of the city. . . .

Every few days, all through September and into October, bombs were discovered in cafés, public squares and on school grounds, and detonated harmlessly by the bomb disposal squad. There were many false alarms. . . .

After each terrorist attack, Algiers becomes a grimmer place than it normally is. Streets then are nearly deserted after nightfall. Attendance falls off sharply in cinemas and restaurants. . . .

The Casbah, on the other hand, seemed apathetic. Where a few years ago no civilians would dare enter without army patrols, and soldiers with walkie-talkies circulated endlessly, now there was only mild curiosity aroused by the rare European who enters Algerian quarters. From an "average" Muslim and his friends, Henry Tanner reported the following statement: *If elections were free, "99.99 per cent of the Casbah would vote for the F.L.N."* (Italics are the authors'.)

He [the average Muslim] and the two neighbors who came to dinner have no connection with the rebellion. They are trying to live as normally as they can. Nevertheless they are nationalists. . . . All their talk has a central theme: dignity. They want dignity. They feel that they don't have it now. And they feel that the European minority will not let them have it unless it is forced to

320

do so at gunpoint, either by the French or by the rebel army.

'The French are all right,' one of them says. 'De Gaulle is a great man, an honest man. The soldiers, too, are only doing a job—most of them. It's the local Europeans who are causing all the trouble.'

Like almost all young Moslems in Algiers, these men are convinced that their people owe the important gains they have made in the past year (equal voting rights, more schools, more civil service jobs) exclusively to pressure from the rebellion. Discussing General de Gaulle's declaration and future of Algeria, therefore, they defer judgment to the rebel leaders. '*They* are doing the fighting,' they say. '*They* are dying in the mountains, not we. *They* are the ones who have a right to speak.'

Speaking of the "third force" which the French hoped to organize from among the old Muslim elite, the *beni-oui-ouis*, municipal officers, and veterans of the French army, Tanner evokes the words and philosophy of a Muslim civil servant who fought with General de Gaulle's Free French, and is presently an officer in the Home Guard (which de Gaulle subsequently disbanded).

He sounds tired and defeated. Whatever happens to Algeria, he is convinced that he personally will lose. Yet he hopes for peace, even peace at his expense. The French should negotiate with the F.L.N., he says. His family, like almost every Moslem family, has had its sons killed by both sides. . . . 'We have failed,' he says sadly. 'Maybe history will say we lacked courage. Maybe it will say we were gagged by both sides. The fact is that we did not speak. We did not lead our people, who are suffering and have no voice.'

By mid-November, 1959, outward rumors of the split between de Gaulle and the followers of Jacques Soustelle of the Union for the New Republic on the Algerian policy were making headlines in the press. The Gaullists were letting it be known that they accepted only one of de Gaulle's options to the Algerians—integration with France. On November 14 Soustelle, after declaring his perfect fidelity to de Gaulle, spoke only of the "most French solution," careful not to use the word "Francization" or integration. The U.N.R. delegates, debating a motion on Algeria, made it very clear that they were not in favor of any negotiation with the F.L.N. and that they wanted the war to continue until pacification was achieved.

President de Gaulle's preoccupation with national prestige and matters military became apparent in the budget announcement for 1960. In it France took the decision to produce its own armaments even if that method was more expensive than buying certain equipment from the United States; France also entered the atomic field, if not in quantity, then in quality and kind. She planned to develop an atomic striking force of fifty supersonic nuclear fighter-bombers to be manufactured between 1963 and 1966.

The French budget for 1960 and 1961 allocated $85,000,000 per annum to manufacturing jet bombers. $22 million went to the development of intermediate-range ballistic missiles with nuclear warheads, $85 million was allocated to the first French atomic bomb. De Gaulle hoped by this latter plan to become a full-fledged member of the atomic-powered great nations. *La Gloire* came with a big price tag.

THE UNITED NATIONS AGAIN

On November 30, 1959, a new debate on the Algerian question began in the United Nations' Political Committee. The discussion, which continued until a vote was reached, was opened by Mongi Slim, Tunisian delegate and spokesman for the Afro-Asian group. In 1958 in the General Assembly, a resolution on Algeria had been defeated by only one vote. The resolution had asked for recognition of Algeria's right to independence, and for negotiations to settle the long war. President de Gaulle's statement on self-determination, and the offer to hold talks with the nationalists if they would come to Paris, had taken, perhaps, some of the apparent urgency from Mongi Slim's cause. France still adamantly refused to sit in on the Algerian debate and stated once more that the U.N. had no right to interfere in her internal affairs.

Mongi Slim, speaking to an absent French delegation, presented a demand for French negotiation with the Provisional Government. The fact of negotiations, he added, would not change the French options to Algeria, but would simply determine the procedure for "honest" elections. He said, if the French agreed to negotiate, some additional representatives would be added to the imprisoned Algerian government leaders whom de Gaulle refused to recognize. He emphasized that since both the French and the Algerians agreed on the fundamental doctrine of self-determination, what was left was only to find some viable method of negotiating the cease-fire. Mr. Slim added, "We feel that it is perfectly normal that the Algerian nationalist leaders should wish to discuss the conditions and guarantees for the implementation of self-determination at the same time as they discuss the cease-fire."

During the Algerian debate, twenty-one nations in a draft resolution which was circulated in the Political Committee of the United Nations, urged the United States to intervene with France on behalf of informal discussions with the "Algerian people" to settle the war and the issues of self-determination. The resolution reminded the United States that that country had already expressed hope for a solution of the Algerian problem, "through appropriate means" and in conformity with the United Nations' Charter. But in 1959, after de Gaulle's announcement, the United States through its spokesman, Henry Cabot Lodge, Jr., warned the Political Committee not to pass a resolution which might prejudice the recent attempt of Charles de Gaulle to solve the problem. Spain, the United Kingdom, and Australia also advised a hands-off policy. The Afro-Asian statement demanding pourparlers was signed by Afghanistan, Burma, Ceylon, Ethiopia, Ghana, Guinea, India, Indonesia, Iraq, Jordan, Lebanon, Liberia, Libya, Morocco, Nepal, Pakistan, Saudi Arabia, the Sudan,

Tunisia, the United Arab Republic, and Yemen. In this crucial vote, as in the one of 1958, the United States, caught between its pro-Maghrib desires and its loyalty to France in N.A.T.O., abstained.[41]

Several days afterwards, however, President Eisenhower, stopping in Tunisia on his way to Paris for a meeting of the Western powers, issued a joint communiqué with Bourguiba in favor of the policy of self-determination of the African people. The problem, they said, was mainly to achieve a cease-fire for the continued Algerian war which was a grave cause of international concern.

In Paris a day of strike by the Communist, Socialist, and Catholic labor unions, on December 2, 1959, gave evidence that the Gaullist honeymoon was over. Though part of the displeasure may have been timed for the Algerian debate in the U.N., mainly it was the rise in prices without an equivalent rise in salaries that brought about the short, peaceful, but paralyzing, demonstration. Everything except railways and the Paris subway, from garbage collection to airplane landings, stopped for one day. Another cause of discontent was the debate on the school system.

While the Algerians were organizing their case in the U.N., Debré was reaffirming his old stand on Algeria at the ceremony for the opening of the Sahara oil pipeline. The line carrying oil 400 miles from Hassi Messaoud to Bougie on the Mediterranean was opened and marked the beginning of large-scale production of Sahara oil. Premier Debré called the enterprise "a new chance for union between France and Algeria," and vowed again that the "pacification" of Algeria would be completed by the French army. At Bône he declared it was politically impossible to separate France from Algeria.[42]

In the U.N. the General Assembly finally rejected on December 12 a compromise solution submitted by Pakistan on the Algerian problem. "The resolution would have had the eighty-two nation body call for informal talks on Algeria by France and the Algerian nationalists. It also would have recommended recognition of the North African territory's right to self-determination—already conceded by France." The vote was 39 to 22 with 20 abstentions. "The ballot constituted a gain of one vote over the majority obtained for a somewhat similar move in the Assembly's Political Committee." But it failed to achieve the necessary two-thirds margin which the Assembly required for adoption. Said the Algerian Provisional Government:

> The debates of the 14th Session of the General Assembly of the United Nations on the Algerian Question demonstrated in the clearest way the correctness of the position and preoccupation of the Provisional Government of the Algerian Republic and of the Algerian people fighting for their liberation. The overwhelming majority of the representatives of the member states of this organization strongly supported our point of view: it is not possible to dissociate pourparlers on a cease fire in Algeria from the conditions of the implementation of the right to self-determination.

> The fact that the resolution introduced by the Delegation of Pakistan did not receive the ⅔ vote necessary for adoption by the General Assembly is in contradiction with the consensus of opinion of the majority of the Delegations. In fact, all of the paragraphs of the resolution voted on separately obtained the ⅔ majority by a very large margin. This contradiction is due to the maneuvers and pressures of the Atlantic coalition, which at the request of France, stood firmly against the adoption of any resolution, regardless of content.[43]

On the same day, December 12, Charles de Gaulle graciously accorded the Federation of Mali, uniting the autonomous republics of Sudan and Senegal, its sovereignty within the Community, "not only with the accord but with the aid of France." Mali would remain in the French customs union, use French money, and speak French as the official language. In return France was allowed to keep military bases there. The French Community was beginning to evolve on a political level, and member states so desiring have achieved Republican "sovereignty" with the support, the approval and assistance of France. France has also promised technical aid and assistance to the other states of the Community. In June, 1960, this complex was composed of the Overseas Departments, the Overseas Territories, and twelve new Republics which were: Islamic Republic of Mauritania, Republic of the Upper Volta, Republic of Dahomey, Republic of the Ivory Coast, Republic of the Niger, Mali Federation (Senegal and Sudan), Central African Republic, Gabon Republic, Republic of Chad, Republic of the Congo, Malagasy Republic.

Guinea, of course, had declared its independence in 1958 at the time of the Referendum.

CHAPTER TEN

"THE FOUL BLOW"—JANUARY 24, 1960

MASSU'S FOLLY: INTEGRATION OR ELSE

The incident which triggered the second Algier's rebellion, January 24, 1960, was de Gaulle's removal for insubordination of General Jacques Massu from the command of the Army of Algiers. The president's action followed the publishing of a statement made by Massu to a correspondent of the West German press in which he strongly criticized President de Gaulle's policy of self-determination for the Algerians. Massu said that such a policy was acceptable neither to the army at war to keep Algeria French nor to the Europeans of Algiers who favored a policy of integration. How Massu blundered into this public indiscretion is a mystery but there are rumors that he simply fell into a trap set for him by certain activists who maneuvered the interview. Massu, rugged and outspoken by nature, may well have been the dupe of more subtle politicians. The interview, pretext or not, was accepted by de Gaulle as a challenge. Immediately he yanked Massu back to Paris and summarily relieved him of his command, and the activists were presented with their *cause célèbre* on a platter. Massu, the idol of Algiers, the hero of May 13 and all it represented had been publicly humiliated. Was this not a proof of de Gaulle's real sentiments toward the cause of *Algérie Française?*

It is apparent that the January coup was prepared with the complicity of the Algiers' authorities, the collusion of half a dozen rightist organizations, veterans groups, and some elements of the

327

French army. Since de Gaulle's announcement of a "new" policy of self-determination for Algeria on September 16, 1959, Metropolitan and international opinion had been congratulating itself on a hopeful turn of events. The moderates and even the liberals applauded at least this one act of the president. But Algiers' opinion skyrocketed the other way. The rightists took up the old chant that de Gaulle was selling them down the river, and many officers of the French army claimed that they were in the midst of winning the war and losing the "pacification."

The rebellion had been in preparation for some time. Assured of a large degree of army support, some access to army arsenals and the overt support of the Home Guard (U.T.B.) which had already refused to disband in spite of de Gaulle's express orders, the master minds of the coup felt sanguine of success. After all, Algerian opinion had swayed France once, had actually changed its government, why not twice?

On the other hand:

> While metropolitan opinion was anesthetized by reassuring discourses and drugged dreams, while forms of public life lost all substance, while democracy succeeded in becoming progressively anemic under the Gaullist magic here [in Paris]; during the same period the factions of Algiers were organizing, preparing, with the complicity of the local powers, their arsenals, and the army was progressively enthralled by the certitude of its political mission. Only the great height of de Gaulle, and his past glory, prevented the degradation from being plainly visible to all eyes. Until the day when the veil was torn.

> Until the day when we are able to measure exactly the road covered between May 1958 and January 1960. The compromises which had kept us going, which had founded the new regime abusively labeled democratic, existed without a doubt; they belonged to the army.[1]

Some reports claim that January 22, 1960, was "D" day for the plotters, and according to Joseph Ortiz, one of the leaders of the insurgents, it was not planned for several months. Perhaps he envisioned a new May 13. According to Henri de Turenne, special permanent correspondent of *France-Soir* in Algiers, the movement which culminated in civil strife on January 24 and a manning of the barricades in the early morning of January 25 began with a strike in the suburbs of Algiers, Bab-el-Oued, in the forenoon of Saturday, January 23. That morning—the day that General Crépin took over from General Massu—students and activists of all stripes assembled and marched from door to door, café to café, whipping up enthusiasm. In the noisy and overflowing streets violent projects were broached. A plan to march on Barberousse Prison, where the Algerian terrorists were held pending trial and sentence, was aired; the mob would take justice in its own hand and execute the prisoners then and there. Meanwhile heavy units of gendarmes were installed before the Government House and other public buildings. If on that day no general order for the rebellion seems to have been given, still Deputy Lagaillarde in his paratroop uniform and students of the *Association Générale des Etudiants Algériens* (A.G.E.A.) were prominent among the milling crowd. This was also the morning when Biaggi, the ubiquitous parliamentarian was ignoring orders from France to leave Algiers immediately. Paratroops took up position on the outskirts of the Casbah to "insure order."

A worried Delegate General Paul Delouvrier and General Challe, Commander of the Army of Algeria, made public declarations with intent to calm an army and a citizenry deeply moved by the replacement and rebuke of General Massu. Delouvrier recalled to the crowd the two new promises of General de Gaulle, which were as little reassuring to a liberal solution of the Algerian problem as his action against Massu was promising. They were: a promise of rapid justice to be instigated against Algerian terrorists whose recents acts had thrown new consternation into the hearts of the Europeans—in response to the general unrest four Algerians were to be summarily executed on the morning of January 24 after sentence by a military tribunal—and a special commissioner placed at each detention center to insure against the torturing of suspects. The promise of military justice, of course, made it impossible for the accused to obtain counsel of the kind granted to a civil prisoner. Then de Gaulle once more offered the Algerians his promise that he would never consent to political negotiations with the F.L.N. Having given these indications of his understanding of the viewpoint and the frame of mind of the public of Algiers, de Gaulle next had Paul Delouvrier declare somewhat ominously: "Today's authority is indisputable. The power will not retreat." A little later General Challe made a statement designed to subdue the army's growing discontent: "The union of the army rests high above personalities and loyalty to your chiefs [superior army officers] no matter what might be the nature of your attachment to them."

While Challe and Delouvrier were exhorting calm and compromise, *L'Echo d'Alger,* under a huge headline: *General Massu is relieved of his Command,* ran Alain de Sérigny's provocative article:

> The mutation of a general is an act of the high command which does not concern us. But when it is a question of General Massu, and especially in the circumstances under which the decision was made, we estimate that our silence would be cowardice.

> Massu is another thing. Massu, companion of the Liberation, is a symbol. It is thus proved that between the word of a great soldier and the declarations attributed to him by a foreign correspondent, the choice is made. No denial will serve any purpose. Between the word of Massu and that of a German journalist, no hesitation: Massu is condemned. Massu is relieved from his command, treated as though guilty of a failure in discipline.

> At this point it becomes evident that there is on foot a machination to destroy one of the personalities who is most representative of resistance to the national disintegration.[2]

So the battle with President de Gaulle was joined. The sentiment of de Sérigny indeed echoed that of the citizens of Algiers.

330

The Gaullist counsels of the Delegate General and the Commander in Chief were ignored; the riot grew. Challe declared Algiers to be under a state of siege and recalled a number of "neutral" regiments back into the city.

THE NEW "PATRIOTS"

The apparent leaders of the rebellion were Joseph Ortiz, forty-seven years old, café owner and former Poujadist, who in 1958 formed the paramilitary organization *Front National Français* (F.N.F.) whose emblem, like that of *Jeune Nation,* is the Celtic Cross. Implicated in the bazooka attack on General Salan, he was temporarily imprisoned by Robert Lacoste. At the time of the rebellion of January, 1960, he claimed to have 1,500 militants behind him, and the discipline and order of his men was demonstrated in an assembly held for integrationist Georges Bidault who arrived in Algiers in December to give a series of speeches. (He was subsequently recalled by the de Gaulle government.) Behind the other barricade was the well-known personality, U.N.R. Deputy Pierre Lagaillarde, who had directed the assault on the Government General during the May 13 uprising. He was the former President and motivating force behind A.G.E.A. The new President was Jean-Jacques Susini who, at the time of the rebellion in January, was Ortiz's right hand man and the theoretician for the F.N.F.

Perhaps of more importance, though less picturesque, as symbols of French Algeria, are Robert Martel, whose organization displayed the insignia of Pére Foucauld, a red heart surmounted by a cross, and Auguste Arnould, both of whom were involved in the revolution of May 13. Martel has been the motivating spirit behind a group of farmers and small *colons* sometimes referred to by metropolitan Frenchmen as the "poor white trash" of Algeria. He claims to represent 5,000 people, but Arnould is the man with the greatest potential backing. A pilot of Air Algeria, forty years of age, he was the leader of an association numbering forty-five war-veteran organizations, whose members have been estimated at 50,000.[3]

331

During the afternoon of January 24 a crowd of some 2,500 people, mostly European rightists, had gathered in the Forum and the Place des Glières to protest the replacement of General Massu by General Crépin and also the significant outlines of de Gaulle's Algerian policy of September 16. The crowd had been restless, ominous, but not violent. From time to time it burst forth singing the *Marseillaise* and it chanted the well known slogans of French Algeria. It praised Massu and jeered de Gaulle. In spite of activist hope that the gathering which they had spawned would swell to 150,000 and include not only the French army, the European citizens, but the mass of the Muslims as well, and that this power bloc would force de Gaulle to change his Algerian policy, the first afternoon of the January insurgency did not attract anything like the excitement of the May 13 revolt. It was not until evening when the gendarmes, who had been practicing how to use their gun butts as weapons, put on their steel helmets and armed themselves with tear gas bombs to try to disperse the crowd, that street fighting began. As the police moved into position against the crowd a shot was fired and people began to break and run. The gendarmes returned the fire and took refuge against a parapet of the staircase of the Forum above the square. The shooting did not last long but it resulted in the death of 24 and the wounding of 136 Frenchmen, mostly of the "forces of order." It is interesting to note that this battle at 6:00 P.M. was not offered by the paratroops, who filled the city and the Place des Glières, but by the local police force. The bloodshed had the immediate effect of dispersing idle bystanders and at least temporarily sobering the activists. Here in the face of the guerrilla warfare of the F.L.N., the French of the right were shooting at Frenchmen trying to sustain Republican institutions and the President's policies which were, under the present Constitution, French law. But even the ultimate horror of civil war did not stop the uprising.

Apparently heartened by the inaction of the army during the passage of arms, the insurgents solidified their position during the night of January 25. The bloodshed which stunned the crowd seemed only to strengthen the position of the rebels. Certainly it had put them out on the far limb of legality; their shooting could, or could not, be considered treason, depending on the subsequent action of the French government as manifested through the French army. In any case, on the night of the 25th, complacency or actual complicity of certain elements of the army saw to it that support in the form of heavy arms and supplies of many kinds was brought behind the barricades. The number of men in the redoubts was strengthened by many Home Guards (U.T.B.) who slipped behind the fortifications under cover of darkness. When the morning sun appeared over the Forum, it shone on seven barricades bristling with guns and spotted with military uniforms of one kind or another. At this time, according to some authorities, the insurgents and their adherents in the crowd at large numbered some 20,000. Lagaillarde's men had taken refuge in the buildings of the university, another band of rebels used the post office on Place des Glières for headquarters, and the bank on rue Charles Péguy had become command post for Ortiz's guerrillas.

The 10th Division of Paratroops, not yet replaced by de Gaulle, tried in somewhat desultory fashion to keep people from joining the insurgents or fraternizing with them, but crowds continued to form in the streets and spokesmen from the rebel camp boasted of fighting on to the bitter end. Hopes that sufficient pressure on the French Government might cause it to change its policy or to resign still ran high. A spirit of braggadocio reigned in the rebel camp.

ANXIOUS DAYS: JANUARY 26-28

In Paris de Gaulle spent an anxious night. He cautioned Challe not to fire on the demonstrators unless it was absolutely necessary, but he declared that the barricades must finally be reduced at all costs. Premier Debré was dispatched on a lightning trip to Algiers to restore the authority of the government and make a quick report on the gravity of the situation. The Elysée issued a statement that "The President of the Republic and Government are determined to maintain the Algerian policy they have already adopted and to assure the quickest possible return to public order." But nothing gave.[4] Only more dissidents joined the insurgents and others fêted them with provisions and good cheer from the street side. But as the barricades sat in the warm Algerian sunshine, new units of paratroops, soldiers from the *bléd* who were not stricken with the virus of Algiers, gradually took up position to separate one barricade from another and tried persuasively to discourage civilians from joining the forces of French Algeria.

During January 26 de Gaulle's appointed Delegate, Delouvrier, and General Challe who was in supreme command of the Army of Algeria both received orders from Paris to deal firmly with the uprising. Both of these government spokesmen made statements pleading for peace and the return to order. Thousands of French soldiers began to trek back to Algiers from the battlegrounds in other parts of Algeria. Still the paratroopers who had replaced the police took no active step to remove the barricades or attack the rebels; they simply took up position in the square. Many of them undoubtedly had much sympathy for the cause of the insurgents. Support for the rebellion was built up further by news of demonstrations of unity in other parts of the country. In Oran, to the west, thousands of Europeans surged out in support of *Algérie Française* and built their own barricades from overturned streetcars. These resistants were cut off from the rest of the city by police loyal to the central government who constructed cordons of barbed wire. In Blida to the south and Sidi-bel-Abbès, young activists tried to organize strikes. The seaport of Bône rumbled ominously with anti-Gaullism. At Constantine and Tlemçen, *colons* and even certain army officers made solemn public vows that Algeria would remain forever French.

Premier Debré returned to Paris, after his quick trip to Algiers, a very distressed man. He was obviously caught between loyalty to de Gaulle and his appreciation of the position of the rebels. It is said that at this time he offered his resignation and that de Gaulle refused to accept it, believing rightly that Debré's loyalty in face of his personal convictions was more salutary to the government than his resignation. In an address to the insurgents on behalf of the government, Debré offered certain proofs of the decision of the Fifth Republic never to abandon French Algeria. One of the most interesting, and certainly one of the most important statements he made, at least to those other rebels, the F.L.N., was a promise that "all those will remain French who on this French soil are French, and that nobody will be able to take away from them or even dispute this status for themselves or their children." This phrasing seems haunted by de Gaulle's thoughts on the possible partition of Algeria in case of a future majority secession vote of the Algerian Muslims. It was not only Debré whom de Gaulle had to convince that he would not change his Algerian policy. Soustelle was extremely hostile to it and certain other deputies of the U.N.R. From the highest echelons of the army came great pressure. Marshal Alphone-Pierre Juin, the "first soldier of France" threatened de Gaulle that he would issue a statement opposing his policies should the latter allow or order the army to fire upon the insurgents. General Ely, Chief of Staff of the French Army, was in constant communication with de Gaulle and the Army of Algiers, and it is purportedly because of his efforts of conciliation that the restive elements in the high command and among the colonels of Algiers were once more brought under control. Ely, who had resigned under the Fourth Republic to avoid a split in the army, remained loyal to de Gaulle but at great cost to his personal feelings about the Algerian question.

Though the events of the day indicated stalemate, every hour the defiant barricades remained standing was an affront to the French Government and the person of President de Gaulle—an open challenge to his authority. The position of General Challe was also an agonizing one. Early in the first night of the revolt he called a meeting of the paratroop Colonels Dufour, Broizat, Bréchignac, and Bonnégal. These men explained to him that "certain complicities" made it impossible for them to order their troops to fire on the insurgents. Challe, while relaying to them the unshakable terms of the President realized that at any moment he might be caught between hammer and anvil. On one side it would be impossible *not* to obey de Gaulle. On the other side, would it not be worse to give de Gaulle's orders to the army and find out that they were not obeyed? Hence, in spite of de Gaulle's commands that the revolt be subdued during the first night, there was a long period of temporizing. Obviously many elements in the army were curious to see if de Gaulle would give way under prolonged pressure, and it cannot be denied that power balanced outside of Paris for nearly a week.

The President was disconsolate to hear General Challe's tale of open army complicity. Juin's position was one thing, and a little removed from the actual plot, but Challe's bitter revelations were the hub of the matter. Challe had reported to him:

> Even the men who are eternally faithful to you, such as Generals Gambiez and Olié, believe that the policy of self-determination cannot constitute a principle of war. These sentiments have no connection with those of the ultras who are battling for racist privileges. The army hopes to win the war in the name of French Algeria. Once peace is established, then it is possible to reenvisage the application of self-determination.[5]

And though de Gaulle had been, until this time, impatient of such arguments, this time he listened. His subsequent promises to the army were proof of this. But before the insurgents he ordered Challe to maintain a bold front, and Challe proudly said: "In the Fifth Republic there is no February 6. M. Lagaillarde like M. Pinay, has mistaken his Republic." [6]

The outspoken sentiment of the Army of Algeria was, as has been earlier remarked, that they are winning the war and losing the "pacification." One young colonel is quoted as saying:

> Since the Challe plan a year ago one-half the rebel forces have been destroyed. Nearly forty "Katibas"—one-third of the effective F.L.N. forces have been completely wiped out. There remain no more than 12,000 to 15,000 *fellaghas.*

How the colonel knows whether other F.L.N. soldiers have enlisted or are being drafted to replace the losses is merely conjecture. Certainly the F.L.N. war effort, by all numerical indications, had not slackened during 1959 nor early 1960. Also, it becomes more and more apparent that the French army, as well as the *colons*, do not believe that a free election would result in a "French" solution to the Algerian question. They are afraid that it would, on the contrary, result in Algerian independence. The French army, therefore, whose promises have been made not only to the European population, but to thousands of Muslims who have adopted the French cause, both in civilian life and specially in the ranks of the army itself where there are many Muslim reservists and regular soldiers, feels obliged to live up to these promises. If, under a European solution to the problem, these people might be certain of protection against the F.L.N., how will they fare in an independent state? Would not these "francizised" Muslims be the victims of the new order? This problem is among the burdens on the mind of French soldiers who have been trained for many years to take their political mission seriously.

By January 27 at least two things were certain vis-à-vis de Gaulle and the insurgents. Neither side had given an inch and, if anything, more rebels were managing to sneak behind the barricades. The outlaws were in possession of much heavier armament than they had a day earlier and the army apparently had decided to keep the French Government over a barrel as long as possible. In Paris itself there was much more awareness of the danger of the situation than there had been on May 13, 1958, and this in spite of heavy censorship of the news from Algiers. Almost unanimous support of de Gaulle's position against the insurgents and for his policy of self-determination for Algeria became immediately evident. From the man on the street, a postman, came this thought:

> Once more we have to support de Gaulle, but the next
> May 13 it will be two years that this has been going on;
> and I state, one, that the war goes on, two, that de Gaulle
> says white but the army says black as before, three, that
> the left is not budging. . . .[7]

337

Only in the cabinet and in other parts of the government itself did de Gaulle find metropolitan opposition. Michel Debré and Jacques Soustelle, then Minister of the Sahara, were both said to have refused to approve an order to resolve the rebellion of the settlers by shooting. When de Gaulle sturdily informed the cabinet that he intended to prosecute the insurgent leaders and their accomplices for treason because they had brought upon France, in the midst of a war with the F.L.N., this extra trial, Soustelle and Debré urged tolerance. A little later Delouvrier made, in his own name, a promise to Ortiz and Lagaillarde that they would receive the consideration of "patriots" if they surrendered. This promise was gainsaid by de Gaulle.

In France both the Communists and an important segment of the Socialists, who had, with the possible exception of the statement of September 16, opposed all de Gaulle's projects since his inauguration, now rallied to him and applauded his firm stand against the insurgents and the dilatory army. Even Mendès-France was a Gaullist *de l'occasion*. Again there was a vigorous metropolitan reaction against a descent into the "worst possible political situation"—one involving a rightist settler and army coup, for there were some indications that behind the uprising there was real intent to upset the de Gaulle government even as May 13 had upset the Fourth Republic. Only this time there was no de Gaulle waiting in the wings. Of course groups like *Jeune Nation*, Poujadists, and certain Independent deputies joined with the dissident U.N.R.'s to rail against the policy of self-determination for the Algerians.

On January 27 in Algiers two compromising speeches were made. First, Delegate General Paul Delouvrier made the following temporizing statement to the insurgents.

> Most certainly I understand the motives of those who, with the courage of despair, have hemmed themselves in to bear witness to French Algeria. I know that most people share these motivations. Metropolitan France must know this.
>
> But as representative of the authority of the state,

how can I not disapprove both the form and the consequences of the attitude chosen?

What are the risks? Immense as you know. No one here wants a secession, but it might come. A crisis of the regime? No one here wants it but it might come. And at the end of all that, what? The loss of Algeria.

I am the legal link, but I also feel myself to be, believe me, the personal link between here and Metropolitan France, between you and our fellow citizens on the other side of the Mediterranean.

That is why I entreat you with all my soul, with all my heart, with all my mind to do nothing that might dangerously compromise the future of the country. . . .[8]

On the same day Challe appealed to the army with the first of a series of statements which were intended to help it make up its mind. He ended it with: "I repeat once more, the French Army is fighting so that Algeria remains definitely French." This, of course, is not exactly the reason General de Gaulle would have given, but it represented a government attempt to bring the army back to the fold.

The man chiefly responsible for keeping the army together was, once again, Paul Henri Ely. Again he ran the gamut from Elysée to the High Command in Algeria, as he had in May 13 before he finally chose to resign rather than order the army to obey the government. Now, as Chief of Staff of the Armed Forces of France, against all of his personal wishes he handled the political negotiations between de Gaulle and the colonels, between the government and an army which has repeatedly disobeyed his counsels to remain aloof from politics. Personally loyal to de Gaulle but understanding the sentiment of an army which hates the politicians who have pushed them out of every French stronghold since Indochina and even before, it would have broken his heart to have been forced to ask the army to fight the Home Guard and the civilian insurgents. So Ely was again the bearer of compromises from de Gaulle to the colonels. What these compromises were became apparent early in March, 1960. (Ely has resigned since the settling of the revolt. He is of retirement age and unwilling to stretch his loyalties again.)

While Challe and Ely were working for de Gaulle, Delouvrier in an unauthorized speech on January 28, proved how far he had slipped from de Gaulle's tutelage during the few days since his return from Paris where he received instructions. Hysterical statements which de Gaulle was forced later to deny, escaped him. Announcing his decision and that of General Challe to leave Algiers for Blida where they would be freer of anti-government suasion, he made this statement as part of his farewell address:

> Men and women of Algiers, and all the Algerians who want Algeria to remain French, officers, non-commissioned officers of the French Army, you soldiers of France, do not be stupified and listen to me. It will be long. . . .
>
> I am going to address myself first to the Metropole. . . . *There are still no insurgents in Algiers.* There are resolute men, who are also ready for the supreme sacrifice, men at the hour of truth who want to die to save France.
>
> There is no unruly army. General Challe has told you so. The army is the army of the government and of the Republic. There are resolute men, officers and soldiers, equally ready to die every day in combat against the rebellion.
>
> And these two groups of men have been brought face to face by a tragic misunderstanding. On the one hand, because they think they are no longer going to be French, on the other hand, because they must obey. Face to face and it is so terrible that nobody dares fire. Every bullet weighs on the conscience of he [sic] who fires in killing a brother who fights in the same struggle. . . .
>
> You must understand, Frenchmen of Metropolitan France, that everyone who is living through these mo-

340

ments on the soil of Algeria has a drama of conscience.

Each act produces a crisis of conscience. Between *de Gaulle and bloodshed,* between Frenchmen, that is the choice. . . .[9]

The speech went on to raise the question of the anguish the army would have when faced with such alternatives. Then Delouvrier, not too wisely, called for a spontaneous outburst from the Muslim population, a sign that they, too, had faith in the proposed "Francization" of Algeria. Speaking directly to Joseph Ortiz and Lagaillarde, the insurgent leaders who had promised to die rather than surrender, he promised that he "would walk hand in hand with them to the War Memorial when the trouble was over." De Gaulle was furious when reports of this promise reached him, for he had sworn to prosecute the European rebel leaders to the full extent of the law for treason against the Fifth Republic, and to throw all people guilty of seditious activity into prison. Finally Delouvrier called on the High Command of the Army of Algeria. By name he entreated General Crépin, Massu's replacement, and General Gracieux whose paratroops were silently blockading the barricades, Colonel Arnould, Crépin's Chief of Staff, and Major de Gérminy, S.A.S. officer in charge of the *cité Mahieddine,* a Muslim suburb on the outskirts of Algiers, to remain loyal to de Gaulle.

THE GENERAL BEFORE THE CAMERAS

These first several days of anxiety and wavering, of army complicity and kind words for the insurgents were known to the press as the *"journées Gracieux* ("days of grace"). On January 29 General de Gaulle in his uniform of World War II gave a strong speech which reiterated his former Algerian policy and called the army back into line with dignified authority and heartfelt pleas that France in the middle of one terrible war should be spared the horrors of another. His speech is worthy of inclusion in the text. It ran as follows:

341

If I have put on my uniform today to address you on television, it is in order to show that it is General de Gaulle who speaks, as well as the Chief of State.

In Algeria, we are fighting against a rebellion which has lasted more than five years. France is valiantly continuing to exert the necessary efforts to put down that rebellion.

But she wants to arrive at a peace that is peace; to do what has to be done so that the tragedy does not begin all over again; to act in such a way as not—when all is said and done—to lose Algeria, which would be a disaster for us and for the West. The world, a prey to vast crises and movements which are well known, is watching this struggle which disturbs it and in which the various opposing camps seek to take a hand. It is obvious that the unity, progress and prestige of the French people are at stake, and that the future of this people is blocked as long as the Algerian problem remains unsolved.

Taking all this into consideration, I, in the name of France, made the following decision: the Algerians shall have free choice of their destiny. When, one way or another—through the conclusion of a cease-fire or through total defeat of the rebels—we shall have put an end to the fighting, when later, after a prolonged period of restored peace, the populations will have had a chance to understand what is at stake and, moreover, thanks to us, to achieve the necessary progress in the political, economic, social, educational and other fields—then, it will be the Algerians who will say what they want to be. This will not be dictated to them. For if their response were not really their response, then while for a time there might well be military victory, basically nothing would be settled. On the contrary, everything can be settled and, I believe, settled in France's favor, when the Algerians will have had an opportunity to make known their will in all freedom, dignity and security. In short, self-determination is the only policy that is worthy of France. It is the only possible outcome. It is the policy which has been defined by the President of the Republic, decided upon by the Government, approved by the Parliament and adopted by the French nation.

Now then, there are two categories of people who do not want any part of this free choice.

First, the rebel organization, which maintains that it will cease fire only if I negotiate with it beforehand, by special prerogative, on the political destiny of Algeria, which would be tantamount to building it up as the only valid representative and to elevating it in advance to being the Government of the country. That I will not do.

On the other hand, some persons of French descent demand that I renounce the idea of self-determination, that I say that everything has been done and that the fate of the Algerians has already been decided. That I will not do either. Self-determination is the only means by which the Moslems can themselves cast out the demon of secession. As to the terms of this or that French solution, I mean to have them worked out at leisure, when peace has been restored. After which, I reserve the right to commit myself—when the right time comes—for whatever I shall consider good. You may be sure that I will do this thoroughly.

It was then that, trying to force their pretended claims on the nation, on the State and on myself, certain people in Algiers started an insurrection; it was then that they fired on the forces of law and order and killed fine soldiers, and they are now rising up in arms against the authority of France. Aided in the beginning by the accommodating uncertainty of various military elements, and profiting from the fears and feverish passions stirred up by agitators, they have thus far obtained the support of part of the European population; they have instigated a forced strike, the halting of transportation and the closing of stores. Because of them, there is danger that a

343

disruption of the national unity may occur, to the indignation of the French nation and in the very midst of the struggle being waged against the rebels. There is not a man with any common sense who does not see what the inevitable consequences would be if this dreadful secession carried the day.

In face of the foul blow that has thus been struck against France, I speak first of all to the community of French descent in Algeria. This community has known me for many years. It has seen me many times in its midst, especially during the war, when its sons, in great numbers, were serving in the ranks of the Army of Liberation, or else when, following the upheaval of May 1958, I once again assumed leadership of France in order to rebuild the unity of Frenchmen on both shores of the Mediterranean. Whatever any agitators are trying to make this community believe, there are between it and myself, very special ties that are very dear to me and very much alive. I know perfectly well what services this community renders France through its century of toil in Algeria, what cruel trials it is undergoing, what moving sorrow it has for the victims it mourns. But I must speak to this community in plain and unmistakable words.

Frenchmen of Algeria, how can you listen to the liars and the conspirators who tell you that in granting a free choice to the Algerians, France and de Gaulle want to abandon you, to pull out of Algeria and hand it over to the rebellion? Is it abandoning you, is it wanting to lose Algeria, to send there and to maintain there an army of 500,000 men equipped with tremendous amounts of matériel; to consent to the sacrifice there of a good many of our children; to pay out there, this very year, civil and military expenditures amounting to a thousand billion [old francs], to undertake there a tremendous program of development; to draw from the Sahara, with great

344

difficulty and at great expense, oil and gas in order to bring them to the sea?

How can you doubt that if, some day, the Moslems freely and formally decide that the Algeria of tomorrow must be closely united to France—how can you doubt that anything would bring greater joy to our country and to de Gaulle than to see them choose, between one solution or another, the one that would be the most French? How can you deny that all the work for the development of the Moslem populations, which was initiated eighteen months ago, and is now still being pursued and which, after pacification, will have to be expanded yet more—how can you deny that this work tends precisely to create new and manifold ties between France and the Algerians? Above all else, how can you fail to see that, in rising up against the State and against the nation, you are surely heading toward ruin and at the same time you are running the risk of causing France to lose Algeria at the very moment when the decline of the rebellion is becoming evident? I solemnly appeal to you to return to law and order.

Next, I speak to the Army, which, thanks to its magnificent efforts, is in the process of winning the victory in Algeria; however, some of the elements of this army might be tempted to think that this war is their war, not France's war, and that they have a right to a policy which would not be France's policy. To all our soldiers I say: in your mission there is no room for any equivocation or interpretation. You must liquidate the rebel force, which is seeking to drive France out of Algeria and to impose upon that land its dictatorship of want and sterility. At the same time that you are conducting the battle, you must contribute to the material and spiritual transformation of the Moslem populations so as to win their hearts and minds to France. When the time comes for the people to vote, it will be your responsibility to guarantee the complete freedom and sincerity of this vote.

Yes, that is your mission, as France gives it to you, and it is France that you serve. What would the French Army become but an anarchic and absurd conglomeration of military feudalisms, if it should happen that certain elements made their loyalty conditional? As you know, I have the supreme responsibility. It is I who bear the country's destiny. I must therefore be obeyed by every French soldier. I believe that I shall be obeyed, because I know you, because I have a high regard for you, because I feel affection for you, because I have confidence in General Challe whom I have placed at your head, soldiers of Algeria, and finally, because I have need of you for France.

This having been said, listen to me carefully. In the presence of the insurrection in Algiers and in the midst of the agitation—bordering on a paroxysm—the Delegate General, M. Paul Delouvrier, who is France in Algeria, and the Commander-in-Chief may, on their own responsibility, have not wanted to give the signal themselves for a pitched battle, but no soldier, under penalty of being guilty of a serious fault, may associate himself at any time, even passively, with the insurrection. In the last analysis, law and order must be reestablished. The methods to be employed so that law and order will prevail may be of various sorts. But your duty is to bring this about. I have given, and am giving, this order.

Finally, I speak to France. Well, my dear country, my old country, here we are together, once again, facing a harsh test. By virtue of the mandate that the people have given me and of the national legitimacy that I have embodied for twenty years, I ask all men and women to support me, no matter what happens.

And while the guilty ones, who dream of being usurpers, take as a pretext the decision that I have made concerning Algeria, let it be known everywhere, let it be clearly understood, that I do not intend to go back on that decision. To yield on this point and under these conditions would be to destroy the trump cards that we still hold in Algeria, but it would also be to make the State bow before the outrage that is being inflicted on it and the threat that is aimed at it. Thus France would become but a poor broken toy adrift on the sea of hazards.

Once again, I call upon all Frenchmen, wherever they may be, whoever they may be, to reunite themselves to France.

Long live the Republic.

Long live France.[10]

These were the thoughts of a statesman at grips with a terrible human problem, the thoughts of a man of Promethean stature, who, accepted his responsibility all the while keeping faith with himself and humanity.

INSURRECTION MORTE

Whether it was de Gaulle's speech that brought the end of the ambiguous days or the replacement of the 10th Division of Paratroops and the Foreign Legion by troops of the line, or both together, one does not know. But certainly the army was made aware that it had a chief, a strong one, and the soldiers watching the barricades began to take a tougher attitude toward the insurgents. By Saturday, January 30, the long negotiations between de Gaulle and the High Command in Algeria carried on through the prestidigious General Ely, bore fruit. An order from Challe called the Home Guards into service by ordering them to report to their recruiting stations in uniform. This call to arms brought many of them out from the barricades with the belated realization that the army was not, after all, going to support the rebels of Algiers. On Saturday also the paratroops under Brigadier-

347

General Kléber-Toulouse, who had replaced Gracieux, formed a solid phalanx around the barricades and successfully isolated them from the general population.

Meanwhile Ortiz and Lagaillarde smelled the turn of the wind. They had several anxious meetings with certain army officers and began to discuss terms of possible retreat. They made several offers of "honorable surrender" which the government would not accept. De Gaulle refused to allow them to surrender with arms or return to their homes, nor would he promise them amnesty. On the same day came news that Gaullist support had rallied in outlying areas of Algeria. In Oran, for example, settlers themselves pulled down activist barricades and announced their Gaullist sympathies. General Gambiez of that region, in his double capacity of prefect and commander, broadcast the complete obedience of his troops, himself, and the local politicians to the French Government. From Constantine came other reassurances of loyalty.

On Sunday, January 31, the army with deceptive calm quashed nearly all attempts at fraternization or the delivery of food and supplies to the men behind the barricade. After several minor breakthroughs in the afternoon, the French regulars moved forward quietly and with bodily force and gun butts, slowly pushed the citizens away from the rebel strongholds. Their action cost no more than a few battered noses and bruised heads, but it signified that de Gaulle had finally won his battle short of renewed civil war in which hundreds might have been killed. However, this victory was a painful one. De Gaulle had been forced to endure for nearly a week the sight of central power in the hands of the insurgents and the army. He had also given promises to the army which he might later regret.

Commander-in-Chief Ely's persuasion of the army to continue its loyalty to de Gaulle was perhaps as important to the turn of events as de Gaulle's own steadfast leadership. Ely's performance was all the more impressive when one takes into account the fact that he preferred the army's politics to that of the President's, and that he really believed that de Gaulle faced not sporadic cases of treason in the officers' corps, but a disaffection of the whole body military. De Gaulle's stand against the army, although not without private compromise, was still firmly bound to self-determination for the Algerian people, and it was adamant enough to trigger the worst reaction had it been inevitable. Indeed, Debré, after his trip on January 26 had been convinced that de Gaulle would lose the entire army if he did not amend his statement of September 16, 1959. Ely stated the problem as follows: even if only a few officers had reached the point of overt complicity with the activists, the others "might criticize the companions who were most engaged in political activity. But they could not treat them as plotters and enemies. One cannot fight the partisans of France when one is fighting her enemies." [11]

De Gaulle, who had hoped that the appointment of Colonel Bréchignac and General Gracieux, neither of whom had any connection with the situation in Algiers, might ameliorate the problem, became desolate watching the army, continue day after day to show its face of "complacent incertitude." To make matters worse, Ely had advised de Gaulle that the insurgents had no real reason to give up their positions. Armed as they were, it would have taken a pitched battle and the lives of some seven hundred men to reduce the barricades. Neither he nor the insurgents believed that the army would have the stomach for such action. Apropos the policy of self-determination for Algeria, Ely purportedly said to de Gaulle that the time to see if the army were willing to accept it was after, not before, pacification had been achieved. A French victory would prove that the government was sincere in saying that it wanted a "French" solution in Algeria and would under no circumstances negotiate with the F.L.N. Beyond assurance of this, and the possibility of rebellion without this assurance, Ely did not believe that the army had a candidate to replace the present "patron." One of the young colonel activists remarked, "They wouldn't want, all the same, to replace General de Gaulle with M. Pinay."

So negotiations between the army and the government boiled down to these demands upon de Gaulle: another promise of no negotiations with the Algerian rebels; assurance of a "French" solution to the Algerian problem; and some formula to permit the insurgents to save face. De Gaulle answered that he could not and would not change his offer of self-determination, that he had already stated many times that he would never negotiate with the F.L.N., and that he would, with his council of ministers, decide upon measures to be taken against the insurgents. Obviously he was too intelligent to resort to a bloodbath of *petit commerçants* and hysterical citizenry, but on the other hand he was not going to guarantee the immunity of the rebel leaders. On this point he was both correct and wise, and the army understood. De Gaulle's speech of January 29, strong and reasonable as it was, did much to convince the wavering factions of the army that here was the old de Gaulle, a chief not to be taken lightly. The plain talk between Ely and the General Staff in Algiers convinced sufficient high-ranking officers that their road lay clearly behind de Gaulle. The anguished Challe, who had on two occasions announced that the final assignment of the army was to secure French Algeria, was reassured and took a firmer stand. At Constantine Generals Gandoet and Lennuyeux relaxed, once more succumbing to the magic phrase "the most French solution." And Crépin who had replaced Massu but had not been able to regain authority over his troops, is purported to have said brusquely to the colonels of the General Staff of the Army of Algeria: "You have satisfaction in the essentials. Now you must obey. It is the only condition through which the army will find again any authority under de Gaulle and the government." [12] But underneath the obedience rumbled the question of the army: Have we once more been had as we were on May 13, 1958?

Although de Gaulle via the army had demanded unconditional surrender of the insurgents, the military managed to find a "face-saving expedient" by allowing the surrendered rebels to remain "in operational units to be attached for the time being to the First Paratroop Regiment of the Foreign Legion." [13] Of the three insurgent leaders, Martel, Ortiz, and Lagaillarde who a few hours before had sworn to fight and die for the stand they had taken, only one, the young Pierre Lagaillarde, a deputy in the French National Assembly, gave himself up without any guarantees of protection, to the custody of the army. Ortiz fled over the barricades into the tortuous streets of Algiers during the night before the surrender, to be reported later in Belgium, and Robert Martel conveniently disappeared. The Home Guards who had not responded to General Challe's order of mobilization were told to report to battalion headquarters. Civilian rebels were allowed to surrender their arms and return to their homes if they chose.

Early on Monday morning, February 1, Lagaillarde and the group of men who had agreed to put themselves at the disposal of the army, marched out of their redoubt, their complement now reduced from the 1200 men who were holding out the night before to 420. Carrying their arms, which they surrendered, and a French flag, they were taken by truck to the rest camp of the First Regiment of the Foreign Legion at Zeralda, twenty-five miles west of Algiers. Lagaillarde and his men were roundly cheered by the residents of Algiers as they drove out through the now peaceful city. But apparently the patriotic zeal of many of the new volunteers (including that of Lagaillarde's father) waned before sunset. General Crépin announced that the former insurgents might prove their patriotism by forming special units which would remain temporarily attached to the regiment of Legionnaires. One commando, named "Alcazar" after a unit of pro-Franco cadets in the Spanish Civil War, thus came into being.

From Reuters came the official translation of the surrender issued by Crépin:

> The redoubt set up since Sunday, January 24, was evacuated today beginning at 1100 hours (5 A.M. E.S.T.). It had been agreed on the night of Sunday-Monday that the occupants could either return home individually after handing over their arms to the authorities or, as for the U.T.B., return to their general headquarters, or for those who so desired, to remain at the disposal of the army in the framework of special operation units and, at least for a time, with the First Paratroop Regiment of the Foreign Legion.

The evacuation of the barricades took place according to plan and in the best order. Apparently the insurgents' last few hours had been filled with bitterness. There was spleen between the followers of Ortiz and those of Lagaillarde, and most of Ortiz's men had fled over the barricades during the night. There had been real anguish at the "betrayal" of the army and the sudden indifference of the citizens, and the fear that the army might fire at them had been very real once the Tenth Division of Paratroops had been eased out of the city. After the regulars from the *bléd* and the *djebels* had moved into Algiers, most of the insurgents had realized that the game was up.

While the surrender was taking place in Algiers, in Paris a general strike requested by de Gaulle gave evidence that the left supported the President in at least one phase of his politics —the Algerian policy. A work stoppage of less than an hour— between 11:00 A.M. and noon, was called by France's three largest trade unions in response to de Gaulle's appeal. Strikers of the C.G.T., the F.O. and the C.F.T.C. issued a manifesto against the ultras and for self-determination of the Algerians. All the political parties, except some right-wing Independents and certain dissident members in the government itself supported de Gaulle in his stand against the insurgents. But even as the left rallied, de Gaulle took steps to increase his power to absolute dictatorial status until April 1, 1961. Once again the paradox of the Gaullist regime became apparent. Supported for the first time by the Communists, both Socialist groups—*Union de la Gauche Socialiste* and *Parti Socialiste Autonome*—and by such offshoots of the old Radical Socialist Party as Mendès-France, de Gaulle moved closer to the position they most abhor, that of absolute authority under the guise of Republican government.

MORE POWER TO DE GAULLE

On Tuesday, February 2, after a debate of only three hours, the Assembly voted by a very strong majority (441-75 and the Senate 226-39) to accord de Gaulle the exceptional powers he demanded for the government. The Independents remained divided, but the U.N.R. in spite of the politics of Soustelle's followers, came through without a trace of weakness. Guy Mollet assured the Assembly that de Gaulle had promised him that morning that the powers would be used "profoundly to cleanse the administration, the army, the services of the Algiers administration."

Article 38, which was at this time legally invoked by the Assembly for the government of Michel Debré, gave de Gaulle the authority to legislate by ordinance or decree upon matters relating to security of the state, the administration of Algeria, and indirectly through these to control public liberties of all kinds. Article 38 extended broad powers.

> The Government may, in order to carry out its program, ask Parliament to authorize it, for a limited period, to take through ordinances measures that are normally within the domain of law.
>
> The ordinances shall be enacted in meetings of the Council of Ministers after consultation with the Council of State. They shall come into force upon their publication, but shall become null and void if the bill for their ratification is not submitted to Parliament before the date set by the enabling act.
>
> At the expiration of the time limit referred to in the first paragraph of the present article, the ordinance may be modified only by law in those matters which are within the legislative domain.

Jacques Fauvet has declared this article of the Constitution to be of all of them: "the most convenient, the most unjustified, the most dangerous perhaps." One of de Gaulle's spokesmen said for him in this regard:

> General de Gaulle has decided to proceed to a vast and rapid purge of the army, of the administration and of the magistrature. He does not wish to have to make concessions with this or that army clan to elaborate his Algerian policy. The recent experience has demonstrated

353

to him that simple mutations of superior officers were insufficient to re-establish his authority over the army. He wants to go on to more radical measures which concern all the levels of the military hierarchy. He does not wish to see his decisions contravened by the reticence of magistrates as they were in the abortive arrest of Le Pen [Poujadist Deputy of the Assembly]. He wants to be able to send a colonel to Nouméa without having to name him a general.[14]

Article 38 gave Charles de Gaulle, who is in reality the "government of Michel Debré," the right to assume many functions which were normally under the jurisdiction of Parliament. Parliament, however, must have these ordinances or decrees of de Gaulle submitted to it for ratification by April 1, 1961, at the latest. And Article 38 is null and void if Parliament is dissolved.

The Assembly, in giving de Gaulle special powers for the "maintenance of law and order, the safeguarding of the state, and the pacification and administration of Algeria," was treated to the following *"exposé des motifs."*

> Once again, France is being put to the test by serious events. Doubtless the authority of General de Gaulle and the unity of the nation behind the Chief of State have succeeded in saving the Republic from a major crisis, whose consequences would have been incalculable. But, in the over-all situation in which the country finds itself, and considering the extraordinary nature of the Algerian problem, the risk of deep-seated disturbances remains hanging over the state.
>
> In order to enable the Republic to surmount this risk in every case, it is essential, in accordance with Republican tradition and in implementation of Article 38 of the Constitution, to give the executive the means of dealing with a very unusual situation and to make appropriate use of the authority of the State, which is the primary

condition of the nation's future. In other words, the Government must be able to take by ordinance the measures necessary for the maintenance of law and order, the safeguarding of the State. . . .

Thus the purpose is neither to embark, through this means, on a series of comprehensive reforms nor to reconsider the fundamental principles of our public law. It is merely necessary—but this is fundamental—to give the words "Republican (form of) Government" the meaning they must have in a period of extraordinary difficulty. . . .[15]

On the same day Premier Debré made a speech, which after stating that those Frenchmen implicated in the civil strife in Algeria would be brought to judgment and made to face the responsibility of their actions, had these important paragraphs.

. . . from these barricades, from this outbreak, from the actions which preceded and accompanied them, there are lessons to be learned.

All ambiguity must be removed from France's policy in Algeria. The State must be put in a position to face the harsh tests of this difficult century in which we live. . . .

What matters above all is to understand and to make it understood that France can settle this tragedy only to the extent that her line of policy is not doubted, to the extent that all the authorities and administrations responsible for the future of Algeria base their actions on this policy alone, and also to the extent—and this is of prime importance—that there can be no doubt as to the stability of the institutions and the firmness of the State.[16]

The section dealing with the possible end or continuance of the war in Algeria, still euphemistically termed the "pacification" was also most interesting both to the F.L.N. and the world in general. From it only one conclusion could be drawn—the war will continue. Debré said:

> An offer has been made in the name of France which is called a 'cease-fire.' Its terms and conditions have been defined. There has been no response to it up to now. Consequently, as was provided and has always been said, the effort of pacification will be carried on until it has been completed and France will continue to make the effort which is necessary so that—throughout all Algeria—order in the towns and the countryside and security for all the citizens may reign again. . . .
>
> The second aspect, the second step, is self-determination for the Algerians. When peace has come, *when the necessary—and long—cooling-off period has been completed, the men and women of Algeria will choose their destiny*. (The italics are the authors'.)

Debré finally joined de Gaulle's team.

These paragraphs were the crux of the speech; and they tipped off an anxiously waiting F.L.N. (which had looked with expressed approval on some aspects of de Gaulle's manipulation of the right) that, in spite of particular action taken against certain enemies of the state, nothing had really changed. In fact, the September 16 announcement was once again vitiated in the statement concerning "the long cooling-off period." Hopes for a Gaullist settlement which had begun to rise in the autumn now waned in additional bitterness.

The particular steps de Gaulle's government has taken against certain activists implicated in the January rebellion have in themselves pleased the majority of citizens in metropolitan France. The implication that the war will no doubt go on and on has pleased them less. And the broad basis of power from which de Gaulle must operate, or so he believes, to secure the State from treason, is something most suspect to them. They would look upon the assumption of Article 38 with even more dismay and aversion if it were not for the element of personal trust which remains between most Frenchmen and de Gaulle, and of de Gaulle for his "old and dear country." Once again Charles de Gaulle has proved to be that dangerous thing, the indispensable man, and once again the country realizes what violence might be done if his personal regime should be terminated by death or rebellion. They are also uneasily aware that the great beast of the army still stirs with disaffection, its huge strength in the most part unaffected by French opinion at home.

CLEANING THE FRENCH HOUSE

Four days after the assumption of special powers de Gaulle took the following steps to purge the government. Pierre Messmer replaced M. Pierre Guillaumat as Minister of the Armed Forces. Guillaumat was shifted to the post of Delegate to the Prime Minister, thus kept in the government but shorn of special or dangerous powers. Roger Frey was succeeded as Minister of Information by M. Terrenoire, another Deputy of the U.N.R. Frey was also made a Delegate to the Prime Minister. The most resounding slap in the face was reserved for Jacques Soustelle, champion of the May 13 revolt and beloved of the Europeans of Algeria. De Gaulle ordered him to resign because of his outspoken support of the policy of integration in face of the new government policy of self-determination. Soustelle's former province, which included Sahara and the Overseas Territories, and atomic energy, was divided between Guillaumat (atomic energy) and R. Lecourt, an M.R.P., who took over the Sahara and Overseas Territories. The Ministry of Public Communications, formerly in the hands of M. Cornut-Gentille, U.N.R., was given to Maurice Bokanowski, U.N.R., who was moved up from a position within the ministry of the interior to take a cabinet post. Jean Foizet was made Secretary of State for Community Relations. After the shuffling among the ministers, the cabinet remained divided in this fashion. There were twelve non-parliamentarians, five U.N.R.

members, two M.R.P.'s and two Independents. Both Messmer and Terrenoire are old friends and followers of de Gaulle and comrades of the Resistance.[17]

Jacques Soustelle made this strong declaration to the press on the day of his curt dismissal from the government.

> Nineteen years, seven months and eighteen days after the date on which I answered the call of General de Gaulle; one year, eight months and twenty-three days after May 13, 1958, I am excluded from the government to the applause of those who have never pardoned me for the part I played in the founding of the new regime.
>
> No one can pretend that I have not successfully acquitted myself of my functions: the results obtained in the Sahara, overseas, and in the atomic domain speak for themselves.
>
> As to the tragic events of these last days, it is established that I took no part and have no responsibility: the highest authority of the state gives evidence for me on this point. Thus the exclusion of which I am the object has no other motive than the attachment that I seem to hold in spite of everything for the cause of French Algeria.
>
> On this point nothing or no one can swerve my conviction. I can only obey my conscience.
>
> At the moment when I am evicted from the government, I reiterate with more force than ever the warnings which I have multiplied in vain these latter days.
>
> First nothing of any avail will be accomplished in Algeria while the rigors of republican law are not visited upon the Communists and defeatists, accomplices of the F.L.N., whose impunity has pushed to despair the unfortunate victims of terrorism and whose insults have demoralized the army.[18]

358

In Algeria under the orders of Delouvrier and Massu's successor, General Crépin, police activity was increased. Five activist organizations were dissolved and outlawed. They were Ortiz's group, the F.N.F., the M.P. 13 (*Mouvement Populaire de 13 Mai*), the Movement for Installation of a Corporate Order, the M.N.E. (National Student Protection and Assistance Movement), the A.G.E.A. of Lagaillarde and Susini, and the *Comité d'entente,* a committee which served to integrate the activity of the other five. Two legal processes were opened in Paris and Algiers, one for homicide resulting from the shooting on January 25, and one for attempt to overthrow the government. Under these counts some seventeen people are being prosecuted by the French Government.

Under house arrest was Alain de Sérigny whose *Echo d'Alger* had for years been pouring the idea of French Algeria at any cost, and later Soustelle's philosophy of integration, into the minds of Algerian citizens. A temporary Gaullist, de Sérigny took great care that the people should not be made aware of the support de Gaulle had in France and in the world at large when he offered his Algerian policy of September 16. From this moment on he became openly critical of French policy, as indeed he had been during the Fourth Republic. Since the banning of the opposition press in Algeria, the *Echo* had gradually assumed the quality of a huge brain-washing apparatus, and de Sérigny, ancient Pétainist and potential fascist, became more and more offensive in his editorials until he made the final open challenge to de Gaulle over the withdrawal of Massu.

It is said that the Muslims of the Casbah of Algiers could hardly believe that "Mr. *Colon*" himself had been hauled away to jail. (He was picked up on a ship he owned leaving for Marseilles.) Lagaillarde was tucked safely away in the Santé prison from which Ben Bella and associates had recently been graduated. Ortiz, the object of wide police search, was still at large. Doctor Lefevre of May 13 fame, and Messieurs Parachini, Schambill and Féral, the latter president of the N.M.E., were also arrested. Deputy Jean-Baptiste Biaggi who barely escaped arrest under the Fourth Republic was apprehended at Orly Field, and in spite of "parliamentary immunity" joined Lagaillarde at the Santé. His traveling companion Deputy Mourad Kaouah was also arrested and both were charged with having plotted against the internal security of the state, a crime liable to the death penalty. Two other Deputies and long-time troublemakers, Jean Demarquet and Jean-Marie Le Pen were the objects of government search. Jean Meninghaud who carried the word from the Ortiz redoubt to the army, Robert Martel of the U.F.N.A., and Maurice Crespin, his right arm, Doctor Perez, former President of the F.N.F., Jacques Susini of the A.G.E.A. and M. Michaud, President of the university movement, were all apprehended or sought. It is interesting to reiterate once more that most of these men were active in May 13 plotting and have, in comparative safety, multiplied their revolutionary activities since the beginning of the Fifth Republic.

The reshuffling within the army subsequent to the January uprising has been the object of widespread rumors, the most drastic of which declared that forty colonels or other high-ranking officers had been placed under house arrest. It is known that some officers who had responsible parts in the uprising have been recalled to Paris. Among them are Colonel Argoud, Chief of Staff of the Army of Algiers. Lieutenant-Colonels Broizat of the Tenth Parachute Division, Gardès of the *Cinquième Bureau* (intelligence), and Colonel Bigeard, serving in the South Oran zone, were also recalled. Colonel Yves Godard, who was in charge of the police of the city of Algiers, both civil and military, was arrested and so also Gaston Trouja, police commissioner of that city. Auguste Arnould, head of the C.A.N.A.C. which claimed the backing of 50,000 veterans, was arrested on February 11.

By the last week in April, 1960, de Gaulle drastically altered the high command in Algeria. Generals known to be solid Gaullists—often they held the *Compagnon de la Libération* award, the top decoration awarded personally by de Gaulle to a small number of outstanding Resistance leaders—and generals who never mixed soldiering with politics took over at the President's order. Whether this really brought the army to heel under civil command or not was still an unanswered question, but the purpose was clear. Jean Crépin, a "no-nonsense" general assumed Challe's post as High Commander of the Army of Algeria. With a distinguished record in the Resistance and an outspoken dislike for politically-minded army officers, he seemed perfect for the job de Gaulle wanted done. Another *Compagnon de la Libération*, Lieutenant-General Adolphe Vezinet, assumed Massu's old command in the highly important Algiers district. The famous and notorious Tenth Parachute Division was relinquished by Brigadier-General Jean Gracieux, considered a political general, to another Resistance hero, Brigadier-General Bernard Saint-Hillier. Admiral Philippe Auboyneau, who held the line against "the foul blow," kept his command of French naval forces in the Western Mediterranean. As important as this change in the high command, were the new assignments right down the line to the rank of lieutenant, where known Gaullists and politically disinterested officers earned promotions and enlarged responsibility.

In Paris, under the direction of special magistrates who were appointed after the vote of "special powers," the investigation of treasonable activity continued. Inquests dealing with the several truckloads of ammunition which were found behind the barricades at the time of surrender proceeded, and rightist arms traffic between France and Algeria fell under examination. These investigations led to a shake-up of no small dimension. "Leather nose" Thomazo of May 13 fame, now a deputy of the U.N.R., was subject to house search, and in subversive centers, such as Lyon and Toulouse, raids and seizures were made which produced heavy documentation of the extent of the subversion against the regime. In Lille a plot against the life of de Gaulle was investigated.

In spite of this crack-down, *Le Monde* asserted a week after the barricades were reduced (therefore quite early for mature judgment) that the Bureau of Psychological Warfare was still maintaining its old line. It continued to publish leaflets declaring that the army was in Algeria for the sole purpose of keeping that colony French. On February 10 the Bureau was closed down and

Major Victor Sapin-Lignière, commander of the U.T.B., arrested, and the Home Guard unit dissolved. Major-General Faure was called to Paris and removed from his command although, serving in Kabylia, he was not known to have direct connection with the latest coup of the activists. In any case he had been sufficiently damned by ancient evidence.[19]

Early in February, for the first time since January 23, metropolitan newspapers, which the army had kept from circulation in Algiers during the insurrection, were back in the streets.[20] But during the time of the insurrection the insurgents had had no way of knowing that the opinion of Paris, indeed, of the world at large, was against their operation. Along with liberal news came a group of devoted officials to take over the legal and police functions in Algiers. They were Attorney-General Robert Schmelck, Jacques Aubert, Director of the Secret Police for Algeria, and Jean Fachot, Police Commissioner of Algiers. According to Henry Tanner, Schmelck was Secretary General of the Control Commission that supervised the Referendum and national elections in the Fall of 1958, and he was heavily criticized by army officers and extremists. Aubert was an administration man in Constantine and had a reputation of being "a friend of the Muslims." Fachot, like so many of the people now working with the de Gaulle government, is an old Resistance comrade from the Free French forces. "M. Schmelck demanded at his installation today that the courts give fair but heavy punishment to the men who have been criminal or crazy enough to attempt a coup while our men are fighting in the mountains." [21]

With the authority of the state seemingly re-established and the army experiencing a coming-to-terms with the central government that it has not had to make for several years, there are many hopeful aspects of the abortive revolution of January, 1960. It would be nice to believe that it will soon be possible, as a young officer on leave humorously remarked, to be an outspoken partisan of self-determination in Algeria and a Gaullist as well. The draftees served the state well during the period of uncertainty. Aghast at having to come in from the mountains and the *bléd* to defend the Republic against Frenchmen, they managed

362

to accomplish that task with the minimum of disaster. It must have been quite a shock for the activists to see, for a change, men in the uniform of the French army answering *"vive de Gaulle"* to their cries of *"De Gaulle Assassin," "De Gaulle au poteau."* And it must have been surprising for the Home Guards and the men behind the barricades to learn that there was a portion of the army ready to isolate them from their source of supplies, strength and affections, in fact, to reduce them, if necessary, in the name of the French government.

It was also heartwarming to see that rightist attempts to stir up the Casbah did not work. It was good that the activists did not direct their venom against their Muslim "brothers" as well as their brother Frenchmen. And while the French Algerians marched about demanding Massu's return, the "defender of the Casbah" was himself the object of calumny. Muslim bands, small, and mainly children, formed parades crying *"Massu au poteau"* and *"Vive de Gaulle."* But what hope for the future does this aggregation of favorable signs have?

PEACE OR WAR

De Gaulle, while declaring that he had offered the F.L.N. a cease-fire, has continually refused to discuss with them any facets of the Algerian political future. Since the settlers' rebellion of January, 1960, he has stated that the Algerian Provisional Government has chosen to continue the war by refusing to accept his offer of pourparlers. This is a very clouded issue, certainly clouded from the French side, where de Gaulle, while promising self-determination, puts it in a future of his choosing after a pacification of his determination, and then promises the French army that it can guarantee the fairness of the election. While hoping that the Algerians will vote for a French solution of a federated nature, de Gaulle is by no means certain that a free vote would result in this kind of Algeria. Apparently the settlers and the army are even less sure. And yet he has promised that no French citizen who wishes to remain one can be allowed to be anything but French. But he has also spoken of an "Algerian Algeria." It would seem that he has ideas, perhaps of a last resort, of a population and nationality division for Algeria. Such a partition would, of course, be abhorrent to the F.L.N. for it would leave the French in possession of the richest and most developed land. It would also secure the Sahara for them. This kind of self-determination would not be acceptable to those Algerians who have for nearly six years been fighting for independence of an Algeria defined by its present boundaries.

Ferhat Abbas, on the other hand, called de Gaulle's bluff when the latter said it was evident that the F.L.N. did not really want a cease-fire. The head of the Algerian Provisional Government offered the prospect of immediate pourparlers and immediate peace. He has chosen on one, or perhaps two occasions, a representative Algerian group to meet directly with de Gaulle. His latest offer in spring 1960 de Gaulle denies having received, saying it was not a "written" one and that it did not come through proper channels, i.e., the Moroccan or Tunisian embassy. But all of this is and remains double talk. Perhaps there is some of it on both sides. It is very likely that de Gaulle, with free hands, would not temporize in such a fashion with the problem of cease-fire. It is even possible that he might see his way clear to negotiate directly with the F.L.N. if it were not for the phobia the European extremists and the rightist army chiefs have to any kind of pourparlers with the rebels. They believe that negotiation is the first step toward selling France in Algeria "down the river." Although de Gaulle will not accede to this pressure sufficiently to change his publicly stated and internationally well-received policy of self-determination for Algeria, he was obliged once more to give them some kind of a guarantee. And that has been that the army will *not* leave Algeria until it has been conquered, pacified, if you will, and the revolutionaries made subservient to the French. The army still apparently believes in its two-handed mission, fighting and developing, coercing and killing, and persuading by loving kindness and automatic weapons, even by torture. Surely de Gaulle must know the hopelessness of this formula, so long a failure, but he is shielding himself while he must with Olympian ambiguity all the while hoping public opinion in France and in the world at large must, at some time in the near future, sway the views of the army and the *gros colons*.

Observers of both camps made much of the fact that de Gaulle during his trip to Algeria and tour of the army posts early in March, 1960, promised the army that they should organize the political consultation which he hopes will take place after peace has been achieved. This sounds like a retreat into the worst days of Franco-Algerian relations. The Provisional Government of the Algerian Republic, which, as we have remarked, emitted certain hopeful sounds when it got wind of the massive retaliation against the right that de Gaulle had organized, stiffened visibly and declared that there was no possibility of anything but a long and bitter war when it heard he had promised the army the right of electoral control. On the other hand, observers aware of the Gaullist way of nibbling a bit at a time of the desired solution, also point out that de Gaulle did not say that other neutral observers might not be present during the elections.

The crux of the Algerian situation remains whether or not authority has really been permanently returned to the head of the state or whether in actuality it rests in the hands of a brooding army licking its wounds and biding its time. Whether or not the rebellion strengthened de Gaulle or weakened him is also difficult to decide at this time. The fact that, after nearly two years of international acclaim for the man who had "stabilized" France, put her back on her feet, his authority was denied by Frenchmen, and above all by French army officers, for a period of several days cannot help to raise questions in the minds of observers. De Gaulle has painted a certain picture of La France in the hope that seeming, when relied on long enough, will actually become being. An enormous number of people have already been taken in. America is full of people who keep saying both privately and through the mediums of news magazines, that de Gaulle is just a step away from solving the Algerian question. In fact these people are simply mouthing what they would like to believe. The American government, above all, would like to believe it, otherwise France in N.A.T.O. is going to demand more and more in the way of Western support of the French Algerian policy. Because this is a hard fence to straddle, many of our commentators are trying to help make de Gaulle's seeming become true. A recent column of Walter Lippman, declaring that we should support de Gaulle's Algerian policy "now that it had been made clear" is a perfect case in point, and also an article in *U. S. News & World Report,* February 15, 1960. *Why France turns to a "Dictator."* In a paragraph headed *UP TO MOSLEMS NOW* there is this statement:

'It is up to the Moslems now,' said one French official. 'De Gaulle has shown them that he is strong enough to negotiate peace which will permit independence if the Moslems of Algeria want it. Now it is up to the rebels to accept negotiations.'

In commenting on the speculations of the American press, the representative for the Algerian Office in New York declared that in them the "clear-cut positions of the Provisional Government of the Algerian Republic were either misunderstood or distorted." The following letter from A. Chanderli, the permanent Representative of the Algerian Front of National Liberation is here appended to give the other side of the picture.

LETTER TO THE NEW YORK TIMES OF THE PERMANENT REPRESENTATIVE OF THE ALGERIAN FRONT OF NATIONAL LIBERATION, January 28, 1960

Dear Sir:

In their respective declarations of September 16 and September 28, 1959, the French Government and the Algerian Provisional Government accepted the principle of self-determination as the basis for a peaceful and just settlement of the Algerian problem.

What is the explanation of the fact that since this time, the prospects of a rapid solution and an immediate peace have not appeared?

The Algerian Provisional Government's statement of September 28 declared its readiness at any moment to enter into pourparlers with the French Government to discuss the conditions and guarantees for the application of self-determination. As Premier Ferhat Abbas reaffirmed yesterday (January 27, 1960), eventual negotiations with France about self-determination and a cease-fire do not concern 'the future of Algeria.' 'From the moment that the Algerian people's right to choose its own destiny was recognized, there is no longer any place for a pre-determined status. . . . The object of the negotiations are the means and guarantees for the applications of self-determination and the conditions of the cease-fire.'

While the French Government has until now refused to enter such pourparlers, the most responsible French authorities have issued a series of declarations and messages—statements which were designed to minimize the content of self-determination and assure its eventual application by the French army and administration. In the light of such statements which removed the very essence of meaning from self-determination, it was not only logical but indispensable that there be discussion of the conditions and guarantees for the application of self-determination.

The events of the past week have shown even more dramatically the necessity for such discussions.

The armed colons in Algeria, backed up by certain Deputies in the French National Assembly, have now publicly denounced the principles of self-determination. And the commander-in-chief of the French armed forces in Algeria, General Maurice Challe categorically affirmed on January 28, 1960:

'The French Army is fighting so that Algeria remains definitely French.'

The responsibility for the continuation of the war in Algeria is clear.

And yet, in your January 28th editorial, commenting on General de Gaulle's offer of self-determination, you wrote: 'The folly of the Algerian rebel leaders in not grasping this opportunity when it was offered and when it could have been put into effect ought to be obvious.'

On the contrary, it is obvious that without firm guarantees no certainty could exist that real self-determination will be 'put into effect.'

Sincerely yours,
A. Chanderli
Permanent Representative of
the Algerian Front of National
Liberation.[22]

In a similar rebuttal to the *New York Herald Tribune,* February 4, 1960, Chanderli pointed up certain facts that are still little known to the average American. First he maintained that the struggle between the Algerian rebels and the French army is a full-scale war, not a repression of a few criminal outlaws and terrorists. After all, the French Army in Algeria numbers more than half a million men, and the Army of National Liberation has kept them stalemated for over five years. "Military communiqués," he says, "published in your own newspaper report the daily field battles which continue to claim monthly casualties of more than 3,000."

Chanderli also mentions that, although the press is quick to mention the "terroristic nature" of the war waged by the Algerian rebels, it is reluctant to accuse the French army of such proved excesses as torture, reprisals against villages, and concentration camps. Although *Le Monde,* January 5, 1960, in Paris published the report of the International Committee of the Red Cross which gave documentary proof of the deplorable conditions in the French camps of resettlement in Algeria, small coverage has been given in the U. S. press to the plight of the some 2,000,000 Muslims detained in the regroupment areas by the French. He then rebutted the argument concerning the folly of the establishment of the Algerian Provisional Government. The editorial had stated that the formation of the G.P.R.A. had been a blunder because "negotiating with them would be tantamount to recognizing their sovereignty." In answer Chanderli declared that the Algerian Provisional Government, as its name suggests, considers itself only "the trustee and guarantor of the interests of the Algerian people until this people shall freely pronounce itself."

In commenting upon the long history of *"élections à l'Algérienne,"* Chanderli noted de Gaulle's statement of January 29, 1960, to the army which proposed still one more. The French president said, "When the time comes for the consultation, you will have to guarantee its complete and sincere freedom." Chanderli considered this arrangement to "subordinate the free choice of a people to the 'good will' of an army of occupation." [23]

Just four days before the settlers' uprising in Algiers, the National Council of the Algerian Revolution (C.N.R.A.) published a text explaining certain modifications of the apparatus of the Algerian Provisional Government. Covering the progress of the war, the government's foreign policy and the coordination of aid and support to the Algerian Revolution from "nations devoted to liberty," the text also confirmed the fact that the Algerian Provisional Government had recognized (September 28, 1959) the recourse to self-determination as "one of the ways of regaining independence." The bulletin further claimed that after this position had been taken, peace could have been immediate if the French had been willing to accept the designated negotiators (among whom were Ben Bella and the other imprisoned Algerian leaders) of the Algerian Provisional Government. Instead, the French government, ignoring the *ruse de guerre* which cast these leaders into jail, answered in Gaullian tones that it was unable to negotiate with Algerian deputies who were *hors de combat.*

In answer to de Gaulle's offer of self-determination *after* a successfully conducted pacification, the C.N.R.A. "stressed the basic contradiction which existed between the recognition of the principle of self-determination and, on the other hand, the refusal of negotiations and the pursuit of the war by the French

369

Government—a long war for which it is preparing by mobilizing new draftees and strengthening the means of destruction at the disposal of its army." [24]

Speaking in general terms of the sacrifice of the Algerian soldiers and martyrs during the long war, the document pays specific homage to the "500,000 Algerians in France who are carrying on an anti-racist and anti-colonialist combat." Making good use of the Red Cross International Committee's material on the French internment centers in Algeria, the text denounced the regroupment in camps of "so-called" *hébergement* (regroupment) of millions of men, women, and children in conditions of famine, misery, and death.

In another section of the released text of the C.N.R.A. meetings, December 16, 1959-January 18, 1960, in Tripoli, the use of torture, "carried to such a degree of perfection that it is now a subject of instruction in the specialized schools of the French army," is noted. The report accuses the United States Government of continuing support for the war policy of France and of furnishing that nation with matériel to wage the Algerian war in return for France's cooperation in N.A.T.O., whose resources, it claims, are also mobilized against the Algerian people. Condemning the U. S., the Algerian Provisional Government, on the other hand, is warmly grateful for the "constant support" given its cause by the socialist countries.

According to a publication of December 16, 1959, the composition of the Provisional Government of the Algerian Republic was as follows:

> Premier: Ferhat Abbas
> Vice-premier and Minister of External Affairs: Krim Belkacem
> Vice-premier: Mohamed Ben Bella
> Ministers of State: Hussein Ait-Ahmed, Rabah Bitat, Mohamed Boudiaf, Mohammed Khider, Said Mohammedi
> Minister of Social and Cultural Affairs: Abdel Hamid Mehri

Minister of Armament and Communications: Abdel Hafid Boussouf

Minister of Finance and Economic Affairs: Ahmed Francis

Minister of Information: M'hammed Yazid

Minister of Internal Affairs: Lakhdar Ben Tobbal

Interministerial Committee of National Defense: Krim Belkacem, Lakhdar Ben Tobbal, and Abdel Hafid Boussouf

On January 29, 1960, as the settlers' revolt was being painfully brought under control in Algiers, the G.P.R.A. issued another interesting statement. The gist of it was that the French Governments (apparently those of the Fourth and Fifth Republic are lumped together) have never been able to control the 'ultras' who have dictated French Algerian policy for many years. It is in the intransigence of this group which will not recognize the right of the Algerian people to self-determination that blame for the prolonged war must be placed. It is against this group that the G.P.R.A. needs guarantees of a free consultation, not against the average Frenchman of the Metropole.

> The present events in Algeria are ample demonstration—if there is further need for this—that the Provisional Government of the Algerian Republic had every reason to call for these guarantees (when asking for pourparlers). The French people can recognize the Algerian people's right to self-determination. But that does not settle the problem since the application of this right remains subordinate to the good will of the army of occupation and the 'ultras.'

.   .   .   .

> Aware that the 'ultras,' in agreement with certain French generals, were waiting for what they called the 'international storm' to pass to re-open the entire matter, the Provisional Government of the Algerian Republic, helped by its friends, tried to have a resolu-

371

tion adopted by the United Nations in order to consolidate the position of those in France who sincerely desire a peaceful settlement. The western powers who opposed any resolution at all today contemplate the consequences of their policy. Today, Algiers is in the hands of the adventurer, Ortiz, of the killer and torturer, Lagaillarde, and their gangs. The unarmed civilian population is the object of pressure from those who are trying by force to use them in their action. Already, Algerian workers have fallen under the murderous bullets of colonialists at Mostaganem.

The menace hanging over our people in the form of this uncontrolled army risks endangering the peace of the world. The Provisional Government of the Algerian Republic is not remaining passive before this situation. . . .[25]

A few days later, however, statements from an "authoritative observer" in Tunis in February gave cautious Algerian nationalist approval to General de Gaulle's purges in the army and the government. Apparently the G.P.R.A., after its blasts of the month before, was somewhat mollified by the sturdy Gaullist stand. According to Thomas Brady of the *New York Times,* (February 11, 1960) the Algerian nationalists did not seem to be particularly upset by the purported de Gaulle concessions to the army. Instead, they declared that parallel guarantees to them regarding a "neutral" observation force in an election for self-determination would be sufficient to meet their demands. The spokesman also announced that the General's action against the 'ultras' was an important step along the road to peace. It was made clear in the same interview, however, that the nationalists would not accept the idea of partition in any form. They refused to discuss a federal plan to split Algeria along the line of ethnic enclaves, because the future of all of Algeria must be in the hands of the Algerian people and such decisions could not be made for them prematurely either by the French or the G.P.R.A.

From this conciliatory statement Ferhat Abbas advanced even

farther. On February 17 he opened a "peace offensive" designed
to appeal to the moderate Algerians, both Europeans and Muslims. But the difference between his appeals, he said, and the
case of de Gaulle before the moderates was that de Gaulle in his
heart hopes that the Muslims will choose a "French" solution,
while Abbas wants an Algerian one. His wise and moving speech
of February 17, 1960, to the *Europeans of Algeria* stated:

> The settlement of this problem (the Algerian prob-
> lem)—I mean by this a just, viable and definitive
> settlement—depends first and foremost upon the Alge-
> rians themselves, that is, upon you and us. It is useless
> to deceive oneself. The hour of truth has arrived for
> our common country. In the interest of our children, in
> the interest of their future, it is essential that this truth
> be affirmed.
>
> To call upon the French Army to assure your security
> and this future, to hand over the majority of Algeria's
> inhabitants to repression and torture, to reinstate the
> 'Arab Bureaus' by means of the 'Special Administrative
> Sections,' in brief, to perpetuate colonial domination
> and racial discrimination would be to condemn our
> country to an endless war.
>
> There is no army which can assure your future in the
> colonial framework. Only the construction of an Algerian
> state can permit us to live together and to guarantee the
> future of our children.
>
> The war in Algeria is not the war of Arabs against
> Europeans or Moslems against Christians. Nor is it the
> war of the Algerian people against the French people.
> It is war imposed upon a people who for a long time
> lived on false premises, the source of its misfortunes. It
> is the war of a people who have been scorned for a long
> time. It is the war of a people deceived for a long time.
> It is time to become aware of the true nature of our
> struggle, of the legitimacy of our combat.
>
> Europeans of Algeria,

In the last century, the century of colonization, you came from all over, from France, Italy, Spain, and from Malta to settle in our midst. The colonial conquest opened the doors of our country to you. It gave you exorbitant rights which it systematically took away from us.

This colonial regime went further. It gave you the illusion that these stolen rights were owed to you, that you were superior men and that the Arabs were to be put upon and used at will. It is from this illusion that you are dying today. . . .

But this era has ended, it is completely finished. The 'Algeria of Papa' is dead. It is not General de Gaulle who destroyed it, but the Algerian people, through their struggle. What could have been understood in your fathers can no longer be understood in you. In today's world there is no longer any place for the colonial concept, there is no longer place for racial supremacy.

Therefore, do not cling to the contradictions and consequences of a corrupting past. Do not be the prisoners of a false dilemma: to destroy the Algerian people, or to leave. Do not play into the hands of the 'ultras,' . . .

Algeria is the patrimony of all. For several generations, you have called yourselves Algerians. Who denies you this title? But, in becoming your country, Algeria has not ceased to be ours. Understand and admit that, for us, Algeria is the only possible fatherland.

The Algerian patriots who have accepted to die in order to live in freedom do not begrudge you the right to enjoy the same liberty. If they refuse to be second-class men, if they refuse to recognize you as super-citizens, on the other hand they are ready to consider you as authentic Algerians.

Algeria for the Algerians, for all Algerians, whatever be their origin. This formula is not a fiction. It translates a living reality, based on a common life. It is the earth which forms man. And the earth of Algeria has formed us. It has marked us so deeply that we can live together. From now on, we are all Africans, compelled to undergo the same ordeals and to nourish the same hopes. . . .

The independence of Algeria, like that of Tunisia and Morocco, like that of all the colonized countries, is inevitable. It is written in the march of history. Already Guinea, the Cameroon, Togo, Nigeria and the Congo are independent or on the verge of independence.

Today you dread this independence. Tomorrow, you will call for it with all your hearts, for only this independence can reconcile us with ourselves, by freeing us from servitude, hatred and fear.

In the Algerian Republic which we shall build together, there will be room for all, work for all. The new Algeria will not know of any racial barrier, nor religious hatred. It will respect all values, all legitimate interests. . . .

Will Algeria live? This question was put thirty years ago. Let me give you, without passion and without hatred, the answer of those Algerians who are fighting to be free: Algeria will live because it is now, by itself, building its destiny. We want you to participate in this construction. Your honest and sincere adhesion to self-determination offers you the means. . . .

No imposed statute can establish peace and guarantee the future.

The victory to be won is over ourselves. Our salvation is within us.[26]

All the salutary moderate efforts that both the French and the G.P.R.A. seemed to have made were dissipated by news of the talks of De Gaulle and the army on March 5, 1960, in Algeria. In these conversations de Gaulle used a new phrase, that of "Algerian Algeria," a little redundant perhaps, but no doubt happy-sounding to the ears of those so long offended by

"French Algeria." He said that he believed that self-determination would eventually lead to the formation of an Algerian state tied to France. De Gaulle, avoiding the city of Algiers and going by helicopter to the army units stationed in the mountains near the Tunisian border, told the officers:

> A negotiated cease-fire with the nationalists has become improbable because they are not likely to lay down their arms. After 'pacification' has been completed, Algerians of all religious and ethnic groups will determine the future of Algeria. They are likely to reject both Francization and independence. The latter would be 'a stupidity and a monstrosity.' Officers must understand that Algeria is not the only problem that France has to solve and that the French army will not always be the Army of Algeria.[27]

Continuing the prosecution of the ultras, the government took into custody Dr. Jean-Pierre Perez, an organizer of military units for the insurgents, and Jean-Jacques Susini, President of the Algiers Student Association. These two men joined the six other members of the ultras' high command who, by May, 1960, had been rounded up; eight other leaders remained fugitives from justice. Twenty army officers and an equal number of police officers have been replaced. Beyond that it does not seem possible that the government will go, and the pamphlets from rightist organizations are still being published and distributed in Algiers. The question is, has anything basic been changed? The Algerians say no. Even though they believe that General de Gaulle is sincerely hopeful of terminating the war they think that he cannot follow his own wishes because the French Army still has his hands tied. So hopes for peace once more fell.[28]

In a text of March 14, 1960, the Provisional Government of the Algerian Republic declared that President de Gaulle's speech to the French Army Expeditionary Force in Algeria had literally closed the door to negotiations for peace. "The old colonial concepts reappeared." Of course this business of who closed the door on whom and whose desire for peace was the most honest can be bandied back and forth for a long time, and certainly there are elements on both sides who wish the war to continue. Speaking of the de Gaulle talks to the French officers, the text declared:

> From the recent declarations of General de Gaulle, it is clear that the French Government fears the popular verdict. This is why it has removed the substance from self-determination and is trying to revive the illusion of a military solution. . . .
>
> As to the menace of partition and the division of Algeria into ethnic and religious communities, as to the cantonal elections and the project of a statute imposed with the complicity of prefabricated elected officials, the only result of all this will be to perpetuate the war. . . .
>
> The perspectives of peace in Algeria appear remote. As of now, the responsibility for the pursuit of the war is established. The world has already taken note of this.[29]

As for the real war, not the war of words, there were supposedly as many monthly casualties early in 1960 as in the peak year of 1958. The terror, too, continued at a steady pace with both sides trying to win through intimidation.

In summary we might say that if the original sin of President de Gaulle was to hate the Fourth Republic so much that he was purblind to the weakness of the right and the army cabals, then it must be admitted he has paid a partial price for his guilt. If he took, on the other hand, a calculated risk to form a government of men loyal to the ideas of May 13, of ministers who believed in the possibility of "pacification" and integration, if he left an army fuming with dissidence categorically unchanged, and allowed the machinations of Lagaillard, Ortiz, Martel, Lefevre and many others to grow in power and virulence, his risk failed. Things got worse instead of better.

If he believed that his nominal leadership would be enough to put the army back in a vest-pocket, he has had a sobering lesson. For the army, though technically mutinous in limited instances, showed on the whole a vastly sulking spirit. It sat back on its haunches like some great beast waiting to be placated, expecting to be fed its regular meal, the raw meat of *"Algérie Française."*

Now the redoubts have been reduced, and significant purges, perhaps two years later than would have been wise, have taken place in the French Government, in the Algerian administration, and in the army and the police. But has the battle with the ultras really been won? It is hard to believe so. It is much more likely that the right is involved in a waiting game realizing that time plays into its hands in two ways. The chief becomes older; the war becomes more terrible in its senseless duration. The elements of violence grow.

There has been a subtle alteration in President de Gaulle's policy of self-determination. Both the French army have perceived it and the Army of National Liberation, even if the press at large and public opinion choose to soft-pedal the uncomfortable truth. Though he apparently clings vigorously to the idea of self-determination for the Algerians, he has surrounded this offer in the mist of many exceptional conditions—conditions so subtle that it seems almost certain that the war will go on if only because the F.L.N. cannot believe that self-determination surrounded by so many "ifs" will ever become a concrete fact. The war will also go on because the French army needs it as a *raison d'être*. If indeed de Gaulle has hoped to move little by little to his own personal ending of the Algerian problem, so slowly that he would not catch the army in a great schism, then he has had to take a few discouraging steps backwards.

His justifiable severity to the insurgent leaders did a great deal toward reinstating his prestige, which had been very high before the recent challenge, in the eyes of the world. But the longer both sides, and particularly the French, obfuscate possible pourparlers for a cease-fire and postpone negotiations toward electoral guarantees, the more world opinion will swerve to the Algerian cause. De Gaulle's request for special powers giving him nearly dictatorial authority have further isolated the Gaullist concept of "Republic" from the general idea. More than ever alone, he is more than ever strong and yet curiously vulnerable because he formally assumes his will to be both just and justified. Once more it has become horrifyingly apparent that the person of de Gaulle remains the sole bulwark between French Republicanism and what is known in France as the *"politique du pire"* of the army and the ultras. If he should disappear from the scene before there is a negotiated settlement and the formation of an "Algerian Algeria" of some kind, one can envisage a military dictatorship, civil war, and even the secession of French Algeria. And the most discouraging of all appearances is that both sides have regretfully laid aside the "liberal" attitude of February for a dug-in, stubborn, long-war philosophy. The problem seems endless even though the beauty of Ferhat Abbas' appeal to *Algerians,* rather than to Muslims or French, represents the faintest glimmer of hope on the horizon.

CHAPTER ELEVEN

UNFINISHED BUSINESS

ALGERIA IN 1960

In February, 1960, Robert C. Doty in an article "What Price Algeria?" in the *New York Times* summed up the French effort of pacification. De Gaulle had just restored the authority of Paris over the rebels of the ultra group in Algiers, but domination of the nationalist Muslims seemed as far away as ever.

> In blood and money the price is an average of seven soldier-deaths a day and at least one billion dollars a year. Even this is minor compared to the truly exorbitant price—the erosion of French world influence, the sapping of France's moral position through the excesses of repressive war, the injection of the Army into politics, the atrophy of political life and a subtle deterioration of the psychological climate of the country.
>
> The price tag on the alternative—the sudden outright loss of Algeria—is also excessive. For this would entail massive displacement of the European population in Algeria, isolation of France from her other African interests and, certainly, political turmoil on both sides of the Mediterranean.[1]

Doty pointed out that thirty-nine nations voted against France in the fall 1959 meeting of the United Nations. Although de Gaulle believes that the most important job for the western democracies is the social development of the two-thirds of the world's population in Asia and Africa, it is interesting to note

380

that almost all of the African and Asian states have taken a stand against France because of the Algerian problem. Indeed many of them are giving material support to the G.P.R.A. De Gaulle's western allies are torn over the Algerian problem, their desire to propitiate the Arab world, and their need for France in N.A.T.O. A basic feeling for democracy, the heritage of the British and the Americans, is outrageously alienated by many of the practices of the Fifth Republic—its camps of *hébergement,* its treatment of the Algerian rebel, captured gun in hand, as a common criminal. Police and army excesses, the new racialism and neo-fascism that is tempting France, even the special powers that de Gaulle was forced to take to settle the January rebellion all trouble France's allies, and these happenings are creating a vision of France repellent to Western eyes. No amount of grandeur, new atomic weapons exploded in the Sahara, no amount of financial stability and Common Market success can quite make the French puzzle fit together in a pleasing pattern. The cost of Algeria is, in fact, world esteem.

And yet it cannot be denied that France, under cover of the brutal pacification, is *legally* improving the Muslim status in noticeable fashion. We have already mentioned the single college and equal voting prerogatives, all "firsts" in Algeria. The proportional representation of Muslims in the National Assembly was increased by the ordinance of October 16, 1958, and in the Senate on April 22, 1959. However, representation in Algeria is not taking place on an equal basis with Metropolitan France. The Europeans of Algeria continue to have twice the number of representatives as an equivalent number of Frenchmen in France.

1 for 48,000 Frenchmen in Algeria
as compared to
1 for 100,000 Frenchmen in France.

"Equal" representation between Muslims and French in Algeria is:

1 million French $=$ 21 representatives
9 million Muslims $=$ 46 representatives [2]

Election control commissions have been set up for all elections since de Gaulle's coming to power. This, of course, does not insure democracy or fair elections in a country torn by civil strife. There was also an increase in the number of civil servants in Algeria, and a merging of the civil service cadres of Algeria and France. Algerian Muslims were now legally permitted to fill certain A and B categories in the Algerian administrations.

A certain amount of emancipation of the Muslim women has been provided for. Recently, marriage contracts have been changed so that the minimum age of marriage for women is fifteen and for men eighteen. Personal consent freely given is required, and a judicial procedure is necessary for the dissolving of a marriage contract and the entailed responsibilities. Algerian school enrollment has been accelerated in an attempt to eliminate illiteracy over a period of eight years, and a budget of $49,000,000 was set aside for education. Arabic was now to be taught in the French Algerian schools; more Algerians were permitted in public employment; vocational training is being expanded and certain social legislation for Muslims in France with families in Algeria has been set up.

Various measures of economic coordination between France and Algeria have been passed by the government of the Fifth Republic. Algeria has greater representation in the state Economic and Social Council; Algeria has been brought into international trade channels because of the Common Market; and Algeria is included in an insurance and marketing of agricultural products plan. The grain markets of Algeria and France have been merged; also railroads and gas and electricity have been nationalized.

Land reform (banning of collective ownership) and reclamation of about 50,000 acres of recently "pacified" land have been undertaken. In the field of industrialization a national agency, Development Fund for Algeria, has been created to pump state and private funds into the newly coordinated Algerian budget. In 1959 capital investment, according to official French sources, reached $427,000,000 as against approximately three-quarters of that figure in 1958. Transportation of oil and gas has been regulated and rates lower than in Metropolitan France have been established.

Fifteen per cent of state contracts are reserved for Algeria. In these, flexible contracts for new industries, the state has promised a minimum appropriation of 100 billion francs a year (about $200,000,000). Also, Algerian taxes were raised. All of this represents an enormous effort of integration.[3]

Early in 1959 France signed an agreement with Standard Oil of New Jersey to participate in the Saharan development. An official contract of twenty-one American banks opened to France a credit of $200,000,000 for two years. Before this time France had always demanded a 51 per cent control over Saharan oil, but she accorded Standard a contract of 50 per cent. In the new code of French oil policy, foreign countries were offered the most favored conditions granted by any country today.

Free Algeria, a publication of the Algerian Office in New York, issued a news bulletin early in 1959 protesting the fact that France was disposing of the Algerian patrimony, and even the French patrimony, in estimated reserves of 1,450 million tons of oil (estimated developed production to be 70 million tons per year, 18-25 million tons by 1962) and an estimated 2,000 billion cubic meters of natural gas. Speaking of the Saharan Petroleum Code, *Free Algeria* added: *"The sale price of raw or unfinished products must be the going price of the international market. . . . which itself is unilaterally determined by the price of a barrel of oil in Texas—by far, the most expensive in the world."* The editors judged the French government's motive, in extending these favorable terms to foreign companies, to be the quest of short-term capital and political support.[4]

The Provisional Government of the Algerian Republic defined its position on this question on January 28, 1959.

> We must stress the precarious nature of the contracts recently concluded with France by foreign petroleum companies. Our people and our Government are not bound by agreements concluded with our enemy in time of war, and consider them as an act of hostility with

383

regard to the Algerian people. The cooperation of foreign capital in the development of the natural wealth of our country can be conceived only within the framework of an independent Algeria and a united North Africa.[5]

These business mergers of France and American firms, it has been argued, make it more likely that the United States will continue a hands-off policy in French North Africa. How these developments relate to and square with stated Paris and Washington policies of self-determination for peoples is another difficult question.

All this accomplishment, all this money, all this blood give strong evidence of the French desire to keep Algeria and the Sahara complex under their direct control. All of these measures are *de facto* integration, and add up to a truer picture than the lone statement of de Gaulle regarding self-determination. In May, 1960, France once more scheduled local elections—this time cantonal elections—for Algeria. This was the fourth elective consultation organized by France for Algeria in the two years of de Gaulle's power. In the face of almost universal criticism of the meaningless mandate of Algeria, the government of the Fifth Republic goes on searching for a "third force" group of pro-French Muslims with which it can negotiate.

Around the person of Messali Hadj, called a traitor to the French government as a member of the M.T.L.D. and subsequently the M.N.A., imprisoned for many years, and released from jail at the time of de Gaulle's first clemency measures, a controversy swirls. Around him the French have tried to build an Algerian counter-force to the F.L.N. This rallying of the Messalistes has resulted in bloodshed between the Muslim groups, for Messali now speaks out for continued union with France. The F.L.N. in a booklet entitled *"De la contre-révolution à la collaboration, ou la trahison des Messalistes"* accuses Messali's men with the responsibility of much of the terror in the Metropole and in Belgium, and of strife between Muslims in Algeria.[6] The massacres of Melouza and Villeurbanne are laid at the door of

Messali's revived M.N.A. which is accused of working hand and hand with the French police and army. All such material is, of course, so highly propagandized that it is impossible at the present time to evaluate its truthfulness. Certainly there has been internal strife in the F.L.N., and possibly it has been fomented by the old M.N.A. which could not bear to lose its effectiveness and leadership. But there is no evidence of the existence of a third force which is anything but *beni-oui-oui.* Certainly the Muslims who represent Algeria in the National Assembly do not represent an Algerian point of view. They are simply pulled along by French coattails and find living that way somewhat easier than life in camps of resettlement (where by May, 1960, between 1,500,000 and 2,000,000 Muslims are existing), or fighting the French army in the mountains.

It would be hard for an outside observer not to believe that the best Algerians, the most politically mature, the most motivated, are not by now committed either outwardly or inwardly to the struggle for independence. Many reputable sources, newspaper men from Morocco and Tunisia, for example, have placed the figure of Algerians who support the revolution either overtly or covertly, at 99 per cent. This, too, is only conjecture, but how, in face of the other evidence, not to believe a good part of it?

In spite of an increased French force (the Algerians say that in the first few months of 1959 the French had some 800,000 soldiers and police plus two-thirds of the French airforce and half the French navy in Algeria) the war does not diminish. In fact Algerian casualties for that period were heavier than they had ever been:

Killed or Wounded for January — 3,545

February — 2,846

March — 3,817 [7]

In 1960 some 3,000 Algerians are reported killed or wounded each month.

Brave statements of the Fifth Republic cover a censorship of questions military. The French Government recently declared to the French officers that any figures on battle casualties not made public by the government itself was a secret of national defense and its revelation would be punishable by law.

While all official French publications laud the benevolent hand of France in Algeria, other sources of French activities mushroom from the press of the Algerian Bureau and the F.L.N. These are, unfortunately for the peace of mind, corroborated by neutral sources in the press and in special publications. *The Report of the International Committee of the Red Cross on Torture and Inhuman Treatment of Algerians Held in French Prisons and Camps* submitted detailed findings to the French Government confirming the fact that brutality, torture, and subhuman standards of living are commonplace in Algeria for the Algerian detainees. The report, which was at first published in *Le Monde* was seized and torn up in Algeria although allowed to be circulated in Paris. Said David Schoenbrun, C.B.S. correspondent in Paris:

> Paris is suffering from a case of suppressed shame, shame about the revelations of tortures and inhuman conditions in Algerian internment camps, revealed two days ago in a report by the International Red Cross. This report and the shame it provoked have been generally suppressed, however, partly by Government pressure, partly by a curious self-censorship of the French press, which rarely prints unpleasant truths about Algeria.[8]

The report of the Red Cross Committee itself, in describing a tragic situation, strikes a balance which is about as fair as human beings can be, and can scarcely be accused of conscious impartiality.

> The situation in a certain number of camps appeared less satisfactory, without being completely bad. In these camps, the members of the commission, were unable to meet some inmates, although their names were listed among the camp's inmates; they were in the charge of the army, either for the transportation of material, or

386

for 'operational work'. Almost everywhere, when they were able to talk privately with the delegates, the inmates charged that they had been tortured, treated by 'electricity' or 'water' during their questioning. . . . sometimes, although rarely, this had occurred in the camp itself. . . . more often, it took place outside, at the moment of arrest. In every case, the commander, for his part, affirmed his indignation, declared that inhumane treatment was formally prohibited, and promised to investigate and give the necessary instructions so that such practices would cease. As will be described later, in several camps the doctor participating in the mission was able to make examinations whose results unhappily appeared to confirm the charges.

Particular mention is made of the frequency of deaths said to be the results of 'attempts to escape'. The report on the camp at Bou-Gobrine notes: 'This question deserves closer study in view of the frequency of such cases.'

The camps where conditions appeared acceptable are those of Azazga (133) in Kabylie, at the C.D.R. of Bou-Gobrine (58) and at the Camp-des-Chenes, at La Chiffa. The latter is a clandestine Center of Transit and Interrogation (C.T.T.) whose existence was only revealed to the delegates by a chance meeting on the road, of some twenty civilian prisoners escorted by soldiers, and whom they questioned about their destination. At Orléans (26) at the Casino de la Corniche at Algiers (43), at Maison-Carrée (30), at Orléansville (194), and finally, at Tizi-Ouzou (248), while somewhat primitive, the conditions of internment and the treatment of prisoners appeared fairly correct.

Foremost among the camps which were most strongly criticized was Bordj-Menaiel, in Kabylie. From a total of 524 inmates, 15 were on 'operational work.' The men sleep on the ground. The lodgings are qualified as 'disastrous' in virtue of their extreme precariousness and total discomfort. Although the camp has been in existence for more than three years, the inmates still have no blankets or eating utensils at their disposal, and eat out of cans. Discipline is exceptionally harsh, and all the isolation cells were occupied. Moreover, an earlier visit by the previous mission on December 11, 1958, had pointed out the same facts, and had emphatically called the attention of the authorities to conditions in this camp.

This time, the mission made two successive visits to the camp of Bordj-Menaiel. On October 30, it found the inmates 'completely terrorized', begging the delegates not to reveal their declarations 'from fear of being beaten or even killed in reprisal'. While recognizing that the attitude of the camp guard was correct, the inmates charged that inhumane treatment and torture had been practiced during the interrogation in quarters annexed to the camp.

The report noted: 'About 60 sick or suffering inmates were suddenly removed from the camp before our visit'. In one solitary confinement cell, the delegates found an inmate with large scars covering his face, swollen and disfiguring marks on his chest, broken ribs, numerous scratches on his legs, and circular scars on both ankles. According to the man's statements, these wounds were inflicted upon him during a questioning period. He was left without medical attention for 48 hours.

A little later, the report declares: 'The earlier visits, and the talk that we had just had with the officers-in-charge plus their negative attitude, confirm our impression that, on their part, it is a question of a position taken, and any request for improvement is useless. We cannot prevent ourselves from thinking that the miserable conditions in this camp are desired and form part of a system. If, in the short run, this attitude can procure some results (by these methods, the intelligence service

388

appears to have obtained some important results) it is on the other hand, inhumane, and in flagrant contradiction to elementary humanitarian principles.'

The committee immediately asked to see General Challe. Following this meeting, an investigation was ordered. On November 24, the mission returned to the camp of Bordj-Menaiel. The barracks had been repainted, cleaned up, and the general conditions of internment were improved. The report notes: 'We had private talks with several inmates. The general atmosphere is changed. There is no longer any serious complaint. The cruel treatment during questioning has been stopped.'

During the time between the two visits, the total number of persons held in the camp dropped from 524 to 363. The normal capacity of the camp is 300 according to the camp directors, but in the opinion of the mission, it is between 120 and 150.

The same criticism, but somewhat less acute and general is directed against the camp of Bou-Gobrine (152), where six deaths occurred during the past month, all described as taking place during 'attempts to escape while being taken to the interrogation officer'; at Bouira (98), at La Bouzareah (15); at Cinq-Palmiers near Warnier, which is both a Center of Transit and Interrogation and a Military Internment Center; at Damiette (716); at the Chenu Farm near Blida (101), and in its two connecting camps; finally, at Paul-Cazelles (104). In the pages of the report, it appears that during the visit to the Center of Transit and Interrogation at Cinq-Palmiers, a cell was discovered in which six inmates were held—three with marks of recent bruises,—and in their midst, the corpse of a man who had died during the night still lay (the visit took place much later, at 11:30 in the morning). The Commission, having requested the death certificates for five deaths which occurred between October 12 and 18, noted that all

389

carried the same prognostic: 'prolonged poisoning by tear gas'. The men had been forced out of a cave several days earlier by means of tear gas. The mission expresses astonishment that they were neither hospitalized, nor treated, and that one of them died—as a result of this— more than a month after his capture. The mission protested the total absence of blankets and demanded that the ground be covered by a layer of wood or straw. They were answered that wood is expensive, and funds are lacking. The mission also protested against the absence of an infirmary, and that the wounded were left without care, lying on the bare ground, without any covering.

In most of these camps, the mission noted that many inmates had been kept for more than three months, sometimes even for more than a year, whereas the legal detention period in a Camp of Transit and Interrogation is officially limited to three months.

Finally, in the report on the camp of the Casino de la Corniche d'Alger, the following paragraph appears:

'With regard to cruel treatment inflicted during questioning, the colonel in charge explained that "the fight against terrorism makes certain methods of questioning indispensable, methods which permit human lives to be spared and new attacks prevented." He assured us, however, that in his sector, these methods are reserved for certain special cases, that they are not generalized, and are only applied under the responsibility of an officer.' [9]

The Red Cross investigation, made at the end of 1959, covered prison camps, *centres d'hébergement* (regroupment camps) now enclosing two million souls according to Algerian Office figures, military internment camps, and screening camps as well as three hospitals. In these, a heavy toll of life and morale was taken by idleness, starvation, improper shelter and hygiene. A Muslim living in such conditions, without anything to do, divorced from his village which is perhaps totally destroyed, becomes a nonentity. He may not make a good revolutionary, but he will not make a good Frenchman either.

It must be admitted that de Gaulle, between May, 1958, and January, 1959, released, according to official figures quoted in the *New York Times,* January 20, 1959, between 8,000 and 10,000 prisoners, but an equal number of new arrests have been made. *El Moujahid* refers to the psychological measures used against detainees against whom the French have little or no evidence. Often they are kept for weeks, treated without violence and sufficiently nourished while they are indoctrinated with what the French are now prepared to do for Algeria. To all of this the Muslims mutely submit; but their great silence is the veil of much more political knowledge, at least in urban centers, than is outwardly apparent. The behavior of the Casbah of Algiers during the January 24 uprising is a good example of this.

Because of the great inhumanity of the Algerian war, on April 11, 1960, the Algerian Provisional Government announced its decisions to ratify the Geneva Conventions. In its recently published *White Paper,* the G.P.R.A. urged the French Government, a signatory to the Conventions, to live up to them in regard to the French-Algerian war. France, maintaining that it was involved in "pacification," not war, that the Algerian rebels are common criminals, has avoided condemnation under the Geneva articles on the mistreatment of prisoners and the abrogation of human liberties. The Algerians maintain that the struggle involves over half a million French forces in Algeria and the Army of National Liberation which has grown from 3,000 men in 1954 to 130,000 men in 1960.[10] They declare that the war is costing France $3,000,000 a day. French official casualty figures, no longer published in daily communiqués to the press, rose to a total of 13,000 French soldiers by November 1, 1959, and 145,000 Algerians. In effect, the G.P.R.A. reported, "Algerian casualties (which included many civilians) have reached a total of well over 600,000." Military experts believe, also, that French estimates of their own losses are extremely low. To these Algerian figures can be added the between 1,500,000 and 2,000,000 in-

391

ternees, 100,000 Algerians held in transit and interrogation centers, camps and prisons, and some 300,000 Algerian men, women, and children who live as refugees in Tunisia and Morocco.[11] There is also an army of 10,000 Algerians outside the borders of that strife-torn country. Now this is war in any man's language, and the Algerians' plea that international pressure be put upon France to live up to Articles 3 and 4 which concern the humanitarian treatment of prisoners might be said to make good propaganda against the French. But it also makes good sense and human charity. There is little doubt that France has violated the following sections of Article 3:

> a) Violence to life and person, in particular, murder of all kinds, mutilation, cruel treatment and torture;
> b) Taking of hostages;
> c) Outrages upon personal dignity, in particular, humiliating and degrading treatment.
> d) The passing of sentences and the carrying out of executions without previous judgment pronounced by a regularly constituted court affording all the judicial guarantees which are recognized as indispensable by civilized peoples.[12]

The White Paper has impeccably documented sources to prove these charges in incident after gruesome incident. Of course, neither the bomb-throwing terror of the Muslims in the cities nor the murder and mutilation of Europeans in outlying districts when captured by the *fellagha* make a pretty picture. But there is evidence, in the documentation of the A.L.N. treatment of French prisoners, that the Algerian Government is working toward a civilized approach to its own behavior as well as the French, in this, one of the messier kinds of modern war.

Article 4, which deals with the treatment of civilians, is also one the French can look upon with chagrin. The practice of reprisals committed with the purpose of bombing-out villages en masse has become only too commonplace in the latter years of the war. One typical operation is described:

The reprisals, relatively rare in the early days, became massive operations towards the end of my period of service. . . . A double assassination (two officers of the battalion) set off the start of the repression. . . . The first operation lasted for two days. All the huts and stacks of hay were burned—this representing the entire winter food supply for the population. . . . Then, all the inhabitants were driven away and I would not venture to guess where they finally ended up. About 100 men considered as suspects were brought to headquarters, where, lacking space in the prison, we placed them outside in a cage of barbed wire: they spent three days and three nights there, in the wind and rain, so crowded together that they could barely all sit down at the same time. . . . Previously, six village men, who were reported to have 'admitted' either making or placing the mine, had been shot in the village square. The village was declared out of bounds, and the next day, 40 blasts of cannon were aimed at it. An officer told me that the Prefect had originally planned to destroy the village with its entire population, but the General had ordered the evacuation before launching the mortar and artillery operation.[13]

Some 300,00 refugees have fled from the French army's operations over the borders of Morocco and Tunisia. The *Economist*, London, May 2, 1959, declared that these refugees, almost as numerous as the Hungarian refugees, have received almost no publicity and little aid. About 85 per cent of them are women and children. Their men are often fighting with the rebels. These people are without food, work, or shelter in Tunisia and Morocco, which states are also struggling to care for their own underprivileged people. Charges of genocide against the policy of the camps of *hébergement* have been levied by distinguished scholars against the French. Also charges having to do with the neglect of human rights.

As for individual liberty, it may be suppressed at any time without any judicial indictment, by means of an administrative internment warrant which is equivalent to a veritable *lettre de cachet.* . . .

Concerning the rules for criminal examination, besides the fact that certain protective provisions for the security of the accused are no longer applicable in Algeria, these are reduced to naught as the accused is brought before the court after a detention period of from two weeks to two months and even longer, held in special premises where he makes 'spontaneous confessions.' . . . We must here denounce the 'legal procedure' employed in the attempt to legitimize these lengthy internments, authorized by no legislation—however unfair to individual rights—for persons whom it wishes to interrogate at leisure, a warrant giving as their 'residence' the very premises wherein they are incarcerated.

Systematic reassignments from civil courts to military courts. Sentences are most frequently pronounced on the basis of confessions obtained during the inquest, despite the most vehement subsequent retractions. Some trials take place in an atmosphere quite incompatible with the serenity of justice;

Constant violations of the rights of defense. The free choice of counsel, already hampered by many pressures put upon the prisoners, is now nothing but a deception, since the Algerian attorneys who ordinarily used to defend political prisoners have themselves been interned or kept from the free exercise of their profession. As for the Parisian attorneys, they are often faced with the greatest difficulties in the accomplishment of their mission. . . .

Means of legal recourse have finally been reduced to the possibility of review before the military court of appeals, which passes judgment in Algiers itself under particularly hasty conditions.[14]

The conclusions to all this are simple and appalling. Since 1955 and perhaps earlier, a mass of growing documentation proves the French guilty of most of the crimes that the more naïve part of the Western world in the twentieth-century has so far been only able to associate with Nazi practices and the concentration camps of World War II. Genocide, though not a boasted state policy, is certainly a concomitant of the taking of hostages, mass reprisals, the torture of prisoners, arrest and imprisonment for indeterminate lengths of time; the non-voluntary regrouping of great masses of people at starvation levels without proper housing or hygiene, and, above all, without the chance to work to support the remnants of a dislocated family increase the indictment. To revenge the isolated murder of a French soldier, a whole village may be bombed and a year's grain burned—and this in a country which even in full peace and prosperity cannot sufficiently feed and house its people. For at least three years now the International Committee of the Red Cross has made a detailed and sober report of these appalling conditions. In 1957, 1958, and 1959 the French Government has appointed a Commission for the Safeguard of Individual Liberties. Each year this body has also made serious and increasing charges against the conduct of the Algerian war in which soldiers are still treated as common criminals even when captured with full F.L.N. insignia and weapons in hand. Each year the French public, losing some of its ostrich-like determination to ignore those problems, sends more documents of protest to the international press. Each year international feeling for France becomes more horrified as a vicious system, long signalled, perpetuates itself and becomes more and more documented with the incidents of its horror. A file on *"disparus"* has now appeared, listing 150 cases—and this is certainly minimal—of Algerians who were rounded up for interrogation, often without any specific charges, and never heard of afterwards. Death by torture? The old wood chopping expedition from which no prisoners returned? Shot while trying to escape? All this and much more can be laid at the door of the French forces of "pacification"— often well-meaning tools of policies which, by their very nature, involve injustice to a nation in its élite citizenry and also in its most innocent and humble denizens.

As early as 1957, as we have mentioned, 357 eminent Frenchmen addressed a letter to President René Coty protesting this state of affairs. Jean-Paul Sartre posed the question with greater eloquence than anyone when he said:

> Appalled, the French are discovering this terrible truth: that if nothing can protect a nation against itself, neither its traditions nor its loyalties nor its laws, and if fifteen years are enough to transform victims into executioners, then its behavior is no more than a matter of opportunity and occasion. Anybody, at any time, may equally find himself victim or executioner.[15]

It is hard to know whether to end this book on an emotional level which implicitly condemns "pacification" in all its forms, or by quoting the latest report on the "strides toward victory" which come from French army headquarters, which, as we have mentioned, are no longer giving weekly news bulletins on casualties or engagements. According to the French army, in March, 1960, "the number of nationalist rebel regulars has fallen from 26,000 at the beginning of last year to fewer than 16,000. Over the same period rebel losses, including about 10,000 imprisoned, are also said to be 26,000. "Practically no reinforcements have been able to reach nationalist forces in Algeria from Tunisia and Morocco since the beginning of last year." Stating somewhat ambiguously that the number of terrorist attacks had declined, the spokesman added that "there had been an increase in the number and effectiveness of attacks against civilians."

Appalling as is the suffering of the Algerian Muslims, as is the behavior of the French military and the police both in France and Algeria, most saddening of all is the depth and breadth of corruption which has attained deep hold within France because, and there seems to be no other sufficient explanation, the French people can still identify themselves with the high moral tone of their President and his policies of reconstruction in Algeria, while both he and they seem actually powerless to change the

396

measures which the active force of the government, its army branch, has found it expedient to apply to an oppressed people in the name of all the traditional French liberties. It does not seem too categorical to say "There is no health in it." It does not seem too categorical to believe that de Gaulle's present policy has no meaning because of the manner of its implementation. It would seem, too, that he must be aware of this, and one can only assume that in spite of the illusion of French grandeur which he carefully fosters, France will remain a very sick country until the resolution of the Algerian War.

Time alone can make of a policy of self-determination a logical outcome for Algeria. Time and above all, peace time. Freedom from fear is the only environment in which a people, particularly one lacking in breadth of political maturity, can express an honest voice. And how can this be obtained if one enemy, the great colonial power refuses to negotiate with the other? How, on the other hand, can the rebels lay down their arms? One solution seems as impossible to the philosophy of the partisans as the other. And France will not recognize the international voice, the world sentiment rising against her. The Algerians speak often and openly of their desire to resort to the arbitration of world opinion. They have agreed that de Gaulle's offer of self-determination is acceptable to them if guarantees are provided. They have made a brave fight against great odds and have taken a more logical and responsible world position than has the French nation. It is difficult to see how their power and prestige cannot grow even in the face of greater French use of force, more weapons, more men, and more repression in its most brutal sense.

There have been many intelligent solutions, and not a few fantastic ones, offered to the Algerian question. There are, of course, de Gaulle's and Ferhat Abbas's. The S.F.I.O. has recently suggested one which involves negotiation and eliminates the "pacification" so necessary to Gaullist plans. Alain Savary and certain other political scientists have their concepts of a just and, they hope, viable solution. The present authors can envisage a somewhat similar one based on negotiations, a healing time-elapse, and, finally, a guaranteed democratic procedure for the Algerian people.

The necessity of the element of self-determination for the Algerian nation, itself agreed upon in both official camps, stands out as a primary condition for an enduring solution. The wisest approaches also hinge upon the passage of time to allow for a cooling of the blood and a renewed objective examination of what the French presence really means to Algeria and to France. No solution which seems practical and just espouses integration, the favorite answer of the *colons* and the despair of the Algerian nationalists who say the vast majority of their people oppose it. "The Muslims are Muslims," is Charles de Gaulle's answer to the integrationists. His favorite theory—Algerian autonomy within a French framework—while reasonable enough and moderate seems to fall upon deaf ears. Yet there is considerable support on both sides of the Mediterranean for a future Maghrib entente or federation which might remain indefinitely within a

French or at least Western sphere of influence. At this moment in history the undetermined status of Algeria prevents such an evolution advocated by fair-minded students such as Lorna Hahn.[1]

Most students are agreed that the long war and the surging African nationalism have antiquated the formerly attractive prospect of an autonomous Algeria linked to France. Algerian Algeria seems to command the long range future. Therefore, all the positive aspects of de Gaulle's Algerian policy—and they are manifold—might as well be flushed down the drain if he expects by them to keep Algeria French.

Every feasible Algerian solution, however, stems from one beginning—the necessity for a cease-fire and therefore pourparlers between de Gaulle and the representatives of the Provisional Government of the Algerian Republic. Every solution seems to be put beyond the pale of possibility by the stubborn French refusal to consider the Algerian rebels representative of their state, the continuance of "pacification" and its ultimate goal, submission of the Algerian nationalists. What we theoreticians cannot know is whether or not de Gaulle would enter into pourparlers were it not for the pressure of the French army and *colons*. It seems likely he would not be stopped by the representatives of the "Algeria of Papa" which he has long since forsworn. With the army a different relationship prevails. De Gaulle has significant ties with this strong and sometimes threatening power factor in the Fifth Republic. Still there is some evidence that he would be courageous enough to risk a showdown here, too, if it could not be avoided.

Taking this idea one step farther, we are caught on the horns of the unpleasant dilemma. If he would, why hasn't he? If he can't, the army, then, is the *de facto* determinant of France's Algerian policy.

If this is indeed the case, there is only the glimmer of hope that the viewpoint of the army can slowly be changed, permeated by the more emancipated concepts of metropolitan France and by international opinion. It would be an interesting test to ask the French nation in a referendum to say yes or no

399

to pourparlers with the Provisional Government of the Algerian Republic. A yes result would undercut at least an important part of the army high command and place it in the position of going against the national will. International opinion is besmudged with Saharan oil and suffocated by natural gas. A recent yarn from the *Algérie Française* camp in Paris has Nasser insisting that the Algerian Liberation Army fight on indefinitely in order to tie up oil deliveries, thus safeguarding Suez tolls and the Near Eastern oil royalties. It is a fair guess that where Nasser's interests conflict with the Algerian nationalist program, they will be stymied. The Maghrib is not the Near East; it is not even Arabic in its majority, nor is its economic orientation similar.

Both France and the world at large are becoming much more vocal regarding the Algerian war, and the French policy receives more damnation at home and abroad for its tough aspects than praise for its *"mission civilisatrice."*

If de Gaulle were to adopt a possible face-saving offer of the United Nations to perform good offices, it is possible that the French army would feel obliged to accept the decision, particularly if sanctions were promised. But de Gaulle's nature is not susceptible to the shuffling off of French problems on other shoulders.

While de Gaulle lives, perhaps a certain equilibrium can be maintained, and the ultimate offer to the Algerians will not grow less generous. If he should pass from the scene, the worst possibilities of an army coup and perhaps an Algerian secession, engineered by an army-*colon* alignment, must be envisaged. What we can most heartily hope is that Charles de Gaulle, who has undoubtedly a magnificent sense of history, great personal courage, and support in the Western world, can find a way of negotiating with the Algerian nationalists and still control the army. The hope is not great but it is fervent.

If a cease-fire were once achieved and the right to free discussion between *all* elements of both sides established, then an eventual democratic process would make sense. Both sides have agreed to it in advance, and in the world's eyes it seems the most just course of action. A democratic solution would pose many problems for the European community of Algeria, and, no doubt, for Algerian nationalists. Granted—but unjust situations, created by history and made to appear more unjust by the passage of time and new conditions, are rarely ameliorated without pain. It does not seem possible that negotiation and *free* discussion could bring about as much evil and injustice to so many innocents on both sides of the Mediterranean as the continuation of the program of "pacification," bloody warfare, and the maintenance by naked power of French Algeria.

Charles de Gaulle has underlined the necessity of finding an end to the Algerian war in these strong words:

> It is clear that the unity, progress, and prestige of the French people are in jeopardy and that their future is blocked as long as the Algerian problem remains unresolved.

CHAPTER ONE

NOTES

1. *Africa, a Study Prepared at the Request of the Committee on Foreign Relations, United States Senate,* by Program of African Studies, Northwestern University, Melville J. Herskovits, Director. (Washington: U. S. Government Printing Office, 1959, p. 2. Prepared for the 86th Congress, First Session.

2. Arthur Layton Funk, *Charles de Gaulle, the Crucial Years, 1943-1944* (Norman, Oklahoma: University of Oklahoma Press, 1959), p. 107n.

3. Quoted from *Le Sémaphore,* March 30, 1830, by Charles-Henri Favrod, *La révolution algérienne* (Paris: Plon, 1959), p. 1.

4. The figures cited above in this paragraph come from official French statistics and from the Algerian Office in New York under A. K. Chanderli, 236 East 46th Street. The situation in 1891 is described in Augustin Bernard, *L'Algérie* (Paris: Plon, 1930), p. 414. This is Volume II in *Histoire des colonies françaises et de l'expansion de la France dans le monde,* edited by Gabriel Hanotaux and Alfred Martineau.

5. The Maspétiol Report, *Rapport du groupe d'étude des relations financières entre la Métropole et l'Algérie,* Direction Générale des Finances, Algiers, 1955; the Delavignette Report, *Situation économique et sociale de l'Algérie,* Avis et Rapports du Conseil Economique, Paris, 1955. A most useful examination and analysis of these documents by a trained

403

economist is Melvin M. Knight, "The Algerian Revolt: Some Underlying Factors," *The Middle East Journal*, X (1956), pp. 355-367.

6. The statistics used in the above two paragraphs come from the Maspétiol Report, pp. 14, 69, 73, and 80. Some of the interpretations are from Knight, pp. 359-360.

7. David S. McLellan, "The North African in France; A French Racial Problem," *Yale Review*, XLIV (1955), p. 422.

8. Quoted by Alain Savary, *Nationalisme algérien et grandeur française* (Paris: Plon, 1960), p. 27.

9. *Ibid.*, pp. 28-29.

10. Bulletin of the Government General, June 26, 1956, cited by Knight, p. 360.

11. Raymond Aron, *L'Algérie et la république* (Paris: Plon, 1958), p. 18, citing Laurent Schiaffino in the *Tribune Libre du Monde*.

12. Knight, pp. 360-361; Aron, *L'Algérie*, pp. 22-23; Germaine Tillion, *Algeria, the Realities* (New York: Knopf, 1958), p. 4.

13. Ambassade de France, Service de presse et d'information, "Basic Facts on Algeria," November, 1955, p. 6, based upon official statistics of 1954.

14. Knight, p. 362.

15. These figures come from official French sources and may be conveniently found in Ambassade de France, Service de presse et d'information, "Basic Facts on Algeria," November, 1955, pp. 5, 7.

16. Aron, *L'Algérie*, p. 18. The year for which these figures were assembled is not clear, but it apparently represents the situation as of, roughly, 1954, and this aspect of the European problem is rather static. The broken down figures are: 26,476 European industrial and commercial enterprises employing 305,000 salaried personnel against 7,224 Muslim enterprises employing 23,314. The total *chiffres d'affaires* amounted to 900 billion francs of that time, of which 69 billion went to Muslims (*ibid.*, pp. 17-18).

17. These figures for 1954 come from Ambassade de France, Service de presse et d'information, "Basic Facts on Algeria," November, 1955, p. 4; the later report is *ibid.*, "Algeria," August, 1957, p. 5.
18. Savary, p. 17; see also p. 18 for actual members within each category.
19. Tillion, p. 11.
20. McLellan, pp. 421-438.
21. Quoted by Favrod, p. 66.
22. Charles-André Julien, *L'Afrique du nord en marche, nationalismes musulmans et souveraineté française* (Paris: René Julliard, 1952), p. 34; Bernard, pp. 493-495.
23. Julien, pp. 112-113; Hildebert Isnard, "Aux origines du nationalisme algérien, *Annales, Economics, Sociétés* (October, 1949), p. 467; Raymond Kierstead, "The Political Status of Algeria, 1943-1947," unpublished seminar report in History E 45, Northwestern University, 1958, p. 3.
24. Quoted from Julien, p. 116; quote within quotes from *"circulaire Michel."*
25. Quoted by Julien, p. 116n.
26. Quoted by Favrod, p. 69.
27. Quoted by Jacques Chevallier in the parliamentary debate on Algerian policy, *Annales de l'Assemblée Nationale,* 1947, August 20, 1947, p. 4493; Kierstead, p. 4.
28. Quoted by Julien, pp. 110-111 from *L'Entente,* February 23, 1936.
29. Quoted by Julien, p. 115 from *Ach Chihab,* April, 1936.
30. Quoted by Julien, p. 126.
31. Quoted by Julien, p. 127 from Abbé Gabriel Lambert, *L'Algérie et le projet Violette* (Oran, s.d. 1937?).
32. This First All-Muslim Congress represented such diverse groups as the *Fédération des Elus Musulmans* (Bendjelloul, Saadane, Bentami, Abbas), the Ulema (Ben Badis, El-Okbi), the *Etoile nord-africaine* (Messal Hadj), and the Algerian Communist party (Ben Ali Boukhort). The Second Congress held in July, 1937, supported the Blum-Violette

proposal. Messali Hadj's influence sagged against the combined opposition of the *Fédération des Elus Musulmans*, the Ulema, and Communist representatives (Julien, pp. 131-132).

33. Julien, 133-136.
34. *Ibid.*, pp. 136-137.
35. Messali Hadj's publication, *El Oumma*, thundered against colonialism and denied Algerian loyalty to France, a position which contributed to his arrest in August, 1939.
36. Julien, p. 138.

CHAPTER TWO

NOTES

1. *New York Times*, October 22, 1943; Charles-André Julien, *L'Afrique du nord en marche, nationalismes musulmans et souveraineté française* (Paris: René Julliard, 1952), pp. 270-275.
2. Dwight D. Eisenhower, *Crusade in Europe* (New York: Doubleday, 1948), Permabook 1952 edition cited here, p. 153.
3. Quoted from Mme. Jeanne Scelles-Millie, *L'Algérie en 1945 et la presse musulmane algérienne*, un rapport documenté, January 25, 1945, by Julien, p. 275.
4. A. J. Liebling, "Monsieur Flandin's Domaine," *The New Yorker*, September 13, 1958, p. 87.
5. William L. Langer, *Our Vichy Gamble* (New York: Knopf, 1947), pp. 399-400 for the text, and pp. 272 and 388 for estimate.
6. Quoted by Langer, p. 333 from "Murphy to Giraud," November 2, 1942, in OSS files. In a letter "Robert Murphy to Richard Brace," January 25, 1960, Murphy wrote: "In re-

sponse to your letter of November 28, I have no particular recollection of the discussions in Algeria in 1943 to which you refer [his purported discussions with Ferhat Abbas], although the archives of the Department of State may include some record of such conversations. Our policy at that time was that the future of France would have to be determined by the French themselves after the war. This principle of self-determination of course continues to be the basis for our approach to such matters."

7. *New York Times,* November 8, 1942, p. 8.
8. Elliott Roosevelt, *As He Saw It* (New York: Duell, Sloan & Pearce, 1946), p. 111.
9. *Ibid.,* 114-115; see also Arthur Layton Funk, *Charles de Gaulle, the Crucial Years, 1943-1944* (Norman, Oklahoma: University of Oklahoma Press, 1959), pp. 54-100; Winston S. Churchill, *The Second World War; the Hinge of Fate* (Boston: Houghton Mifflin, 1950), pp. 674-695, for the Casablanca Conference; Kenneth W. Pendar, in his *Adventure in Diplomacy, Our French Dilemma* (New York: Dodd, Mead, 1945) p. 150, records President Roosevelt's interest in and grasp of Islamic problems, based upon a conversation held in Marrakech after the Casablanca Conference.
10. Pendar, p. 42.
11. Gabriel Esquer, *Histoire de l'Algérie (1830-1957)* (Paris: Presses Universitaires de France, 1957), p. 79; Julien, p. 282.
12. Quoted by Esquer, p. 82, from Ferhat Abbas's statement in May, 1946. For the Manifesto, see *ibid.,* p. 80-82 and Julien, pp. 284-285.
13. Funk, pp. 101-148; Charles de Gaulle, *The War Memoirs of Charles de Gaulle, Unity, 1942-1944,* translated by Richard Howard (New York: Simon and Schuster, 1959, pp. 115-166; Langer, pp. 382-398; George F. Howe, *United States Army in World War II, the Mediterranean Theater of Operations, Northwest Africa: Seizing the Initiative in the West,* Office of the Chief of Military History Department of the Army, (Washington: Government Printing Office, 1957), pp. 54-55; 358, 360 and *passim.*

14. Julien, pp. 286-287; Esquer, p. 82.
15. Georges Catroux, *Dans la bataille de Méditerranée* (Paris, 1949), p. 432, cited by Julien, p. 294.
16. Quoted by Julien, p. 296. Ferhat Abbas and Saydah Abdelkader were released in December, 1943.
17. De Gaulle, *Unity*, p. 206.
18. *Ibid.*
19. *Ibid.*, p. 207.
20. Michael K. Clark, *Algeria in Turmoil, a History of the Rebellion* (New York: Praeger, 1959), p. 28.
21. Quoted by Julien, p. 299.
22. Julien, pp. 299-300.
23. Esquer, p. 84.
24. *New York Times*, June 1, 1945.
25. Julien, p. 304.
26. *Ibid.*, p. 305.
27. Manfred Halpern, "The Algerian Uprising of 1945," *The Middle East Journal*, II (1948), p. 196.
28. Julien, p. 305.
29. Clark, p. 31.
30. Halpern, pp. 191-202; Julien, pp. 305-307; Esquer, p. 84; Thomas J. Hamilton in *New York Times*, April 29, 1946.
31. *Débats de l'Assemblée Consultative Provisoire, 1943-1945*, p. 1402; Raymond Kierstead, "The Political Status of Algeria, 1943-1947," unpublished seminar report in History E 45, Northwestern University, 1958, pp. 13-14.
32. Cited from *L'Echo d'Alger*, June 8, 1945, by Julien, p. 307.
33. Charles-Henri Favrod, *La révolution algérienne* (Paris: Plon, 1959), p. 76-76n.
34. Julien, p. 308; Esquer, pp. 90-91.
35. *Débats de l'Assemblée Consultative Provisoire, 1943-1945*, July 10 and 18, 1945, pp. 1349, 1357, and 1402; Kierstead, pp. 12-17.
36. *Débats*, p. 1412.
37. *Ibid.*, July 11, 1945, pp. 1373-1374.
38. Julien, p. 309; *Le Monde*, October 24, 1945. Of the 60,000

Muslims eligible to vote for the first college, no more than 32,000 registered. Reluctance of officials (mayors) and employers to administer the law, plus the boycott of the elections by the P.P.A. and A.M.L. help explain this situation.

39. For the picture of the Algerian deputies in Paris, see Gordon Wright, *The Reshaping of French Democracy* (New York: Reynal & Hitchcock, 1948), p. 102; Julien, p. 311, quotes the U.D.M.A. slogan. Highlights in the debates on the amnesty can be followed in *Annales de l'Assemblée Nationale Constituante,* June-October, 1946, (hereinafter cited *Annales*), February 28-March 1, 1946, p. 507, 535, 537; Kierstead, p. 18.

40. *Annales,* p. 1520.

41. *Annales,* pp. 1506-1507; Raymond Aron, *L'Algérie et la république* (Paris: Plon, 1958), p. 36.

42. *Le Monde,* August 25, 1946, for the official election statistics.

43. Wright, pp. 189-190, 192, 204; Robert Montagne, "Evolution in Algeria," *International Affairs,* January, 1947, p. 48.

44. *Annales,* p. 3260; Kierstead, p. 25.

45. *Annales,* August 23, 1946, pp. 3272-3273.

46. *Annales,* pp. 3280-3281.

47. Wright, pp. 202-205; 213-215, for an excellent discussion of the French Union in the Second Constituent.

48. Quoted from *Annales de l'Assemblée Nationale Constituante, June-October,* 1946, September 28, 1946, and translated by Kierstead, p. 29.

49. *Annales,* September 28, 1946, p. 4231; Kierstead, p. 29; Wright, p. 215.

50. *Le Monde,* April 4, 1952, quoted by Clark, p. 43.

51. Julien, pp. 315-316; *Le Monde,* November 15, 1946, for the official figures of the popular vote.

52. This moderate Muslim leader's body was found in December, 1954; apparently he was an early victim of the F.L.N. At the time he was president of the *djemaa* of Ain el Ksar.

53. Dorothy Pickles, *French Politics, the First Years of the Fourth Republic* (London: Royal Institute of International Affairs, 1953), p. 79; Julien, pp. 316-319; the Ramadier gov-

ernment's proposal is in *Annales,* August 10, 1947; Kierstead, p. 32.

54. *Annales,* August 20, 1947, p. 4465.
55. Clark, pp. 46-47, for a good discussion and a different interpretation.
56. *Annales,* August 20, 1947, p. 4500.
57. *Ibid.,* August 20, 1947, p. 4505; Kierstead, pp. 32-37.
58. The full text is in *Annales de l'Assemblée Nationale, 1947,* August 23-27, 1947, pp. 4600-4729. Excellent summaries are in Julien, pp. 322-323 and Kierstead, pp. 36-38; the most caustic evaluation we have seen is Clark, pp. 44-50. Originally the Statute provided for three departments (Algiers, Oran, and Constantine). In 1955 Bône became the fourth, and in 1956 Sétif, Batna, Tizi Ouzou, Orléansville, Médéa, Tiaret, Mostaganem, and Tlemçen raised the total to twelve. In 1957 two departments, Saoura and Laghouat, were created in the Sahara.
59. In placing the budget under the joint control of the governor general and the Algerian Assembly, the Statute terminated the function of the Financial Delegations which for a half-century before 1945 advised the governor general. Created by the law of August 23, 1898, the Financial Delegations were intended to provide the governor with advice from a fair cross-section of Algerian opinion. In those earlier days they served as a sort of Assembly. The original law created three delegations—the *colons,* represented by twenty-four men whose interests were colonization and agriculture; the non-*colons* had a similar number of representatives of commerce, industry, and labor; finally the natives or *indigènes* had twenty-one members, six of whom were Kabyles and fifteen of whom were Arabs. Each delegation first deliberated separately, then met in plenary session to vote the budget. European members had to be twenty-five years old, French citizens for twelve years, and to reside in Algeria for three. The *indigènes,* according to the 1898 law, were elected by the municipal councils of the French communes (*com-*

410

munes de plein exercice) and by the municipal committees in "mixed communes" (Augustin Bernard, *L'Algérie* (Paris: Plon, 1930), p. 432. With minor changes this arrangement carried until 1945.

60. For persons unfamiliar with the term "mixed communes," it is necessary to know that as early as 1863 the French Empire substituted the *douar*-commune for the tribal unit. The *douar* was governed by an assembly of notables called a *djemaa*, which, until 1919, was appointed by the French army. "The decree of 29 August 1937 made the *douar*-commune an intermediary municipal center between itself and the mixed commune of which it continued to be a part." The *djemaa* had powers similar to the municipal councils. By 1945 the administration of the mixed communes received broad powers which previously were held by the prefects. The 1947 Statute called for a progressive elimination of mixed communes. During the period of transition the *djemaa*(s) were elected by direct universal suffrage of the Muslim members of the second college using the secret ballot (Esquer, pp. 91-92). By 1947 there were seventy-eight mixed communes and 332 self-governing communes where most Europeans lived. The difficulty was that many of these self-governing units were surrounded by the mixed communes, which, according to the Statute, were to be abolished. Since the administration of the Statute in this question was left to the Algerian Assembly, whose European majority opposed the change, mixed communes still operated on April 11, 1956, the day the Algerian Assembly was dissolved by Guy Mollet's government (Jacques Soustelle, *Aimée et souffrante Algérie* [Paris: Plon, 1956], p. 71).

61. Quoted by Alexander Werth, *France, 1940-1955* (New York: Holt, 1956), p. 391; for a clear statement of the Mayer Plan see Pickles, p. 87.

62. Julien, p. 326, citing Pierre Frédérix in *Le Monde*, April 3, 1952.

63. Julien, p. 327; the quote is from Pickles, p. 30.

64. 1948, p. 58.
65. Julien, p. 330; see also pp. 327-334 for the evidence of electoral fraud, 1947-1952.
66. Naegelen transferred Laussel, the civil administrator at Khenchela to Chateaudun-du-Rhumel, a demotion, for having shown partiality in the February, 1951, elections in Algeria. Hachémi Benchennouf, who was retiring as an M.R.P. representative, stood for the Algerian Assembly. In order to insure against administrative interference Benchennouf imported three M.R.P. deputies from Paris to observe the elections. His subsequent victory apparently upset Naegelen who took it out on Laussel who in turn was defended in Paris by Benchennouf's M.R.P. friends. Finally, Henri Queuille, then president of the council, ordered Laussel back to his post in Khenchela. Naegelen offered his resignation and was surprised when it was accepted (Clark, pp. 62n-63n).
67. Werth, p. 573.
68. *Ibid.,* p. 571 notes the Truman administration as being anti-colonial—helping to hold down the French repressive colonial policies and, through the C.I.O. and A.F. of L., the trade union movement in Tunisia and Morocco. This, Werth sees, coming to an end with Eisenhower's victory in 1952, after which the French were given a free hand with the Arabs "no doubt in return for certain assurances concerning Europe and Indo-China." The French then pushed the tough policy in Morocco and Tunisia; in the latter it was already very tough.
69. James M. Laux, *French Economic Policy Since the Liberation,* 1944-1954 (Evanston, Illinois: unpublished doctoral dissertation but available on film, 1956), see Chapter XII.
70. During Queuille's first government, which lasted thirteen months beginning September, 1948, no member of the North African lobby sat in the cabinet. However, during the decade following 1944 M.R.P. members such as Bidault, Schuman, Pleven, and Teitgen served as watchdogs over French colonies and defended the Indo-China imbroglio. See Robert F.

Byrnes, "The Christian Democrats," in *Modern France, Problems of the Third and Fourth Republics,* ed. by Edward M. Earle (Princeton: Princeton University Press, 1951), pp. 172-178, for a thoughtful statement on the M.R.P.

CHAPTER THREE

NOTES

1. Serge Bromberger, *Les rebelles algériens* (Paris: Plon, 1958), pp. 1-13.
2. *Ibid.,* p. 14, calls the O.S. (*organisation spéciale*); Charles-Henri Favrod, *La révolution algérienne* (Paris: Plon, 1959), p. 107 calls it *organisation de sécuritié.* Bromberger seems to be correct, and all the Algerian nationalists we have spoken with call it *organisation spéciale.*
3. Bromberger, p. 19.
4. Michael K. Clark, *Algeria in Turmoil, a History of the Rebellion* (New York: Praeger, 1959), p. 364.
5. Bromberger, p. 20.
6. *Ibid.,* pp. 20-21; Clark, p. 343.
7. Gabriel Esquer, *Histoire de l'Algérie (1830-1957)* (Paris: Presses Universitaires, 1957), p. 106, relates the C.R.U.A. to Ben Bella and says the C.R.U.A. was formed in Algeria.
8. Favrod, p. 91.
9. Bromberger, p. 21.
10. Quoted by Favrod, p. 92.
11. Bromberger, pp. 16-17 (map), 22; Clark, pp. 95-96.
12. Quoted by Favrod, p. 93.
13. Favrod, p. 93.
14. *Alger Républicain,* January 29, 1954.
15. *Ibid.,* November 3, 1954.

16. *Ibid.*, November 6, 1954.

17. *Alger Républicain,* November 26, 1954.

18. Quoted by Stanley Clark, *The Man Who Is France, the Story of General Charles de Gaulle* (New York: Dodd, Mead, 1960), p. 221.

19. Favrod, pp. 222-224.

20. *L'Echo d'Alger,* November 2, 1954; *Le Monde,* November 2, 1954; *Alger Républicain,* November 2, 1954; Michael Clark, pp. 3-4, 105-106.

21. *Alger Républicain,* November 4, 1954.

22. Quoted by Michael Clark, p. 119; see also *Journal Officiel,* for debate of November 12, 1954.

23. *Alger Républicain,* November 13, 1954.

24. *Ibid.*, November 26, 1954; Clark, p. 123.

25. Bromberger, p. 45.

26. *Ibid.*, p. 34.

27. *Ibid.*, p. 62.

28. *Ibid.*, pp. 66-67; Clark, p. 137.

29. Bromberger, pp. 69-70.

30. *Ibid.*, p. 71.

31. Favrod, p. 115.

32. Bromberger, pp. 71, 87.

33. Quoted by Favrod, p. 100.

34. Quoted by Bromberger, p. 90.

35. Other members of the committee arrested within a year of its secret formation were: Jacques Salort and Henri Alleg, both of the *Alger Républicain,* Lucette Manaranche and Célestin Moreno. The political bureau membership included André Moine, Kaidi Lakhadar, and André Ruiz. Moine directed propaganda—*Liberté* was one publication—from a bookstore in Algiers. Abd-el-Kader "Lucien" Gerroudy, a former school teacher in Tlemçen, commanded the Fighters for Liberation also from Algiers. Forces were divided between those operating in the cities and those who fought in the countryside (Bromberger, p. 99). Alleg went to prison.

36. Bromberger, pp. 108-118; Clark, pp. 344-347.

37. *The Freedom Fighter,* Central Organ of the Algerian Libera-

tion Front, Special Issue, n.p., n.d., p. 5, irregular spelling preserved; Favrod, p. 108.

38. See Favrod, p. 109; Bromberger, p. 63; Clark, p. 246, for differing views.
39. *The Freedom Fighter*, Special Issue, pp. 6-7; Favrod, p. 110.
40. Raymond Aron, *On War*, translated by Terrence Kilmartin, (New York: Doubleday, 1959), p. 85.
41. *Manchester Guardian*, July 31, 1957.
42. *The Baltimore Sun*, September 7, 1957.
43. July 29, 1957.
44. *Manchester Guardian*, July 13, 1957. The Algerian Front of National Liberation, "The Algerian Question, An Army and a People, The Algerian Army of National Liberation." Background document prepared for the 12th Session of the General Assembly of the United Nations has printed excerpts from these newspaper articles, Series B, No. 1.
45. Quoted by Favrod, p. 95.
46. *The Freedom Fighter*, Special Issue, p. 21.
47. Favrod, p. 179 for three paragraphs omitted from *The Freedom Fighter* cited above in note 46.
48. *The Freedom Fighter*, Special Issue, p. 22.
49. Clark, pp. 314-320.

CHAPTER FOUR

NOTES

1. Alexander Werth, *Lost Statesman, the Strange Story of Pierre Mendès-France* (New York: Abelard-Schuman, 1958), p. 171.
2. Quoted from the speech by Charles-Henri Favrod, *La révolution algérienne* (Paris: Plon, 1959), p. 221.

3. Jacques Soustelle, *Aimée et souffrante Algérie* (Paris: Plon, 1956), p. 109.

4. Raymond Aron, *L'Algerie et la République* (Paris: Plon, 1958), pp. 13-47.

5. Ambassade de France, Service de presse et d'information, "A New Agrarian Policy in Algeria, the Soustelle Plan," November, 1955, pp. 1-8.

6. Jacques Soustelle, "The Wealth of the Sahara," *Foreign Affairs,* XXXVII (1959), p. 630.

7. Soustelle, *Aimée,* p. 109.

8. *Ibid.,* 144; Michael K. Clark, *Algeria in Turmoil, a History of the Rebellion* (New York: Praeger, 1959).

9. United Nations, General Assembly, *Official Records,* 10th Session, 530th Plenary Meeting, September 30, 1955, p. 196.

10. Mohamed Alwan, *Algeria before the United Nations* (New York: Robert Speller and Sons, 1959), pp. 60, 77.

11. Soustelle, *Aimée,* p. 152.

12. *Ibid.,* p. 158.

13. Quoted by Soustelle, *Aimée,* pp. 160-161; all the quotations in this paragraph are from these pages.

14. For convenient summaries see Soustelle, *Aimée,* pp. 160-165; Clark, pp. 229-233.

15. Soustelle, *Aimée,* p. 164.

16. *Ibid.,* p. 163.

17. *Ibid.,* p. 95.

18. Jacques Beaufort, "Lacoste Speaks Up," *The Mediterranean and Eurafrica,* I (1958), p. 7.

19. Text in Soustelle, *Aimée,* pp. 82-83.

20. *Ibid.,* p. 181.

21. Gunnar Myrdal, *Economic Theory and Underdeveloped Regions* (London: Duckworth, 1957), pp. 60-61.

22. Quoted from Ambassade de France, Service de presse et d'information, "The New French Assembly," February, 1956, p. 3.

23. *Ibid.,* p. 4. In 1956 there were no deputies from Algeria, hence the total membership was 30 less than in 1951.

24. January 4, 1956.

25. *New Yorker*, January 14, 1956, p. 79.
26. "Auguste Martin to Richard Brace," January 20, 1956.
27. *Programme d'action du parti socialiste S.F.I.O.*, Supplément au "Populaire Dimanche," No. 358, pp. 13-14.
28. Ambassade de France, Service de presse et d'information, "Principles of French Policy in Algeria," February 16, 1956.
29. *Ibid.*, "Statement on Algeria Broadcast to the French People," February 28, 1956.
30. Quoted by Favrod, p. 223.
31. Clark, p. 299.
32. Favrod, p. 224; Clark, p. 351; Jacques Fauvet, *La IVᵉ république* (Paris: Fayard, 1959), p. 319.
33. Ambassade de France, Service de presse et d'information, "Algeria," August, 1957, pp. 2-3.
34. Fauvet, p. 319.

CHAPTER FIVE

NOTES

1. *New York Times*, June 25, 1956.
2. *Ibid.*, June 16, 1956. We are indebted to the work of Roger Keith, "The United States and Algeria, 1942-1957," unpublished seminar report in History E 45, Northwestern University, 1958, pp. 19ff.
3. *New York Times*, June 21, 1956.
4. *Ibid.*, May 9, 1956.
5. *Ibid.*, September 5, 1956.
6. *U.S. News and World Report*, March 16, 1956, p. 36.
7. Quoted by Theodore Draper, "The Legacy of Suez," *The Reporter*, March 31, 1960, p. 23.
8. *Ibid.*
9. *New York Times*, October 3, 1956.

10. Jacques Fauvet, *La IVe république* (Paris: Fayard, 1959), pp. 321-322. For a convenient summary of French official policy during the Suez crisis, texts, and speeches, see Ambassade de France, Service de presse et d'information, August 20, 1956, "Text of Speech delivered by Christian Pineau, French Minister of Foreign Affairs, at the London Conference on August 17, 1956"; *ibid.*, "Text of Speech Broadcast to French Nation by Premier Mollet on September 12, 1956"; *ibid.*, "Summary of France's Position on the Suez Issue as Put Before the Security Council," October 10, 1956.
11. Fauvet, p. 323.
12. J.-R. Tournoux, *Secrets D'Etat* (Paris: Plon, 1960), pp. 127-128. The account of the capture of Ben Bella which follows is based on this source, unless otherwise noted, see pp. 127-136.
13. Tournoux, p. 137.
14. *Ibid.*, p. 139.
15. Charles-Henri Favrod, *La révolution algérienne* (Paris: Plon, 1959), pp. 154-157.
16. Tournoux, p. 137n.
17. Cited from *Archives inédites*, location unspecified by Tournoux, p. 43.
18. *Ibid.*, p. 144.
19. Tournoux, p. 165.
20. Quoted by Tournoux, p. 166 from *Archives inédites*.
21. *Ibid.;* Fauvet, p. 325.
22. Ambassade de France, Service de presse et d'information, "Statement on the Cease-Fire in the Middle East made by Premier Guy Mollet before the French National Assembly on November 7, 1956," November 8, 1956.
23. *New York Times*, October 24, 1956.
24. Ernest O. Hauser, "Is France Still Our Ally?" *Saturday Evening Post*, April 6, 1957, p. 95.
25. Mohamed Alwan, *Algeria Before the United Nations* (New York: Robert Speller, 1959), pp. 60-63, 78-80.
26. "The U.S.—and an Idea," *Newsweek*, February 18, 1957, p. 40.

27. *New York Times,* February 7, 1957.
28. *Ibid.,* January 14, 1957.
29. *Department of State Bulletin,* March 11, 1957, p. 422.
30. "Le récit de Germaine Tillion," L'Express, August 28, 1958.
31. Serge Bromberger, *Les rebelles algériennes.* (Paris: Plon, 1958), p. 213.
32. *New York Times,* March 29, 1957.
33. *Le Monde,* March 22, 1957.
34. Fauvet, pp. 328-331.
35. *New York Times,* March 20, 1957.
36. *Ibid.,* May 14, 1957.
37. *Ibid.,* June 29, 1957.
38. *Congressional Record,* Vol. 103, Part 8, 85th Congress, First Session, July 2, 1957, p. 10780.
39. *Ibid.*
40. *Ibid.,* p. 10781.
41. *Ibid.,* p. 10786.
42. *Ibid.,* p. 10782.
43. *Ibid.,* pp. 10783-10784.
44. *New York Times,* July 4, 1957.
45. *Ibid.,* July 8, 1957.
46. July 22, 1957, p. 143.
47. Dean Acheson, *Power and Diplomacy* (Cambridge, Massachusetts: Harvard University Press, 1958), p. 123.
48. *Congressional Record* (daily edition), July 8, 1957, p. 9878.
49. *Ibid.,* July 23, 1957, p. A5919.
50. Gunnar Myrdal, *Economic Theory and Underdeveloped Regions* (London: Duckworth, 1957), p. 77.
51. Ambassade de France, Service de presse et d'information, "Bourgès-Maunoury outlines his Governmental Program," June 13, 1957.
52. Quoted by Fauvet, p. 333.
53. Ambassade de France, Service de presse et d'information, "Premier Félix Gaillard outlines his Governmental Program," November 5, 1957.
54. *New York Times,* September 12, 1957.
55. *Ibid.,* November 16, 20, 1957.

56. Alwan, pp. 63-65; A. K. Chanderli, "The Algerian Question at the United Nations," *The Arab World* (Sept., 1959), p. 3; *New York Times,* December 11, 1957.

57. Ambassade de France, Service de presse et d'information, "Text of the Institutions of Algeria Commonly Known as the Loi-Cadre," February, 1960.

58. The figure for freedom fighters is taken from Bromberger, *Les rebelles,* p. 249, and represents a compilation from *Le Petit Matin,* the Neo Destour organ at Tunis, printed a few hundred yards from F.L.N. headquarters in that city.

59. Tournoux, pp. 234-236; Fauvet, pp. 339-341.

60. Bromberger, p. 256; Favrod, p. 228.

61. Quoted by Favrod, pp. 214-215.

62. Favrod, p. 215.

CHAPTER SIX

NOTES

1. Merry and Serge Bromberger, *Les 13 complots du 13 mai* (Paris: Librairie Arthème Fayard, 1959), p. 24. Hereinafter cited as "Brombergers."

2. This phrase has been translated since the time of the French Revolution of 1789 as "Public Safety" but the real meaning of *Salut* is well-being, health, or welfare in the widest sense. We will continue to use the traditional term or the initials PS to designate *Salut Public* or CPS for Committee of Public Safety.

3. Michael K. Clark, *Algeria in Turmoil, a History of the Rebellion* (New York: Praeger, 1959), p. 364.

4. Brombergers, p. 26.

5. Jacques Soustelle, *Aimée et souffrante Algérie* (Paris: Plon, 1956), p. 35.
6. Brombergers, pp. 35-36.
7. Alain Jacob in *Le Monde*, May 20, 1958.
8. Paris: René Julliard, 1958.
9. Paul Gerin, *L'Algérie du 13 mai* (Paris: Librarie Gallimard, 1958), p. 141, for both quotations.
10. Henri Alleg, *The Question* (New York: George Braziller, 1958), pp. 57-59.
11. Brombergers, p. 45.
12. Gerin, pp. 131-132.
13. Brombergers, p. 67.
14. *Ibid.*
15. The Brombergers (p. 69) say of General Descours, "un des anciens chefs de réseau O. R. A. pendant la guerre. . . ." De Gaulle (*War Memoirs, Unity, 1942-1944*, p. 315) in describing the resistance in the Isère in 1944, mentions Colonel Descour, "chief of our forces in the Isère." These may be the same person, and, if so, Descour(s)' loyalty to de Gaulle dates back to the Occupation period.
16. Alexander Werth, *Lost Statesman, the Strange Case of Pierre Mendès-France* (New York: Abelard-Schuman, 1958), pp. 168-177; Soustelle, p. 1.
17. Soustelle, pp. 31-50; p. 43 for his four points; p. 48 for the quotation directly above.
18. Gerin, p. 195.
19. Brombergers, pp. 97-110.
20. Charles de Gaulle, *War Memoirs, Unity, 1942-1944.* Translated by Richard Howard (New York: Simon and Schuster, 1959), p. 75.
21. Brombergers, p. 112.
22. Dominique Prado, *13 mai, histoire secrète d'une révolution* (Paris: Editions de Paris, 1958), pp. 11-15.
23. *Ibid.*, p. 12.
24. Clark, p. 371.
25. Brombergers, p. 62.

26. Prado, p. 13.
27. "Salan to Ely," night of May 9-10, 1958, text in Alain de Sérigny, *La révolution du 13 mai* (Paris: Plon, 1958), pp. 30-31.
28. Quoted from *El Moujahid* by Clark, p. 369.
29. Brombergers, p. 146.
30. *Ibid.*, p. 153.
31. Brombergers, p. 158.
32. *Ibid.*, p. 159.
33. Sérigny, p. 47.
34. *Ibid.*, p. 59.
35. Gerin, p. 41.
36. *Ibid.*, p. 43.
37. *Ibid.*, pp. 44-45 for the text.
38. Brombergers, p. 187.
39. Sèrigny, p. 64.
40. Brombergers, p. 177.
41. *Ibid.*, p. 198.
42. Gerin, p. 51.

CHAPTER SEVEN

NOTES

1. Paul Gerin, *L'Algérie du 13 mai* (Paris: Librairie Gaillimard, 1958) p. 58.
2. *Ibid.*, pp. 90-91. The Casbah C. P. S. contained twenty-five Muslims, four Jews, two Christians; in addition to four army officers, and two non-coms (Michael K. Clark, *Algeria in Turmoil, a History of the Rebellion* (New York: Praeger, 1959), p. 393n.
3. Merry and Serge Bromberger, *Les 13 complots du 13 mai* (Paris: Librairie Arthème Fayard, 1959), p. 207.

4. Quoted by Clark, pp. 383-384.
5. The C. P. S. activists in Algeria warned Pflimlin by telegram that they would prevent his Minister for Algeria, the Independent André Mutter, from reaching Algiers. This did not deter Mutter whose party chief, Pinay, thought he should refuse to offer himself as a hostage. Mutter was reported to have said, "I will put on my decorations. I will take the plane. I will get off in Algeria, and I will say, 'Here I am!'" (Brombergers, p. 214; *L'Express,* May 22, 1958.)
6. Brombergers, p. 231.
7. *Le Monde,* May 17, 1958.
8. Brombergers, p. 298.
9. *Ibid.,* p. 318.
10. Quoted by Clark, p. 404.
11. *Le Monde,* May 20, 1958; Joel Colton, "The Passing of the Fourth Republic: The Spring of 1958," *South Atlantic Quarterly,* LVIII (1959), pp. 337-350.
12. For Gaullist activity in Corsica in 1943 and Henri Maillot's part see Charles de Gaulle, *War Memoirs, Unity, 1942-1944* (New York: Simon and Schuster, 1959), pp. 158-159.
13. Brombergers, p. 339.
14. *Le Monde,* May 27, 1958.
15. Brombergers, p. 384.
16. *Ibid.,* p. 402.

CHAPTER EIGHT

NOTES

1. Quoted from Mendès-France's speech of investiture of June 3, 1953, by Ambassade de France, Service de presse et d'information, "Tradition and Innovation in the French Constitution," September, 1958, p. 3.
2. The quoted passage here is from Edgar S. Furniss, Jr.,

France, Troubled Ally; De Gaulle's Heritage and Prospects
(New York: Harper & Brothers, 1960), pp. 363-364. There
are many places where texts of the Constitution can be
found. Various drafts were printed by the French Press in
the month of September. For English readers there are two
convenient sources for the final text of the Constitution:
Ambassade de France, Service de presse et d'information,
"The French Constitution, French Text and English Translation," available at 972 Fifth Avenue, New York 21, New York,
1958; and Nicholas Wahl, *The Fifth Republic, France's New
Political System* (New York: Random House, 1959), pp.103-
126.

3. Ambassade de France, Service de Presse et d'information,
   "Tradition and Innovation in the French Constitution,"
   September, 1958, pp. 8-9; Wahl, pp. 45-47; Furniss, pp. 351-
   372.

4. *L'Express*, September 25, 1958.

5. Ambassade de France, Service de presse et d'information,
   "Birth of a New Community of Free Peoples," October,
   1958, p. 8.

6. For the complete list of members of the Government see
   ibid., "First Government of the Fifth Republic, the Debré
   Cabinet," January, 1959.

7. *Le Monde*, December 2, 1958.

8. *Ibid.*, November 25, 1958.

9. Paris Herald Tribune, September 20-21, 1958; *Free Algeria*,
   September 19, 1958.

10. This list is from *Free Algeria*, September 19, 1958, original
    spelling preserved.

11. *Le Monde*, August 29, 1958.

12. Ambassade de France, Service de presse et d'information,
    "Text of Speech Delivered by General Charles de Gaulle at
    Constantine, October 3, 1958," October, 1958.

13. *Ibid.*, "The Constantine Plan Gets under Way," February 1,
    1959.

14. Ambassade de France, Service de presse et d'information,
    "Inauguration of De Gaulle as President of the Republic and

of the Community and the Full Text of the Inaugural Address," January 8, 1959.

15. *Ibid.*, "Full Text of the Policy Statement on Algeria by Premier Michel Debré to the National Assembly on January 9, 1959," January 15,1959.
16. Charles de Gaulle, *The War Memoirs of Charles de Gaulle, Unity, 1942-1944* (New York: Simon and Schuster, 1959), pp. 164, 168-169, 197; *ibid., Salvation, 1944-1946* (New York: Simon and Schuster, 1960), pp. 133-139.
17. Alexander Werth, *Lost Statesman, the Strange Story of Pierre Mendès-France* (New York: Abelard-Schuman, 1958), p. 61.
18. De Gaulle, *Salvation, 1944-1946,* pp. 136-137.
19. Furniss, p. 407.
20. *Ibid.*, pp. 407-408.
21. *Le Monde*, January 30, 1959; Furniss, p. 414. These figures are rounded off. By dividing them by 500 the dollar equivalents come out to total: $34 billion; housing: $6 billion; energy: $5 billion; agriculture and fishing: $4 billion; processing industries: $3 billion. Since the Plan ran 1958-1961, there would be some error in this process. The 1958 franc stood at 420 to the dollar officially and varied upward to around 500 on the free market, thus 500 is a reasonable divisor, particularly in light of the value of the new franc.
22. Furniss, p. 421.

CHAPTER NINE

NOTES

1. *Le Monde,* June 11, 1958.
2. *Ibid.*, June 12, 1958; also quoted by Edgar S. Furniss, Jr., *France, Troubled Ally; De Gaulle's Heritage and Prospects* (New York: Harper & Brothers, 1960), p. 425.
3. *Le Monde,* October 14, 1958.

4. Alain Savary, *Nationalisme Algérien et grandeur française* (Paris: Plon, 1960), p. 133; Ambassade de France, Service de presse et d'information, "Premier de Gaulle Outlines his Program for Algeria, Text of the Speech delivered at Constantine, October 3, 1958," October, 1958.
5. Quoted by Savary, pp. 133-134.
6. Quoted from *Der Tag* (West Berlin newspaper) by *Le Monde,* October 15, 1958; see also Furniss, p. 431.
7. Savary, pp. 135-136 for the quotation.
8. Savary, pp. 136-137. The quoted passage is on p. 137.
9. Savary, pp. 120-123.
10. Savary, p. 125.
11. Quoted from *France-Observateur,* July 16, 1959, by Savary, p. 129.
12. Furniss, p. 429.
13. Thomas Brady in *New York Times,* April 17, 1960.
14. Quoted by Savary, p. 131.
15. Furniss, p. 434.
16. *Le Monde,* January 17, 1959.
17. Quoted by Savary, p. 138; see also *Le Monde,* June 25, 1959, for other portions of the speech.
18. Savary, p. 141.
19. Quoted by Savary, p. 142.
20. Jean Daniel in *L'Express,* February 5, 1959.
21. *Ibid.*
22. *L'Express,* February 12, 1959.
23. Volney D. Hurd in the *Christian Science Monitor,* March 14, 1959.
24. *El Moujahid,* March 17, 1959.
25. Eugene Mannoni in *Le Monde,* April 21, 1959.
26. *Le Monde,* April 21, 1959.
27. Quoted by *Le Monde,* April 21, 1959.
28. *Le Monde,* April 23, 1959.
29. Algerian Office, "Review of Developments in Algeria, December 15, 1958-January 15, 1959," New York, 1959.
30. *The Gangrene,* translated by Robert Silvers (New York: Lyle Stuart, 1960); *France-Observateur,* June 25, 1959; *Nation,* July 18, 1959, pp. 23-27.

31. *Arab News and Views,* Arab Information Center, 120 East 56th Street, New York, V (September 1, 1959).
32. The full text is to be found in the Reuters official translation in *New York Times,* September 17, 1959. Ambassade de France, Service de presse et d'information, "Address by General Charles de Gaulle, President of the Republic and of the Community Broadcast over the French Radio and Television Network on September 16, 1959," is not a complete text.
33. *Ibid.*
34. *New York Times,* September 17, 1959.
35. Quoted by Thomas Brady in *New York Times,* September 17, 1959.
36. Thomas Brady in *New York Times,* September 29, 1959.
37. Algerian Office, "Text of the Declaration Made by the Provisional Government of the Algerian Republic in Tunis, September 28, 1959," New York, 1959.
38. *Ibid.;* Reuters from Tunis, *New York Times,* September 29, 1959.
39. Paul Ghali in *Chicago Daily News,* September 29, 1959.
40. *New York Times,* September 30, 1959.
41. Algerian Office, "The Question of Algeria, the Debate in the United Nations, December, 1959," New York, 1959, pp. 1-5.
42. Henry Tanner in *New York Times,* December 7, 1959.
43. Algerian Office, "The Question of Algeria, the Debate in the United Nations, December, 1959," New York, 1959, pp. 4-5.

CHAPTER TEN

NOTES

1. Jean-Jacques Servan-Schreiber in *Express,* February 4, 1960.
2. Quoted from Robert Soule in *France-Soir,* January 24-25, 1960.
3. *New York Times,* January 26, 1960; *France-Soir,* January 26, 1960.

4. Henry Giniger in *New York Times,* January 26, 1960.
5. Jean Daniel in *Express,* January 28, 1960.
6. *Ibid.*
7. Jean Cau in *Express,* February 4, 1960.
8. *New York Times,* January 28, 1960.
9. *Ibid.,* January 29, 1960.
10. *Ambassade de France,* Service de presse et d'information, "Address by General de Gaulle on Algerian Policy Delivered on Radio and Television, Friday, January 29, 1960," pp. 1-4.
11. A. Delcroix in *France-Observateur,* February 4, 1960.
12. Eduard Roermond in *France-Observateur,* February 4, 1960.
13. Thomas Brady in *New York Times,* February 2, 1960.
14. *France-Observateur,* February 4, 1960.
15. *Ambassade de France, op. cit.,* "French Government Granted Special Powers for the Maintenance of Law and Order (,) the Safeguarding of the State and the Pacification and Administration of Algeria," February 4, 1960, pp. 1-7.
16. *Ibid.,* "Statement of Premier Michel Debré to the National Assembly on February 2." Excerpts. Pp. 2-7.
17. *Le Monde,* February 6, 1960.
18. *Ibid.*
19. *New York World Telegram and Sun,* February 10, 1960.
20. Thomas Brady in *New York Times,* February 4, 1960.
21. Henry Tanner in *New York Times,* February 10, 1960.
22. *Algerian Office,* "The Algerian Political Issue: Points of Clarification," February, 1960, pp. 1-2; see Jean Knecht in *Le Monde,* February 6, 1960, for a resumé of opinion in the United States.
23. *Algerian Office,* "The Algerian Political Issue," Section 2, pp. 1-2.
24. *Algerian Office,* Text of the "Meeting of the National Council of the Algerian Revolution at Tripoli (Libya) December 16, 1959-January 18, 1960," pp. 1-5.
25. *Ibid.,* "The Declaration of the Provisional Government of the Algerian Republic, Tunis, January 29, 1960," pp. 1-2.
26. *Ibid.,* "Text of the Appeal of Premier Ferhat Abbas to the Europeans of Algeria, Tunis, February 17, 1960," pp. 1-5.

27. Henry Tanner in *New York Times,* March 6, 1960.
28. Those in prison at this time were: de Sérigny, A. Arnould, head of the veterans' organization, Major General Sapin-Lignière of the Home Guard, Dr. Bernard Lefevre, head of a fascist group, Jean-Maurice Demarquet, right-wing deputy, and Dr. Fernand Feral, chief of a vigilante organization.
29. *Algerian Office,* "Text of the Provisional Government of the Algerian Republic, Tunis, March 14, 1960" p. 1.

CHAPTER ELEVEN

NOTES

1. *New York Times,* Magazine, February 7, 1960, p. 15.
2. Algerian Office, "French Elections in Algeria," New York, December, 1958. A background document prepared for the 13th Session of the General Assembly of the U.N. See p. 2.
3. Ambassade de France, Service de presse et d'information, "Algeria after a Year of Political, Administrative, Social and Economic Measures—June, 1958-June, 1959," August, 1959, pp. 1-13.
4. *Free Algeria,* Front of National Liberation Delegation, New York, "Are International Trusts Joining France in a Mid-20th Century Colonial Exploitation of Algeria" (February, 1959).
5. *Ibid.,* p. 4 for the quoted material; see also Alain Savary, *Nationalisme Algérien et grandeur française* (Paris: Plon, 1960) pp. 72-84 for a general discussion of the oil question.
6. Etudes et documents édités par la Front de Libération Nationale (Fédération de France), "Da la contre-révolution à

la collaboration, ou la trahison des Messalistes" (Paris, August, 1959), pp. 3-95.

7. Algerian Delegation New York, "Report on the Latest Developments in Algeria Presented by A. Chanderli, Representative of the Algerian Front of National Liberation, to the Members of the Afro-Asian Group at the United Nations," May, 1959.

8. Quoted by Algerian Office, "The Report of the International Committee of the Red Cross on Torture and Inhuman Treatment of Algerians Held in French Prisons and Camps," New York, January, 1960, p. ii, from C.B.S. World News Roundup, January 6, 1960. *Le Monde's* detailed analysis of the Red Cross Report appeared in the January 5, 1960, issue.

9. The long quotation is from Algerian Office, "The Report of the International Committee of the Red Cross on Torture and Inhuman Treatment of Algerians Held in French Prisons and Camps, New York, January, 1960, pp. 3-5. This report has been checked against the text of the Red Cross Committee Report to the French Government, "Septième mission du comité international de la croix-rouge en Algérie (octobre-novembre [1959], Rapport communiqué au gouvernement français," *Cahiers du temoignage chrétien,* Cahier 39 (Paris, 1960), pp. 4-42, which itself is not a complete text of the Red Cross Report, and the data used by the Algerian Office is accurate, and the quotations have been verified. The numbers in parentheses seem to refer to the number of persons in the camps.

10. Algerian Office, *White Paper, on the Application of the Geneva Conventions of 1949 to the French-Algerian Conflict* (New York, 1960), p. 6.

11. *Ibid.,* p. 7.

12. *Ibid.,* p. 26.

13. *Ibid.,* p. 37, letter from a French priest serving as an officer in the Grand Kabylia, reprinted from *Des Rappelés Temoignent* (Paris: Comité Resistence Spirituelle, 1957), pp. 81-82.

14. *Ibid.,* pp. 48-49.

15. Quoted by *ibid.,* p. 58.

EPILOGUE

NOTES

1. Lorna Hahn, *North Africa: Nationalism to Nationhood* (Washington: Public Affairs Press, 1960), pp. 250-253. For a recent analysis see also, Raymond Aron, *France: Steadfast and Changing, the Fourth to the Fifth Republic* (Cambridge, Massachusetts: Harvard University Press, 1960). Two worthwhile analyses of the Fifth Republic which appeared in late summer 1960 are: Philip M. Williams and Martin Harrison, *De Gaulle's Republic* (New York: Longmans, 1960); and Roy C. Macridis and Bernard E. Brown, *The De Gaulle Republic* (Homewood, Illinois: Dorsey Press, 1960).

Amis du Manifeste et de la Liberté, A.M.L. Algerian political party, organized in 1944, opposed to continued colonial status and in favor of autonomous federal republic in Algeria. Favored by both Ferhat Abbas and Messali Hadj in the beginning.

Armée de Libération Nationale, A.L.N. Algerian Liberation Army, the F.L.N.'s fighting force.

Association Générale des Etudiants Algériens, A.G.E.A. Association of Algerian Students, the French student organization in Algeria.

Beni-oui-oui Muslims in Algeria who always agreed with the French often for reasons of personal gain, thus "yes men" or "stooges."

Berbers The indigenous people of Algeria whose origins are disputed but who lived there long before the Christian epoch. They are Muslims, though not Arabic in origin, and they make up at least 75 per cent of the Muslim population.

bey Assistant to a beylerbey. See beylerbey.

beylerbey or beylerbeg Ruling Turkish official in Algeria.

bicot Slang (French) for Algerian.

caïd Muslim chief.

bléd Country or countryside as distinct from city.

C.C.E. See Committee of Coordination and Execution.

Comité d'action des Associations Nationales des Anciens Combattants, C.A.N.A.C. Action committee of veteran organizations who in Algeria stood for integration and the continued French presence and against negotiations with the F.L.N.

Chaouia   Berber tribes in the Aurès Mountains.

colon   Settler, planter, colonist (European in Algeria). *Gros colon*—wealthy planter dedicated to maintaining himself in Algeria which explains why he insists that France remain in Algeria.

Comité Révolutionnaire d'Unité d'Action, C.R.U.A.   Founded by the leaders of the *Organisation Spéciale* in March, 1954 to organize the armed insurrection of the Algerians for independence. Later absorbed by the F.L.N.

Committee of Coordination and Execution, C.C.E. of the F.L.N. Composed of five members (probably colonels of *wilaya*) whose names remained secret, elected by the National Council of the Algerian Revolution, C.N.R.A. C.C.E. headquarters were inside Algeria; this is the interior high command.

Committee of Public Safety, C.P.S.   Committees composed mainly of Europeans with some *beni-oui-ouis* favoring French retention of Algeria and opposing any concessions made to the F.L.N. These Committees took form in Algeria first in February, 1956, and again in May, 1958 when they helped overthrow the Fourth Republic; then again in January, 1960 when they tried to defy de Gaulle. Army officers, *colons,* activists all belonged. In 1958 one central committee functioned in Algiers and local committees in the other cities and countryside. De Gaulle ordered army officers to resign from this political action in 1958, but some of them persisted. The Committee of Public Safety first entered French history in April, 1793, during the First French Republic as an instrument of national defense and centralized wartime government.

C.N.R.A.   See *Conseil Nationale de la Révolution Algérienne.*

C.P.S.   See Committee of Public Safety.

dey   Ruling official in Algiers under the corsairs.

Direction de Surveillance Territoire, D.S.T.   The French Security police, operating in France and Algeria.

djebel   Mountain.

Djemaa   Muslim assembly of notables.

douar   Muslim village or tribal unit which in recent times had its own budget, administered by an assembly of notables, *Djemaa,* elected by direct male suffrage by Muslims in the Second College.

D.S.T.   See *Direction de Surveillance Territoire.*

Ecole Jeanne d'Arc   Unofficial school where French army officers in Algeria studied revolutionary tactics.

L'Etoile nord-Africaine   Literally, North African Star. Algerian political party founded in Paris 1924 by Hadj Abdelkader. Dissolved by French government in 1929; revived as *Parti du Peuple Algérien,* Algerian People's Party 1937; dissolved 1939; secretly revived later. Taken over by Messali Hadj in 1925.

Fédération des Elus Musulmans d'Algérie   Moderate Algerian political party under Dr. Bendjelloul in 1930's. After 1938 Ferhat Abbas led one wing of this party and fused it with the *Union Populaire Algérienne,* U.P.A.

fellaghas   Highwaymen or robbers in Arabic, but in the revolutionary vocabulary fighters on the side of Algerian independence. *Fellah* means farmer or peasant; *fellahin* is the plural form.

fidayines   Partisans of the F.L.N. who fight out of uniform, like the *moussebilines,* usually serving in their own villages.

F.L.N.   See *Front de Libération Nationale.*

French Socialist Party   See S.F.I.O.

Front de Libération Nationale   The National Liberation Front of Algerian nationalists which began the Rebellion against France in 1954, and became the Provisional Government of the Algerian Republic on September 19, 1958.

Front National Français, F.N.F.   Political party in Algeria organized in 1958 by Joseph Ortiz. It favored integration, permanent French control over Algeria. Active in the January, 1960 Algiers uprising against de Gaulle, paramilitary in organization.

G.P.R.A.   See Provisional Government of the Algerian Republic.

hébérgement   Relocation camps, centers where Algerians taken off their land or picked up in the villages and cities are regrouped or lodged. In these centers they are detained, interrogated, screened and finally relocated or held. The apparent aim is to reduce F.L.N. support among the general Muslim population by punishing it or moving it. Or, put another way, to save the unengaged Muslim population from getting into trouble with the F.L.N. or suffering retaliation from French forces.

imam   Priest who performs or leads the regular service in a Mohammedan mosque.

Jamaa or *Djemaa*   See *Djemaa*.

Kabyles   Berber people who inhabit Kabylia Mountains.

Kanum   Unwritten Berber code protecting individual liberties against community interest.

khamessa or khammessat   Muslim tenant farmer system which granted tenant one-fifth of produce; altered in 1956 to increase tenant's share to one-half.

loi cadre   Basic law(s) or governing statutes (of Algeria) of which there was one in 1947, another in 1958.

loi d'urgence   Emergency powers, extended, since 1955, to various French governments which in turn pass them on to civil and military authorities in Algeria. They include the right to suspend regular legal procedures in pacification of Algeria. They facilitate arbitrary arrest, imprisonment, and torture of suspects.

Maghrib, also *Moghrib*   Means "the West" in Arabic and today refers most often to the area of Tunisia, Algeria, and Morocco. Also Africa Minor.

marabout, Arabic *murabit*   A Mohammedan hermit or saint, holy man but not a serious theologian.

mechtas   Hamlets.

Messalistes   Followers of Messali Hadj.

mise en valeur   To develop (a colony).

M.N.A.   See *Movement National Algérien*.

moujahid, plural *moujahidines*   Algerian freedom fighter; soldier in the Algerian Liberation Army; *jihad*, Arabic, combatant.

Mouvement National Algérien, M.N.A.   Messali Hadj's organiza-

436

tion created in 1955 to compete with the F.L.N. It attempted to infiltrate and dominate the F.L.N. and was quite unsuccessful in Algeria, possibly a little more successful in France. It stands as a rival to the G.P.R.A., which it does not recognize. A trump for French policy of trying to divide Algerian nationalists. Violence between F.L.N. and M.N.A. partisans in Algeria and France.

Mouvement pour le Triomphe des Libertés Démocratiques, M.T.L.D. Algerian political party organized by Messali Hadj in 1946, a successor to the outlawed P.P.A., and, like it, drawing recruits from the Algerian working classes.

moussebilines Partisans of the Algerian Liberation Army, serving out of uniform in various capacities, often becoming full fledged freedom fighters, *moujahidines* in uniform, after promotion.

M.T.L.D. See *Mouvement pour le Triomphe des Libertés Démocratiques.*

muphti or mufti An official expounder of Mohammedan law, sometimes an assessor to a court.

Mzabites Berber people in the south.

Organisation Spéciale, O.S. Algerian organization of active militants founded in 1947 by Aït Ahmed, dedicated to independence and to the use of force. Fused with F.L.N. in 1954.

O.S. See *Organisation Spéciale.* Also called *Organisation Secrète.*

Parti du Peuple Algérien, P.P.A. Algerian People's Party of Messali Hadj, organized in 1937, dissolved in 1939, secretly revived and forerunner of various other parties organized by Messali Hadj such as M.T.L.D. and the M.N.A.

Parti Populaire Français, P.P.F. French party of the right with fascist proclivities in late 1930's. Jacques Doriot leader in 1939.

Parti Social Français, P.S.F. French party of the right in 1930's with fascist principles under Colonel de la Rocque.

Parti Socialiste Autonome A socialist party formed in 1958 upon the split in the old S.F.I.O. over that party's position on the referendum of de Gaulle's constitution of the Fifth Republic and the later economic, social, and Algerian policies of the

Debré government. Mendès-France is a member of this party which opposes Mollet's opportunism, is anti-nationalistic, and usually opposes de Gaulle.

Provisional Government of the Algerian Republic, G.P.R.A. Formed from the F.L.N. in September, 1958, while the Fifth Republic of France was in birth. Recognized by various Muslim, African, and Asian powers.

Rassemblement du Peuple Français, R.P.F. French People's Rally, Gaullist party organized in 1947, rather unsuccessful and split up; died out in early 1950's.

Rassemblement Franco-Musulman Algérien, R.F.M.A. Organized 1938 by Dr. Bendjelloul to unite moderates, the ulema, the P.P.A., and various other Algerian action groups.

ratissage From the French verb *ratisser*, to scrape or rake, in French military slang to rake out the traitors or rebels.

rattachement French policy of governing Algeria through the equivalent ministeries in Paris. Tried momentarily in 1848 and during the period 1881-1896; it reduced power of the governor general.

Sahara Literally "emptiness" or "nothing" in Arabic; the Sahara desert.

Sections Administratives Specialisées, S.A.S. French Specialized Administrative units in Algeria whose officers at best were sincere social and economic workers trying to build Algeria to make the French presence indispensable, and at worst welfare storm troopers defending integration at the expense of the will of the indigenous population.

S.F.I.O. French Socialist Party formed in 1905, literally *Section Française de l'Internationale Ouvrière*. Split in 1958.

Tell Meaning the "hill" in Arabic. Refers to the fertile hilly area stretching inland from the Mediterranean to depth of fifty to one hundred fifty miles along the Maghrib.

Tuareg (plural form) Berber people inhabiting the south, Sahara Atlas, and Sahara, monogamous matriarchal society.

U.D.M.A. See *Union Démocratique du Manifeste Algérien*.

ulema Turkish *ulema*, Arabic *ulama*, learned men; scholars trained in Islamic theology and law and recognized as authorities who played an important role in developing cultural nationalism in the Maghrib.

Union de la Gauche Socialiste A new socialist group (party) which took form in 1958 in protest against S.F.I.O. party elders like Mollet who endorsed the coup of May, 1958 and the subsequent Gaullist constitution. This party, like the *Parti Socialiste Autonome,* sought new approaches to social and economic improvement. Opposes de Gaulle's economic policy on the grounds that it stabilizes at the expense of the working classes.

Union Démocratique du Manifeste Algérien, U.D.M.A. Algerian political party organized in 1945 by Ferhat Abbas, supporting an autonomous Algeria federated to France.

Union Française Nord-Africaine Organization of French *colon* leaders Boyer-Banse and René Reygasse, dedicated to keeping Algeria French.

Union Général des Etudiants Musulmans Algériens, U.G.E.M.A. Algerian Students' Union which favored independence and therefore outlawed by French government.

Union Générale des Travailleurs Algériens, U.G.T.A. The F.L.N.'s trade union organized in March, 1956 and officially recognized by the International Confederation of Trade Unions, I.C.F.T.U., in July, 1956, at the expense of Messali Hadj's U.S.T.A. The U.G.T.A. had the effect of winning Algerian workers away from the Communist dominated French C.G.T. and the other French unions, the F.O. and C.F.T.C. Trade unionism was thus linked with Algerian nationalism.

Union pour la Nouvelle République, U.N.R. The Gaullist party organized in the summer of 1958 which dominates the new National Assembly with about 20 per cent of the popular vote by virtue of its affiliation with *beni-oui-oui* representatives from Algeria and electoral laws which favor it.

Union pour le Salut et le Renouveau de l'Algérie Française, U.S.R.A.F. Union for the Safety and Renewal of French Algeria, political group dedicated to the purpose set forth in its name which took form in 1956 and was supported by Jacques Soustelle.

Union Syndicale des Travailleurs Algériens, U.S.T.A. Messali

Hadj's trade union organized February, 1956 and briefly recognized by the International Confederation of Trade Unions, I.C.F.T.U., then dropped in favor of the F.L.N.'s U.S.T.A.

Unités Territoriales Blindées, U.T.B. Home guards of Europeans in Algeria.

Units within the Algerian Liberation Army:

fauj A group, composed of 11 men, including one sergeant and 2 corporals. The half-group equals five men and a corporal.

ferka A section, composed of 35 men (3 groups plus the head of the section and his assistants).

katiba A company, consisting of 110 men (3 sections plus 5 officers).

failek A battalion, consisting of 350 men (3 companies plus 20 officers).

U.N.R. See *Union pour la Nouvelle République.*

wilaya A military province of the Algerian Liberation Army. There are six including the Sahara.

441

Index

Index

Index

Index